3-11-01

D0172313

INSIGHT GUIDES

IRELAND

DISCOVERY CHANNEL

APA PUBLICATIONS
Part of the Langenscheidt Publishing Group

L

ABOUT THIS BOOK

Editorial

Project Editor
Brian Bell
Principal Photographers
Geray Sweeney
Thomas Kelly

Distribution

UK & Ireland
GeoCenter International Ltd
The Viables Centre
Harrow Way
Basingstoke
Hants RG22 4BJ
Fax: (44) 1256-817988

United States
Langenscheidt Publishers, Inc.
46–35 54th Road
Maspeth, NY 11378
Fax: (718) 784-0640

Worldwide
APA Publications GmbH & Co.
Verlag KG (Singapore branch)
38 Joo Koon Road
Singapore 628990
Tel: (65) 865-1600
Fax: (65) 861-6438

Printing

Insight Print Services (Pte) Ltd
38 Joo Koon Road
Singapore 628990
Tel: (65) 865-1600
Fax: (65) 861-6438

©1999 APA Publications GmbH & Co.
Verlag KG (Singapore branch)
All Rights Reserved
First Edition 1986
Sixth Edition (updated) 1999

This guidebook combines the
interests and enthusiasms of
two of the world's best known
information providers: Insight
Guides, whose titles have set the
standard for visual travel guides
since 1970, and Discovery Channel, the world's premier source of
nonfiction television programming.

The editors of Insight Guides provide both practical advice and general
understanding about a destination's
history, culture, institutions and
people. Discovery Channel
and its popular Web site,
www.discovery.com, help
millions of viewers explore
their world from the com-
fort of their own home
and also encourage them
to explore it firsthand.

How to use this book

For this new edition of
Insight Guide: Ireland, all
the maps have been redrawn, all the
Places chapters have been rewrit-
ten and the rest of the book has
been thoroughly updated. These
major changes were made in order
to reflect the speed at which Ireland
itself has been changing. In the
Republic, social reforms in areas
such as divorce have combined with
closer links with mainland Europe to
create a new confidence and dyna-
mism, and in Northern Ireland there
has been much renewal following decades of terrorist
bombings. *Insight Guide:
Ireland* reflects these
changes through its for-
mat of informative, en-
tertaining and well
written text paired with
vivid photojournalism.
The book is carefully
structured both to con-
vey an understanding of
the country and its cul-

EXPLORE YOUR WORLD'
Discovery
CHANNEL

Trinity College's Long Room Library.

ture and to guide readers through its sights:

◆ To understand Ireland today, you need to know something of its past. The first section covers its history and culture in lively, authoritative essays written by specialists.

◆ The central Places section gives a full run-down of the attractions worth seeing. Places of interest are co-ordinated by number with the maps.

◆ The Travel Tips section is a point of reference for information on travel, hotels, restaurants, shops and festivals. Information may be located quickly by using the index printed on the back cover flap – and the flaps are designed to serve as bookmarks.

◆ Photographs are chosen not only to illustrate geography and buildings but also to convey the many moods of the country and the everyday activities of its people.

The contributors

This edition was produced by Insight Guides' editorial director, **Brian Bell**, an Irishman who began his publishing career as a journalist in Belfast. Most of the chapters on the Republic were restructured and updated by **Rachel Warren**, a West Cork-based writer with an encyclopedic knowledge of Ireland's attractions. **Ian J. Hill**, a prominent Belfast journalist, did the same job on the Northwest and Northeast chapters, as well as providing entirely new text for the chapters on Belfast and food. The Dublin chapter was updated by its original author, **Liam McAuley**, an editor on the *Irish Times*; he also wrote the piece on horses and is the author of the detailed *Insight Compact Guide: Dublin.*

Other *Irish Times* contributors include **Eugene McEldowney** (Song and Dance), **Seamus Martin** (Pubs), and **Fintan O'Toole** (The Church). **Niall Stokes**, founder of the leading Dublin magazine *Hot Press*, wrote the chapter on Youth.

Much of the material for the chapters on Folklore, Sport and the Far West is based on the work of the late **Breandán O hEithir**, who wrote authoritatively for the first edition. Other writers whose work for earlier editions is partly retained include **Peter Kellner** and **Naomi May**. The Introduction and History chapters were written by **Brian Bell**.

Many photographers are represented in this book, notably **Geray Sweeney**, a Belfast photographer who has also shot Insight Compact Guides to *Dublin* and *The West of Ireland* and an Insight Pocket Guide to *Ireland's Southwest*, and Limerick-born **Thomas Kelly**, who now lives outside Dublin.

Map Legend

▬ ‥	International Boundary
‒ ‒ ‒	County Boundary
⦿	Border Crossing
⋅•⋅	National Park/ Nature Reserve
‒ ‒ ‒	Ferry Route
✈	Airport
🚌	Bus Station
🅿	Parking
❶	Tourist Information
✉	Post Office
✝ ♂	Church/Ruins
☪	Mosque
✡	Synagogue
♖	Castle/Ruins
∴	Archaeological Site
∩	Cave
★	Place of Interest

The main places of interest in the Places section are coordinated by number with a full-colour map (e.g. ❶), and a symbol at the top of every right-hand page tells you where to find the map.

CONTENTS

Maps

Ireland **136**

Dublin **138**

Dublin's Suburbs **161**

Around Dublin **166**

DART Rail System **337**

Southern Region **170**

Cork City **194**

Killarney **209**

The Midlands & West **230**

Northern Region **260**

Derry City **280**

Belfast **316**

Ireland **Front flap**

Dublin **Back flap**

Introduction

The Irish Character 15

History

Chronology **22**

Ireland's Invaders **25**

The Making of a Nation............**33**

Living with Partition **45**

Ireland Today.........................**53**

Features

The Role of the Church **69**

The Youth Explosion **78**

Song and Dance **85**

The Irish Way with Words **93**

Fairies and Folklore **98**

Racing Certainties **105**

The Games People Play **110**

The Serious Business
of Drinking **119**

A Fresh Approach to Food......**125**

Round tower at the Rock of Cashel, Co. Tipperary. About 70 round towers still exist in Ireland.

Travel Tips

Getting Acquainted **330**

Planning the trip **331**

Practical Tips **333**

Getting Around **336**

Where to Stay **340**

Where to Eat **351**

Nightlife **361**

Cultural Attractions **362**

Shopping **368**

Sports **369**

Full Travel Tips index

is on page 329

Insight on....

Ireland's Architecture **62**

Ireland in the Movies **96**

The Travelling People **188**

The Burren **228**

The Men Who March **310**

Places

Introduction **135**

Dublin **141**

Day Trips from Dublin **164**

The Southeast **175**

Cork City & Surroundings **193**

The Southwest **201**

The Shannon Region **219**

The Midlands **235**

The Far West **249**

The Northwest **265**

The Northeast **279**

Belfast **315**

THE IRISH CHARACTER

Take generous portions of charm, wit, congeniality and loquacity. Then mix in
melancholy, daydreaming and a tendency to violence. Stir gently

"How do you recognise an Irishman in a car wash?"
"He's the one sitting on the motorbike."

The Irish take a perverse delight in the universal jokes made against them. Indeed, they even print selections on linen tea-towels, which they sell at fancy prices in souvenir shops. That explains the perverse delight, of course: there's money to be made in conforming to a stereotyped image and, by appearing to be dim, the Irishman can benefit from the dimness of others.

Thus a guileful guide, deploying words like grapeshot, can charm the most sceptical travellers into paying good money to kiss the Blarney Stone in County Cork, at the same time reassuring them fulsomely that its promised ability to confer eloquence on all who kiss it is, in itself, just a bit of blarney.

Millions of visitors respond to this captivating charm by falling in love with Ireland at first sight. The national tourist slogan, *Céad Mile Fáilte*, fulfils its promise of "a hundred thousand welcomes" and the people's informal friendliness makes it exceptionally easy to take things easy. Rural values survive: after achieving independence from Britain in 1921, an event accompanied by bloody internal strife, the new Republic signalled its priorities in its currency, with coins displaying images not of rulers or tyrants but of pigs, hens, hares and salmon.

But only the coins of *the Republic*, of course, for there are two Irelands. One consists of the 26 counties of the Republic, which evoke images of black beer and green shamrock, of still sunsets over Galway Bay and statues of the Virgin Mary that, according to thousands of eyewitnesses, miraculously move. Then there are the six counties of British-administered

---

PRECEDING PAGES: farm children, Connemara; an evening out at Bad Bob's bar, Dublin; traditional rural cottage and locals; Dublin's Georgian doorways.
LEFT: the Republic's flag at a football game at Croke Park, Dublin. **RIGHT:** paper boy, Belfast.

Northern Ireland, a harder place where a celebrated slogan daubed on the side of a derelict house asked: "Is there life *before* death?"

Endless paradoxes ambush the unwary. It doesn't take long for the enquiring visitor to begin pondering such puzzles as why a Dublin Roman Catholic will in all probability hate the

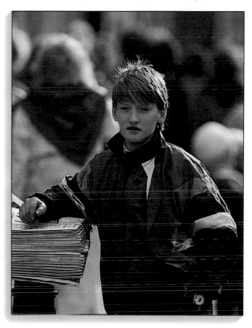

British but respect the English, while a Belfast Protestant will badmouth the English yet swear eternal loyalty to the British. Non-residents should enter this debate only if they relish taking sides in marital conflicts.

Such stereotypes, naturally, soon turn into absurd over-simplifications. An English journalist, for instance, despatched to Northern Ireland to seek out why its Protestant and Roman Catholic communities were at each other's throats, reported: "They are incomparably more pleasant to the outsider than any other people in the British Isles. Even the terrorists have excellent manners." It was the German writer Heinrich Böll who identified the two turns of speech most characteristic of the Irish as "It could be worse" and "I shouldn't worry." In a world where worries proliferate daily, Ireland has more to offer than pigs, priests, potatoes and patriots: it has insane optimism.

Naturally the Irish have written down this philosophy on linen tea-towels, which they will sell to passers-through at a decent profit. It reads: "There are only two things to worry about: either you are well or you are sick. If you are well, then there is nothing to worry about. But if you are sick, there are two things to worry about: either you will get well or you will die. If you get well, then there is nothing to worry

acter with a liking for alcohol and argument, preferably indulged in simultaneously. But the Irish readily collaborated.

Unarguably, there is a strong theatricality about their character. There's a recklessness, a tendency towards exaggeration. There's a love of "codology", the Irish equivalent of "leg-pulling." But there's an introversion, too, the proneness to melancholy captured by George Bernard Shaw in *John Bull's Other Island*, a play set in the land of his birth: "Your wits can't thicken in that soft moist air, on those white springy roads, in those misty rushes and brown bogs, on those hillsides of granite rocks and

about. If you die, there are only two things to worry about: either you will go to heaven or to hell. If you go to heaven, there is nothing to worry about. But if you go to hell, you'll be so damn busy shaking hands with friends, you won't have time to worry. Why worry!"

A strong theatricality

Not that the Irish won't give you cause enough for perplexity. Their character is as elusive as the fairy gold to be found at the end of Irish rainbows and the conversation as elliptical as an incomplete jigsaw puzzle. Hollywood, as so often, is partly to blame; it perpetuated the image of the stage Irishman, a clownish char-

magenta heather. You've no such colours in the sky, no such lure in the distance, no such sadness in the evenings. Oh the dreaming! the dreaming! the torturing, heartscalding, never satisfying dreaming, dreaming, dreaming."

You can sometimes sense this aspect of the Irish character in a pub when, after the talk – once called "a game with no rules" – has achieved an erratic brilliance, the convivial mood abruptly changes to one of wistfulness and self-absorption, and you know it's time to go. This contradictory character led the 19th-century philosopher Søren Kierkegaard to muse that, if he hadn't been a Dane, he could well have been an Irishman: "For the Irish have not the heart to baptize their children completely, they want to preserve just a little paganism, and whereas a child is normally completely immersed, they keep his right arm out of the water so that in after-life he can grasp a sword and hold a girl in his arm."

The Irish themselves look less whimsically at their native land. The poet Louis MacNeice, for example, described it as a nation "built upon violence and morose vendettas". Today, because of the guerrilla warfare that has been waged in the northeast of

EXPATRIATE IRISH

Almost 3 million Irish citizens live outside Ireland, including 2 million in Britain, 500,000 in the US, 213,000 in Australia and 74,000 in Canada.

Micheál MacLiammóir, "no European island lies in so lamentable and hostile a solitude as Ireland, who has no neighbour on her right hand but her conqueror, and nothing at all on her left hand but the desolate ocean, not one dry step until you get to America."

This "wretched little clod, broken off a bigger clod, broken off the west end of Europe," as Shaw called it, has had a turbulent history, whose unfinished state is reflected in the island's partition. The current "Troubles" blighting Northern Ireland

the island since 1969, this dark side of the Irish character is much more in evidence than it was half a century ago, when John Wayne and Maureen O'Hara rollicked their way through the virulently green landscapes of *The Quiet Man*. As one commentator observed: "The quiet Irishman is about as harmless as a powder magazine built over a match factory."

Perhaps the island's location is to blame. "With the exception it may be of Malta and of Iceland," wrote the actor and theatre director

LEFT: the wearing of the green.
ABOVE: although nearly half the population is under 25, Ireland retains its respect for the older generation

were at first seen by the world as a curious religious conflict, an inexplicable throwback to the Reformation. In reality, religious affiliation has been mostly a symbol. The conflict has had little to do with God but everything to do with nationalism. The doctrine of the Transubstantiation may be debated from the pulpits of fundamentalist preachers, but what everyone else is arguing about is the conflicting secular loyalties of 1 million Protestants, who want to stay British, and half-a-million Roman Catholics, who feel a bond with the Republic. It's partly a question of insecure national identity, partly a realisation that, in an area with too few jobs to go round, each tribe has to fight for its fair share.

What these divisions indicate is that there is more than one "Irish" character. The Northern Protestant is generally regarded as being more earnest, more unimaginative than the Northern Catholic, who is in turn seen as less outgoing, less impulsive than the Southern Catholic. The Irish refine these distinctions even further, giving the sense of place an importance seldom found elsewhere in the world.

But is too small a place for many. In *Mother Ireland*, the novelist Edna O'Brien described the constricting parochialism and the awful predictability that led her to flee to London: "Hour after hour I can think of Ireland, I can imagine without going too far wrong what is happening in any one of the little towns by day or by night... I can almost tell you what any one of my friends might be doing, so steadfast is the rhythm of life there."

A strong theatricality

It's a rhythm, though, that's well liked by most visitors. It is an echo of an 18th-century pace of life that has not completely faded away, a psychological climate in which a racehorse attracts more admiring glances than a Rolls-Royce. It reflects the values of the railway guard answering a traveller who complained that the train was already half an hour late: "You must have a very narrow heart that you wouldn't go down to the town and stand your friends a few drinks instead of bothering me to get away."

It's this attitude to life, never far beneath the surface, that makes Ireland such a rewarding place to visit. As the American-born novelist J. P. Donleavy, an exemplar of the less folksy style of Irish writing, expressed it winsomely in *The Ginger Man*: "When I die I want to decompose in a barrel of porter [*dark beer*] and have it served in all the pubs of Dublin. I wonder would they know it was me?"

THE IRISH DIASPORA

As many as 70 million people throughout the world can claim Irish descent, and the Irish are generous in granting citizenship. It can extend to the grandchildren and great-grandchildren of people born in Ireland, the argument being that they were prevented from being Irish only because their forebears had to emigrate for economic reasons.

RIGHT: Dublin society spends a day at the races.

Decisive Dates

ca 7000BC: Archaeological evidence of Mesolithic hunter-fisher people (flints, etc) along the coast dates from this period.

From ca 3000BC: The Neolithic period sees megalithic tombs appear. Signs of prolonged settlement, agriculture and cultural sophistication (portal tombs) grow more frequent.

From ca 500BC: The migration of Celts from Britain marks the start of Ireland's Iron Age.

ca AD300: Stone-carved inscriptions appear in the 'Ogham alphabet', a rune-like script.

431: The Pope sends Palladius as a bishop to Ireland. This implies that Christian communities existed before St Patrick arrived.

ca 432: St Patrick (later to become Ireland's patron saint) comes back to Ireland as a missionary. At 16, he had been abducted from Britain to Ireland, but later fled to France.

From ca 800: Viking attacks begin. After a series of raids (many monasteries are plundered) the Norsemen found settlements which grow into harbour towns (e.g. Dublin).

976–1014: Brian Ború, crowned King of Munster in 976, proclaims himself High King of Ireland in 1002 and defeats the Vikings near Clontarf in 1014. After his murder that same year, the kingdom falls apart again.

From 1169: Anglo-Normans – sent to Ireland by the English king Henry II after a request from Dermot MacMurrough, who is losing the fight for the Irish throne – conquer large areas of the island and settle there. Feudalism is introduced and castles built.

1366: The Statutes of Kilkenny represent an attempt by the English crown to stop its barons from assimilating, marrying Irishwomen or speaking the Irish language.

From 1541: England's Henry VIII declares himself King of Ireland and begins asserting British supremacy over the Irish clan princes.

1607: The most powerful Irish clan princes flee to Spain (the "Flight of the Earls"), marking the end of Gaelic supremacy.

1608: James I starts systematic settlement of Protestant Scots and English ("the Plantation of Ulster").

1641–53: A rebellion by Irish Catholics against the English settlement policy is initially successful. In 1649, after his victory in the English Civil War, Oliver Cromwell conquers Ireland in a merciless campaign.

1690: England's Catholic King James II loses his throne to William of Orange at the Battle of the Boyne in 1690, and the period of "Protestant Ascendancy" begins.

1691: The Irish-Protestant parliament in Dublin passes the "Penal Laws" which exclude Catholics from public office, deprive them of their property and hence of their right to vote, and make it difficult for them to practise their religion.

1791: Influenced by the revolutions in France and America, the United Irishmen movement is formed in Belfast. Its leading light, Wolfe Tone, is a Protestant coachbuilder's son.

1800: The Act of Union makes Ireland part of the United Kingdom. The parliament in Dublin is dissolved and Ireland is represented by 100 MPs in the House of Commons.

1829: A Catholic politician, Daniel O'Connell ("the Liberator"), forces the London parliament to pass a law emancipating Catholics.

From 1840: Nationalist movements gain strength (Irish Republican Brotherhood founded in 1858, Irish National Land League founded in 1879), and are accompanied by a renewed interest in Gaelic culture (Gaelic League formed in 1893).

1845–51 The Great Potato Famine deprives more than one-third of the Irish population of their main source of nutrition (the unusually warm winters mean that the fungus blighting the crops cannot be destroyed). An estimated 1 million people die between 1846 and 1851 of malnutrition, typhus and other diseases; 1 million others emigrate.

From 1880: The Land League and the Irish Home Rule Party led by Charles Stuart Parnell employ parliamentary means in their struggle for Irish autonomy and land reform. In 1886, the first of several draft resolutions for Irish independence is rejected.

1905–08: The group known as Sinn Féin ("We Ourselves") is formed "to make England take one hand from Ireland's throat and the other out of Ireland's pocket".

1912: Almost three quarters of all Ulster Protestants sign a solemn pledge to stop all attempts at autonomy "by all necessary means". The Ulster Volunteer Force is formed in 1913 to enforce the pledge.

1916: On 24 April around 1,800 volunteers, led by Pádraig Pearse and James Connolly, occupy public buildings in Dublin and declare the formation of an Irish Republic. This "Easter Rising" is put down six days later. Britain's harsh response backfires and support strengthens for the nationalist cause.

1918–23: In elections to the UK Parliament, Sinn Féin wins 73 of 105 Irish seats. Their MPs announce the formation of an Irish parliament in Dublin, with Éamon de Valera as president; the British government sends in troops. During the Anglo-Irish War of 1919–21 the Irish Republican Army gradually gains the upper hand against the British. In 1922 the Irish Parliament narrowly accepts the Anglo-Irish treaty for the foundation of an Irish Free State excluding the six counties of Northern Ireland with Protestant majorities. Civil war ensues between forces in favour of a Pan-Irish Republic and the pro-treaty Free State government, which wins.

1937: The Free State (Éire) adopts its own constitution.

1939: Éire declares its neutrality during World War II. Germany tries to damage Britain's interests by supporting the IRA.

1949: Éire leaves the British Commonwealth to become the Republic of Ireland.

1969–70: A demonstration by the Northern Irish Civil Rights Movement is attacked by loyalists in 1969. Mounting violence prompts the British to send in troops. The IRA, which has been fighting for a united Ireland since the 1930s, splits into two factions in 1970. The Provisional IRA intensifies its "armed struggle" in Northern Ireland.

1972: The situation becomes volatile when 13 demonstrators are shot dead by British soldiers on "Bloody Sunday". The parliament in Belfast is dissolved and Northern Ireland is

henceforth ruled directly from London.

1973: The Republic joins the European Economic Community along with Great Britain.

1990: Mary Robinson becomes the first woman president of the Republic of Ireland.

1994: IRA declares ceasefire in Northern Ireland (ends in 1996 with bomb in London).

1997: Divorce becomes legal in the Republic. New talks begin on Northern Ireland's future and the IRA declares another ceasefire. A general election in the Republic puts a Fianna Fáil-led coalition in power. Mary McAleese, a Northerner, becomes president.

1998: A Northern Ireland peace treaty is signed by all parties, including Sinn Féin, but the terrorists refuse to hand over their arms.

IRELAND'S INVADERS

First the Celts came, then the Vikings and Normans. The English decided

to stake a strategic claim, and that's when the trouble really began

Ireland, it is said, has no ancient annals: all its history is contemporary because yesterday's myths mould today's thought in an astonishingly direct way. In the words of the 19th-century historian Thomas Babington Macaulay, dealing with Ireland is like stepping "on the thin crust of ashes beneath which the lava is still flowing."

It's an easy proposition to prove. Volunteer, at an Irish dinner party or in a bar, a statement about any aspect of the country's turbulent past, and a catalogue of heroism and hatreds, claims and counter-claims, murderers and martyrs, decisive dates and disputed deeds will pour out with vehemence and wit, populated with a cast of characters ranging from Brian Ború to Oliver Cromwell, from William of Orange to O'Connell the Liberator, from Henry VIII to Margaret Thatcher. Nowhere else does the ordinary citizen delight in interpreting today's political deeds through such detailed and comprehensive reference to centuries-old events.

The next-door neighbour

The reason for this lack of historical perspective lies in the extraordinary love-hate relationship that Ireland has had with its more powerful neighbouring island to the east. Ireland's history, in a nutshell, is its resistance to England. In this geographically forced marriage, the dominant partner sometimes deliberately abused the weaker, more often unthinkingly ignored her; yet the Irish, while hating the English for their arrogance and neglect, also admired them for their character and achievements and, until a surprisingly late stage, had no great wish for the marriage to be totally dissolved.

It is a tragic national drama, full of tantalising might-have-beens, and the English have long been resigned to the fact that they are cast as the villain. "Go into the length and breadth of the world," England's reforming prime minister William Ewart Gladstone told his parliament a century ago, "ransack the literature of all countries, find if you can a single voice, a single book... in which the conduct of England towards Ireland is anywhere treated except with profound and bitter condemnation."

Those seeking to understand rather than condemn must begin by travelling back several cen-

turies before the birth of Christ. It was then that Ireland's first conquerors, the Celts (or Gaels), quick-tempered masters of horsemanship, came west from the mainland of Europe, mainly from France and Spain, to this wild, wet island at the continent's outermost fringes. They brought with them a loose tribal structure, the blueprint for building a civilization, and had little trouble in overcoming the natives, an obscure, primitive people called the Firbolg ("Big Men").

But old traditions of magic and wizardry survived so strongly that to this day you can find reverence for holy wells and for clumps of trees inhabited by "the fairies". Evidence of much earlier inhabitants survived, too, in the form of

LEFT: The Arrest of Christ from the *Book of Kells*.
RIGHT: Tara brooch from the 8th century.

thousands of megalithic burial chambers. The Newgrange passage-grave in the Boyne valley, near Dublin, for example, is thought to be 5,000 years old. From the Bronze Age, when Ireland was one of the world's largest metal producers, beautifully crafted leaf-shaped swords and gold ornaments are preserved.

Europe's next conquerors did not get as far as Ireland. The Roman legions, hard pressed to hold southern Britain against incursions by Picts and Scots,

TOO MANY MONARCHS

Because kingship was elective, not hereditary, power struggles were inevitable, especially since there were as many as 150 kings in a population of 500,000. They reigned, it was said, but didn't always rule.

Christianity had been brought to the island by an English-born rustic missionary, St Patrick, who had been kidnapped as a youth and taken to Ireland to tend sheep. Later, he travelled widely in France and Italy, returning to Ireland in 432 to spread the word of Christ through the trackless forests. He found, in this land of which he was to become the patron saint, a largely peaceable people, though there was intermittent feuding between various provincial kings.

were disinclined to take on more trouble by adding the Gaels to their empire. Their inaction had far-reaching consequences: if Julius Caesar had successfully ventured west, it is unlikely that Ireland's character today would be so distinct from Britain's. What's more, the roads might have been better.

The Golden Age

The divergences between the two cultures widened still further when the fall of the Roman Empire plunged Europe into the Dark Ages. Ireland, in contrast, entered its Golden Age, becoming a lone beacon of learning and civilization – "the Land of Saints and Scholars".

In the absence of a Roman substructure of towns and cities, monasteries became centres of population. The kings kept their treasures there, which made the monasteries a target for plundering bands of Vikings, who sailed to Ireland in their high-prowed ships from northern Scandinavia. Tall round towers, many still standing, were built by the monasteries to serve as lookouts and refuges as well as belfries. Also surviving are some of the monks' exquisitely illuminated manuscripts, such as the *Book of Kells*, which the Vikings, being unable to read, ignored. Ireland's strong tradition of storytelling dates from this period. It can be seen on the many sand-stone high crosses, designed to teach

Bible stories by means of elaborate carvings.

The Norse tyranny was destroyed at the Battle of Clontarf in 1014 by the most celebrated of the High Kings, Brian Ború, who saw himself as Ireland's Charlemagne. But he himself died in the battle as he was praying for victory.

Less destructive but no less ambitious visitors were the Norman adventurers such as Strongbow, who came looking for land. His real name was Richard, second Earl of Pembroke, and he was answering a call for help from Dermot MacMurrough, a local chieftain, who had outraged rivals by stealing another prince's wife – an offence which, not for the first time, was to change the course of history.

England gets involved

The Norman lords' pedigrees were longer than their purses. Having gained a toehold, they began enriching themselves by building a power base, complete with fortified stone castles. This alarmed England's king, Henry II. He promptly paid a visit to Ireland, inaugurating an involvement between the two countries that was to last, with immeasurable bloodshed, for 800 years.

Over the next three centuries, the Normans, intermarrying with the natives, expanded their influence. Many of the country's elaborate castles, such as Blarney in Co. Cork and Bunratty in County Clare, date from this time. In 1429, Henry VI subsidised each new castle to the tune of £10, then a sizeable sum.

But, as the barons thrived, the English Crown's authority gradually shrank to an area around Dublin known as "the Pale". It was Henry VIII, determined finally to break the local nobles' power, who proclaimed himself "King of this land of Ireland as united, annexed and knit for ever to the Imperial Crown of the Realm of England". Henry tried to make himself the source of all land ownership by demanding that the lords surrender their lands to him, then have them "regranted by the grace of the king". When many refused, Henry seized their lands, resettling them with loyal "planters" from England and Scotland.

His daughter, Elizabeth I, fought four wars in Ireland. As well as trying to impose the Refor-

mation on the country, she wanted to protect England's right flank against an invasion from her principal opponent, Spain.

Later, James I defeated a particularly powerful baron, Hugh O'Neill, Earl of Tyrone, at the Battle of Kinsale and planted new settlers on O'Neill's lands in six of the nine counties of the ancient province of Ulster. The new settlers were Protestants, firm believers in the Calvinist work ethic, and the racial mix that they created is still causing strife in Ulster today.

An early sign of the troubles ahead came in 1641, when Ulster Roman Catholics, hoping to recover their confiscated lands, rebelled at Por-

tadown. The facts of the rebellion were rapidly overwhelmed by the legend as lurid tales spread of a drunken Catholic pogrom against the God-fearing settlers, with 12,000 Protestants knifed, shot and drowned, pregnant women raped, and infants roasted on spits. Whatever the death toll really was, the Protestants were never to forget the threat represented by 1641.

The Gaelic Irish had further cause to worry when, after Charles I was beheaded, the new Puritan Parliament in England began suppressing the Roman Catholic religion. Fanned by the flames of this resentment, a new Catholic revolt began to spread. This "Great Rebellion" was ruthlessly suppressed by the English Protector,

LEFT: England's Richard II made two expeditions to Ireland, in 1394–95 and in 1399. **RIGHT:** Walter Devereux, 1st Earl of Essex, was despatched in the 1570s by Elizabeth I to colonise Ulster.

Oliver Cromwell, whose 20,000 Ironside troops devastated the countryside. By 1652, about a third of the Catholic Irish had been killed. Much of their land was handed over to Protestants.

When the monarchy was restored, Charles II disappointed Catholics by throwing his support behind the Protestants, on whom he depended for power. His successor, James II, himself a Roman Catholic, raised hopes by introducing an Act of Parliament that would have ousted the Protestant settlers; but, before it could be put into practice, James was defeated in 1690 at the Battle of the Boyne, near Dublin, by William of Orange. William had been called in by the Eng-

was broken up between all his sons instead of passing to the eldest – unless one son turned Protestant, in which case he got the lot. By the middle of the 18th century, only 7 per cent of land was in Catholic hands.

The land problem

Any threat from the trading class was removed when swingeing restrictions were imposed on commerce between Ireland and England. The country was left with only the land to rely on and the peasants put in the position of slaves. No hope of redemption was offered: if a tenant worked hard to improve his holding, the land-

lish establishment to end James's "Popish ways" and his success in doing so is still commemorated annually on 12 July with mammoth parades by Protestant Orangemen throughout Northern Ireland.

From that day in 1690, Roman Catholics became a persecuted majority in Ireland. Their share of land ownership tumbled to just 15 percent. New anti-Catholic legislation, the "penal laws", barred them from all public life and much social activity. They weren't allowed to buy land or rent it profitably. When a Catholic landowner died, his property

THE POVERTY TRAP

The king's representative, the Viceroy, reported in 1770 that Irish peasants were "amongst the most wretched people on earth".

lord would raise his rent.

But the people blamed their plight not on the king but on the landlords. Even the Catholic gentry did not resent the king's control; indeed, when the American colonies declared their independence in 1776, the Catholics reaffirmed their allegiance to George III. Also, many of the middle-class "Ascendancy" were prospering. Arthur Guinness, for instance, introduced his famous stout in 1759.

But trouble was inevitable and, gradually, violent groups of men began to ride out at night avenging themselves on their oppressors –

maiming landlords' cattle, burning barns, firing shots through windows. These secret societies, with names such as the Whiteboys and the Ribbonmen, deflected much of the masses' energy from more political aims. Jonathan Swift, the Irish-born dean of St Patrick's Protestant Cathedral in Dublin and the author of such incisive satires as *Gulliver's Travels*, had a more political sensibility: he endorsed the call to his fellow countrymen to burn everything English except their coal, and he advo-

THE FRENCH LESSON

The echoes of the French Revolution of 1789 were heard loudly in Ireland.. Fashionable Dubliners addressed one another as "Citizen". Demands grew for Catholic emancipation.

fourths of the population) were still denied any political role and the extensive patronage at the disposal of the English parliament allowed it easily to manipulate policy in Dublin.

The government in London thought it had done rather well to pass two Catholic Relief Acts giving Roman Catholics limited voting rights and allowing them once more to own or lease land. As so often in Ireland, however, a well-meaning policy gave birth to anarchy. Catholics began buying land in Ulster, forcing up

cated a separate parliament for Ireland.

Pressure for political change was applied by Protestant patriots such as Henry Grattan. The threat of physical force was added in the shape of the Irish Volunteers, 80,000 strong by 1782. London caved in and agreed to a separate parliament in Dublin. At last Ireland was an independent nation – although only legislatively, since allegiance was still owed to the British Crown. Also, a fatal flaw in the new arrangement was that the Catholic majority (three-

LEFT: William of Orange, victor at the Battle of the Boyne in 1690. **ABOVE:** Powerscourt, in Co. Wicklow, was one of the grandest English-built mansions.

prices and alarming the Protestants, who formed a vigilante outfit, the Peep o' Day Boys, to burn out Catholics in dawn raids. The Catholics set up their own vigilante force, the Defenders. The lines of a long conflict were drawn.

A secret society is born

Yet Ulster was the cradle in 1791 for a brave attempt by Protestants and Catholics to fight together for reform. Wolfe Tone, the son of a respectable Protestant coach builder, set up the first Society of United Irishmen club in Belfast and a second soon opened in Dublin. It began well, largely as an enlightened debating society, but was suppressed within three years when

William Pitt, the British prime minister, feared an alliance between Ireland and France, with whom Britain was then at war. Tone, condemning England as "the never-failing source of all our political evils", fled to America.

Government anxiety increased when the United Irishmen, largely a middle-class Protestant group, began forging links with the Defenders, who were mostly working-class Catholics. And soon an even more threatening alliance was being forged: the United Irishmen persuaded Tone, who had been thinking of settling down near Philadelphia as a farmer, to sail to France and rally support against Britain. Tone assured

Catholic Irish peasants, began arresting the organisation's outlawed leaders, identifying them as a result of information partly provided by informers, partly extracted through brutal beatings. Soon Ulster was in the grip of terror and the stage was set for a significant new group to enter the Irish drama. These were the Orangemen, whose role in Ulster remains central today.

The movement began in 1795 after a bitter clash between Protestant Peep o' Day Boys and Catholic Defenders at the Battle of the Diamond, near Armagh, in which 30 men died. The Protestants, fearing worse was to come, reorganised as the Orange Society, named after their

the French that their arrival in Ireland would trigger a national uprising, supported by the Irish militia, and on 16 December 1796 a French battle fleet of 43 ships set sail.

It was the weather that came to England's rescue. Severe storms dispersed the fleet, and the few troops who landed at Bantry Bay, on the southwest coast, were greeted rather unenthusiastically by the Irish peasants, who believed that the French really had been sent by the northern Protestants to suppress them further.

In the end, it was the United Irishmen who were suppressed. Pitt, fearing a second French expedition, imposed harsh martial law in Ulster. The army, four-fifths of whom were themselves

hero, William of Orange, and preyed as lawless bandits on Catholics. In defeating the United Irishmen, the government was glad of their vicious support.

The Great Rebellion

Disaffection with English rule climaxed in May 1798 in a major rebellion. But by then so many of the United Irishmen's leaders had been arrested that most of the risings throughout the country were too ill-organised to succeed. Also, the native yeomanry, revealing a disturbing aspect of the Irish character, reacted by torturing and shooting indiscriminately, often butchering the rebels after they had surrendered.

Within six weeks, it was all over. Perhaps 50,000 had died, giving birth in the process to countless ballads commemorating a small nation's struggle for freedom. The notion of an Irish patriotism independent of England's fortunes was taking root with a vengeance.

Napoleon Bonaparte, pressed by Wolfe Tone not to abandon French support for Ireland, belatedly agreed to another expedition, which set sail that August. But again the French had been misinformed. When one party

MASSIVE CORRUPTION

Irish leaders who wavered about union with England found themselves offered peerages, offices of state and huge financial bribes.

Pitt's exasperated response was to propose a full union between Britain and Ireland. The 300-seat Irish parliament in Dublin would be abolished and 100 seats for Irish representatives would be created within the Imperial Parliament in London. Englishman, Irishman, Welshman and Scot would be treated equally. Opinion in Ireland was split, less on any patriotic principles than on cool appraisals of individual self-interest and economic prospects. But London's mind was made up and, after a period of

landed at Killala, County Mayo, having been led to expect enthusiastic, disciplined battalions, they found instead supporters whom they could at best regard as rapacious simpletons. Tone landed with another party at Donegal, was captured and died in prison after an attempted suicide. His martyrdom was assured, but the French declaration of an Irish republic was as insubstantial as so many other Irish dreams before and since.

LEFT: Protestant prisoners are executed at Wexford in 1798 in what was regarded as a "murder without sin" (MWS). ABOVE: Thomas Robinson's *Battle of Ballinahinch* portrays a clash the same year in County Down.

political wheeler-dealing on an ambitious scale, a majority of five voting *against* the union was turned into a majority of 46 voting *for* it. Ireland's parliament had, in effect, abolished itself.

On 1 January 1801, with all the pomp and circumstance that attend such occasions, Britain and Ireland entered, in Pitt's phrase, their "voluntary association" within the Empire with "equal laws, reciprocal affection, and inseparable interests". As with most marriages, the intentions were good. Perhaps the two partners might even live happily ever after.

It was not to be. No one present on that day early in a promising new century could have imagined the terrible suffering that lay ahead.

THE MAKING OF A NATION

The union with Britain brought little happiness to either partner. And the divorce would involve more than a century of bitter bloodshed

None of Ireland's basic problems had been solved by the union. The peasants who worked the land still had no rights to it and no alternative employment had been created. They did not applaud or even notice the new arrangement, and agrarian disturbances continued, as the Anglo-Irish historian William Lecky put it, "like the passing storms that sweep so rapidly over the inconstant Irish sky".

This was the situation that Robert Emmet found when he returned from France in 1802 after the Peace of Amiens had ended hostilities between Britain and France. Emmet, a Protestant doctor's son, had been much influenced by the United Irishmen and concocted a plan to seize Dublin Castle, the seat of Britain's administrative power in Ireland, in July 1803.

The rebellion, like so many others, misfired. For one thing, Emmet had kept it such a well-guarded secret that too few supporters knew it was happening; for another, the last-minute organisation produced a comic opera of incompetence, with fuses for grenades being mislaid and only one scaling ladder being completed. Thirty people died in fitful rioting. Emmet, soon captured, was sentenced to be hanged, drawn and quartered. It could have ended there, but for the condemned man's inspiring speech from the dock. "Let no man write my epitaph," said Emmet. "When my country takes her place among the nations of the earth, then and not till then let my epitaph be written."

The rise of Daniel O'Connell

A more democratic approach was taken by Daniel O'Connell, a Catholic lawyer from a well-off Kerry family. Like many of his contemporaries, he had been educated in France and the ideals of the French Revolution had entered his thinking. He wanted no revolution in Ireland, though, not even a separation from the British Crown. What he campaigned for, with powerful oratory, was the right of Catholics to become Members of Parliament. Soon landlords were alarmed by the success of O'Connell's Catholic Association, particularly when its leader, standing for parliament in 1828 as a "Man of the People", had an overwhelming victory. Sir Robert Peel, Britain's prime

minister, was forced to introduce a Catholic Emancipation Bill, which was passed.

Once in the House of Commons, O'Connell, by now "the uncrowned king of Ireland", began to rally support for his next cause: a repeal of the union. When his appeals struck few chords in parliament, he took his arguments to his fellow country-men, holding monster rallies throughout Ireland. At one meeting attended by 300,000 at Tuam, a Union Jack flew from the cathedral spire to underline O'Connell's insistence that Ireland did not wish to relinquish its loyalty to King or Empire but merely sought the right to run its own internal affairs. Also, he told the crowds, there must be no violence.

LEFT: emigrants bound for a new life in America.
RIGHT: absentee landlords continued to evict the poor who didn't keep up with their rents.

Ireland's greatest disaster

At that point, fate intervened in the form of the Great Famine that began in 1845. In reality, it wasn't a true famine at all; rather a failure of the potato crop. At its height, wheat and barley were being freely shipped to England, together with tens of thousands of cattle, sheep and pigs. But such produce was beyond the pockets of the peasants, whose every penny went towards paying rent to the series of middlemen – often as many as seven – who stood between them and their land's ultimate owner. All they could afford was the humble potato. When it was blighted, they starved.

The crop failed again and mothers were reported to be eating flesh from their dead babies. The *Mayo Constitution* reported: "The streets of every town in the country are overrun by stalking skeletons." And, all the while, food exports to England remained buoyant.

England's refusal to provide relief is regarded today as a horrifying failure of imagination, one of the worst in its colonial history. Even compassionate and otherwise enlightened men lacked the vision to question the wisdom of the prevailing economic orthodoxy, the rigid belief that it would make matters even worse to interfere with natural economic forces. The same

Twenty years before the famine, the novelist Sir Walter Scott had written of the Irish peasantry: "Their poverty has not been exaggerated: it is on the extreme verge of human misery." And, as their numbers grew – the population doubled to 8 million between 1800 and 1840 – so their misery deepened. Evictions began as the first potato crop's failure left tenants unable to pay their rents. An English MP described one large-scale eviction as "the chasing away of 700 human beings like crows out of a cornfield".

THE GREAT HUNGER

A Mayo curate wrote in 1846 of the people's plight: "They are to be found in thousands, young and old, male and female, crawling in the streets and on the highways, screaming for a morsel of food."

principle was applied to the industrial working classes in England's factories, but their lot was less desperate than that of the Irish peasants.

A million people died in the Great Hunger and well over a million set off in squalid emigrant ships for a new life in America, where they would pass down to future generations a deep anti-British resentment. Around a third of the land in Ireland changed hands as estates went bankrupt, but the new landlords, who were mostly Irish (of both religions, now that

Catholics were allowed to buy land), were even harsher than their predecessors in increasing rents. O'Connell's talk of non-violent nationalism seemed quite irrelevant and a group of his middle-class supporters broke away to form the Young Ireland movement, which was prepared to use the threat of violence. O'Connell himself died in 1847, aged 71, his dreams shattered.

In 1848, a year which saw nationalist uprisings in several countries of Europe, an attempted rising in Kilkenny was easily put down; it was a bungled fiasco, with little support from a weakened populace and none at all from the influential priesthood. A few wild

WHAT KARL MARX THOUGHT

In a letter to Friedrich Engels in 1856, Karl Marx analysed Ireland's down-trodden populace in terms of a class struggle: "By consistent oppression they have been artificially converted into an utterly demoralised nation and now fulfil the notorious function of supplying England, America, Australia, etc with prostitutes, casual labourers, pimps, thieves, swindlers, beggars and other rabble."

plans, like one to kidnap Queen Victoria during her visit to Dublin in 1849, didn't materialise. The Irish genius seemed to be for theatricality, not for effective action. As one disconsolate patriot put it: "God knows, if eloquence could free or save a people, we ought to be the freest and safest people on the face of the globe."

Revolution in the air

Tenant rights were talked about regularly by Irish MPs in the House of Commons, but good

LEFT: the formidable Daniel O'Connell, "the Liberator"; an Irish kitchen in the 1840s was far from primitive.
ABOVE: cows shared space with a cottage industry.

harvests after 1851 seemed to lessen the urgency. In 1856, James Stephens, a Kilkenny railway engineer, came home from France and took what he called his "3,000-mile walk" through south and west Ireland talking of an independent republic. But, failing to interest either the gentry or the tenant farmers, he concluded that perhaps only the labourers could be stirred to revolution. On St Patrick's Day, 17 March 1858, Stephens founded a society which later came to be known as the Irish Republican Brotherhood, dedicated to the idea of an independent democratic republic and branding its opponents as "ruthless tyrants" and "an alien aristocracy". An American branch was set up, called the Fenians after ancient Gaelic warriors. The American Civil War, Stephens noted, had given his supporters there valuable experience of battle. After a skirmish in Canada, Fenian participants were referred to as "The Irish Republican Army." It was the IRA's first appearance on the world stage.

Stephens was deposed as leader after his failure to organise an army of liberation from the United States, but by 1867 armed and well-drilled bands had been set up throughout Ireland to revolt. During one of the risings, some trains were derailed, marking the arrival in the country of a strategy that would shape Ireland's strug-

other Irishmen from Clerkenwell prison in London killed 12 Londoners and maimed 30.

The fight for Home Rule

But it was not terrorism that was to further Ireland's cause most at this time. The two principal engines of change were driven by William Ewart Gladstone, who came to power as Britain's prime minister in 1868, and Charles Stewart Parnell, an English-educated Protestant landowner from County Wicklow.

Gladstone's approach was far removed from the indifference of his predecessors. "My mission," he said, "is to pacify Ireland." He began

gles until the present day: guerrilla warfare. A ship, *Erin's Hope*, sailed from New York carrying much needed modern rifles and ammunition, but it reached Ireland too late and nobody could be found to receive the consignment.

The same year, too, England learned for the first time what it meant to have Ireland's grievances brought to its own door-step. A prison van carrying two captured revolutionary leaders was ambushed near Manchester, a police sergeant being shot dead in the raid. When three of the rescuers were caught and sentenced to death, an emotional appeal from the dock about the nobility of their cause transformed them into martyrs. Soon afterwards, an explosion meant to spring

in 1869 by removing one chronic grievance. Since the Reformation, the Protestant church had been the established church in Ireland, although it represented only a sixth of the population. Gladstone abolished this privileged position. Next, he introduced a land Bill designed to make it less easy for landlords to evict tenants. Sensing new hope, nationalists began to demand once more that Ireland should have its own parliament to administer Irish affairs, leaving international matters to the Imperial parliament in London. This aspiration became known as Home Rule.

Parnell, son of an Irish father and an American mother, had an arrogant personality and a political pragmatism that enabled him to take on even Gladstone without the slightest senses of inferiority. On reaching the House of Commons, in 1875, he scorned its cozy, club-like conventions and perfected filibustering techniques for blocking parliamentary business: proposing endless amendments, and making speeches lasting several hours. In one case, he forced an infuriated House into a continuous 41-hour session.

He had reason for concern

BOYCOTT'S LEGACY

An effective technique was to ostracise anyone who took over an evicted man's land; it was applied so successfully to a Captain Boycott in County Mayo that his surname entered the English language.

emigrated to Lancashire in England, where Davitt lost an arm in a factory accident when he was 11. By the time he returned to Ireland, he had embraced Fenianism, completed a term of penal servitude, and was convinced that the only hope for tenants was to have rents reduced by law to a realistic level and then to devise a scheme enabling them gradually to own their own land.

Once again, across Ireland, massive demonstrations were held. Funds from America

about Ireland. After several relatively good harvests, 1877's summer was wet and a flood of cheap grain carried from America by the new fast steamships was lowering prices to a point where tenants could no longer afford their rents. A new wave of evictions was threatened. With Michael Davitt, Parnell set up the National Land League of Ireland.

Davitt's parents, evicted from their Mayo landholding in 1852 when he was five, had

LEFT: two great opponents in the London parliament, William Ewart Gladstone (left) and Charles Stewart Parnell. ABOVE: an 1874 St Patrick's Day parade in New York features a bust of Daniel O'Connell.

flowed in to help the victims of oppression and threats of violence, frequently carried out, gave teeth to the Land League. In parliament, Parnell officially deplored the violence, and one Irish MP condemned the practice of shooting landlords because the gunmen often missed and hit the wrong person. At home the agitators gained some invaluable allies: the Catholic priesthood, which had previously stood aside from nationalist movements. Soon no-go areas were established within which justice was in the hands of the Land League.

Gladstone's 1881 Land Act was regarded as revolutionary. It granted fixity of tenure to tenants who paid their rent; laid down that a tenant should be paid when he vacated a holding for improvements he had made; and decreed that fair rents should be defined not by the landlord but by a Land Court. Progress seemed possible. But then Lord Frederick Cavendish, the new Chief Secretary for Ireland and Gladstone's nephew by marriage, was knifed to death in Dublin. Reform slid down the agenda.

Parnell's next move was to found the Irish National League to campaign uncompromisingly for Home Rule. A general election in 1885 gave him control of 85 of the 103 Irish seats in the House of Commons and ensured that he held the balance of power between Gladstone's Lib-

erals and Lord Salisbury's Conservatives. Suddenly, Home Rule became the main issue in English politics.

The Conservatives found it hard to regard Home Rule as anything other than the thin end of the wedge of full independence. After all, they argued, Home Rule would still leave the Imperial parliament controlling international affairs, war and peace, even customs and excise. How could any Irishman be satisfied with that? And yet the writings of the time show that most educated Irishmen, including nationalists, were happy to remain within the British Empire. All that self-respect required was that they should control their domestic affairs. Had Home Rule

been granted in 1886, therefore, Ireland might well still be part of the United Kingdom, having "a distinct but not separate identity" rather like Wales and Scotland. It is one of the big "ifs" of Irish history.

Ulster goes on the alert

But one significant group would have hotly opposed such an outcome. A million Protestants still lived in Ireland, almost half of them in the northeast area of Ulster, and Home Rule would have severely limited the power of this influential minority. These Ulstermen saw themselves as different, as indeed they were. Their Presbyterian tradition had always been more radical than the loose Protestantism of their southern co-religionists and had given them a formidable self-reliance. Although security of tenure had always been greater in the northeast, the Protestant descendants of the 17th-century Scots settlers felt far from settled; they had retained an ineradicable tribal fear of being dispossessed of their lands by the Catholics.

What's more, they had a lot to lose. England's Industrial Revolution, which had been stopped from spreading to most of Ireland by trade restrictions, had taken root in Ulster. The linen industry, permitted to flourish because there was no equivalent industry for it to compete with in England, had brought prosperity to Belfast. Then, in the 1850s, shipbuilding became a major employer. In those few years, Belfast was permanently differentiated from Dublin. Some saw the city as a New Jerusalem created largely by jerry-builders; others regarded it as an outpost of industrial Britian. Northern Protestants saw their prosperity being threatened by anyone who wanted to weaken the link with England.

This uncertainty was a tonic to the Orange Order, whose belligerent cry of "No Popery, No Surrender" succinctly defined, and still defines, its attitude. Leaders such as the Earl of Enniskillen gave the movement a veneer of respectability, but signs of the Orangemen's violent origins weren't hard to find. Lord Randolph Churchill ringingly reassured the northern Protestants on behalf of the Conservatives that,

BELFAST'S STUPENDOUS GROWTH

Belfast's population jumped from 20,000 to 100,000 between 1800 and 1850, making it Ireland's first – and only – industrial city.

if Home Rule were imposed, "Ulster would fight, and Ulster would be right." But the first Home Rule Bill was voted down in 1886.

England's values, so precious to the Orangemen, were being rejected in the south. A literary revival was growing, creating a new appreciation of Celtic culture and myths and a new respect for the Irish language, hitherto regarded as a fast-dying vulgar tongue. W.B. Yeats, the son of a Protestant Irish artist, published collections of folk tales such as *The Celtic Twilight,* conferring a new dignity on the often ridiculed Irish peasantry. A Gaelic League was set up, declaring itself the archer that would slay the plundering crow of the English mind, its arrow being the Irish language. It was time, said the League, for the Irishman to stop being a "West Briton".

In the political arena, however, there were setbacks. Parnell lost political support when the scandal of his long-time affair with Kitty O'Shea, who had borne him three children, erupted in 1889. Parnell died two years later, after being soaked with rain at a political rally in Galway. Gladstone himself retired from the scene in 1893, aged 84, having failed to get his second Home Rule Bill, which had been approved narrowly by the House of Commons, through the Upper Chamber, the House of Lords. It was time for the baton of the Irish cause to pass to a new generation.

The 20th century

As a new century dawned, a Conservative government in England held out no hope of Home Rule. Queen Victoria's visit to Dublin in 1900 and Edward VII's in 1903 were well received, but new forces of nationalism were being assembled by Arthur Griffith, a Dublin printer and journalist, and John McBride, a Mayo-born republican who had fought against the British in South Africa's Boer War. Griffith and

McBride demanded "an Irish Republic One and Indivisible".

Two general elections in Britain in 1910 left the Liberals and Conservatives almost equally split in parliament. Once again the Irish Party, now led by the moderate John Redmond, used its balance of power to press for a new Home Rule Bill. Such a Bill was introduced in 1912 by prime minister Herbert Asquith and looked likely to become law in the foreseeable future.

The Protestants in Ulster began arming themselves. They found as leader a Dublin MP and brilliant lawyer, Sir Edward Carson, who had been Solicitor General in a Conservative gov-

ernment and who had earlier acted as prosecuting counsel against Oscar Wilde in the writer's celebrated homosexuality trial. What, asked Carson, was the point of Home Rule now that most Irishmen owned their farms, all major grievances had been removed, and even a Catholic university had been set up?

In 1913 recruiting started for a 100,000-strong Ulster Volunteer Force and large consignments of rifles were imported. "This place is an armed camp," said Carson. The southerners responded by setting up a counter-force, the Irish National Volunteers, whose badge carried the Letters "FF", for Fianna Fáil, a legendary band of warriors. The problem, then as now,

LEFT: Orangemen opposing Home Rule march to Belfast's City Hall in 1886. **RIGHT:** Sir Edward Carson, a Dubliner, rallies Protestant Ulster against Home Rule.

could be simply stated. The Protestant majority in the northeast wished to remain full British subjects and were prepared to fight Britain to retain that status. The Catholic minority in the area, like the Catholic majority in the rest of the island, sought a more Irish identity. The two attitudes seemed irreconcilable.

Sir Winston Churchill, then a Liberal Minister, was first to voice publicly one possible solution. Six of the ancient province of Ulster's nine counties – those most heavily settled by Protestants in the early 1600s – might be excluded from any Home Rule agreement. Redmond, under pressure to get results, conceded that

these six counties could *temporarily* be excluded for six years, after which time he hoped the Unionists would see the wisdom of rejoining their fellow Irishmen. From the nationalists' point of view, it was a fatal concession.

The Great War intervenes

Larger problems than Ireland loomed for Britain in 1914 with the outbreak of World War I. A deal was rapidly done under which a Home Rule Act was passed, together with an order suspending its operation for the duration of the war or until such time as an amendment could be added to take account of Ulster's concerns. Ireland was thus bought off, to the extent that a greater pro-

portion of Irishmen volunteered for the British army than any other part of the United Kingdom's population. Irishmen won 17 Victoria Crosses in the first 13 months of the war. Surely, Redmond reasoned, such courage would eradicate even Ulster Unionist worries.

The reality was different. Carson, now a member of Britain's War Cabinet, saw the Ulster regiments' heavy losses in the war, particularly during the Battle of the Somme in 1916, as a subscription towards permanent membership of the UK. In Ireland, many still remembered the old adage that England's misfortune is Ireland's opportunity, and nationalists led by Arthur Griffith began grouping under the broad banner of Sinn Féin (pronounced *shin fayne* and meaning, self-reliantly, "We Ourselves").

James Connolly, a tough-minded labour organiser born into a poor Irish family in Scotland in 1868 and a soldier in the British army at the age of 14, had embraced socialist thinking, setting up an Irish Citizens' Army to defend striking workers against brutal police suppression. Pádraic Pearse, a shy and austere school-master, had developed a mystical belief that bloodshed was needed to cleanse Ireland, in the same way as Jesus Christ, by shedding his blood, had redeemed mankind. Philosophy and physical force came together on the sunny spring holiday morning of Monday, 24 April 1916.

The Easter Rising

As Pearse, commander of the patriots determined to liberate Ireland, set out to march down Dublin's Sackville Street, his sister pleaded with him to "Come home, Pat, and leave all this foolishness." Most Irish people would probably have echoed her sentiments if they'd had an inkling of the ambitions of the small band of unrepresentative middle-class intellectuals behind the Easter Rising. But Pearse proceeded and, with 150 others, armed with a variety of venerable rifles and agricultural implements, took over the city's General Post Office and solemnly read out, to the apathy of bystanders, the proclamation of the new Irish Republic.

Another 800 or so civilian soldiers took over a brewery, a biscuit factory, a lunatic asylum and other key points. Eamon de Valera, a young mathematics teacher born in America of an Irish mother and a Spanish father, liberated a bakery against the wishes of its workers, who had felt that even in a republic people had to eat.

As usual in Irish politics, dissension among the rebel components was rife, some regarding the revolt as "rampant neurotic romanticism". The Rising, planned for the Easter Sunday, had to be postponed for a day, and the chaos meant that only in Dublin was it possible to organise anything, and even there only 800 of a hoped-for 3,000 soldiers showed up.

Soon Dublin ground to a halt. Alarm and rumours spread. The poor looted stores and children ran-

REACTION TO THE RISING

The Rising was unexpected. A quarter of a million Irishmen were fighting in France at the time, and Dublin housewives, regarding the rebellion as treachery and madness, made tea for the troops sent in to quell it.

Sinn Féiners," one leading Irish MP wrote to his party leader, Redmond. "But a reaction might very easily be created." He then added the prophetic words: "Do not fail to urge the government not to execute any of the prisoners."

But Redmond's urgings went unheeded and on 3 May the first three leaders, including Pearse, were shot at dawn. The next day, four more were shot. On 5 May, one more. On 8 May, four more. On 12 May, two more – including Connolly, who,

sacked sweet shops. A British gunboat on the River Liffey began to shell the rebel strongholds. The inevitable end, when it came, was swift. The British set fire to the area around the GPO, burning out the rebels. By the time Pearse surrendered on the Saturday, 64 rebels, 134 police and soldiers and at least 220 civilians had died. The centre of Dublin lay in ruins. Martial law was imposed and 4,000 jailed. "So far the feeling of the population in Dublin is against the

LEFT: James Connolly, labour organiser and one of the rebel leaders in 1916. **ABOVE:** Dublin's O'Connell Street in ruins after being shelled by British gunboats during the Easter Rising; the pillared Post Office survived.

because a bullet during the fighting had fractured his ankle, sat in a chair before the firing squad. Nobody knew how long the executions would go on. It was, someone said later, "like watching a stream of blood coming from beneath a closed door". Slowly, in Ireland, derision for the upstarts turned to sympathy, then support. As Yeats wrote in a famous poem, the rebels had been "changed, changed utterly. A terrible beauty is born."

That Christmas, as a goodwill gesture, David Lloyd George, the "Welsh wizard" who was now Britain's charismatic prime minister, released 560 Irish internees from prison in England. Among them were Arthur Griffith, Sinn

Féin's founder, and a 27-year-old west Cork man, Michael Collins, formerly a clerk in London with the British civil service. Another batch of prisoners given an amnesty at Easter 1917 included Eamon de Valera, the sole surviving Easter Rising commandant. The cast was in place for the climactic act of Ireland's drama.

The hunger strikes begin

The new men wrote a script which was to be revived with uncanny fidelity in the 1970s and 1980s. They opposed Redmond's party at by-elections with Sinn Féin candidates, who began winning. Jailed supporters, on having their

Church's hierarchy condemned conscription – which turned out to be unnecessary anyway, as the war was soon to end – and the Irish Party walked out of the House of Commons. Sinn Féin had found a rallying cry, which it put to effective use, winning sweeping victories in the post-war general election of December 1918.

The new MPs boycotted the House of Commons forming their own parliament, Dáil Eireann, in Dublin's Mansion House. As president of their new "republic", they elected de Valera; the fact that he was languishing in jail at the time was probably worth an extra vote or two.

Standing behind Sinn Féin were the Volun-

demand to be recognised as political prisoners turned down by the authorities, staged hunger strikes. When one striker died after being force-fed, Collins organised a show funeral, massively attended. Arms were stockpiled. Lawlessness reminiscent of the 18th century started spreading in rural areas. By the time Redmond died (of natural causes) in March 1918, his hopes of bringing about Ireland's independence peaceably had turned to dust.

The next month, panicked by a setback in the war in France, Britain finally extended conscription to Ireland, throwing in as a sop new Home Rule legislation based on partitioning the island. It was a foolish move. The Catholic

teers, known in the countryside as the Irish Republican Army, who increasingly saw violence as an effective weapon. They began killing anyone in uniform who stood in their way, then progressed to selective assassinations. Like so many Irish conflicts, this one rapidly took on some of the characteristics of a civil war. The corpses found labelled "Spy – Killed by IRA" were usually those of Irishmen.

After an attempt was made in broad daylight on the life of Viceroy, the king's representative in Ireland, England, perplexed as ever, suppressed Sinn Féin. "The English government in Ireland," jeered Arthur Griffith, "has now proclaimed the Irish nation, as it formerly proclaimed the Catholic Church, an illegal assembly." Undeterred, Sinn Féin did well in the municipal elections held in January 1920.

When some of the boycotted police force – about one in 10 – resigned, they were replaced by recruits from England, many of them demobilised soldiers hardened to killing on the battlefields of France. Forming motorised anti-terrorist squads, they hit back quickly at any sign of trouble. But there were areas into which even they dared not go. In these, policing was taken over by the trench-

A NEW COUNTRY

The 1921 Treaty styled the 26 counties the Irish Free State, a literal translation of the Gaelic word *Saorstat*.

Sunday", Michael Collins had 12 British officers shot dead, mostly in their beds. That afternoon, at a Gaelic football match in Dublin's Croke Park, police shot dead 11 civilians. In the countryside, fearful families took to sleeping in hedgerows to escape the revenge killings. Guerrilla warfare spread, out of control.

In May 1921 Britain tried out a new idea, holding elections for two Irish parliaments, one in the North, one in the South. Sinn Féin swept the board in the South and the Unionists dominated the North.

coated Volunteers, who arrested and sentenced petty criminals such as house breakers and cattle stealers and enforced licensing laws. The government, with 10,000 police and 50,000 troops, was humiliated.

Run-up to a Republic

Before long, the police began fighting back, carrying out undisciplined reprisals after every IRA atrocity. On 21 November 1920, "Bloody

LEFT: Ireland's independence did not end the bloodshed on the streets of the capital. **ABOVE:** children in Dublin wave American flags to celebrate the ending of the Anglo-Irish war in 1921.

Partition appeared inevitable. That October, a conference was called in London at which Britain and Ireland, faced with the prospect of declaring war on each other, sat down to thrash out a settlement.

The compromises were agonising. But on 5 December 1921, at 2.20 in the morning, a deal was done, a document signed. The consequences would be enormous, for this was the first fissure, signalling the eventual break-up of the British Empire. To those present, the significance was somewhat narrower. Eight centuries of attempts by England's monarchs and ministers to rule their neighbouring island had, with surprising abruptness, come to an end.

LIVING WITH PARTITION

Instead of coming together, the Catholic South and the Protestant-dominated North ignored each other for 50 years. Then civil strife erupted in the North

To David Lloyd George's dexterous political mind, the fact that the Anglo-Irish Treaty gave everyone *something* they wanted but nobody *everything* they wanted meant that it must stand some chance of success. This was the old mistake: the belief that the Irish were really Englishmen with brogues. In reality, the two peoples' expectations were quite different and, after eight centuries during which Irishman had fought Irishman over conflicting national allegiances, the first fruit of independence was true civil war.

The treaty gave the nationalists more than many had expected: an Irish Free State with a dominion status within the British Empire similar to Canada's. This was far greater freedom than Home Rule had ever promised.

The border question

But one dark cloud cast a shadow over the deal. Six counties of Ulster – Antrim, Down, Tyrone, Fermanagh, Armagh and Derry – were retained within the United Kingdom, the British having recognised that even the deluge of a world war had not softened the resolution of the northern Protestants. Sir Winston Churchill expressed the dilemma graphically: "As the deluge subsides and the waters fall short, we see the dreary steeples of Fermanagh and Tyrone emerging once again. The integrity of their quarrel is one of the few institutions that has been unaltered in the cataclysm which has swept the world."

To sell the long-resisted division of Ireland to nationalists, the government added a proviso: a Boundary Commission would decide which Roman Catholic-dominated areas of Northern Ireland would later be incorporated within the 26 counties of the Free State. This promise permitted patriots such as Michael Collins to swallow the bitter pill of partition: after the Catholic areas of Tyrone, Fermanagh and south Armagh

had been removed, they reckoned, what would remain would not leave the new north-eastern state a viable entity.

But Collins's hopes, faint though they were, were not universally held. Ferocious arguments split the infant Free State, laying bare long suppressed personal animosities. On the one side

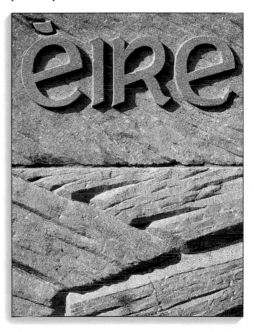

stood the pro-Treaty provisional government led by Arthur Griffith; on the other, the anti-Treaty forces massing behind Eamon de Valera. After a bitter 12-day parliamentary debate, the Treaty was carried by 64 votes to 57.

It was too narrow a margin to ensure peace, especially since the Irish Republican Army, mirroring the split in the country, was marching in opposite directions; about half with Collins, transforming itself into the regular army of the Free State, and the other half refusing to recognise the new government, relying instead on force to win them a free and united Ireland.

By 1922 Dublin's O'Connell Street was in flames again, with 60 dying in eight days of sav-

LEFT: a farewell to empire as Queen Victoria's statue is removed from outside Ireland's parliament building.
RIGHT: the new nation looked to the Gaelic language to help mould a new identity.

age fighting. Northern Protestants, looking on, vowed to have nothing to do with any redrawing of borders, declaring: "What we have, we hold." Fighting broke out in Northern Ireland, too, with the death toll rising to 264 within six months.

The new Ireland's first prime minister did not live to see the end of the struggle: in August 1922, heavily overworked, Griffith collapsed and died. Collins had a more violent end, being shot dead in an ambush on the Macroom to Bandon road in his

STATE EXECUTIONS

The Free State government, in its first six months, executed 77 Republicans – far more than had been shot by the British in the preceding Anglo-Irish War.

effective surrender. But it was to dominate every aspect of political life in the Free State for the next half-century. The country's two main political parties today, Fine Gael (meaning *Tribe of Ireland*) and Fianna Fáil (*Warriors of Ireland*) are direct descendants of the pro- and anti-Treaty forces.

In 1927, de Valera entered parliament (the Dáil) at the head of Fianna Fáil. He came to power in the 1932 election, ushering in a new era of pious respectability and vowing to reinstate the ancient Gaelic lan-

native County Cork. He had been expecting just such an outcome: after putting his name to the Anglo-Irish Treaty, he had written to a friend: "Will anyone be satisfied with the bargain? Will anyone? I tell you this – early this morning I signed my death warrant."

De Valera's vision

The Boundary Commission recommended only minor adjustments, and even these were never implemented. De Valera's view of the border as "an old fortress of crumbled masonry, held together with the plaster of fiction" had proved false. Permanent partition had arrived.

The civil war ended in 1923 with de Valera's

guage and culture. "No longer," declared de Valera, "shall our children, like our cattle, be brought up for export." His vision was later spelt out in a famous St Patrick's Day address, in which he described his ideal Ireland as "a land whose countryside would be bright with cozy homesteads, whose fields and villages would be joyous with the sounds of industry, with the rompings of sturdy children, the contests of athletic youths and the laughter of comely maidens, whose firesides would be forums for the wisdom of serene old age." It was a noble enough aim. It just didn't particularly belong to the 20th century.

In the following three decades, de Valera built

Fianna Fáil into a formidable populist political movement, drawing support from small farmers, the urban working class and the newly moneyed. Fine Gael's heartland was among larger farmers and the professional classes. The Labour Party, which pre-dated partition, found it hard to build support: the trade unions, while nominally pro-Labour, often did deals with Fianna Fáil, and the Church's anti-communist propaganda encouraged a fear of the Left.

Endless emigration

"Dev", as he became affectionately known, pursued a policy of economic nationalism, raising social scale from the farmhands, the once affluent Anglo-Irish – sometimes called the Protestant "Ascendancy" – fell into decline and their "Big Houses" at the end of long, tree-lined avenues began to look dilapidated.

Many southerners began to question the wisdom of following their leader's "Small is Beautiful" signposts. "It was indeed hard," said one observer, "to muster up enthusiasm for the cargeen moss industry, in the possible utilisation of the various parts of the herring's anatomy, down to the tail and the fin, in portable, prefabricated factories themselves made of herringbone cement along the west coast."

tariff barriers against England, which retaliated. A tax was even imposed on English newspapers. Yet not everyone was thrilled when, for example, Dev announced that Ireland was self-sufficient in shoelaces. Emigration, mainly to England and America, claimed yet another generation of younger sons unable to inherit the family farm and younger daughters unable to find husbands. In the early 1920s, an astonishing 43 per cent of Irish-born men and women were living abroad. At the opposite end of the

LEFT: Eamon de Valera's vision for a new Ireland had a strong rural emphasis. **ABOVE:** a turf gatherer in the remote west of Ireland

But what was the alternative? Certainly not to imitate the United Kingdom, Dev insisted, and, to emphasise the point, he produced a constitution in 1937 which abolished the oath of allegiance to England's king and claimed sovereignty over all 32 counties of Ireland. But it also underlined the pervasive influence of the Roman Catholic Church, thus alienating northern Protestants for good. The poet W. B. Yeats, a member of the Irish Senate, had warned him of the dangers. "If you show that this country, Southern Ireland, is going to be governed by Catholic ideas and by Catholic ideas alone, you will never get the North," said Yeats. "You will put a wedge into the midst of this nation."

The new constitution created a curious equilibrium. The bishops in the South and the Orangemen in the North each exercised a sectarian and politically conservative pressure on their respective parliaments.

Although the Unionists would have been happy to remain an integral part of Britain, Lloyd George, emphasising Ulster's "otherness", had given them their own parliament, Stormont – built on the outskirts of Belfast in the style of Buckingham Palace, only grander. And they had lost no time in making their makeshift state impregnable. London, relieved to be rid of the perennial Irish problem, did mended Catholic pipes. An all-Protestant part-time special constabulary (the "B" Specials) maintained close links with the Orange Order and helped the police keep dissension under control. The IRA, making little headway in Ulster, began a campaign in English cities in 1938, setting off suitcase bombs.

World War II

While Irish history was repeating itself, European history concocted another world war. The Unionists felt their self-interest had been justified when, as soon as Britain declared war on Germany in 1939, de Valera announced that

nothing to stop them. Nor, fatally, did the Roman Catholics' elected representatives, who boycotted Stormont. The assembly, the Unionists boasted, was "a Protestant parliament for a Protestant people." The historic hatreds between the two communities were left unhealed.

If anything, they were deepened. Taking advantage of the nationalists' boycott, the Unionists made sure that the plum jobs and the best housing went to their own supporters. Two distinct communities developed: Protestant dentists pulled Protestant teeth, Catholic plumbers

WARTIME VOLUNTEERS

Although the Free State stayed neutral in the war, 50,000 southern Irishmen joined the British forces.

Southern Ireland would remain neutral. Behind the scenes, Sir Winston Churchill, Britain's new wartime leader, offered de Valera a united Ireland at some point in the future if Ireland were to enter the war and allow the British navy to use its ports. De Valera said no.

Churchill's fears had not been unfounded. The Germans had been planning an invasion of Ireland, "Operation Green", as a springboard to an assault on Britain. In a handbook designed to brief their battalions, they noted that "the Irishman supports a community founded upon equality for all, but associates with this an extraordinary personal need for independence which easily leads to indiscipline and pugnacity."

Northern Ireland became a target. A ferocious night raid on Belfast in April 1941 killed more than 700 people. The Unionists claimed that the neutral South's lack of a blackout helped German bombers pinpoint their targets in the darkened North. Another grudge was chalked up on the blackboard of Irish history.

Over the years even the name of the Free State had been fiercely argued about. Both the English and the Irish seemed to find "Eire" (Gaelic for "Ireland") acceptable. But in 1948

also by the restrictions placed on entertainment. In 1954 a record 1,034 books were banned, and cinemagoers, if they wished to follow the plots of many films, had to cross the border to see the unscissored versions. London's more lurid Sunday newspapers published tamer Irish editions.

Northern Protestants looked askance at what they saw as the southern state's unacceptable intrusion into personal freedoms – its outlawing of divorce, for example, and its ban on the importation of contraceptives. Northern Ireland, Britain had pledged when the Republic left the Commonwealth, could remain part of the United Kingdom as long as a majority of its

a coalition government fixed the name of the country as the Republic of Ireland. Britain declared that, as a result, Ireland was no longer part of the Commonwealth. At last, Ireland – or at least 26 counties of it – was truly free.

Politically free, at least. Economically and culturally, Ireland remained chained. Emigration reached epidemic proportions, triggered not only by the loneliness, dullness and generally unattractive nature of life in rural Ireland but

---

LEFT: Stormont, symbol of power in British-ruled Northern Ireland. **ABOVE:** Nelson's pillar in Dublin's O'Connell Street was illegally blown up in 1966 to mark the 50th anniversary of the Easter Rising.

people wished. Since Protestants outnumbered Catholics by two to one in the Six Counties, that might mean forever. Some Protestants were so fervently "loyalist" that they would not even think of setting foot in the alien republic.

The green consumers

As Britain rebuilt its economic strength in the 1950s, Northern Ireland began to feel the benefit of its welfare state and industrial incentives, while the Republic remained essentially a humdrum peasant economy. In 1958, under the premiership of Sean Lemass, Ireland decided to rejoin the 20th century. He set out vigorously to create new jobs by opening up the economy to foreign investment, attracting light engineering, pharmaceutical and electronics companies. The dream of Eamon de Valera – who was now president, a largely symbolic office – faded fast. Interest in Gaelic language and culture waned and the voice of management consultants was heard in the land. The Irish, embracing consumerism with relish, seemed destined to become indistinguishable from the English.

Even the IRA failed to command much support in its continuing fight for a united Ireland. A campaign of border raids between 1956 and 1962 netted a few arms hauls but gradually petered out. By 1965, it seemed the most nat-

ural thing in the world for Lemass to have a good-neighbourly meeting with Northern Ireland's premier, Captain Terence O'Neill. But it seemed shockingly unnatural to hardline Unionists. Uncompromising voices, including those of several Cabinet colleagues and a popular fundamentalist preacher, the Reverend Ian Paisley, reminded him that Lemass's Republic still claimed jurisdiction over the Six Counties.

O'Neill, with his upper-class background, was ill-equipped to cope with the Pandora's Box that was opened just three years later. It began routinely enough, when a Unionist-controlled council in Caledon, County Tyrone, where many Catholic families were badly in need of

housing, allocated one of its dwellings to a young, single Protestant girl. Local nationalists, following the example of blacks in the United States, first staged a sit-in, then a civil rights march. A second march was planned for October 1968, inside the walled city of Londonderry. This is a symbolic place for Unionists, who still commemorate the breaking of the city's siege in 1689 when Protestant supporters of William of Orange defeated Catholic supporters of James II, thus cementing Protestant supremacy (Nationalists, equally tutored in the city's history, reject its "English" name in favour of the original Derry).

O'Neill's government, viewing the march not as a civil rights protest but as a nationalist conspiracy, banned it. Two thousand people marched anyway, and were met by the massed forces of the Royal Ulster Constabulary, complete with two mobile water cannon. Television viewers around the world were treated to the ensuing battle, as the RUC took their truncheons to the demonstrators with what looked suspiciously like enthusiasm. "It was as though they had been waiting to do it for 50 years," said a young civil rights leader, Bernadette Devlin.

Further marches ended in violence and O'Neill, having seen his dreams for a civilised relationship between the two Irelands consumed by the fires of sectarian hatred, was forced out of office by militant Unionists.

British troops march in

Almost inevitably, the Protestants' annual march through Londonderry in August 1969 sparked off violence. Petrol bombs were hurled, along with broken-up paving stones. The police replied with CS gas. Fighting spread to the Catholic Falls Road and the Protestant Shankill Road. The RUC, hopelessly out of its depth, appealed for reinforcements and, on 16 August, a reluctant British government sent troops on to the streets of Derry and Belfast "in support of the civil power". What was the choice? Northern Ireland was, after all, part of the UK.

It was an emergency measure, a temporary arrangement. Nobody imagined, in their wildest nightmares, that the troops would still be there three decades later.

LEFT: Bernadette Devlin, the fiery civil rights leader who became an MP. RIGHT: the Rev. Ian Paisley, rallying Protestants in the late 1960s.

IRELAND TODAY

*Leaving the North to fight its ancient battles, the South looked to Europe,
transforming in the process its economic and social values*

At first the British soldiers arriving in what was technically British territory were welcomed as saviours. Catholic housewives, many of whom had been preparing to take refuge in the Republic, plied them with endless cups of tea. Girls smiled sweetly at them. Perhaps, it seemed for a moment, all would be well. But it was already too late for such hopes, for this latest chapter of Ireland's Troubles had caused a fearful resurrection: that of the IRA.

As a fighting force, the Irish Republican Army had virtually ceased to exist in 1962. By the late 1960s the declared aim of the small group of Marxists who constituted the rump of the IRA was to overthrow the conservative establishments in both parts of Ireland, then set up an ill-defined workers' republic. Lacking modern weaponry, they were acutely conscious of their failure to protect Catholic communities against Protestant mobs, a failure brought painfully home by graffiti which interpreted IRA as "I Ran Away".

The IRA is reborn

After a stormy meeting in the Republic, the movement split into two groups: the Official IRA, which had Marxist leanings and was interested in infiltrating conventional politics, and the Provisional wing, which combined a more simplistic nationalism with a faith in the efficacy of violence.

Recruitment to the Provisionals ("Provos") soared when the British army embarked on late-night arms searches in Catholic areas. Guns and explosives were found, but the sympathy of moderate Catholics was lost. To keep the two communities apart, the troops erected a ramshackle barrier of building blocks and corrugated iron, "the Peace Line". No one thought that the line would become a semi-permanent concrete and steel fortification, a Berlin Wall within the United Kingdom.

LEFT: Ulster's wall art conveys a sinister sectarian message. **RIGHT:** a Belfast loyalist publicly states her opposition to closer links with the Republic.

Trust and understanding between nationalists and Unionists have always been difficult because the two cultural traditions have so few points of contact. Protestant children still attend Protestant schools supported entirely by the state, while Catholic children go to schools largely financed by the state but managed by

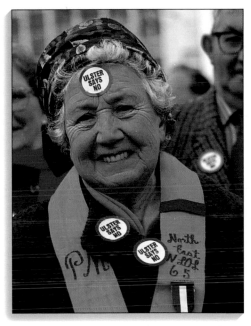

their church. Catholic children are taught Gaelic games, Protestants play cricket. Catholics learn Irish, Protestants don't. Integrating the schools, a policy which might in the long term lessen the inheritance of hate, has proved an impossible nettle to grasp. The Roman Catholic Church in particular argues strongly that Catholic children must have the spiritual nourishment of a Catholic education. And, in any case, so few communities remain in which Protestants and Catholics live side by side that integrated schools would mean bussing thousands of children from one area to another.

In the anarchy of the early 1970s, relationships within Ulster were corroded further as shopkeepers in both Catholic and Protestant areas were visited regularly by vigilantes from their own communities demanding what amounted to protection money. Most paid up; those who didn't frequently found their premises burned to the ground soon afterwards. Gangsterism, divorced from any political objective, was added to the witches' brew of violence.

The IRA's armed offensive gathered pace, spreading terror by means of snipers' bullets, booby-trapped vehicles and bombs placed in crowded bars.

DIVISIONS RUN DEEP

Even underground, Ulster's communities are divided. Republicans work in the sewage tunnels in Catholic areas and Loyalists in the tunnels in Protestant areas.

of it, 13 civilians lay dead, shot by paratroopers. The date, Bloody Sunday, became yet another Irish anniversary to be commemorated violently. The following month, as a reprisal, a bomb exploded at Aldershot Barracks in England, killing seven people. As in the 1850s and the 1930s, the Troubles had spread inexorably across the Irish Sea.

Ireland joins Europe

In the Republic of Ireland, where many IRA men on the run took refuge, leading politicians

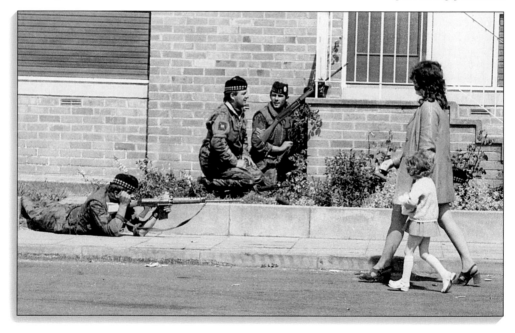

In the Catholic ghettos, the initial songs of praise for the British army had turned into a ghoulish refrain: "If you kill a British soldier, clap your hands." Protestant vigilante and terrorist groups such as the Ulster Defence Association and the Ulster Volunteer Force began to match violence with violence. Britain introduced internment of suspected terrorists without trial – a drastic remedy, but one which had worked before. It didn't work this time. The army, having arrived as mediator, was now in many areas the enemy.

The situation worsened dramatically when, on 30 January 1972, shooting broke out at an anti-internment rally in Londonderry. At the end

condemned the continuing violence in the North but were careful to ensure that the South would not easily be drawn into it. For, as bombs and bullets ripped Northern Ireland's economy to shreds, the Republic was enjoying unprecedented affluence. The inward investment policy had brought real, not fool's, gold to the end of the Irish rainbow. Large Mercedes and Toyotas sped German and Japanese executives through rural lanes, adding further unpredictability to Ireland's devil-may-care driving conditions.

After the country's entry into the European Economic Community at the beginning of 1973, financial subsidies descended, as seemingly inexhaustible as Ireland's rain. Former farm labourers, much to their delight, found themselves earning good money assembling electronics components, and one euphoric trade minister dared to describe Ireland as "the sun-belt of Europe".

Culturally, too, the climate was brightening. Writers and artists, once forced to emigrate in search of intellectual freedom, were exempted from paying income tax on their royalties. Some well-known names, such as thriller writer Frederick Forsyth, moved to Ireland to take advantage of the concession. One or two more provocative authors found it peculiar that, while one arm of the government was allowing them

London takes control

In the North, the sky was darkening further. Two months after Bloody Sunday, Britain abolished the 50-year-old Stormont parliament, imposing direct rule from London, and began attempts to persuade Protestant and Catholic leaders to set up a power-sharing executive. To the English, power-sharing seemed a perfectly sensible compromise. But to both tribes in Ulster, it was anathema: the Protestant extremists saw it as the first step towards a united Ireland, and the IRA saw it as a permanent hindrance to such unity. It collapsed and direct rule was reimposed

As atrocities multiplied, the death toll passed

to live free of income tax, another was banning their books.

Feminism reached Dublin, flourishing richly in a climate long hostile to female initiative. In one celebrated protest against the ban on importing contraceptives into the Republic, groups of women staged well-publicised shopping trips by train to Belfast. On returning to Dublin, they made a point of declaring their unlawful purchases to Customs officers and, on being asked to hand them over, informed the embarrassed young men that they were wearing them.

LEFT: In the North, the security forces were very visible.
ABOVE: In the South, poverty remained very visible too.

2,500 and an entire generation reached adulthood without ever having known peace. British governments suggested political formula after political formula, but none was accepted. Even well-tried nationalist tactics were failing to work any more: a hunger strike in an Ulster prison was ignored by Britain's prime minister, Margaret Thatcher, and 10 men starved to death.

British politicians sent across the Irish Sea recalled the plea of one 19th-century predecessor who wrote to the then prime minister, Benjamin Disraeli: "Ireland is an infernal country to manage, statemanship wholly out of place. The only way to govern is the old plan (which I will not attempt) of taking up violently one faction or the other, putting them like fighting cocks, and then backing one. I wish you would send me to India. Ireland is the grave of every reputation."

The truth was that most people in Northern Ireland had adapted to the level of violence. As the estimated 300 to 400 republican gunmen concentrated their fire on police and military targets, it was possible for the average citizen to live a relatively uneventful life. Indeed, it was reported that statistically the combined risk of being killed in the Troubles and on the roads was, at 22 per 100,000 population, much less than the combined risk of being murdered or of being killed on the roads in France (30) or the United States (32).

Hard times

Economic recession, and the reluctance of industrialists to site factories in Northern Ireland, made unemployment seem as great an evil as terrorism. And in this respect the South was faring little better. As the effects of the 1970s oil crisis became felt, industrial unemployment rose and inflation neared 25 per cent. Both governments were chasing the same investors. The North had the bad luck to win the tussle over who should build John de Lorean's gull-wing

CHARLES HAUGHEY: CHARISMA AND CONTROVERSY

Charles J. Haughey's personality would dominate and divide politics in the Republic throughout the 1980s. Well before becoming Taoiseach, he had caused controversy. In 1970, when Minister for Finance, he had been accused – and acquitted – of conspiring illegally to import arms for use in Northern Ireland.

He was also charismatic, as this pen portrait by the historian J.J. Lee makes clear: "An accountant by profession, with a capacity to master a brief quickly, he had abundant flair and imagination, immense public self-control, an ability to cut through red tape with an incisiveness that infuriat-

ed those wedded to the corruption of bureaucratic mediocrity, and an energy capable of sustaining his insatiable appetite for power. He was plainly Taoiseach material. Yet, widely admired for his talents, he was also widely distrusted for his use of those talents. He radiated an aura associated in the public mind with a Renaissance potentate – with his immense wealth (discreetly acquired after his entry to politics), his retinue of loyal retainers, his Florentine penchant for faction fighting, his patronage of the arts, his distinctive personality, at once crafty and conspiratorial, resilient and resourceful, imaginative but insecure."

sports car: the Belfast factory closed after the UK had poured £17 million into it.

The parlous state of the Republic's economy was not helped when Fianna Fáil, out of power since 1973, successfully wooed the electorate in the 1977 general election with an irresponsibly profligate manifesto. State spending, much of it on creating non-productive public service jobs, soared out of control and the state's foreign debt became mountainous.

The Haughey era

In 1979, Jack Lynch, who had followed Sean Lemass as Fianna Fáil leader, resigned as Taoiseach, to be succeeded after a bruising party contest by Charles Haughey. The early years of the "Haughey era" were marked by extraordinary political in-fighting. At one stage in 1981–82, there were three elections within 18 months. The country's complex electoral system of proportional representation meant that Fianna Fáil minority administrations alternated with Fine Gael-Labour coalitions led by Garret FitzGerald, whose genial, absent-minded manner concealed a sharp political brain.

The last of these coalitions, from late 1982 to 1987, had one major achievement: it succeeded in negotiating, with the British Prime Minister Margaret Thatcher, the Anglo-Irish Agreement. This gave the Irish Government a consultative role in the administration of Northern Ireland, while committing British and Irish law and security forces to work together against terrorism and reaffirming that the Six Counties would remain part of the United Kingdom as long as a majority of their people favoured that option.

It was a Haughey administration that eventually introduced fiscal measures brutal enough to halt the Republic's economic deterioration. Public services were cut and unemployment soared, but the ground was laid for better times in the 1990s. That decade was ushered in by the election as Ireland's president of the left-wing Mary Robinson, a leading lawyer and feminist who stood for liberal and pluralist values. In her seven-year term, she was to transform the presidency from being a dumping ground for retired politicans to a force for social change.

Suspicions grew about Charles Haughey's financial probity and in 1992 he was forced

from office, to be replaced by Albert Reynolds, a homelier, less charismatic figure. Five years later Haughey was charged for having received while in office more than £1m of undeclared funds from supermarket tycoon Ben Dunne.

An election in November 1992 confirmed the desire for change that had swept Mary Robinson into the Presidency two years earlier. The two big "civil war" parties, Fianna Fáil and Fine Gael, lost support at the polls, while the Labour Party more than doubled its parliamentary strength to assume a pivotal role in the country's politics. At last, a more modern politics seemed to be gaining ground. But Reynolds managed to

scrape back as prime minister in early 1993 by piecing together a coalition.

The abortion debate

The 1992 election was extraordinary for another reason: the voters also had to adjudicate by referendum on a bizarre debate about abortion. The controversy had erupted just after Albert Reynolds first took office, when it emerged that the attorney-general (the Government's chief legal advisor) had sought an injunction to prevent a 14-year-old rape victim having an abortion in England.

To many people, the proposal seemed both hypocritical and irrelevant since an estimated

LEFT: Charles Haughey, a cunning political magician.
RIGHT: Ireland's first female president, Mary Robinson.

4,000 Irish women travelled to Britain each year for abortions. But after a vitriolic public debate, the Constitution was amended to support the attorney-general's view and defend the right to life of the unborn.

The issue would not die down, and three proposals were put to the electorate. The first guaranteed freedom of travel (thereby ensuring that women could continue to go abroad for abortions). The second promised freedom of information "relating to services lawfully available in another state." The third, and most contentious, outlawed termination of pregnancy unless it was necessary "to save the life, as dis-

Catholic Church and, above all, for the status of women. The most striking feature of the abortion debate was that it was carried on by powerful cliques – politicians, lawyers, clerics, doctors – consisting overwhelmingly of men.

But the ground was shifting significantly and a 1995 referendum on divorce gave the pro-divorce faction the slimmest of majorities: less than 1 percent. Such a result would have been inconceivable a decade earlier. Despite the closeness of the vote, enough politicians of all parties were sufficiently emboldened to ensure that divorce finally became legal in the Republic two years later.

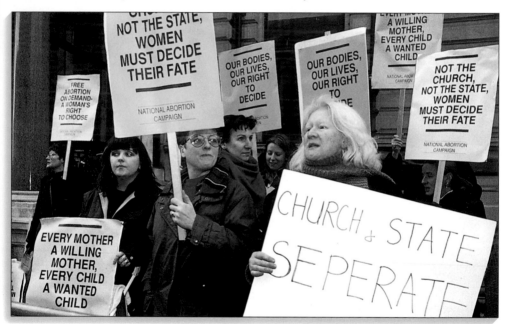

tinct from the health, of the mother." It also specifically excluded the risk of suicide acknowledged by the Supreme Court.

After an acrimonious debate, this last proposal was defeated; the others, on freedom of travel and information, were passed. Abortion therefore remained legal, but in narrow and ill-defined circumstances, and the legislators were faced with tackling an issue that most of them had been all too happy to avoid.

Divorce at last

It was inevitable that the 1992 referendums would provide only a partial answer to a question with crucial implications for the role of the

HYMNS ANCIENT AND MODERN

The traditional rigid division between God and Mammon became more and more blurred as the millennium approached. Newpaper columnist Gene Kerrigan summed up the new attitude rather well: "The best-selling album in Ireland right now is a compilation of old church hymns called Faith of Our Fathers. A decade or so ago, I would have revolted against that album – seeing it as a symbol of repression. Now I enjoy it – because it's nostalgic, and it reminds me of hymns I sang as a kid. Buying a record of hymns nowadays doesn't mean that you're married to the values they represent."

A truce is declared

Suddenly, in 1994, it seemed an end might be in sight to the troubles in the North: the IRA declared a ceasefire and, after initial scepticism, the Loyalist terrorists did the same. As tentative

who stood to lose an average £7,500 a year overtime payments if peace broke out, seemed to have mixed feelings.

Political see-saw

As hope spread in the North, confusion reigned in the South as Albert Reynolds's Fianna Fáil-led coalition collapsed. The cause was a very Irish one: Reynolds tried to appoint as president of the High Court, the state's second highest judicial post, a former attorney-general, Harry Whelehan. But Whelehan had come under fire for having ignored for seven months a request to extradite for trial in Northern Ireland a priest

talks began between the British and the Irish, it was unclear what had really changed: Republicans still wanted an end to British rule in any part of the island and Ulster Unionists still refused to contemplate abandoning their British citizenship. But, as traffic jams in Belfast were caused for the first time in 25 years not by security checks but by coachloads of Christmas shoppers from provincial towns and from Dublin, there was an intense popular desire to avoid any return to violence. Only the police,

accused (and later convicted) of sexually abusing children. Whelehan had, it was said, been reluctant to embarrass the Catholic Church.

After weeks of political horse-trading, a new coalition emerged led by Fine Gael's leader, John Bruton, portrayed as a colourless politician and more sympathetic than most to Ulster Unionist fears. But he was lucky, too: the economy began to flourish as never before, as did artistic creativity, and the combination gave the Irish a jaunty confidence.

The European Union was largely responsible for the economy's upturn. Economically, jobs were created and roads built as billions of pounds poured into the country from the Euro-

LEFT: women in Dublin protest against anti-abortion laws. **ABOVE:** the Castle Court shopping centre was one sign of a return to more peaceful times in Belfast.

pean social fund. Cheques from Brussels made up almost half the income of Irish farmers. Psychologically, any lingering inferiority complex towards Britain was eroded as the new wealth reduced the country's economic dependence on trade with its larger neighbour.

Ireland began promoting itself as the Silicon Valley of Europe. Its combination of a youthful, well-educated workforce and generous grants and tax incentives lured more than 300 electronics companies to the Republic. Computer giants such as Dell and Gateway 2000 began assembling computers there, and Microsoft established its European operations centre in

Dublin. Thanks to the wonders of satellite transmission, women in remote villages plagued for decades by unemployment began to be offered jobs keying in data for American hospitals and life insurance companies – they were so much cheaper than typists in the United States.

The buoyant job market eroded one of the Republic's most distinctive characteristics: the fatalism with which young people emigrated – at a rate of some 30,000 a year in the 1980s – mainly to Britain and the United States. Suddenly many of those who had gone in the 1980s came home, flaunting the experience they'd gained abroad and grabbing many of the new jobs. This unaccustomed immigration had one

negative effect: it meant that overall unemployment stayed high, at around 12 or 13 percent.

As the transformation of the economy became known abroad, Ireland became a magnet for refugees. Having exported people for centuries, Ireland was unprepared to import them, yet refugees from destinations as diverse as Romania and Zaire, learning of Ireland's comparatively liberal immigration laws, arrived in Dublin. Applications for asylum, which had been only 30 to 40 a year at the beginning of the decade, soared to several thousand a year. Politicians, conscious of the high unemployment figures, feared a backlash if the immigrants proved to be economic migrants rather than political refugees. Perhaps, they mused, Mary Robinson would be able to lend a hand: in 1997 she gave up the Irish presidency to become the United Nations High Commissioner for Human Rights.

A love affair with Europe

Happily, Europe loved Ireland just as much as Ireland loved Europe – if nothing else because its support acted as a useful counterweight to Britain's often antagonistic attitude. Being small and remote lent enchantment, too: Ireland could never have got away with offering corporate tax incentives that made a mockery of EU harmonisation if it had been a serious economic competitor to France or Germany.

The effects weren't wholly beneficial. For example, because agricultural subsidies favoured sheep farming, the republic's sheep population more than trebled to over 5 million and some lush parts of the west looked like being turned into rocky hillsides by overgrazing.

Tourism benefited, though, as Ireland suddenly became a chic tourist destination. Part of this popularity could be traced to the success of bands such as U2 and the international success of Riverdance, the show that sexualised traditional Irish dancing. The Irish talent for making merry was also highlighted by the creation of

THE GAELIC REVIVAL

Although as many as 500,000 people can speak Gaelic with some degree of fluency, it is the everyday language of fewer than 20,000 people. But efforts to promote it continue and in 1996 a subsidised Irish-language TV station, Teilifís na Gaeilge, began broadcasting from a base in Connemara.

more than 1,000 Irish theme pubs overseas, from Durty Nellie's in Amsterdam to O'Kims in Seoul. For the first time, a £30 million advertising campaign promoted both the Republic and Northern Ireland as a joint destination.

Social changes

On the political front, a change of government in Britain in 1997 encouraged the IRA to declare a second ceasefire, and peace talks – this time involving Sinn Féin – were resumed. The optimistic climate, however, did not do John Bruton's centre-left coalition much good in the Republic's general election that year and a cen-

tion of Mary McAleese, a Belfast academic with strong nationalist sympathies, to the presidency. Being a citizen of Northern Ireland, Mrs McAleese could not cast a vote in the Republic's presidential contest, yet she could legally stand as a candidate – and win.

But the Emerald Isle hadn't quite become the Garden of Eden. Dublin in particular was bedevilled by criminal racketeering, much of it centred on the lucrative drug trade and seemingly outside the control of an underfunded police force. The scale of the problem became apparent to the outside world only in 1996 when the gangs gunned down Veronica Guerin, the

tre-right coalition of Fianna Fáil and the Progressive Democrats came to power. The coalition's leader, 45-year-old Bertie Ahern, was notable for being the first Irish Taoiseach to be separated from his wife and living openly with another woman. This underlined how quickly Ireland had developed into a more liberal, pluralist society – one that might even, some day, win the approval of Ulster Unionists.

The Alice in Wonderland nature of Irish politics was also highlighted in 1997 by the elec-

country's leading investigative journalist.

In Northern Ireland, a peace agreement was signed in the early hours of Good Friday 1998 by all the main political parties, including Sinn Féin. But the Unionists refused to participate in any new governing body until the IRA began handing over their weapons, which they refused to do. Also, more people died violently in 1998 than in either of the two preceding years.

Hope and despair, familiar partners in Irish affairs, continued to keep the outcome uncertain. Realists knew that Macaulay's words remain as true today as ever: beneath the thin crust of the 20th century, the hot lava of history, 800 years of it, refuses to stop flowing.

LEFT: out for a stroll in Dublin's Phoenix Park.
ABOVE: youthful vandals became a major social problem on Dublin housing estates in the 1980s.

IRELAND'S ARCHITECTURE

*Ireland has history like dogs have fleas, and its
buildings reflect not only a catalogue of conquest
but also its roots as a purely agrarian economy*

"Never accept a commission in Ireland," a 19th-
century English architect warned his colleagues.
His fear was that only the most rugged buildings
could withstand the rain and the wind sweeping in
from the Atlantic. In the 20th century, two even
greater threats emerged: bitter warfare which would
see many of the great Anglo-Irish manors burnt to
the ground, and the rapacity of property developers
which would devastate Dublin's Georgian heritage.

Ireland's buildings reflect a history of conquest.
From the 12th century, Anglo-Norman fortresses
were designed to intimidate. But Ireland proved
hard to subjugate and fortified tower houses,
obsolete in the rest of Europe, continued to be built
in Ireland until the end of the 17th century. In the
18th century, the British imported Palladian and
Georgian styles of domestic architecture.

Neo-classical influences spread to humble farm
houses, which embraced symmetry by adopting a
central doorway. But the crude thatched cottage
didn't die: it evolved into the crude modern
bungalows which disfigure the countryside today.

△ **ROMANTIC CASTLE**
Lemaneagh Castle is a striking ruin of an extended tower
house, dating from 1480 and attached to a 17th-century four-
storey mansion. It can be found in the Burren area of Co. Clare,
on route R476 from Kilfenora through Killinaboy.

△ **THE ROMANTIC IMAGE**
The English tradition of fine
carpentry did not extend to
Ireland, and the limestone or
clay thatched cottage was not
built to last. Traditional long-
houses combined a dwelling
with a shelter for animals.
Cottages were built where
there was shelter from the
wind and a spring could
provide water. An open hearth
fuelled by turf provided both
cooking and heating facilities.

▷ **GEORGIAN ELEGANCE**
Dublin became a showpiece
city in the 18th century, with
areas such as Fitzwilliam
Square (right) conveying an
elegant simplicity that implied
social status. It was clearly a
European capital. By contrast,
Belfast was an industrial city,
whose rapid growth in the
19th century produced some
grand civic edifices but mainly
utilitarian Victorian buildings.

◁ **PALATIAL SPLENDOUR**
Bantry House in Co. Cork is about as far as you can get from the cliché image of an Irish cottage, and hints at the lifestyle enjoyed by the Anglo-Irish aristocracy. When the 2nd Earl of Bantry inherited this Georgian house in 1845, he began turning it into a repository for the art and antiques he collected on his world travels. An amateur architect, he had a theatrical sense of design. Parallels with the Capitol Building in Washington DC reinforce the claims of Charles Frederick Anderson, who emigrated to the US, that he had a hand in both. Its collection of carpets, tapestries and furniture is open to the public, and it offers one of the best views over Bantry Bay.

▽ **POLITICAL RETREAT**
Avondale House, a classic Georgian building in Co. Wicklow, was the birthplace of the leading politician Charles Stewart Parnell (1846 91). Now a museum, it is surrounded by a forest park.

◁ **COUNTRY LIVING**
Kilruddery House in Bray, Co. Wicklow, is an example of a grand country house within easy reach of Dublin. Built in the 17th century, it was later remodelled along neo-Eliza-bethan lines. A conservatory was added in 1852, its walls being masonry instead of glass because it was meant to house not only plants but also the statues collected by its owner, Lord Meath.

THE FIGHT FOR OLD DUBLIN

Dublin in the 18th century was one of the ornaments of Europe, its Georgian buildings expressing a distinctive graciousness. In 1757, it established the Wide Streets Commission, Europe's first town planning authority.

Much of that heritage was destroyed in the unregulated explosion in property specu-lation during the 1960s. Whole streets were razed and replaced by often unsympathetic office blocks. Classic Georgian terraces vanished. Protests peaked in the late 1970s after an important Viking site at Wood Quay was obliterated in order to build offices for city officials.

The recent record has been better. CIE, the state trans-port authority, began buying up property in the Temple Bar area south to the Liffey with the intention of building a huge bus depot. They temporarily rented out some of the small shops to artists, designers and restaura-teurs and the district took on a bohemian atmosphere. Eventually public pressure killed off the bus depot scheme and the narrow cobbled streets of Temple Bar have now become the city's liveliest artistic and gastronomic quarter. The tide may have turned.

THE ROLE OF THE CHURCH

Once, when a priest pronounced on any subject, no-one dared question his authority. Then, suddenly, the Church's power began slipping away

In English, the days of the week take their names from a curiously promiscuous collection of gods – Roman, Viking, and Pagan – from Saturn to Woden and the Moon. In Irish, three days are named after, not Gods, but penitential religious practices. The Irish for Wednesday translates as "first fast", for Friday as "the fast", and for Thursday as "the day between the two fasts". Wednesday and Friday were, in the great Irish monasteries, days of fasting and mortification. Thus, in Ireland, the everyday has been literally defined, not by wandering gods, but by religious practice. For much of Irish history, the sacred and the secular have been virtually indistinguishable.

Church and State

Catholicism in Ireland has long been a nationality as much as a religion. The words "Irish Catholic" do not denote merely a person of a specific faith born in a specific country. They have also come to stand for some third thing born out of the fusion of the other two – a country, a culture, a politics. Catholicism in Ireland has been a matter of public identity more than of private faith, and the struggle to disentangle the two is what defines the Irish Church now.

In Ireland, as in some other atypical European countries such as Poland and Croatia where political nationality was often tenuous or submerged, the Church became a kind of surrogate state, the only organised expression of nationality. Modern Ireland, in its attempt to become a European republican democracy, has had to struggle with the fact that the Church was there *before* the state, that it can claim, and often has claimed, prior rights over the territory. The state is young and fragile, with less than 80 years behind it. The Church is old and seasoned – so old that its language and culture, its imagery and its power, have seeped into the society.

PRECEDING PAGES: pilgrimage to Croagh Patrick mountain; church procession on the Aran Island of Inishmore.
LEFT: a cross on Inishmore. **RIGHT:** a detail from the pulpit in St Werburgh's Church, Dublin.

It is not just a matter of a strongly religious culture, though it remains true that Ireland is exceptionally religious by the standards of the western world. More people attend church once a week (86 per cent of the overwhelmingly Catholic population) than in any other Judeo-Christian society in the world. Asked how

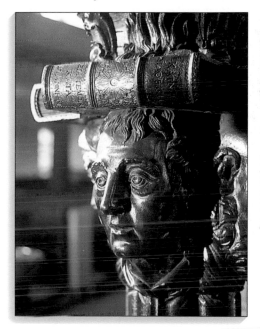

important God is in their lives, the Irish come out far ahead of any nation in Europe.

When it comes to belief in the existence of the soul, in life after death, in heaven, in prayer, the Irish score so much higher in surveys than the rest of the developed world as to seem not part of that world at all. Yet even this is not what is at issue, for such things remain, however deeply-held, still matters of private belief.

It is the public nature of Catholicism in Ireland that has really marked it off. The founding act of the modern Irish State – the 1916 Rising – was a religious as much as a political act, and was conceived by its leader, Pádraic Pearse, as such. Its symbolic occurrence at Easter and its conscious imagery of blood sacrifice and redemption shaped a specifically Catholic political consciousness that belied the secular republican aims of many of the revolutionaries.

Irish nationalism, the primary driving force of Irish politics for most of the 20th century, became, in both its constitutional and its violent manifestations, intimately entwined with Catholicism. Eamon de Valera, the nationalist politician who dominated the State's politics for 40 years, saw fit to get John Charles McQuaid, the Catholic Archbishop of Dublin, to help him to write the Constitution. In the early 1980s, IRA prisoners in Northern Ireland staged a

hunger strike whose imagery and effect were inextricable from Irish Catholicism's traditions of penitence and martyrdom.

In less directly political ways, too, the Church had an enormous public presence. The sociologist Tom Inglis has pointed out that in Ireland it was the Catholic Church which, in the 19th century, taught the peasant Irish not merely what to believe but how to behave. It was the Church which took an agricultural people used to landscape and the rhythms of the farming day, and taught them how to inhabit public spaces and respect modern, industrialised time-keeping.

And if the Church "civilised" the Wild Irish, it also provided the trappings of a state where

there was no state. The Church successfully outmanoeuvred the British government's attempts to construct a secular education system, and built its own mass education system under the control of religious brothers and nuns. It founded its own universities and hospitals.

Having built all of these institutions as alternatives to British rule, the Church retained them in an independent Ireland, and remains a massive temporal power, controlling most of the health and education systems and having a large influence in all other social services. Most primary schools are in Church ownership, as are 90 per cent of secondary schools. Teacher training is Church-controlled, as are most of the training hospitals in which nurses and doctors are formed.

Loss of authority

Yet this great monolith is not all that it seems. The Irish Catholic Church is also a troubled institution, suffering a serious loss of authority. Its strengths throughout the centuries have also become weaknesses in the Ireland of the 1990s. It is afflicted with a paradox: it cannot hope to retain power without giving up power.

The first strength that is now becoming a weakness lies in the very nature of Irish Catholicism itself. It achieved and retained its power through the centuries not by being simply the rock of Peter, but by being something much more like a geological section in which layer after layer of rock is submerged beneath the surface. It grew and consolidated itself not by obliterating what was there before, but by adding another layer to its surface.

Early Irish Christianity, for instance, flourished not by wiping out the earlier Celtic beliefs, but by adapting them. To this day, the annual

FROM THE CRADLE TO THE GRAVE

Irish people were, and are, likely to be born in a Catholic hospital, educated at Catholic schools, married in a Catholic church, have children named by a priest, be counselled by Catholic marriage advisors if the marriage runs into trouble, be dried out in Catholic clinics for the treatment of alcoholism if they develop a drink problem, be operated on in Catholic hospitals, and be buried by Catholic rites. In a sense, the Roman Catholic Church in Ireland anticipated European social welfare systems.

pilgrimage on the last Sunday in July up Croagh Patrick mountain in County Mayo re-enacts the worship of the mountain gods in a Catholic context. Early Irish Christian spirituality is marked by both the intimacy of a tribal society and by a use of natural imagery bordering on pantheism. John Scotus Eriugena (the name meaning John the Irishman, born in Eire), the greatest philosopher and theologian of the early Middle Ages, was indeed accused of pantheism, his great book *De Divisione*

MOVING EXPERIENCES

From time to time, there are outbreaks of superstitious enthusiasm, such as the craze for "moving" statues of the Blessed Virgin which swept much of the country in 1985 and 1986.

At a popular level, and often to the discomfort of the Catholic hierarchy, early pagan Catholicism remains very much alive. In many rural areas, acts of devotion at, for instance, holy wells, vestigial shrines of forgotten water spirits, survive in a Christianised form. In some places, such as Knock, in County Mayo, visited by Pope John Paul II in 1979, this religion of magic has been fully institutionalised by the Church. But in others, it remains on the fringe of Catholicism, barely

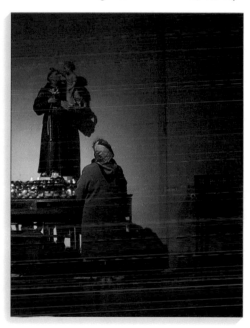

Naturae burned in 1210 and banned in 1685.

This tendency to localism and independence, to build on what is in Ireland rather than on a simple universalism, helped Irish Catholicism to survive under centuries of British rule. But it also forged a kind of Catholicism that is highly dependent on the nature of Irish society. So long as the society remained relatively stable, this rootedness was a huge strength. But, in a shifting society, the Church's very close relationship to the place and the people means that the Church feels the pressure of change intimately.

FAR LEFT: a pilgrim on misty Croagh Patrick mountain.
ABOVE: religion still looms large, at home and in public.

accommodated by a church all too aware of its capacity to take on a life of its own.

The modern Irish Church, however, was built in the 19th century by the imposition on this native layer of religion of a particularly harsh and autocratic combination of sexual puritanism and centralised bureaucracy. Both owed their success to the trauma of famine, the catastrophe of the mid-19th century which halved the population in a few decades. Because the Famine had been caused at least in part by over-population, the new combination of French Jansenism and English Puritanism which the Church adopted made a kind of bitter economic sense and eventually led to a situation in the 1950s where Ireland had the lowest marriage rate in the world.

At the same time, the institutionalisation of the Church as an obedient, highly organised, highly efficient bureaucracy also had economic roots in the Church's position after the Famine as one of the few sources of wealth, development and social services that the Catholic Irish had. On the one hand, the jobs of priest and nun provided an acceptable economic status for surplus children. On the other, the massive church and school building programmes undertaken in the latter half of the 19th century were Ireland's form of infrastructural development.

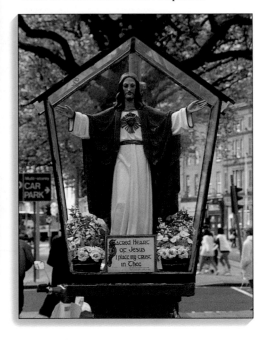

A religion that had been local, intimate and more spiritual than devotional became a massively effective power structure. Between 1850 and 1900, Mass attendance rose from an estimated 30 to 40 per cent to the 90 per cent level which it retained up to the 1980s. However, as the Redemptorist priest Father John J. O'Riordain has put it: "The whole progress of the 19th century in Ireland, with its renewal of church structures, training of clergy, building of churches, expansion of religious life, and devotional revolution, might well be seen as one triumphal march. But the truth, to my mind, is less flattering. Success there was beyond doubt. But the progress was not so much earned as gained in a somewhat dishonest manner. At best it was a display of wealth by somebody who had received a legacy."

That legacy, though, lasted well into the 1980s. The groundwork laid down in the 19th century was the basis for the Church's triumph in independent Ireland.

Holding on to power

Yet this very success also carried the seeds of failure. Because its triumph was so complete, the Irish Catholic Church did not have to develop the kind of complex lay culture which the Catholic Church built in other European Catholic countries such as France, Spain and Italy.

Because the media was mostly very respectful towards the Church, there was no need for specifically Catholic newspapers or broadcasting stations. Because the trade unions were only marginally "infested" by Marxism or secular radicalism, there was no need for specifically Catholic trade unions. Because all of the functioning political parties were fundamentally Catholic, there was no need for a specifically Catholic political party. Thus, Ireland, the most unequivocally Catholic society in Europe, has none of these things to this day.

Essentially, the Catholic Church exercised its power at the top and at the bottom, but not in the middle of the social process. At the top, there were secret meetings with Government Ministers and political leaders at which the Church could exercise great influence. At the bottom, there was the long-term power of controlling education and shaping minds. But in the middle, there was no genuinely Catholic intelligentsia and no Catholic civil society.

In the 1980s, the top and bottom layers of influence ran into deep trouble. At the top, the Church's political influence has become

THE CHURCH'S NEW INFLUENCE

After Ireland achieved independence, the Catholic Church became the effective arbiter of social legislation, having a ban on divorce inserted into the Constitution, encouraging the introduction of draconian censorship of books and films, delaying the legalising of artificial contraception until 1979, retaining largely unquestioned control over schools and hospitals funded by the taxpayer, resisting the slow development of a welfare state.

steadily more marginal. The Church scored two great political victories: by using its influence in favour of a constitutional amendment to ban abortion, and against a constitutional amendment to permit divorce. In both cases, it was on the winning side, and succeeded in holding the line against the march of secular liberalism.

Both victories were Pyrrhic, however, achieved at the cost of a break in the politico-moral consensus that ultimately undermined the Church's authority as being "above politics". By 1990, it was possible for the leader of one of Ireland's major political parties, aligned to the Christian Democrats in Europe, to refer to an

the Supreme Court, faced with the case of a 14-year old girl who had been raped and was pregnant and suicidal, decided that, under the "pro-life" clause itself, she had the right to an abortion in Ireland.

In the subsequent referendum to roll back this judgement, the Church, for the first time in living memory, was clearly divided and marginalised, with the bishops collectively telling the faithful that they could vote either way, but with individual bishops, including the powerful Archbishop of Dublin, Desmond Connell, taking a much harder line. The magisterial authority of the Church had been fatally undermined.

unnamed bishop in public as a "bastard".

In 1997 Ireland finally had to introduce divorce laws – almost inevitable after a 1995 referendum gave the advocates of legalising divorce a wafer-thin majority. In the case of abortion, the 1983 "pro-life" amendment to the Constitution recognising the right to life of the unborn foetus not only made abortion a matter of public controversy and thus increased public support for it in certain circumstances; it also led to the legalisation of abortion itself. In 1992,

LEFT: religious statues can be seen even in central Dublin. **ABOVE:** a Madonna at Ballinspittle, Co. Cork, created a sensation when it was said to move in 1985.

Too few priests

For different reasons, the bottom layer of influence has also become much more tenuous. Keeping control of schools, hospitals and other public services is a highly effective way of maintaining power, but it is also highly labour-intensive. It requires the kind of mass recruitment of clergy and nuns which made it possible up to the early 1970s for most Irish families to boast a member in holy orders. Such recruitment fell away almost completely during the 1970s, and has not recovered since.

The shock troops of Church control in education, the Christian Brothers, are moribund, with barely enough recruits to look after aged members in retirement, never mind teach in hundreds of schools. Likewise with most orders of nuns and priests. In the 1990s, the Church has retreated further into management of schools and hospitals, leaving the groundwork to lay personnel who are increasingly hard to control.

At the same time, there is increasing radicalism among those who do join or stay in religious orders. The extraordinary missionary tradition which sent thousands of Irish priests and nuns to a "spiritual empire" in Africa, Asia, and Latin America has, in a sense, reversed itself, with returned missionaries importing ideas which threaten, rather than reinforce, the remember that "male geriatric dictatorship may well have been what finally toppled Communism in Eastern Europe."

Recognising that its power was threatened at the top and at the bottom in these ways, the Irish Church began to slowly accommodate itself to what was in the middle: the new Irish civil society which emerged from urbanisation and industrialisation in the 1960s. By the early 1970s, the Church was trying to jettison paternalism and present the image of bishops who could sing on TV chat shows.

It had, however, underestimated the omnivorous power of the new media. By 1992, the

Church's place within Irish power structures. Much of the most radical campaigning on poverty and exclusion in Ireland has come from the Conference of Major Religious Superiors, representing the large orders of priests and nuns.

A woman's place

Perhaps even more profoundly threatening to the institutional power of the Church is the quiet spread of feminism within its ranks. Nuns, for so long the obedient servants of the magisterium, have begun to threaten its authority, causing the eminent Catholic sociologist Father Liam Ryan to remark that the Church treats women like second-class citizens but must

bishop who was best at singing on chat shows, Bishop Eamonn Casey of Galway, appointed as the friendly face who could win through media charm the authority which the Church had previously maintained by haughty power, himself became a victim of the ultimate resistance to authority of the modern media. The *Irish Times* uncovered the fact that Bishop Casey had used diocesan funds for payments to the mother of his secret son in America. A sex scandal in the highest ranks of of the Irish Catholic Church, the last unthinkable event, had happened, and the Church discovered it could not be both magisterial and populist, that if you tried to show a friendly face, you could not control what might be revealed. An avalanche of reports on priestly misdemeanours followed: one died in a sex club for gays, another was tried for child abuse…

This final loss of authority has placed the Irish Church on an inexorable path of institutional change. It also explains why the Church cannot retain power without giving up power. At the level of institutional, bureaucratic and political power that it attained for itself in the 19th century, the Irish Church is mortally wounded. Its institutions are challenged from

HE WAS WRONG

In the early 1960s the Archbishop of Dublin, John Charles McQuaid, told his Irish flock: "Allow me to reassure you; no change will worry the tranquillity of your Christian lives."

decline. The Church on which it imposed itself – the intimate, pantheistic and spiritual Church which had shown itself to be virtually invulnerable to persecution and poverty even if Mass attendance was relatively low – shows no sign of rapid decline.

What Father Liam Ryan describes as the four deadly sins of Irish Catholicism – "an obesssion with sexual morality, clerical authoritarianism, anti-intellectualism or, at best, non-intellectualism, and the creation of a ghetto mentality" – will,

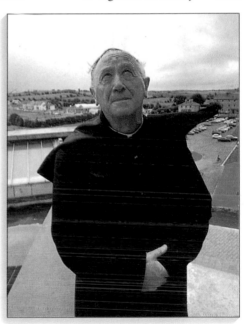

within, and its political power, though still exercised, is on the wane. The demands of a young, educated population and the needs of a pluralist society to disentangle itself from the tribalism that has made violence endemic in Northern Ireland both mean that the Church's grip on power will continue to weaken.

What the future holds

But it is important to remember that it is really only this 19th-century Church that is in sharp

ironically, become less important as the faithful vote with their feet and choose simply to ignore Church teaching on sexuality, to disregard clerical authority, to develop their own intellects, and step out of their ghettoes.

In a sense, the more easily Irish Catholics are able to reject the Church for its sins, the more easily will the religious culture which, like it or not, they have inherited, sit with them. Indeed, the Irish Church at the dawn of the 21st century looks remarkably similar to what it looked like at the dawn of the 19th: a focus for a relaxed but nevertheless deep spirituality in which the broad culture is what matters, not the minutiae of devotional and behavioural rules.

LEFT: pilgrims in Knock, Co. Mayo, "the Lourdes of Ireland". **ABOVE:** pro-abortion protests called into question the traditional moral authority of priests.

THE YOUTH EXPLOSION

With half the population under 25, old values are coming under attack

"This is no country for old men." This dramatic assertion by the poet William Butler Yeats, framed in the opening lines of *Sailing to Byzantium* in 1926, would have seemed like a sad anachronism to the vast majority of young people reared in post-war Ireland. This was no country for *young* men and women in the 1950s, and the mail boat to England claimed some of the brightest talents of a generation.

Not that emigration was confined to the educated classes; it cut right to the core in a society which had been conned by the provincialism of the Republic's founder, Eamon de Valera, out of its colour, its vibrancy, its life force – and out of much of its potential. Socially, Ireland was a drab grey landscape, morose in its conservatism, backward-looking and defensive.

The tunnel of grey

All the while, the country's lack of resources (and so of employment) ensured a constant seepage. Those who went, however, were to return, bringing with them intimations of other cultures, other influences, other possibilities.

By the 1960s the Irish reached the end of the long tunnel of grey. The driving force was money: it was an era of economic expansion and many in Ireland wanted a slice of the international cake. Foreign capital was flowing in as investment. Export markets were opened. Aerials sprouted on roofs as RTE television programmes began. They sprouted especially high so that they could pick up TV programmes from Northern Ireland and Britain. It was a period of extraordinary excitement, and new influences were afoot.

Emigration dwindled with the economic expansion, and the population began to expand. The Irish were producing children faster than anyone else in Europe and, as infant mortality

PRECEDING PAGES: the face of young Ireland. **RIGHT:** the average size of families has been falling, but there's still an urgent need to create new jobs for the young.

fell, the children grew up to find jobs in the Republic and to procreate as well. The changes wrought were profound. Although legislatively backward, Ireland by the 1980s had become in most respects a modern, vibrant young society. International culture had made an impact, sometimes sitting uneasily alongside traditional values, sometimes embracing them.

In search of the grail

The effects were most tangible in the area of music, where there had been a rich folk tradition. Pop audiences' interest in folk music during the 1960s had brought new enthusiasts to

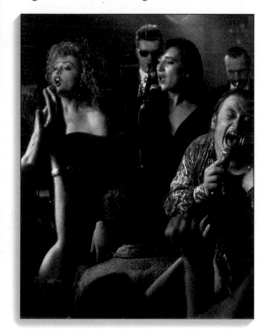

traditional music sessions throughout the country. But while the wave peaked and faded elsewhere, interest continued in Ireland. The transcendent magic of the music attracted many thousands of American, British and, above all, European young people to come in search of the grail. To many, Ireland seems the last refuge of the irrational – and in many ways it is. Modern institutionalism hasn't penetrated too deeply into the countryside or psyche, and even Dublin retains a sense of community rare in cosmopolitan capitals. The characteristic Irish qualities of spontaneity and gregariousness have begun to reassert themselves. Visitors provoke inquisitiveness rather than paranoia.

With such a significant proportion of the population younger than 25 – the figure is just below 50 per cent – the rate of change is accelerating. These children of the 1960s generation entered their teens with totally different expectations. International pop culture vies with school, church and parents as the dominant influence in their lives. The new range of "youth" magazines and TV and radio programmes has made young people more sophisticated, more cosmopolitan, more informed – and more demanding. It hasn't yet made them more radical politically, though that change may come soon.

Young people are no longer prepared to sit around and wait for things to be done. The success of pop groups such as U2 and the fund-raising for famine relief of Bob Geldof are mirrored in the energy being invested in music, film, video and radio by thousands of youngsters. This energy was vividly captured in Alan Parker's 1991 film *The Commitments*, the tale of the rise and fall of a Dublin band that gained credibility not only through its realistically scatalogical dialogue but also because it managed to avoid tacking on a Hollywood-style happy ending. Riverdance, which debuted by filling an interval in the Eurovision Song Contest, became an international phenomenon. It's clear that, if the Irish have special gifts and aptitudes, it's in the area of communications and music.

Ireland's real appeal

These qualities act as a magnet each year for thousands of curious young visitors. The grandeur of the west coast appeals to those who have searched in vain throughout civilised Europe for a taste of gritty authenticity. West Cork, Dingle in Kerry, the Burren in Clare, Connemara in Galway and Gweedore in Donegal – each has its special charm; but the secret of real satisfaction lies in stopping long enough in one spot to get the feel of the authentic culture.

Despite the fresh air blown into the country in the past 30 years, Ireland is still too much a place for old men, with many lingering attitudes that Yeats would readily recognise. But the beauty of the new Ireland is that it has increasingly become a place for young people too.

LEFT: a scene from *The Commitments*, Alan Parker's 1991 hit movie set in Dublin. **RIGHT:** more opportunity for leisure in districts such as Dublin's Temple Bar.

SONG AND DANCE

Irish musicians from the Dubliners and the Chieftains to U2 and Van Morrison
have had global success. And Riverdance has reinvigorated Irish dancing

An English traveller, writing from Ireland in the 17th century, had this to say of rural diversions on a Sunday afternoon: "In every field a fiddle, and the lasses footing it till they are all of a foam." No doubt the writer exaggerated, for if a fiddle was to be provided for every field in the country, it would have kept several factories operating around the clock. But his comment echoes the experience of thousands of visitors to Ireland in the intervening years and bears out the general view that the Irish are a remarkably musical people. Time after time, in letters and reminiscences, we find references to music, dance and song.

You'll still find in every town and hamlet, particularly at weekends, a traditional music session taking place in some pub or other. And it won't be laid on for tourists: it will reflect an authentic tradition going back hundreds of years, mixing haunting airs, lively jigs and soul-stirring ballads, and revealing the influences of classical, Italian and even Spanish music.

Reinventing tradition

While other countries have seen their traditional music wither under the assault of mass-produced pop music, Ireland has witnessed a minor miracle: thousands of youngsters have been picking up the old tunes and songs and carrying them forward into the 21st century. With the international success of such groups as the Chieftains, Clannad, and the Furey Brothers, Irish music has taken on a new lease of life at home and abroad, and the Riverdance troupe catapulted Irish dancing into the 1990s in spectacular fashion. In the pop charts, the remarkable success of Irish groups such as U2, Boyzone, the Corrs and B*witched sent record producers scurrying to Dublin to sign up the next pop phenomenon.

But what exactly *is* Irish traditional music? Since the Irish are a disputatious people, there is no single answer. True *aficionados* would prob-

ably frown on songs such as "Galway Bay" and "Danny Boy", songs regarded internationally as typically Irish. Although "Danny Boy" undoubtedly has deep roots, the folk music purist would consider such songs too modern. To the purist, material can be properly classified as traditional only if it is several hundred years old and fits a

closely defined style of playing or singing.

Yet, in fairness, it is common at traditional music sessions to hear quite modern melodies, such as emigrant songs or patriotic songs of the past 100 years, or even songs composed in recent times such as the haunting anti-war song "The Band Played Waltzing Matilda".

The national instrument

Indisputably, the instrument most associated with Ireland is the harp. As the national emblem, it even appears on the coinage. References to the harp can be found in documents dating back to the 11th century, when it was used to accompany the poetry of the Irish bards at the courts

---

PRECEDING PAGES: traditional music in Hughes Bar, Dublin and, **LEFT,** in the street. **RIGHT:** traditional Irish dancing at the Galway Oyster Festival.

of the Gaelic kings and princes. However, as the ancient Gaelic civilization began to break down under English pressure in the 17th century, harpists had to find a new role. Many, taking to the roads, travelled the country, entertaining the aristocracy in the "Big Houses" of the time.

Other instruments used by the ancient Irish include the bagpipes, which were similar to the modern Scottish equivalent. In time, though, these gave way to a uniquely Irish instrument, the uillean or union pipes. These are played by using a bellows rather than blowing to inflate the bag. They are outstanding among the pipes of the world for their sweetness of tone, and are one of the principal instruments used by today's leading traditional musicians. Others include the fiddle, concertina, flute, tin whistle, guitar and bodhran (a round goatskin tambourine or drum played with a small stick).

Pipers call the tune

Closely allied to the playing of traditional music was Irish dance, which came into its own in the late 18th century. Travellers of the period have remarked that dancing was so widespread among the poor that dancing masters would tour the countryside from cabin to cabin, accompanied by a piper or fiddler, and would be paid by the peasants to teach their children to dance.

Each master had a defined territory and would settle into a district for up to six weeks, ensuring that there would be a festival of music and dancing for the duration. Stories are told of rivalry between various dancing masters for control of certain districts, and at fairs and sporting events they would often hold solo exhibitions of their prowess to decide who was best. A visitor to a town in County Kilkenny recounts seeing a large crowd gathered around two dancers who were taking it in turns to perform on the soaped head of an upturned barrel. They were, he was informed, dancing masters contesting which of them should "own" the parish.

The main occasions for dancing appear to have been Sundays, fair days, at sporting events – and, of course, at weddings, where the musician would be paid for his performance. For many of them, indeed, it was their only means of livelihood. The dances themselves involved communal and group dancing between the sexes to a variety of tunes and tempos which are

LEFT: blowing with brio at Enniscorthy, Co. Wexford.

known today as jigs, reels and hornpipes. There was also great interest in individual prowess, such as dancing within a confined patch of ground. When it was raining, the events were held in barns. In fine weather, they would take place in level fields, or often at a crossroads.

Many of the tunes and songs heard on these occasions had been handed down from one musician to another. A lot would have been lost to modern ears, though, if it hadn't been for the work of several great music collectors who began to travel the country in the early 19th century annotating and writing down the tunes.

Spurred on by nationalism

Another boost to tradition came at the end of that century from the growth of nationalism and a revival of interest in the Irish language and culture generally. After the founding of the Republic, the teaching of folk music and traditional dancing in schools was emphasised. The new state's broadcasting station, Radio Eireann, devoted much air-time to the native culture. More recently, interest has been stimulated by respected composers such as the late Sean O'Riada and his group Ceoltoírí Chualann, the forerunner of the Chieftains. The Clancy Brothers were a great popularising influence.

But perhaps the greatest credit should go to the Comhaltas Ceoltoírí Eireann, the body which looks after traditional music and song. It has hundreds of branches, in every county of Ireland and abroad, and organises regular festivals which culminate every summer in a three-day event called the All-Ireland Fleadh Ceoil. Usually held in a town in the west of the country, it can attract more than 100,000 people and answers the wildest prayers of local publicans.

Major centres such as Dublin, Belfast and Cork hold their own festivals. In addition, there are specialist festivals such as the one devoted to uillean piping. This event, held in Milltown Malbay in County Clare each July, is named after a famous Clare piper, Willie Clancy.

In the tourist season, many hotels lay on after-dinner dancers and traditional musicians. Medieval castles do the same sort of thing in grander style: near Shannon airport in the west of the country, for example, you can find Knappogue Castle, Quin, County Clare; Dunguaire Castle, Kinvara, County Galway; and Bunratty Castle, Bunratty, County Clare. But for authenticity you can't beat the musicians who sing and play primarily for their own pleasure rather than for the tourist coach parties – and you'll mostly find them in plain, unadorned pubs.

Reliable venues

Dublin alone has dozens of regular events, most held in the backrooms of pubs. In the city centre, pubs such as O'Donoghue's in Merrion Row have long been a magnet for lovers of traditional music. It was from O'Donoghue's that the world-famous Dubliners were launched in the early 1960s, and most nights of the week a lively session gets under way in the same back room. Other reliable venues include the Brazen Head, one of the city's oldest pubs, located in Lower Bridge Street; Slattery's of Capel Street; An Beal Bocht in Charlemont Street; and the Wexford Inn, Wexford Street.

To the north of the city, in the picturesque fishing village of Howth, the Abbey Tavern's reputation for traditional music and song (and good food and drink) is still justified despite increased commercialisation in recent years. On the south side of the city, the headquarters of the Comhaltas in Monkstown hosts regular events.

LEFT: exuberant performers dominate a Dublin pub, but traditional music **(RIGHT)** remains very popular.

THE IRISH WAY WITH WORDS

Whether in the theatre or the street, in parliament or the pub, the Irish are renowned for having the gift of the gab. Where did they get it from?

The Irish are noted for their ability to perform remarkable conjuring tricks with the English language, written and spoken. This gift ranges from the calculated blarney of the professional tourist guide or the frothy whimsicalities of a Dublin pub through masters of conversation like Oscar Wilde and Sir John Mahaffy to some of the greatest names in world literature, from Jonathan Swift to George Bernard Shaw, Edmund Burke to Samuel Beckett.

And yet James Joyce, the ultimate virtuoso of the English language, noted wryly in *A Portrait of the Artist as a Young Man* the cultural alienation that underlies its use by an Irishman. In this novel, Joyce's *alter ego*, Stephen Dedalus, uses a word unfamiliar to the Dean of Studies at his university. The Dean, Father Darlington, an Englishman, suspects wrongly that the word is Irish in origin, which prompts Stephen to reflect: "The language in which we are speaking is his before it is mine. How different are the words *home*, *Christ*, *ale*, *master* on his lips and on mine! I cannot speak or write these words without unrest of spirit. His language, so familiar and so foreign, will always be for me an acquired speech. I have not made or accepted its words. My voice holds them at bay. My soul frets in the shadow of his language."

A minority language

Indeed, few visitors realise how recent is the general use of English in Ireland. Few know that Irish, not English, is still the official first language of the state and that, in matters of law, the Irish-language version of the constitution holds superior authority.

In 1835 there were an estimated 4 million Irish speakers, most of whom belonged to a deprived rural class devastated by the Great Famine of the 1840s and subsequent mass emigration. By 1891 the number of Irish speakers

had tumbled to 680,245. Today, the everyday use of Irish is almost exclusively confined to the officially designated Gaeltacht areas along the western seaboard, whose combined population is around 75,000. Yet over a million people claim some knowledge of the language, thanks to compulsory instruction at school.

The ancient Irish language survived repeated waves of invasion by Vikings, Normans and English planters. In 1366, so many of the Anglo-Irish settlers had "gone native" that the Statutes of Kilkenny forbade the use of Irish in a vain attempt to stop Celtic customs and language spreading among the colonisers.

The decisive abandonment of Irish in the 19th century was brought about not just by the impact of the famine but by the introduction of the National School System in 1831. This system decreed that English would be the proper language of instruction, and children who spoke the native tongue were beaten or gagged. Surprisingly, the system was condoned by national

PRECEDING PAGES: a performance in Dublin's Abbey Theatre of Sean O'Casey's play *Shadow of a Gunman*. **LEFT:** Oscar Wilde and, **RIGHT**, George Bernard Shaw, two Irish-born playwrights who found fame in Britain.

leaders such as Daniel O'Connell, who, although a native Irish speaker himself, declared that he was "sufficiently utilitarian not to regret its gradual abandonment."

Far different was the attitude of the 20th-century leader Eamon de Valera, who somewhat surprisingly said that "Ireland with its language and without freedom is preferable to Ireland with its freedom and without its language." The virtual extinction of Irish as a living language was certainly a tragedy. *Gan teanga, gan tír* was the slogan of the revivalists – "No language, no country" – and a certain element of the Irish identity withered as English took over.

Why Irish is unique

Irish had a venerable tradition, being the earliest variant of the Celtic languages and the earliest language north of the Alps in which extensive writings survive. It had a special alphabet of distinctive, beautiful characters. This script was, in a strange quirk of history, carried over into print by order of England's Queen Elizabeth I, who commanded a fount to be cut in 1571 for an Irish version of the Protestant catechism.

Unfortunately this elegant script was officially superseded by Roman script in the 1960s in an attempt to make the language more "modern" and accessible, and the use of Irish script is now rare. Outstanding examples can be seen in the *Book of Kells* or the *Book of Armagh*, kept in Dublin's Trinity College library, or in the *Book of the Dun Cow* in the Royal Irish Academy. A section of this last book appears on the back of the Irish pound note.

The 19th-century shift from Irish to English was so sudden and so resented that the mark of the earlier language was imprinted on its successor. Initially, Irish was regarded as "talk", the language of communication and imagination, whereas English was a necessary and utilitarian, but not fully understood, vehicle. During the 19th century it became commonplace for many people to think in Irish, then translate their thoughts into English. This process led to the development of the so-called Hiberno-English dialect, and sometimes produced effects of great beauty and elegance, even in the simplest phrases. Thus the bald statement in English "that is true" becomes either "'Tis true for you" (Hiberno-English) from *Is fíor é sin* (Irish) or

PLAYING WITH WORDS – AND WINNING

A classic illustration of the Irish love of language is the story of a battle of words between the patriot Daniel O'Connell and an old Dublin fishwife, reported to have the most virulent flow of invective in Ireland.

A colleague bet O'Connell that even he could not best this woman in dispute. He accepted the challenge and, on the appointed day, a quarrel was deliberately engineered. The old harridan attacked O'Connell with all the considerable verbal venom at her disposal. He bided his time and, when she was finally exhausted, let fly at her, eschewing vulgar obscenity, employing instead only the terms of Euclidian geometry. When he reached a climax of mathematical abuse, describing her as a shameless parallelogram, an inveterate isosceles triangle and an unregenerate hypotenuse, she collapsed in tears, protesting her virtue. O'Connell was the victor.

It is no accident that it was an Irish playwright, Richard Brinsley Sheridan, who created the immortal Mrs Malaprop in his comedy *The Rivals* (1775). She resents "an aspersion to my parts of speech" and avers that "if I reprehend anything in the world it is the use of my oracular tongue and a nice derangement of epitaphs."

"There's not a word of a lie in it" from *Níl aon focal bréige ann.*

What's more, received standard English is a language that is imperial and rational, its preoccupations administrative and its social tone most characteristically represented by the genius of Jane Austen. No Irish hand could have written the celebrated opening line of *Pride and Prejudice*: "It is a truth universally acknowledged that a single man in possession of good fortune must be in want of a wife." For all its wit and elegance, it is too precise, too conscious, and, above all, too lacking in the essentially subversive irreverence. Anglo-Saxon precision is

alien to the Irish mind, which would be more at home with Humpty-Dumpty's dictum: "When I use a word it means just what I choose it to mean – neither more nor less."

In the 20th century, a new generation of writers rediscovered the collision of sensibility between the Irish mind and the English language, and set out to explore its literary potential. William Butler Yeats and Lady Gregory, instrumental in founding Dublin's Abbey Theatre, decided that the Irish peasant was essen-

LEFT: James Joyce, who arm-wrestled English into startling new forms. **ABOVE:** Sean O'Casey, who dramatised 20th-century Ireland's political anguish.

tially a noble creature, and they determined to correct the balance of earlier representations by giving him a speech that was real and melodic rather than phonetic and contrived.

John Millington Synge (pronounced *sing*) had the added benefit of being fluent in Irish, and carried the experiment even further, although his lilting stage speech was sometimes dismissed as "Synge-song". In the preface to his controversial play *The Playboy of the Western World*, he wrote:"Anyone who has lived in real initimacy with the Irish peasantry will know that the wildest sayings and ideas in this play are tame indeed when compared with the fancies one may hear in any little hillside cabin in Geesala or Carraroe or Dingle Bay."

A web of lyricism

Synge manufactured a convincing theatrical language from a small number of Irish-derived constructions: ending a phrase with *surely* as in "It's destroyed he'll be surely"; using *do be* in the sense of a continuous present, as in "In the big world the old people do be leaving things after them for their sons and children"; and inserting the adverbial *and*, as in "There were two men and they rowing." Synge used these simple devices as a frame over which he stretched the web of a remarkable new lyricism.

When one considers the contribution of Irish writers to literature in this century, even an incomplete list astonishes: Yeats with his poetry of the Celtic Twilight and beyond; Sean O'Casey with his miraculous ear for the cadences of the Dublin slums; Frank O'Connor's powerfully humorous but unsentimental stories of childhood in Cork; the plays of Samuel Beckett and George Bernard Shaw; Somerville and Ross's world of the Irish RM (resident magistrate), in which tweedy English officialdom gets its come-uppance from the brilliant improvisations on language of the Irish peasantry; the poetry of Patrick Kavanagh, Brendan Kennelly and Seamus Heaney.

The fine tradition of short-story writing is carried on by practitioners such as Neil Jordan (better known as a film director), John McGahern, Brian Friel, Benedict Kiely and William Trevor.

Although very different in their genius, most of them share one thing in common: an almost physical delight in words that springs from a sharpened sensitivity to a language that is never entirely their own.

IRELAND IN THE MOVIES

Bejasus, it's them leprachauns again! The cinema has played a big part in reinforcing the stereotyped image of the Irish. Do they care? No, it spells profit

Ireland's first dedicated cinema, the Volta in Dublin's Mary Street, was opened in 1909 by none other than James Joyce – an indication that the Irish have always valued the word more than the visual. But the country had no film studio until 1958, when Ardmore Studios opened in Bray, Co. Wicklow. Significantly, its first effort was an international production, *Shake Hands with the Devil*, starring James Cagney.

It was thus left to Hollywood to portray Ireland to the world, and it did so by appealing principally to the huge audience of urban Irish-Americans who, though they may have never set foot in the Emerald Isle, had a sentimental attachment to a pastoral ideal. There emerged a land of thatched cottages and infectious whimsicality where people drank all day and greeted each other with cries of "Top o' the morning" – a mythical world whose most potent portrayal was in John Ford's *The Quiet Man*. The Irish, who were in reality facing economic hardship and chronic emigration, didn't object in the slightest to such a benign portrayal: indeed, they proceeded to build a thriving tourist industry on it.

A NEW REALISM

Three decades of terrorism have produced a muted response from international film makers – Neil Jordan's *The Crying Game* was a rare success. But recently, in the search for new locations for its thrillers, Hollywood directors, including Quentin Tarantino, have shown a close interest in Dublin's gangland.

◁ **POTS OF GOLD**
A pre-007 Sean Connery (complete, as always, with Scottish accent) sang and danced with Janet Munro and gangs of leprachauns (above) in *Darby O'Gill and the Little People* (1959). No cliché was left unturned, but the pot of gold at the rainbow's end went to Walt Disney.

◁ **REVIVING THE DEAD**
Veteran Hollywood director John Huston, who came of Irish stock and had a home in Ireland, captured the country's Chekovian melancholy in his last film, James Joyce's *The Dead* (1987), starring his daughter Anjelica Huston.

▽ **WAYNE'S WORLD**
The movie that did most to cement the image of the Irish as fighting boyos with a pre-feminist outlook was John Ford's 1952 production *The Quiet Man*, in which John Wayne slugged it out with Victor McLaglen and Maureen O'Hara in a virulently green landscape. The Irish loved it.

▽ **FIGHT FOR FREEDOM**
Michael Collins (1996) was dubbed Ireland's first national epic film, yet it was financed by Warner Bros. Although director Neil Jordan sacrificed historical detail for dramatic impact, Liam Neeson in the title part conveyed the mixture of romanticism and ruthlessness that characterised Ireland's fight for freedom.

HERBERT J. YATES presents
JOHN FORD and MERIAN C. COOPER'S
Argosy Production

"THE QUIET MAN
starring
John   Maureen   Barry
Wayne   O'Hara   Fitzgera
with Ward BOND, Victor McLAGLEN,
Mildred NATWICK, Francis FORD
Colour by TECHNICOLOR
Directed by John FORD

A HOME-GROWN FILM INDUSTRY

In 1990 Richard Harris (above) played a farmer in *The Field*, a grim story of life on the land in the 1920s. It was part of a spate of local films which had begun with the launch of the Irish Film Board in 1981 and included such varied offerings as Neil Jordan's moody IRA thriller *Angel* (1982) and *Eat the Peach* (1986), the quirky tale of one man's bid to build a motorcycle wall of death.

Irish governments had long realised that film-making created employment and attracted foreign investment. But actively encouraging the industry had been difficult as long as the Catholic church exercised a tight grip on moral values: in the first 40 years of the Republic's independence, an average of 75 films a year were banned and another 200 censored.

With the Irish box office representing less than 0.5 per cent of the global market there was limited scope for purely Irish films. So the government tempted in foreign producers with tasty tax breaks. This persuaded Mel Gibson, for instance, that, although his 1995 *Braveheart* portrayed a legendary Scottish hero, the stirring battle scenes would look no less patriotic if they were filmed in Ireland.

△ SINGING THE BLUES

Although directed by an Englishman (Alan Parker) and financed from America, *The Commitments* (1991), from the novel by Roddy Doyle, captured the mood of modern young Dubliners, expletives and all. This was no feel-good tale of a pop group on the make – it chronicled their disaffection with life in Dublin and referred to Ireland as a Third World country.

▽ WHIMSICAL HUMOUR

The 1990s saw some gentler films taking a fanciful and melancholy view of Irish life. Albert Finney made a convincing Irishman in *The Playboys* (1992) and, below, *A Man of No Importance* (1994).. *Hear My Song* (1991),with Ned Beatty as tenor Josef Locke, was a return to whimsicality..

◁ MODERN MAYHEM

Movies dealing with IRA violence tended towards melodrama, but Neil Jordan's *Angel* and, left, his 1992 hit *The Crying Game* analysed the often conflicting emotions in Ireland's killing fields. Here the IRA man (Stephen Rea) prepares to kill a captured British soldier. The movie was filmed partly on location in Bettystown and Laytown, Co. Meath.

FAIRIES AND FOLKLORE

From leprechauns to giants, there
are Irish tales to suit all tastes

During the summer of 1985 thousands of people began to go on pilgrimages to Marian shrines, in various parts of the country, because people claimed to have seen them move. After a time the phenomenon became a national and international news story; much to the indignation of the country's advanced liberals who saw these pilgrimages as a further manifestation of national obscurantism. The Catholic Church authorities, in the areas where pilgrims collected, counselled caution. They advised people to seek physical and rational explanations for what was happening rather than supernatural ones. But still the thousands travelled until the strange happenings ceased just as suddenly as they had commenced.

By then a book had been produced, in which, tucked away among the eyewitness accounts from the contemporary pilgrims and descriptions of apparitions from the past, there was a contribution by a lecturer in the Department of Folklore in University College, Dublin. This erudite essay showed that the phenomenon of moving statues originated in the early Middle Ages, was well-known in Ireland, and was the subject of many tales and legends.

Heroic tales

This is just one manifestation of Irish folklore, as well as being an example of the past returning to embarrass the present. Other forms of folklore were used to good effect by writers such as W. B. Yeats and J. M. Synge. Then there were the heroic tales concerning Fionn MacCool, leader of Fianna Eireann, and his band of warriors. They defended Ireland against invaders, hunted and indulged in feats of strength between May and November. Then, for six months, they retired to the winter quarters where they feasted, told tales, listened to the

RIGHT: Irish illustrator Jim Fitzpatrick's drawing of an early Norse invader from *The Silver Arm*.

harp and played chess. The ancient Irish had only two seasons, summer and winter, and in rural Ireland May Day and Hallowe'en still mark the beginning and end of the agricultural year. Potatoes that have not been dug before Hallowe'en will remain in the ground, and children will not pick blackberries after that date.

Other writers drew inspiration from tales of spirits, benign and malign, and the little people, sometimes called leprechauns, who guarded hidden treasure and had a thousand tricks to distract the greedy mortals who sought it. They also indulged in games of hurling, sometimes borrowing a champion from the world of mor-

changing a word or an emphasis. Some of these tales, concerning personages such as "The King of Ireland's Son" and his adventures in Spain and Africa, could take more than two hours in the telling. About six really top-class storytellers still survive and their art has now been preserved on film for posterity.

One of the principal reasons why so much of Ireland's past lives on today is to be found in the method St Patrick used to propagate the Christian message when he arrived in 432. He found a people immersed in pagan beliefs and rituals. His debates with the Druids (the pagan priests) enliven much of early Irish literature. He even

tals to assist them. If they won, he was suitably rewarded. It was believed in Sligo that the great traditional fiddle player Michael Coleman, who recorded all his music in New York, had learned his flawless bowing technique from a band of little folk whom he had befriended.

The oral tradition

The storytellers who preserved most of these tales, before the scholars came to write and record them, were custodians of a very ancient oral tradition. They were called *seanachaidhe* from the Irish *seanachas* meaning lore. Some could relate more than 300 tales, learned by rote from their elders, and could recite them without

debated with Oisín, son of Fionn MacCool, who had unwisely returned from the land of Eternal Youth only to become an old man as soon as he touched the soil of Ireland.

St Patrick helped preserve Ireland's social structure and many of its customs even as he changed fundamental beliefs. He clearly did not believe in the politics of confrontation – which is as good a proof as any, some say, that he was not an Irishman. When he ascended Croagh Patrick, Ireland's holy mountain in Co. Mayo, the peak was sacred to the pagan god Crom. When he descended, after battling for 40 days and nights with a legion of evil spirits, including the Devil's mother, he declared the summit sacred to the Christian God. The people were to continue paying homage, but in a new form. So it came about that every year tens of thousands of pilgrims, from all parts of the country and beyond, converge on Croagh Patrick on the last Sunday in July (still called Black Crom's Sunday in the Irish language). They climb at dawn, many of them barefoot, to the oratory on the summit.

But what is sometimes regarded as mere superstition is often based on something very different. For example, the

PAGAN TRADITIONS

Many holy wells, where people come to pray and pay penance, were also deemed to be holy in pre-Christian times.

area of folk cures and folk medicine. It is an area in which one finds that received wisdom and superstition have become inextricably mixed.

How is it that only a member of the Doogan clan can guarantee that earth from Tory Island, off the Donegal coast, will banish all rodents from your home by handing it to you? Why is the seventh son of a seventh son capable of curing certain ills and ailments, depending on which family he comes from? If he is a Shanaghan, for instance, he has the cure for whooping cough.

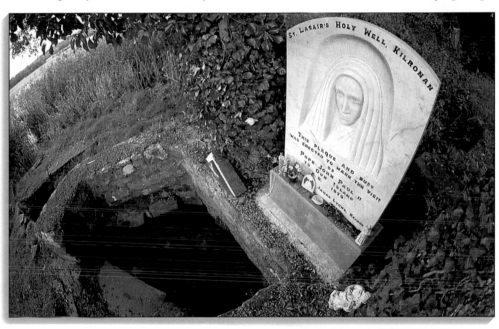

white thorn bush frequently found growing on wheat and barley fields is untouched by the farmer supposedly because "it is a fairy tree and bad luck will quickly follow the person who disturbs it." But the truth is that "fairy forts" are old burial places and the picturesque tale merely serves to strengthen reverence for the dead.

Folk medicine

Another form of folklore, which is now getting a new lease of life because of the increased interest in herbs and alternative medicine, is the

LEFT: a fairy ring, said to possess magic powers.
ABOVE: a holy well, keeping alive old superstitions.

Why is it that direct acceptance of financial reward will remove the capacity to cure, while indirect payment, or payment in kind, will not?

Of course, folklore never ceases to evolve in an island the size of Ireland in which traditions linger on and emerge in new guises when least expected. Television may have hastened the death of the gatherings around the storyteller at the fireside, but it has not yet fully demolished the delight Irish people take in listening to a tall tale well told. Contemporary moving statues have created enough stories to ensure that another generation will have another folk-memory passed on to them orally. That is how it all begins; and that is how it all began.

LOT NO. 376   IR. GNS. 2900000
GNS. 2465000
Fr. F. 29232000
US $ 3166000

RACING CERTAINTIES

Whether they're breeding them, racing them, exporting them or betting on them, the Irish have an extraordinary affinity with horses

In County Cork in the year 1752, a Mr Edmund Blake and a Mr O'Callaghan raced each other on horseback across the countryside from Buttevant Church to the spire of St Leger Church 4½ miles away, jumping hedges, walls and ditches on the way. As a result, a new word, "steeplechasing", entered the English language, and a new sport was created.

Steeplechasing was soon all the rage. Races were run, like the original, across open country from one point to another with the precise course to be taken left largely to the discretion (or indiscretion) of the riders. A 19th-century Englishman returning from a holiday in Ireland wrote that steeplechasing was "a sort of racing for which the Paddies are particularly famous, and in which, unless the rider has pluck and his prad (*horse*) goodness, they cannot expect to get well home." Fortunately, Ireland had no shortage of plucky riders and good horses. *The History and Delineation of the Horse* recorded in 1809 that "the Irish are the highest and the steadiest leapers in the world." They still are.

Great breeding

The pre-eminence of Irish-bred steeplechasers and hurdlers on the racecourses of Britain today is undisputed; and it is remarkable, given the legions of horses exported annually to trainers in England, that the greatest steeplechasers of modern era have also been trained in Ireland. Perhaps the greatest of all was Arkle, who won the Cheltenham Gold Cup, British steeplechasing's equivalent of the Derby, three years in succession in the 1960s, in the process humiliating the cream of the English racehorses to the undisguised glee of all Ireland.

All horse-racing is sport, but some forms are more sporting than others. The Irish prefer the reckless and often threadbare thrills of steeplechasing to its rich relation, racing "on the flat". Whereas top-class flat-racing throughout the

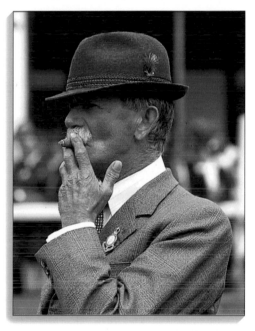

world is dominated by the commercial requirements of the multi-million dollar bloodstock industry, this aspect is absent from racing "over the sticks" for nearly all jumpers are geldings.

The winner of a great flat race like the Irish Derby may become worth tens of millions of dollars because he may breed future winners of great races. The winner of a great jump race earns his owner only the prize-money – modest by comparison – the proceeds of a winning bet, perhaps, and the glory. But what glory. Had Arkle been entered in a referendum for the Irish presidency, the world might well have had its first equine statesman since Caligula.

The origins of horse-racing "on the flat" are lost in pre-history. We know that the Red Branch Knights of pre-Christian Ireland raced each other on horses and that horse-racing was an essential part of public assemblies or fairs in the early centuries AD. According to John Welcome's history, *Irish Horseracing*, "these fairs were held for the purpose of transacting all sorts

---

PRECEDING PAGES: a race at Leopardstown.
LEFT: a bloodstock sale in Co. Kildare.
RIGHT: studying form at the Dublin Horse Show.

of business—marriages were celebrated, deaths recorded, laws debated and defined, methods of defence agreed; but always they were followed by sports and games, and of these sports and games the most popular was horseracing." The greatest fair was held at the Curragh – a wide, grassy plain in what is now County Kildare, across which a horse can gallop to exhaustion.

Racing went on, especially at the Curragh, through Norman and Elizabethan times, and

IRELAND'S SECRET

Horses are said to thrive in Ireland because of the moist climate, which produces some of the world's lushest pastures, and the limestone subsoil, which makes the grass rich in bone-building calcium.

Its headquarters, naturally enough, are at the Curragh, still the heartland of Irish racing. Its 6,000 windswept acres (2,400 hectares) are the home of many training stables. On most days, the gaunt grandstands of the Curragh racecourse overlook the plain silently, like a stranded liner; but on big race days, they overflow with a restless throng of owners, trainers, spectators, bookmakers and hucksters.

A race meeting is a heady mixture: the lean, hard-muscled

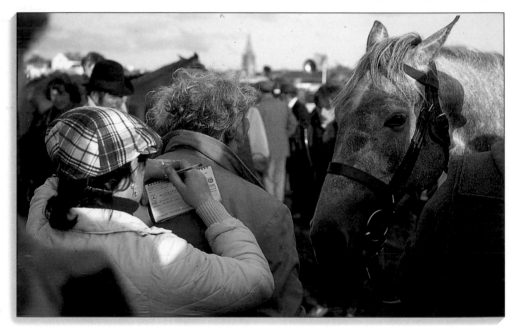

through the succeeding centuries, despite an attempt by Oliver Cromwell's Puritans to stamp it out as a work of the devil. But it wasn't until the middle of the 18th century that the results of races at the Curragh were recorded. In 1790, Irish racing was organised under the aegis of a governing body, the Turf Club. Today it continues to be responsible for the integrity of horse racing at Ireland's 27 tracks, licensing and registering all participants, and overseeing the annual race calendar. The Irish Horse Racing Authority, a semi state body, was set up in 1994 to oversee the financing of racing and the provision of Totaliser betting on the 25 courses in the Republic.

horses, the small, scrawny jockeys in their vivid silks, the eager gamblers thrusting handfuls of banknotes at the bookmakers, who shout and signal to each other constantly, chalking up odds on their blackboards and rubbing them out again with an air of obsessive duty. Wealthy women in their finery, bowler-hatted remnants of the Anglo-Irish gentry, down-at-heel city-dwellers, red-faced farmers... all human life is there.

The thrill of the race

Just before the start of each race, there is a last flurry in the dance around the book-makers. Then a tense stillness as the race commentator's voice echoes over the stands. Batteries of binoculars are trained silently on the runners. But as the horses round the final bend, a murmuring in the crowd rises like a gathering storm until the commentator's voice is drowned in a cacophony of supplication, triumph and despair. Hats are thrown in the air in delight, losers' betting tickets fall to the ground like confetti.

The Curragh is the setting for all the Irish classic races: the 2,000 and 1,000 Guineas, the Derby, the Oaks and the St Leger. The most valuable of these, in terms of prize-money, is the Derby, sponsored since 1986 by the US brewer Budweiser. The total prize fund is now IR£750,000, and can be expected to keep rising.

Although it is contested by fewer runners than its English counterpart, the race is arguably a truer test of a horse's ability, as the Curragh has none of the topographical eccentricities of the Epsom Downs. Winners include some of the world's greatest racehorses: Nijinsky, Shergar, El Gran Señor, Zagreb and Desert King.

The Derby is always a thrilling spectacle. Like all classic races today, it is also a superb shop-window for the international bloodstock industry, in which Irish breeders play a vital and

LEFT: signing a cheque at the Ballinasloe Horse Fair.
ABOVE: to some, fashion is as important as fillies at the Dublin Horse Show.

growing role. Ireland developed into Europe's leading nursery for thoroughbred racehorses: in 1985, for the first time, more foals were born in Ireland than in Britain.

In spring, the migration of birds from their winter quarters to sunnier climates is paralleled by a migration of hundreds of mares (mainly from the US, Britain and France) to be mated with the many former leading males of the turf who have retired to stallion duties in Ireland.

The recent prosperity of the Irish bloodstock industry owes much to a 1969 government concession under which fees received for the services of thoroughbred stallions are fully exempt from tax. Its effect was shown dramatically in the turnover of Ireland's leading bloodstock auctioneers, Goffs of Kildare, which rose from around IR£2 million in 1974 to more than £40 million a decade later, settling at an average of about £35 million. Nice work if you can get it.

An affinity with horses

Then there's the natural ability of many Irish people to understand and handle horses, whether as breeders, stud managers, stud and stable hands, jockeys or trainers. This justly celebrated Irish way with horses was apotheosised in the dapper and diffident personage of Vincent O'Brien, who, until he retired in 1993, had a training record that stretched credulity and defeated even Irish superlatives. His son-in-law, John Magna, carries on the family tradition at Coolmore Stud where he continues to dominate the stallion world, thanks partly to his extraordinary premier stallion, Sadler's Wells.

Summertime visitors to such top-class tracks as the Curragh and Leopardstown are likely to see runners entered by leading trainers such as Aidan O'Brien (no relation to the legendary Vincent) and John Oxx. Most likely two-year-olds are introduced to the duties and rigours of racing life before being sent across the Irish Sea in search of a big-race win to set them on their planned careers as classic victors and, later, top-priced stallions. But their odds are likely to be prohibitively short – and, as racegoers quickly learn, favourites don't always win.

Other leading Irish trainers include Dermot Weld and Jim Bolger. The most successful jockeys of recent years have been Michael Kinane – whose services are in demand worldwide – John Murtagh and Christy Roche.

Apart from the aforementioned tracks, there

is racing "on the flat" and "over the sticks" at 25 other racecourses throughout Ireland. They include Fairyhouse, venue for the Irish Grand National, held on Easter Monday; Punchestown, which holds an historic three-day festival meeting in late April; Killarney and Galway, both of which hold meetings in holiday-time high summer with a festive, not to say Bacchanalian, tinge.

A race across the beach

Perhaps the unlikeliest venue is Laytown, a small holiday resort on the east coast, about 30 miles (50 km) north of Dublin. Racing is held there on only one day a year, in July or August, on a date determined as much by the tidal movements of the Irish Sea as by the Turf Club – for when the tide is in at Laytown, the racecourse lies under a metre or more of water. The Laytown Strand Races is Europe's only official race meeting to be held on a beach.

There is no grandstand at Laytown – and, strictly speaking, no racecourse at all, just a long, gently-sloping beach. A group of marquees serve as the racecourse offices, tea-room and bar. The racetrack is marked out with flags on the sands at low tide.

The atmosphere is extraordinary. In the field above the beach, horses parade in the paddock, owners and trainers confer, punters debate the form, bookmakers shout the odds, drinkers drink – all much like an ordinary race meeting.

But down on the beach hucksters sell candy floss and fish-and-chips and fizzy drinks and toys and raffle-tickets and souvenirs; small-time bookmakers splash barefooted through small pools left by the receding tide; children run about yelling and eating ice-cream; strangest of all, huntsmen on horseback in their red-coated regalia ride back and forth, policing the crowds clear of the racetrack. At times, the races themselves seem a bit like a sideshow.

Laytown is a world away from the Curragh on Derby Day, from big prize-money and bafflingly high bloodstock prices. It has none of the glamour of the top meetings – and little of the tension. But, although the Laytown Races are unfashionable by the standards of today, they are maybe not so far in spirit from the races that thrilled fair-goers in ancient Ireland.

LEFT: the extraordinary Laytown Races, Europe's only official race meeting to be held on a beach.

THE GAMES PEOPLE PLAY

Hurling and Gaelic football make soccer seem tame by comparison. And then there are oddities like road bowls

All the major international sports are played to some extent in Ireland and only a few are affected by the political division of the island: the main exceptions being soccer, athletics and hockey. But the most popular sports in the island are the native ones of hurling and Gaelic football. These are truly amateur games, organised on the smallest social unit of population, the parish, and controlled by a body called the Gaelic Athletic Association.

The GAA was founded in 1884, in Thurles in County Tipperary, by Michael Cusack, a fiery nationalist from the Burren in County Clare, who was immortalised by James Joyce as "The Citizen" in *Ulysses*. Its purpose was as much political as sporting: to revive the native games, under native control, as a means of strengthening national self-respect at a time when national morale was at a low ebb. The association also organised athletic contests in opposition to the Ascendancy-controlled organisation which banned "artisans" from its competitions and, because of a mixture of exclusivity and Sabbatarianism, held its contests on Saturdays. At the time, all but the professional classes worked a six-day week and Sunday was the only day left for organised games.

How to understand hurling

Hurling has been played in Ireland since prehistoric times and the oldest sagas tell of hurling matches that went on for days. It is the fastest of all field team games and its rules are relatively simple, although those who see it played for the first time have some difficulty following the flight of the ball.

Played between teams of 15 a side, it gets its name from the stick, a hurley, used by the players. Made from ash, the hurley is about 3½ ft (1 metre) long with a crooked blade which is about

RIGHT: hurling, one of the world's toughest, fastest and most exciting ball games.

3 inches (8 cm) across at its broadest. The ball consists of yarn, tightly wound round a ball of cork and covered with hard leather, stitched along the outside in a ridge to facilitate handling. The goal-posts stand 21 ft (6.4 metres) apart and are 21 ft high, with a crossbar 8 ft (2.5 metres) from the ground. A goal (three points) is scored when the ball is sent between the posts under the bar. A single point is scored when the ball goes between the posts and over the bar.

The ball can be propelled

FOOTBALLING ICONS

In Kerry, photographs of famous Gaelic football teams and players hang on the walls in the company of the Sacred Heart of Jesus, the Pope and Jack Kennedy.

a ball similar to that used in soccer, Gaelic football is to a great extent an invented game. The rules are therefore imperfect and subject to constant revision. Players can handle the ball, lift it off the ground with the foot, run with it while passing it between hand and foot, kick it, or fist it, or play it with the feet on the ground as in soccer. Its main flaw is that there is no clear method of dispossessing a player in possession. But it is a spectacular game, and attracts the biggest crowds of any sporting event in Ireland.

along the ground or hit in the air. It can only be taken into the hand if caught in flight, or if lifted from the ground with the stick. Skilled players can take the ball onto the hurley, from the ground, while running at full speed and carry it, balanced or bouncing, on the broad end before passing or scoring. The main traditional hurling areas remain south of a line from Dublin to Galway, with a small pocket in the Glens of Antrim. Cork and Kilkenny are the top hurling counties.

Football, Gaelic-style

Gaelic football is also played by teams of 15 a side and the layout of the pitch and methods of scoring are the same as for hurling. Played with

Australian Rules, although played with an oval ball on an oval pitch, has features similar to those of Gaelic football. Irish emigrants were no doubt responsible for the long kicking and the great leaps in the air to catch the ball. In an attempt to gain an international dimension for a game played only in Ireland (with the exception of Irish emigrants in the USA and Britain) the GAA has organised tours to and from Australia, with games played under compromise rules. The fact that the Australian players are all professionals have so far given the contests more bite than was anticipated. Professional players do not like being beaten by amateurs.

Hurling and Gaelic football are organised in a

variety of competitions, graded according to age up to senior level, for county and then provincial championship. The high point of the GAA year is in September with the All-Ireland hurling and football Finals in Dublin's Croke Park.

Bowling along

Road bowling is a strange game, played only in South Armagh, Cork and parts of Waterford and Limerick. The game is very simple: two players throw or bowl an iron ball along an ordinary public road, and the winner is the one who covers a set distance with fewer throws. The bowl, or "bullet," can be 28, 21 or 16 ounces (between

Hares and horses

Greyhound racing (on tracks) and coursing in enclosed fields with live hares are very popular sports in Ireland. The breeding and export of grey-hounds is a minor industry and prize-money is now increased by sponsorship. The fact that races are over in a matter of seconds is no deterrent to the small army of punters who attend. Bookmakers attend all kinds of dog- and horse-races, in competition with the more impersonal tote. In their offices, these "turf accountants" take bets on almost anything, from the World Cup to the papal election.

Coursing is a winter sport which has come

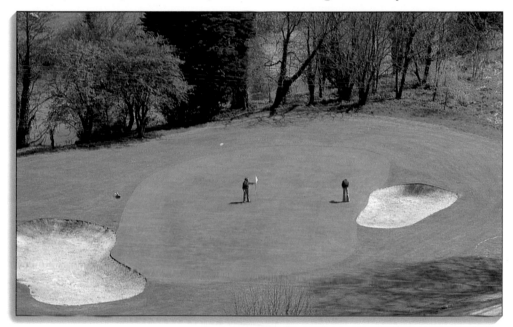

800 and 450 grammes). One of the skills of the game is the negotiation of a bend in the road, either by lofting the bowl over the corner or by curving the throw. If the bowl leaves the road, the player is penalised.

It is a great betting sport and large sums change hands when two noted players meet. Not only are bets laid on the result of the contest; side-bets are also laid on individual shots. Road bowling is illegal as sections of public roads are barred to traffic while the contest goes on. But prosecutions are rare.

LEFT: greyhound racing attracts Ireland's gambling fraternity. **ABOVE:** Dublin's Hermitage Golf Club.

under fire from animal-rights campaigners because of cruelty to hares. Two dogs are slipped simultaneously to chase a hare. Points are scored by deflecting the hare from its course, or by killing it before it gets to the escape exit at the end of the field. Frequently the animal is caught by both dogs and torn apart. But despite violent protests, coursing remains popular in rural areas.

Casual perusal of the sports pages of any Irish daily newspaper will show that an extraordinary range of sports, both national and international, is covered. And, while spectators far outnumber participants, a surprising number excel in a variety of sports at the highest level.

To mention just a few: Sean Kelly dominated the world of professional cycling throughout the 1980s, and in 1987 Stephen Roche won the sport's ultimate prize, the gruelling Tour de France. Dubliner Michael Carruth and Belfast man Wayne McCullough won gold and silver medals respectively in boxing at the 1992 Olympics in Barcelona. In professional boxing, world titles were held by Barry McGuigan and Dave McAuley. Alex Higgins and Denis Taylor both claimed the world championship at snooker. To that list can be added two players with the most international appearances: Mike Gibson, in rugby football, and Pat Jennings, as a soccer goalkeeper.

In international rugby Ireland fields a team drawn from Northern Ireland and the Republic. It's the one international sport (except for professional boxing) that unites all political elements on the island, at least temporarily.

Soccer, the great working-class game, is split by the internal political border. The island fields two international sides: Ireland, as the Northern Ireland team is officially designated, and the Republic of Ireland. Despite limited resources, both have impressed: Northern Ireland qualified for the final stages of the World Cup in both 1982 and 1986, while the Republic caught the eye in the finals of the 1988 European Championships and in the 1990 and 1994 World Cup.

Where golfers link up

Golf is another national passion. Because of the availability of courses, it is played by everyone interested enough to buy a set of clubs. The country is dotted with courses: inland courses like the Curragh (the oldest), Mullingar, Tralee (designed by Arnold Palmer) and the picturesque one at Killarney. There is also a chain of seaside links round the coast from Rosses Point in Sligo, to Lahinch in Clare, to Ballybunion and Waterville in Kerry, Portmarnock and Royal Dublin in the capital, Beltray in Louth and Royal County Down in Newcastle.

So let the non-golfer be warned: Ireland has a higher percentage of golf bores than any other European country. Most of them, though, are also interested in hurling, Gaelic football, soccer, racing, snooker and boxing. Let the non-sportsman be warned.

LEFT: Gaelic football, a spectacular game; the rules, such as they are, are frequently revised.

THE SERIOUS BUSINESS OF DRINKING

The so-called Irish pub has conquered the world. But the only authentic Irish pubs are in Ireland, and their most intoxicating product is talk.

A common stereotype of the Irishman abroad is that of a maudlin drinker seated at a bar in London or New York or Chicago, gazing dolefully into his glass and mouthing inanities to himself about the green fields and the clear mountain streams of his native land. An ill-chosen word from a stranger will quickly rouse his anger and, in the twinkling of an eye, a rip-roaring riot is in progress.

This image of the Irish exile, conveyed principally by movies of a certain vintage, has a strong element of truth in it and so too has the stereotype of the Irish when they are at home. The same movies portray the home-based Irish as jovial, garrulous, welcoming in the extreme and brilliant at the art of conversation. A more realistic view is that the Irish are sad abroad and happy at home because of the drink.

The mystique of Guinness

What makes the Irishman surly in foreign climes is, usually, the lack of quality in, or the total absence of, Guinness. This brew, a strongish black beer with a creamy white head, is, even more than Irish whiskey, the country's national beverage. Brewed in Dublin since 1759, it is a temperamental drink, needing great care in pouring from the tap to the glass. Constant temperature in the cellars, the distance from cask to tap and the frequency of the flow are all considered important factors in the art known as "the pulling of a good pint".

If the pint isn't good, it is sent straight back. Experts embark on long discussions on the pint's quality in different bars throughout the country. Dubliners, who travel frequently inside Ireland, make lists of the provincial pubs which have the best pints. The visitor's best criterion is this: if the place is crowded with locals, then the pint is probably good. And you'll know a good pint when you get one. It won't taste like what passes for Guinness in Britain where the

beer is sloshed into the glass by insensitive barmen, or like the Guinness in America, where the long sea journey from Dublin does nothing for the quality. It will taste, in a good pub in Ireland, as smooth as velvet.

There are other Irish beers, too. Harp, brewed in Dundalk, sells well internationally, particu-

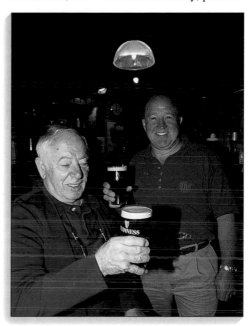

larly in Britain. Smithwick's Ale, lighter than Guinness and darker than Harp, is also popular.

As far as spirits are concerned, the Irish rank highly as connoisseurs. One French Cognac house was surprised to discover that some of the highest sales per head for its premium brandies were in a less than affluent Dublin suburb. But it's Irish whiskey (note the extra "e") which reigns supreme on its home territory. Triple-distilled for purity and lightness, Irish whiskey was overtaken by Scotch on the world market during World War II. One main reason was selfishness on the part of the Irish.

It was an Irishman, Aeneas Coffey, who invented the patent still in the 1830s. This per-

PRECEDING PAGES: Dublin's Brazen Head, a traditional pub. **LEFT:** perfectly poured Guinness. **RIGHT:** enjoying a pint at the Guinness Hop Store bar in Dublin.

mitted the mass production of blended whiskies. Scottish distillers, in the main, switched to the new method. The Irish and the smaller Scottish malt-whisky producers stuck with the old tried and tested "pot still" method, which involved a single whiskey acquiring its mellowness through long ageing. In the 1940s, the Scots diverted their production to export and rationed the sale of their whiskies at home. The Irish did the opposite, keeping their whiskies to themselves. The result was disastrous. GIs from all over America acquired their taste for Scotch in Europe's theatre of war and brought the taste home. Irish whiskey, whose popularity in the royal courts of Europe had inspired Russia's Peter the Great to describe it as "the best of all the wines", went into a decline from which it has only recently begun to recover.

Maturing the malts

The comparative affluence and sophisticated tastes of recent years have stimulated the demand for Ireland's more traditional whiskies as well as Scotland's rarer malts. There are 15 or so different whiskies on sale in Ireland. John Power's Gold Label is by far the most popular. Next come Jameson, Bushmills, Coleraine (which sells in Northern Ireland), Paddy,

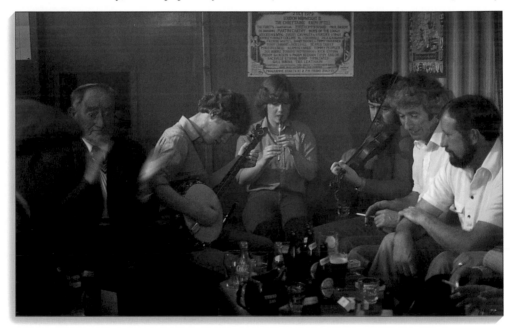

HOW THE IRISH PUB CONQUERED THE WORLD

If America can persuade the world to eat McDonald's hamburgers, can Ireland persuade it to drink Guinness? It seems to be doing just that, judging from the explosive international spread of "traditional" Irish pubs. There are more than 1,000 of them now, from Durty Nellie's in Amsterdam to Finnegan's in Abu Dhabi, from Shifty O'Sheas in Leicester, England, to O'Kims in Seoul, Korea. Most have rumbustious music, and some carry the theme to absurd lengths by incorporating in the decor such Irish Catholic icons as a pulpit and confessional. But they all seem to have one thing in common: they sell lots of beer.

How did it all start? Some trace the trend to the 1994 World Cup when Irish football fans descended on bars around the world, creating the convivial atmosphere of a pub back home. The popularity of Irish culture since then has helped things along.

Never slow to spot an opportunity, brewers such as Guinness set up companies to export the Irish pub concept. They'll help entrepreneurs anywhere in the world to design their hostelry – you can pick a standard model such as Country Cottage, the Victorian Dublin or the Brewery – and also to locate authentic fittings and recruit staff. But of course they're nothing like the genuine article in Ireland.

Hewitt's and Dunphy's. Murphy's sells mainly in the United States, and Tullamore Dew, a particularly light brand, does well in Europe.

Two popular premium brands are Black Bush (from Bushmills in County Antrim, the world's oldest distillery) and Crested Ten, matured for 10 years in the Jameson stable. At the top of the range are liqueur whiskies, among the most exceptional drinks on earth. Bushmills Malt is a single 10-year-old; Jameson 1780 is aged for 12 years; and Redbreast, also 12 years old, is

HOW TO DRINK MALTS

The best Irish malts should be sipped neat like fine Cognacs or Armagnac, although the foreigner is permitted to add just a dash of pure Irish water.

prepared, this secretly distilled drink can seriously damage your health.

But it's not only the drink itself that's important: it's where you drink it. Ireland's rural bars are usually functional in design; nothing to look at from the outside, but warm, cozy and well filled inside.

Picture a bar in a small village on the Atlantic coast. It is 2am, long after the official closing time. There is a rap on the door, sharp enough to suggest authority. A local police sergeant enters, in full uniform, torch-

matured in wood by the house of Gilbey, renowned for its wines, ports and sherries. To put ice in these last three whiskies is an act of sacrilege to an Irishman.

While all the major international brands of gin, vodka and other spirits are readily available, the Irish are inclined to stick to the home products. Thus Cork Dry Gin far outsells the more famous British gins. One often-mentioned drink, poteen, isn't on sale anywhere legally. Some of it can be quite good; but, if carelessly

light in hand. Yet no-one present interrupts the conversation – except for a few visiting English and Americans. Half an hour later, the scene has changed entirely. Not a murmur of conversation is to be heard. The sergeant, his cap placed on the bar in front of him, is clasping a pint of Guinness and, with eyes closed, is singing the old lament "The Blackbird of Sweet Avondale".

This sort of scene can be found easily enough anywhere on the west coast, where the summer tourist season is short and the after-hours trade compensates for the meagre takings in the desolate winter months. In the main cities, however, this laxity does not exist. Drinking-up time is now extended to midnight, Monday to Sat-

LEFT: singing and supping at Megaw's pub in Brookeborough, Co. Fermanagh. **ABOVE:** dogs are welcome, especially at this bar in Crookhaven, Co. Cork.

urda in summer, while it's back to 11.30pm in winter. Sunday closing all year round is 11pm. The law is strictly enforced. Well, fairly strictly.

City pubs are different, too. In Dublin some bars are richly caparisoned in brass and mahogany, with antique mirrors proclaiming the merits of whiskies long since defunct. Some such pubs look much as they did in 1850.

Classic pubs

To experience the value placed on the traditional, visit Doheny and Nesbitt's in Dublin's Baggot Street. This is an old-fashioned pub, long and narrow with a "snug" at each end. A

snug is a small area partitioned off from the rest of the bar in which up to 10 people can drink in almost complete privacy. It even has its own private service hatch, and is a hangover from the days when women who fancied a tipple didn't want to be seen consuming it. The atmosphere is one of talk and more talk, for if there is one thing that is as important as the drink in a Dublin pub it is the conversation. The general appearance is dowdy enough, with hard bar stools and not the slightest attempt at plushness. Yet this bar is the haunt of government ministers, senior public servants, prominent journalists and a group of economists known informally as "the Doheny and Nesbitt School".

Nesbitt's, as it's known for short, fulfills the function that private clubs play in most capital cities, with the distinct advantage that any member of the decent Irish drinking public is free to walk in from the street and join the company.

Other Dublin pubs with good character and conversation include Mulligan's of Poolbeg Street, Neary's of Chatham Street and Ryan's of Parkgate Street. Mulligan's, which welcomed its first customer in 1782, is also divided into sections.The entrance to the left of the building leads into the older part of the pub. Here one finds students, the occasional retired docker and photographers from the *Irish Press,* whose head office is nearby. The door to the right of the building leads to the first of two bars in the slightly more modern section. The first is occupied by newspaper and TV people. Go through to the far bar and you are in left-wing territory.

Neary's is a beautifully furnished old-style pub which attracts permanently posing actors from the Gaiety Theatre. Ryan's, situated in an area a little distance from the centre of Dublin's action, is a real gem: its clients are those who appreciate good conversation, good atmosphere and the traditions of Dublin pub life.

Salmon and singing

Along the Atlantic coast is a tremendous selection of fine pubs, but none better than those in north and west Clare, not far from Galway. In the spa town of Lisdoonvarna, Curtin's "Roadside" tavern smokes its own salmon and has fresh shellfish in season. At night, there are traditional fiddlers, pipers and flute players.

There are about 12,000 pubs on the island, and in them visitors can see something of the real Ireland, both its strengths and its weaknesses. Drinkers will usually respect a stranger's privacy, talking only when a willingness to talk is shown. Those who join in, however, won't forget the experience: the talk's even better than the scenery.

But do the Irish really appreciate what they've got? The curious thing is that, while the rest of the world is discovering the joys of the Irish pub, the latest growth phenomenon in Dublin is the continental café, modelled along the lines of Amsterdam's "brown cafés" where the young and trendy go to converse.

LEFT: a convivial chat in Kenmare, Co. Kerry.
RIGHT: unambiguous message on a Donegal pub door.

A FRESH APPROACH TO FOOD

Despite an abundance of fresh ingredients, the Irish have never
shown much interest in haute cuisine. Until now...

When Irish food is good it is, like the little girl in the nursery rhyme with the curl in the middle of her forehead, very very good. But when it is bad it is horrid.

The distinction begins with the day's first meal. The short-order cry goes out to the cook: "Two breakfasts – one a gentleman's, the other a lady's." Blazing hot plates arrive on the linen tablecloth. Everything on them is fried, not grilled, for this is calorie-cholestrol country. On top of the piles of potato-bread and soda-bread farls, beside the rashers and sausages and black pudding culled from organically managed stock, the tomatoes fresh from the greenhouses, are free-range eggs. The gentleman gets two eggs, his lady one.

If the accommodation is a country house hotel rather than a bed-and-breakfast bungalow, the silver teapot may bear the family crest, and the fried breads – plus the wheaten toast in the rack and the gooseberry jam – come from the house's own walled garden, where the red-faced master of the house, clad in Beford cords and Tattersal checked shirt, forks the soil his ancestors preferred to leave to the gardeners.

The harsh reality

But such heaven is not always available. For, curiously, these simple country skills – bread and jam making, patting butter, letting hens range free – are the exception, not the norm, and they are more likely to have been preserved by what used to be called "the gentry". At too many breakfasts, the juice offered is pasteurised, tasting more of its container than of any orange. Pale flaccid bacon, flecked with a whitish ooze, lies in grease. The eggs' yokes are pale, the store-bought sausages anatomical in colour, shape and aroma. The coffee is stewed, harsh, often instant, poorly disguised by its serving jug.

It's all a long way from the promising "A Taste of..." descriptions in the tourist brochures.

LEFT: the fish should be fresh – Ireland's surrounded by them. **RIGHT:** the country's other culinary glory is its wonderful range of home-baked bread.

Those same brochures promise even greater delights by showing alluring platters of seafood: a salmon, probably, fine as any on an heraldic shield, amongst a throng of lobster, crab, oysters and speckled brown trout.

And so it should be on an island surrounded by relatively unpolluted water. Ireland's coastal

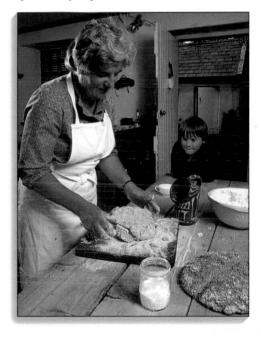

bays are dotted with brightly coloured floats marking pots set to catch European, squat and Norway lobster, and common and spider crab. Vacationing anglers and offshore nets bring wild Atlantic salmon to the table. Raft-hung ropes glisten with plump mussels. Dredgers haul up queen and fan-shell scallops, Venus clams and the one the French call *palourde*. Spanish holidaymakers dig for razorshells on breath-taking strands or scuba-dive for the elusive, scrumptious goose-barnacle (known to locals as the devil's fingernails).

Away from the sea, dun cows browse the wild-flower water meadows, piglets and lambs gain flavour on purple, heathery mountain slopes. Carrots, onions and potatoes prosper in the drumlin's gravelled loam.

But the truth is different. Unlike France's Brittany or Spain's Galicia – both also Catholic, Celtic and projecting into the western Atlantic – Ireland has no hereditary passion for food, seafood in particular. The Anglo-Norman colonists who changed the landscape for ever brought with them tastes more Anglo than Norman-French: woodcock, venison, pheasant, snipe. The Scots Planters who came as their servants and tradesmen did little to redeem the situation: they brought to the table an attitude of Calvinist rigour, not rapture.

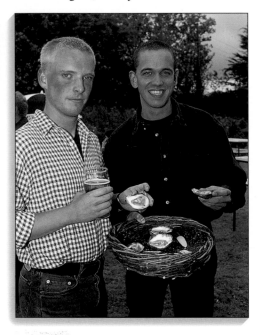

The result? In all too many hotels, chicken, overcooked steak with chips, or "meat and two veg" – both overcooked as well – are the best a traveller may expect. The "fresh" salmon is all too often dull farmed fish, as are the muddy rainbow trout. The increasingly ubiquitous burger bars, pizza parlours and Chinese take-aways are rarely models of their kind, leaving the traditional "fish supper" – heavily battered fish 'n' chips – the best bet.

Another serving of tourist iconography, proferred on so many postcards, are the traditional Irish foods: boxty (raw and cooked potato mashed with butter, buttermilk, flour, then baked), champ (potato boiled and mashed with

butter, milk, scallion, salt), colcannon (champ and cabbage), Dublin coddle (bacon, ham-bone, onion, potato, sausage), Irish stew (mutton, carrot, leek and potato). They're excellent if you can get them – but authentic versions are available in only a handful of places, such as Gallagher's Boxty House in Dublin's *rive gauche*, Temple Bar, or in Belfast's famed Crown Liquor Saloon.

So where does all the fine produce go? Much of it, bought almost before it is caught or killed, is off that night, express, to the markets of Rungis in Paris and Madrid's Maravillas, which between them display more Irish-caught seafood than you'll find on any given day in the whole of Ireland.

The modern approach

Fortunately, there are some saviours at hand. For, just as the great English food writer Elizabeth David rescued her country from roast beef, so the Allen dynasty, from Cork east, have liberated a new generation of Ireland's chefs. Myrtle Allen's Ballymaloe Country House and Restaurant led the revolution, drafting small bands of suppliers together, letting the fine local produce – lamb filets and kidneys in a walnut-oil salad tiede, free-range chicken baked with cucumber, grilled scallions and buttered turnips – speak for themselves. Books, a TV series and a cookery school have helped spread the gospel.

These shops are usually well-stocked with Ireland's other new culinary delight: a great range of farmhouse cheeses. Soft or hard, from cows', goats' or sheep's milk, their arrival on the shelves marks a watershed in the country's new attitude towards its own food products. Fresh herbs, venison and boar sausage, mountain honey and organically grown vegetables compete for shoppers' attention.

There's money to be made, of course, in the new food consciousness. Shannon Basket of Fine Foods in Limerick can export you a preview, or mail you a memory. In September, Galway's riverbank Clarinbridge festival and the Galway International Oyster Festival are splen-

---

FOOD FOR THOUGHT

The novelist William Makepeace Thackeray wrote about Ireland: "We can feel the beauty of a magnificent landscape, perhaps: but we can describe a leg of mutton and turnips better."

did events, as is mid-October's harbourside Kinsale Gourmet Festival.

Now many of the country house hotels – most of which are listed by the Irish Country House Association or by its competitor, Hidden Ireland – are unfurling the fine produce banner. Among the current leaders is Gerry and Marie Galvin's Drimcong House Restaurant in Moycullen, Co. Galway.

Innovative cooking – at a price

Dublin, in particular, has a good spread of first-class restaurants. Some, such as Patrick Guilbaud's eponymous establishment, fly the classic

Belfast, once a foodies' wasteland, has begun providing the lead in a revolution which may even supplant that of its southern competitors. In their restaurant Roscoff, for example, Jeannie Rankin, the Canadian honorary consul, and her Belfast-born husband Paul are aiming to change the face of dining out in Ireland. Surrounded by minimalist decor, fine linen and glass, the Rankins' cuisine embraces marinated olives, oven-hot breads, lobster and herb risotto, char-grilled lamb and couscous. Disciples in Northern Ireland include Shanks, Deane's, Beech Hill Country House, Macnean's and Ardtara Country House.

French flag. Others, including Les Frères Jacques, promote the French provincial style. Johnny Cooke melds Italian and Pacific Rim with panache in Cooke's Café. The Temple Bar *arrondissement* is jammed with multinational tastes and there's an almost Italian quarter, a little south, off Wicklow Street. Visitors, however, can be shocked by the high prices, partly the result of the high rates of value-added tax and duty on wine.

Left: tasting time at the Clarenbridge Oyster Festival.
Above: the traditional utensils behind Irish Stew; today's chefs have learned that visitors prefer their meat not to be overcooked.

At a less elevated level, the baking of bread and cakes anywhere in Ireland is almost always reliable. Brown soda bread made from stoneground wheaten flour is crusty, yet soft inside, and is the perfect accompaniment to seafish. Potato cakes, most popular in the north, are served with bacon and eggs for breakfast. A Barm Brack is a currant loaf traditionally eaten at Hallowe'en (31 October).

Pubs, the social heart of Irish communities, serve food of varying standards. You'll find scary re-heated and re-chilled "lasagnes", but you'll also find excellent home-made sandwiches and the finest of oysters and steaks. And the Guinness is likely to be very reliable.

PLACES

*A detailed guide to the entire island, with principal sites
cross-referenced by number to the maps*

What other city but Dublin, capital of the Republic of Ireland, could boast a General Post Office as a national shrine? Where else but Belfast, capital of Northern Ireland, could have endured a quarter of a century of sporadic terrorist activity and remain so bustling, so commercially alive, so welcoming? How can a country with a tiny population and a reputation for anarchy convince some of the world's biggest computer manufacturers to set up shop there? Why does the South say that the border between the two states has 252 crossing points, while the North insists it has 287?

"Sure," the Irishman will tell you, "it's only apathy that's saving the country from chaos but don't you worry your head at all about it now, the situation may be desperate, but sure it's not serious." Forget the statistics, therefore. Bring a raincoat, an umbrella and sturdy walking boots, but leave your preconceptions at home.

What you'll discover is a beguiling Irish stew of hidden loughs and ancient towns, prehistoric burial chambers and strange stone crosses, round towers and ruined castles, holy wells and high-spirited waterfalls. Racehorses are the local heroes and the villain is anyone too hurried to bid the time of day to a neighbour in a civilised manner. Kerry beckons with opulent valleys, nurturing arbutus, wild fuchsia and scented orchids; Killarney, with jaunting cars and leprachaun lore designed to charm the punts from tourists' pockets; the remote Irish-speaking Gaeltacht in the far west, with its mile after mile of magnificent emptiness; Dublin, increasingly anglicised, americanised and hamburgerised, yet still the least lonely of cities; rivers like the Galway and the Shannon where you could knock a dozen salmon senseless with a single brick; Fermanagh's resplendent lakeland, where boats are still gloriously few and far between; and County Clare's bleak but fascinating Burren.

It is a small country but, like vintage wine, should be savoured slowly. A signpost may present you with three ways of getting to a destination or it may show none. Ask a passer-by and, if he decides you look a bit tired after a hard day's sightseeing and comparing pints of Guinness, he'll probably assure you that it's "just a wee way ahead" because he doesn't wish to distress you by telling you it's really 40 miles by a narrow, twisting road.

Ireland, in the end, is less a place on a map than a state of mind, induced by exposure to its restful yet excitable people, who view life as a chaotic comedy. The inevitable, they promise, never happens in Ireland and the unexpected constantly occurs. Be prepared.

PRECEDING PAGES: the Rock of Cashel; the ancient dolmen at Poulnabrone, Co. Clare; a traditional Connemara farmer – an increasingly rare sight these days.
LEFT: sheep farming at Glenmalure, Co. Wicklow.

Ireland

Dublin

0 — 250 m
0 — 250 yds

Marlborough Rd
North Circular Road
Ross Street
O'Devaney Gardens
Aberdeen St.
Infirmary Road
Dept. of Defence
Parkgate Street
Montpelier
Montpelier Drive
Montpelier Hill
Benburb
St. Bricin's Park
Park
Oxman Town Road
Ben Edar Rd.
Halliday Rd.
Harold Rd.
Manor Place
Mount Temple Rd.
Sitric Road
Ard-Righ Rd.
Arbour
Hill
Place
Collins Barracks
Arbour Hill Prison
Blackhall
Hendrick Street
Street
Prussia
Street
Auburn Walk
Aughrim Street
Ivar Street
Manor St.
Stoneybatter
Kirwan
Street
Grangegorman Lr.
Drumalee Road
Grangegorman Upper

St. Brendan's Hospital
St. Lawrence Hospital
Brunswick Street North
King Street
Queen Street
Smithfield
Bow Street
May Lane
Mary's
Church Street
Constitution Hill
Prebend Street
Church St. Upper
Coleraine St.
North
Beresford
Greek St.
Halston St.
Lane
Chancery Street
Wellington
Fonter
Western Way
Dominick Stre
Henri

King's Inns
34

36
St. Michan
St. Paul
Arran Quay
Hammond Ln.
Chancery
Four Courts
37
Inns Quay
Ormor

Wolfe Tone Quay
Victoria Quay
Ellis Quay
Usher's Island
Island Street
River Liffey
Usher's Quay
Usher
Usher
St. Augustine Street
St.
Merchants Quay
Franciscan Ch.
Cook Street
22
St. Audoen
High St.
Chris
Churc
Cathed
Dublin
Chr
Ch.
Wood
Winetavern
St.

Heuston Station
St. John's Road West
Steevens' Lane
St. Patrick's Hospital
Military Rd.
Bow Bridge
Mount Brown
Bow Lane West
James
Basin
St. Lr.
23 Guinness Brewery (St. James's Gate Brewery)
Watling Street
Bonham Street
Bridgefoot
Oliver Bond Street
John St. West
Bridge Street
Thomas Street West
Echlin St.
Guinness Hop Store
Crane St.
Street
Thomas Court
Hanbury Lane
Rainsford
Robert
Bellevue
Lane
Earl St. South
Meath Place
Meath Street
Cornmarket
Flea Market
Francis Street
Back Lane
John Dillon St.
Nicholas R
Ross R
Bride St.
Bull A
St. Patrick Cathed

St. James's Hospital
Convent
Our Lady's Rd.
Lourdes Rd.
Rosary Rd.
Basin Street Upper
Pim St.
Bond St.
Newport St.
Marrowbone
Summer St. South
Pimlico
Carman's Hall
Swift's Alley
Patrick Street
John Street South
Cork
Street
Chamber St.
Mill Street
Newmarket
Ward's Hill
New Row South
The Coombe
Dean St.
Brown Street South
Convent
Clarence Mangan
O'Curry Road
St. Thomas Road
New Street South
Kevin Str
Vernon
Malpas St.
Long
Daniel

St. James's Walk
Rialto Street
St. Anthony's Rd.
Reuben
Reuben
Circular
Cameron St.
Dolphin's Barn St.
Donore Avenue
Susan Terrace
Donore Rd.
O'Donovan Road
Road
Clanbrassil Street Lower
Blackpitts
Lombard St. We

DOLPHIN'S BARN Road
Coombe Hospital

DUBLIN

It's a small capital and not an especially pretty one – but the vivacity of its citizens and the hospitality they show to visitors have made it one of Europe's most popular destinations

Map, page 138

Dublin means many things to many people. For some, it is a city of writers, the city of Jonathan Swift, Oliver Goldsmith, James Joyce, William Butler Yeats, Sean O'Casey, Brendan Behan, and even Bram Stoker, creator of Dracula. For others, it is a shrine of Irish nationalism. For some, it is the gateway to the fabled Irish landscape. For others, it is a city of talkers, its pubs overflowing with Guinness and jokes. Some come to wander in its Georgian streets, squares and gardens. Others don't know what to expect. But the first thing that must strike nearly all visitors – weather permitting – is its superb natural setting, on a wide plain bisected by the **River Liffey**, overlooked by hills and headlands and facing a broad sweeping bay.

As for the city itself, they cannot help noticing that it looks, well, a bit dingy. Dear, dirty Dublin, someone once called it – and undeniably it does have an untidy, abstracted elegance, as if its mind is on something more important than looking attractive. The once-fashionable clothes are now a little threadbare, but it can still sparkle when it tries.

LEFT: windy perch on the GPO in O"Connell Street. **BELOW:** one of the city's flashy new malls – this one's at St Stephen's Green.

A divided city

Dublin is divided by the River Liffey that flows through its centre and also by the social differences which the river delineates. In the early 18th century, the rich moved north across the river from the old medieval city with its teeming slums to the fine new terraces and squares that were then springing up, such as **Henrietta Street** and **Mountjoy Square**. But within decades they doubled back again to establish fashionable residences on the south side in **Merrion Square** and **Fitzwilliam Square**, continuing in Victorian times through the suburbs of **Ballsbridge** and out along the coast to **Dun Laoghaire** and **Dalkey**.

There are still middle-class enclaves on the northside, but by and large southsiders are better-off, better-dressed and (to their own ears) better spoken. They are also determined and skilful in the preservation of their privilege. Like any snobbery, of course, the north–south chauvinism works both ways, and just as many southsiders "wouldn't be seen dead on the northside", northsiders are inclined to judge that the southside is a wasteland of snobbery and pretension and that "them'uns are welcome to it."

Paradoxes of history

It began by the banks of the Liffey, where Celtic settlements and churches existed at least from early Christian times, near a causeway crossing from which Dublin's Gaelic name, *Baile Atha Cliath*, "The Town of the Hurdle Ford", is derived. But towns as such did not figure in the old Celtic way of things, and it is gen-

The Four Courts, the work of Thomas Cooley and James Gandon, was completed in 1796. The original Four Courts were those of Chancery, Common Pleas, Exchequer and King's Bench.

BELOW: O'Connell Street Bridge.

erally accepted that Dublin was founded in the 9th century not by the Irish, but by the Vikings, who were plundering and colonising all the coasts of Northern Europe. They built a garrison port on the south bank of the river where its tributary, the Poddle, joined it to form the black pool (*dubh-linn*) that gave the city its name. The Poddle, once a fair-sized river, is now an underground stream.

Dublin was soon a lucrative base for both raiding and trading and the Danes hung on to it – despite persistent attacks by local chieftains and a great defeat at the Battle of Clontarf in 1014 – gradually intermarrying with the Irish and adopting Christianity. The Anglo-Normans arrived in the 12th century. But, until Elizabethan times, direct English rule was restricted to a ribbon of land on the east coast known as "the Pale", running roughly from Dundalk to the north to a little way south of Dublin.

The colonisation by landlords from Britain in the 17th and 18th centuries, however, established a stability of Anglo-Irish rule under which the city started to flourish for the haves, if not the have-nots. The 18th century was Dublin's "golden age", when many great buildings were erected and the city's social life was as fashionable as any in Europe. Legislative independence was granted under the English Crown in 1782, but the Irish parliament in College Green was short-lived. After the rebellion of the United Irishmen in 1798, inspired by the ideals of the French and American revolutions, Britain brought Ireland under direct control again and began a long period of decline in Dublin life.

The city was at the heart of the political and cultural ferment that led to the Rising of 1916, the subsequent War of Independence and the establishment of the Free State in 1921. The next 40 years were a time of economic struggle in a puritan atmosphere that was often culturally and socially stifling.

Map, page 138

City centre elegance

A good place to begin a walking tour is O'Connell Bridge. Turn your back on the inviting breadth and bustle of **O'Connell Street** and instead walk down **Westmoreland Street** into **College Green**, which contains two of Dublin's most impressive and historic buildings: the **Bank of Ireland ❶** and Trinity College. You might think that the bank, with its curving, columnar, windowless facade, exudes loftier ideals than those of commerce, and you would be right. It was begun in 1729 to house the Irish Parliament, whose builders could not have foreseen how brief would be its age of glory.

The statue of Henry Grattan, the parliament's greatest orator, stands in the middle of College Green, frozen in mid-gesture, apparently delivering one of his ringing speeches. "Nations," he once said, "are governed not by interest only, but by passion also, and the passion of Ireland is freedom." The eastern front of the bank was added in 1785 by James Gandon, of whom more later. The building is open during banking hours; a liveried attendant will show you around.

Trinity College ❷, whose sober facade is topped by a surprisingly bright blue clock, was founded in 1591 by Elizabeth I on the site of a confiscated monastery, but the frontage was built between 1755 and 1759. The porch inside the main gate leads to a spacious, cobbled quadrangle, on the right of which is the Theatre, or Examination Hall (1779–91), which contains a gilt oak chandelier from the old parliament and an organ said to have been taken from a Spanish ship at Vigo in 1702. On the left is the Chapel (1792) and beyond it the Dining Hall (1743). The 100-ft (30-metre) campanile which dominates the quadrangle was designed by Sir Charles Lanyon and erected in 1853 on a spot supposed to mark the centre of the medieval monastery church.

ABOVE: the Bank of Ireland. **BELOW:** capturing attention in O'Connell Street: a lady preacher and pioneer labour leader James Larkin (1876–1947).

To the right of the second quadrangle is the **Old Library** (1712–32), containing in a glass case the *Book of Kells,* a magnificently ornate 9th-century manuscript copy of the gospels in Latin, which must be seen by any visitor. It is the greatest artefact of the flowering of Irish culture between the 7th and 9th centuries, the era when Ireland was famed as "the land of saints and scholars" and Irish monks re-Christianised Europe after the Dark Ages. Also in the library are the *Book of Durrow* (7th-century), the *Book of Dimma* (8th-century) and the *Book of Armagh* (*circa* 807). Upstairs is the breathtaking **Long Room**, nearly 210 ft (64 metres) in length and containing 200,000 of the college's oldest books.

Embracing a more modern form of communication, the college also houses in the nearby Arts Block the inevitable **Dublin Experience**, a 45-minute multimedia show which operates from late May until early October.

Leaving Trinity by the main gate and turning left, you face the mouth of **Grafton Street**, the southside's principal shopping thoroughfare, now pedestrianised and teeming with people. A statue at the junction with Suffolk Street depicts Molly Malone who, in the famous song *In Dublin's Fair City*, "wheeled her wheelbarrow through streets broad and narrow." With typical Dublin wit, the statue was dubbed "the tart with the cart". Worth a visit for its gregarious atmosphere is **Bewley's Oriental Café**, one of a chain of large, old-fashioned coffee-shops/restaurants that has become a justly beloved Dublin institution. **Johnston's Court**, a narrow alley off Grafton Street to the right, leads to the rear entrance of the **Powerscourt Centre**, a three-storey collection of stylish shops and cafés under the roof of the former Powerscourt Townhouse, built in 1771–74 for Viscount Powerscourt. If you walk through the centre, exiting on William Street South, on your left is the small **Dublin Civic Museum ❸** (Tuesday to Saturday, 10am–6pm, Sunday 11am–2pm), which has a range of artefacts relating to the city's history, including the head of Admiral Lord Nelson from the O'Connell Street pillar toppled by the IRA in 1966 and some interesting prints of the great 18th-century streets.

Map, page 138

St Stephen's Green

On returning to Grafton Street, a right turn and a short walk takes you to the corner of **St Stephen's Green** ❹, a delightful small park bordered by some fine houses, though there has also been some ruinous modern development – particularly on the westside, where the only surviving historic building is the neoclassical **Royal College of Surgeons** (1806). The green, formerly an open common, was enclosed in 1663, but it was not surrounded by buildings until the late 18th century, when it became one of the most fashionable spots in Dublin. The gardens, laid out as a public park in 1880, are a relaxing refuge from the traffic and contain several interesting sculptures.

On the Green's south side are two elegant Georgian houses: **Newman House**, numbers 85 and 86 (June–August, Tues–Fri, noon–5pm, Sat 2–5pm, Sun 11am–2pm), once the seat of the Catholic University of Ireland at which James Joyce, Flann O'Brien and Gerard Manley Hopkins worked or studied; and **Iveagh House**, numbers 80 and 81, which was built for the Bishop of Cork, once housed the Guinness family, and is now part of the Department of Foreign Affairs. The main attraction of Newman House is its fine interior plasterwork, the best of its kind in Ireland. In 1856 John Henry Newman, the English theologian who was rector at the forerunner of University College Dublin, directed the building next door of **University Church**, designed in a colourful neo-Byzantine style.

Newman House's interior shows how European tastes influenced Irish craftsmen.

BELOW: the statue of Molly Malone in Grafton Street.

On the north side of the Green is the **Shelbourne Hotel** ❺, built in its present splendid form in 1865 and the noblest address in the city. Dublin's hotels are much more than places to stay: they have an important role in the social life of the middle classes as places to meet and be seen. In **Earlsfort Terrace**, which branches from the southeastern corner of the green, is the **National Concert Hall**. The building, beautifully renovated, has first-rate acoustics.

Fans of George Bernard Shaw (1856–1950) can divert a few hundred metres southwest to the **Shaw Birthplace** ❻ at 33 Synge Street. Since Shaw moved permanently to England at the age of 20, there's little here to indicate his writing activities, but the house nicely evokes the domestic world of Victorian Dublin.

Official Dublin

The House of Representatives (Dáil) has 166 members (Teachtaí Dála, usually abbreviated to TD), and is directly elected every five years.

Back on the north side of St Stephen's Green, **Kildare Street** leads past the side of the Shelbourne Hotel and a block of modern state buildings to **Leinster House** ❼, built as a townhouse for the Duke of Leinster in 1746 and now home of the Dáil Eireann (Irish parliament). It is flanked by two nearly symmetrical edifices with columnar entrance rotundas. These are the **National Library** and **National Museum** ❽, both built in 1890. Apart from more than 500,000 books, the library has an extensive collection of old newspapers and periodicals. The large, musty reading-room is well worth a look. The museum's exhibits range from pre-history through the early Christian period and the Vikings to the Independence struggle. Opening hours: Tues–Sat 10am–5pm, Sun 2–5pm.

BELOW: the National Museum.

Directly opposite Leinster House is **Molesworth Street**, and a few yards along it is **Buswell's Hotel**, a popular haunt among politicians and political journalists. At its far end the street meets **Dawson Street**, which contains several stylish

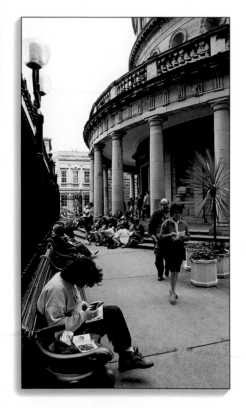

shops. Turning left at the corner you find **St Anne's Church** (1720), a venue for concerts as well as religious services, and a little further on, at number 19, the **Royal Irish Academy**, one of the learned societies of Europe. A few metres up the street is the **Mansion House** ❾, the residence since 1715 of the Lord Mayors of Dublin. A Queen Anne-style house, dating from 1705, it was decorated with stucco and cast iron in Victorian times.

At the lower end of Dawson Street, you can turn right along **Nassau Street** and **Clare Street**, past the Kilkenny Design shop and Greene's fine old bookshop, into **Merrion Square** ❿, one of Dublin's finest. Laid out in 1762, it has had many distinguished inhabitants, Sir William and Lady "Speranza" Wilde, surgeon and poetess, and parents of Oscar, lived at number 1; Daniel O'Connell lived at number 58; W.B. Yeats, who was born in the seaside suburb of Sandymount but grew up mainly in London, lived at number 52 and later at number 83; Sheridan Le Fanu, author of the seminal vampire story *Carmilla*, lived at number 70. The Duke of Wellington, victor over Napoleon at the Battle of Waterloo, was born at number 24 Merrion Street Upper, which runs off the southwest corner of the square towards Merrion Row and St Stephen's Green. The lush gardens in the square are open to the public.

Turning right from the end of Clare Street, along the western side of the square, you find on your right the **National Gallery of Ireland** ⓫. The statue on the lawn is of William Dargan, who organised the 1853 Dublin Exhibition on this site and used the profits to found the collection. To the left of the entrance is a statue of George Bernard Shaw, who said he owed his education to the gallery and left it a third of his estate. Apart from a representative range of Irish work, the gallery contains a small collection of Dutch masters and fine examples of the 17th-century French, Italian and Spanish schools.

Map, page 138

Leaving the gallery and turning right up **Merrion Street Upper** past the lawns of Leinster House, there is a fine architectural view to your left along the south-side of Merrion Square towards the distant cupola of St Stephen's Church (1825). A left turn at the next intersection along Baggot Street, then a right up **Pembroke Street** leads to **Fitzwilliam Square ⓓ**, the smallest, latest (1825) and best-preserved Georgian square in the city. Ireland's greatest modern painter, Jack B. Yeats (brother of the poet) lived on the far side of the square at number 18, on the corner of Fitzwilliam Street, the longest Georgian street in Dublin. In an infamous piece of state vandalism, 26 houses on its eastern side were demolished in 1965 to make way for a new Electricity Supply Board HQ. Perhaps out of shame, the ESB helped restore **Number 29**, in Fitzwilliam Street Lower, as an elegant middle-class house of the late 1700s. Admission is free.

Wander back now to Trinity College, a good starting point to begin exploring the oldest part of the city.

Temple Bar

With your back to the facade of Trinity and the Bank of Ireland on your right, walk along **Dame Street**, passing on your right the imposing, layered structure of the modern **Central Bank**. The network of small streets between the bank

BELOW: the National Gallery; the nursery of Number 29 Fitzwilliam Street.

Some of the converted Temple Bar buildings have retained their elaborate friezes.

BELOW: conviviality at Temple Bar.

and the river quays, known as **Temple Bar** , has undergone a remarkable renaissance in the past few years to become Dublin's "Left Bank", its cobbled streets full of studios, galleries, secondhand book, clothing and music stores, pubs, clubs, cultural centres, restaurants and craft shops. This is very much the "buzz" area of Dublin, especially for young people.

There is no "best route" through Temple Bar; it's essentially a place for browsing. But the map indicates a trail taking in the main points of interest. The area's renewal has been planned around two new public squares: **Temple Bar Square**, seen as a meeting point for shoppers, and **Meeting House Square**, a cultural centre and performance space. Just off Temple Bar Square, Merchant's Arch – a favourite spot for buskers – leads to the river quay and the **Ha'penny Bridge** (1816) – so-called because of the toll once charged for crossing it. This cast-iron pedestrian walkway across the Liffey has become one of the best-known symbols of the city. It is a valuable link between Temple Bar and the bustling shopping streets of the Henry Street area across the river.

The route from Temple Bar Square to Meeting House Square goes through the newly built Curved Street, which houses the **Arthouse** (claimed to be the world's first purpose-built multimedia centre for the arts) and the **Temple Bar Music Centre**, which is both a training centre/workshop and a venue for concerts. You emerge in Eustace Street, which contains the **Temple Bar Information Centre** (useful for details of current events) and the **Ark**, a cultural centre for children. Just up the street from the Ark, a covered passageway leads into Meeting House Square, an outdoor performance venue, used in summer for concerts, theatre and film shows.

To one side of it are two of the area's main cultural attractions: the **Irish**

Film Centre – an arthouse cinema with a bookshop, café/restaurant, bar and film archive – and the **Gallery of Photography**, which shows both Irish and international work and has an interesting range of postcards and books. Just off the other side of the square is **DESIGNyard**, an applied arts centre displaying and selling Irish and international jewellery, glass, ceramics and furniture. Continuing along Essex Street East, you pass the rear of the Clarence Hotel, which fronts onto the river quay. The hotel's current owners include members of the U2 rock band, and its stylish Octagon Bar is a fashionable meeting place.

At the riverside end of the street is Sunlight Chambers, a building with a beautiful Victorian frieze displaying the world according to the priorities of Lever Bros, soap manufacturers: men's toil makes clothes dirty, women's toil (and Sunlight Soap) makes them clean again!

Ancient Dublin

Beyond Parliament Street, Essex Street West leads to **Dublin's Viking Adventure** ⓯ (daily except Tuesday & Wednesday 9.30am–4pm), which offers an "interactive experience" of life in Viking Dublin, using audio-visual gimmicks, a mocked-up street, actors in period dress, and excavated artefacts.

Essex Street ends at its junction with **Fishamble Street**, the medieval "fish shambles", or market, which winds upwards from the quay alongside the Civic Offices. This otherwise unprepossessing street is celebrated as the venue of the first performance of Handel's *Messiah*, conducted by the composer in 1742 in the Charitable Music Society's Hall, long since demolished. Because the hall was cramped and the attendance large, ladies were asked not to wear hooped petticoats and gentlemen not to wear their swords. *Messiah* was an instant

Map,
page 138

The only constants are the sea, the play of light and the same green curve of hills the Vikings saw when they arrived."
—Peter Somerville-Large

BELOW: set dancing in a Temple Bar pub; Dublin's Viking Adventure.

success in Dublin, though London audiences remained cool towards it for several years. A new hotel, named after the composer, stands beside the original site, and the *Messiah*'s birth is celebrated at this spot at noon every 13 April by members of Our Lady's Choral Society, who sing a selection of choruses.

Back on Dame Street, past the Central Bank, you see on your right the ornate Victorian doorway of the **Olympia Theatre** . Despite its modest frontage, it is Dublin's largest; its programme mixes straight plays, musicals and concerts.

Dublin Castle

The street now rises towards the high ground on which the medieval city grew up around Dublin Castle. Just before reaching the castle, you see on your left the Corinthian domed exterior of **City Hall** ⓲ (Mon–Fri, 8.45am–5pm). It was designed in 1769 as the Royal Exchange by the London architect Thomas Cooley (who won a £100 prize for the plan) and served as a prison for rebels in 1798, as a military depot, and as a corn exchange, before being taken over by the corporation in 1852. The entrance rotunda has a splendid illuminated dome. On the mosaic floor is the city's coat of arms, with the rubric in Latin, "Happy the city where citizens obey" – not perhaps the most apposite motto for Dubliners.

Dublin Castle ⓲, built between 1208 and 1220 on the site of an earlier Danish fortress, was the bastion and symbol of English rule in Ireland for almost eight centuries. The building as it now stands is mainly 18th-century; the largest visible remain of the Norman structure is the **Record Tower**, in the lower Castle Yard, which contains the present-day State Paper Office. The **Bermingham Tower**, tallest in the castle, was originally early 15th-century, but was rebuilt after an explosion in 1775. Many celebrated rebels were imprisoned here, in-

ABOVE: stone head in the chapel of Dublin Castle.
BELOW: the interior of Dublin Castle.

cluding Red Hugh O'Donnell and Henry and Art O'Neill, who escaped on Christmas Eve, 1591.

The most impressive parts of the castle are the **State Apartments** – St Patrick's Hall, 25 metres long and 12 metres wide, with a high panelled and decorated ceiling, is probably the grandest room in Ireland. It was used by the British for various state functions and since 1938 has been the scene of the inauguration of Irish presidents. The Gothic-style **Church of the Most Holy Trinity** was built as the Chapel Royal between 1807 and 1814 to a design by Francis Johnston; it was taken over by the Catholic Church in 1943. The exterior is decorated with more than 90 carved heads of English monarchs and other historical figures.

Leaving the castle, retrace your steps a short way down Dame Street and turn right up busy **South Great George's Street**; on the left side is a Victorian shopping arcade containing many interesting and colourful shops and stalls. Continuing into **Aungier Street**, you see on your right the **Church of the Carmelite Fathers**, the only church in Dublin to be re-established on its pre-Reformation site – the order had a church here in the 13th century. Thomas Moore, the 19th-century poet and songwriter, was born at number 12 Aungier Street. John Field, Ireland's greatest composer and pianist, was born nearby in **Golden Lane** in 1782. He created the nocturne and originated the style of romantic pianism which culminated in Chopin's work.

Continue now into **Wexford Street**, turn right, and cross **Heytesbury Street** into **Kevin Street Upper**, where you find **Marsh's Library** ⓳, the oldest public library in Ireland and named after its founder, Archbishop Narcissus Marsh (1638–1713). Among its 25,000 interesting items is Jonathan Swift's copy of Clarendon's *History of the Great Rebellion*, with Swift's pencilled notes.

The next junction marks the beginning of the **Liberties**, an area so named because it lay outside the jurisdiction of medieval Dublin. One of the city's oldest and most characterful working-class areas, it was also filled with some of the worst 19th-century slum tenements. The **Coombe**, which runs westward into the Liberties, was the "coomb" (river valley) of the Poddle.

Make a note to sample the character of the Liberties another time and turn right along Patrick Street to **St Patrick's Cathedral** ⓴. Dedicated in 1192, it has been restored many times and, like Dublin's other cathedral, Christ Church, has belonged to the Church of Ireland since the Reformation. Swift, who was Dean from 1713 to 1745, is buried in it, near his beloved "Stella", Esther Johnson.

Continue now along Patrick Street and Nicholas Street to **Christ Church Cathedral** ㉑, which was founded by Sitric, the Danish King of Dublin, about 1040, and greatly expanded from 1172 onwards under the aegis of Strongbow and St Laurence O'Toole. The central tower was built about 1600 after storm and fire damage to the original steeples. Lambert Simnel, 10-year-old pretender to the English throne, was crowned here by his supporters in 1487. Christ Church became Protestant in 1551, though the Mass was restored for a short period under James II. The structure was greatly

Map, page 138

Swift's self-penned epitaph in Latin reads: "He is laid where bitter indignation can no longer lacerate his heart."

Below: Boyle family monument in St Patrick's Cathedral.

rebuilt in Gothic revival style in the 1870s. Two of the cathedral's many tombs are said to be those of Strongbow and his son, whom, according to legend, he killed for cowardice in battle.

Linked to the cathedral by a covered bridge is **Dublinia** (Apr–Sept, daily 10am–5pm; Oct–Mar, Mon–Sat 11am–4pm, Sun 10am–4.30pm), an exhibition, run by the non-profit Medieval Trust, which recreates the medieval city's growth from 1170 to 1540. Exhibits include a scale model of the old city, various life-size reconstructions, including the interior of a merchant's kitchen, artefacts from the Wood Quay excavations, and a multi-screen historical presentation. From the top of the 200-ft (60-metre) St Michael's Tower, you can enjoy a panoramic view over the city. Admission to Dublinia includes entry to the cathedral via the bridge, but you can also enter Christ Church directly.

Across the river to your left is the stately dome of the **Four Courts**; save it for a later tour.

High Street, which runs off the westside of **Christchurch Place**, was the backbone of medieval Dublin. Part of the old city wall and the only surviving city gate have been uncovered near the partially ruined **St Audoen's Church** ㉒, which can be visited by arrangement. It was named by the Normans after St Ouen of Rouen. Its aisle contains a font dating from 1194; the tower is 12th-century and three of its bells were cast in the early 15th century, making them the country's oldest. On the other side of High Street, in **Back Lane**, is **Tailors' Hall**, the only surviving guild hall in Dublin, and now the offices of **An Taisce**, which works to preserve the country's natural and architectural heritage.

One part of the national heritage which seems well able to look after itself is enshrined half-a-mile further west along Thomas Street: **Guinness's Brewery**

ABOVE: Arthur Guinness. **BELOW:** the brewery tower; the Custom House.

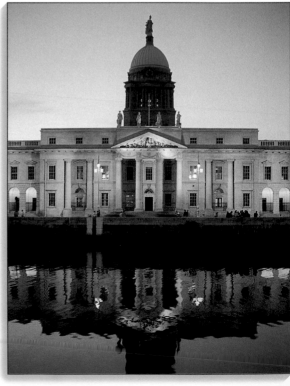

㉓, the biggest in Europe, churning out 2½ million pints of its celebrated black stout every day. The brewery doesn't admit visitors, but the **Guinness Hop Store** in Crane Street, to the left off James's Street, has been converted to house the **World of Guinness Exhibition** (Apr–Sept, Mon–Sat 9.30am–5pm, Sun 10.30am– 4.30pm; Oct–March, Mon–Sat 9.30am–4pm, Sun noon–4pm). There's an impressive and well-displayed series of artefacts – vats, casks and scale-models of ships, a slick audio-visual show, and a souvenir shop selling almost every imaginable article stamped with the legendary trade-name. There's also a bar, of course, where the admission ticket entitles you to a free glass of stout – probably the best-tasting Guinness to be had anywhere, since it hasn't had to travel.

If you don't feel like walking quite so far for a drink, you may enjoy a visit to the **Brazen Head**, nearer at hand in Bridge Street. There is said to have been a tavern on this site since Viking times, though the present premises date from only 1688. It was a meeting place for the United Irishmen. As well as being old, it's odd. On your way back to O'Connell Street Bridge, you could cross over the narrow, arching footpath of the "**Half-penny Bridge**", from which there are fine river views, especially at sunset.

The Guinness Hop Store shows how the brew and its barrels were manufactured.

North of the Liffey

O'Connell Bridge is again your starting-point, but before acquainting yourself with the main features of O'Connell Street, stay a little longer on the southside, walking east along **Burgh Quay** and under the railway bridge for a view across the river to the **Custom House ㉔**, one of the masterpieces of James Gandon, the greatest architect of 18th-century Dublin. Although English, Gandon looked to the Continent for architectural models and it is easier to imagine the Custom House transposed to the banks of the Seine than to the Thames. Finished in 1791, the building was extensively damaged in a fire started by Republicans to mark the Sinn Féin election victory in 1921 and has been largely rebuilt. The central copper dome, 120 ft (38 metres) high, is topped by a statue of commerce by Edward Smyth. The keystones over the arched doorways flanking the Doric portico represent the Atlantic Ocean and 13 principal rivers of Ireland. A **Visitor Centre** (mid-Mar–Oct, Mon–Fri 10am–5pm, Sat–Sun 2–5pm; Nov–Mar, tel: 878 7660 for details) is sited just inside the main riverside entrance, one of the few areas of the interior to survive the fire. Apart from the intrinsic beauty of its neo-classical rooms, staircases and vestibules, the centre offers interesting exhibitions on Gandon and on the work of the various government departments, British and Irish, which have occupied the building.

BELOW: Half-penny Bridge.

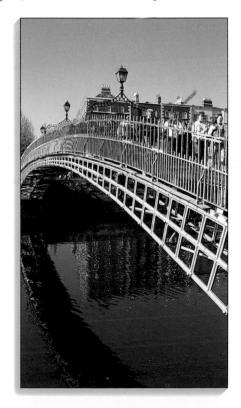

Gandon went on to design Carlisle Bridge (widened and rebuilt in 1880 and renamed **O'Connell Bridge**), the Four Courts, the eastern portico of Parliament House (Bank of Ireland) and the King's Inns.

The gleaming new building just downstream of the Custom House is the **Financial Services Centre**, erected in the late 1980s. The tall, 1960s edifice a little way upstream of the Custom House is **Liberty Hall ㉕**, headquarters of the country's largest trade union, the

Services, Industrial, Professional and Technical Union. Its more modest predecessor was a nerve-centre of the labour struggle early in this century. It stands at one end of a crescent laid out by Gandon and named **Beresford Place** after his patron in the building of the Custom House, John Beresford, Chief Commissioner for the Irish Revenue. At the far end of the place is the **Busaras** (central bus station), a daring work by Dublin standards when built in 1953. More recently it has been described, rather unfairly, as a "hideous edifice".

Walk towards O'Connell Bridge along the north bank and turn into **Marlborough Street**, where you find the **Abbey Theatre** , Ireland's national playhouse. The present building was erected in 1966 to replace a predecessor destroyed by fire. The Abbey, founded in 1904 by W.B. Yeats, Lady Gregory and their collaborators, played a vital role in the cultural renaissance of the time and quickly earned a world reputation through the great works of Synge and O'Casey and for its players' naturalistic acting style. Performances were often turbulent: the most celebrated uproar was that caused at a performance of Synge's *The Playboy of the Western World* by the use of the word "shift" (petticoat). Downstairs in the Abbey is its sister theatre, the **Peacock**, used for experimental work and for trial runs. Turn left now for O'Connell Street, passing on your right the Veritas bookshop, good for religious works.

O"Connell Street

O'Connell Street ㉗ itself is not what it was, though the latter-day rash of fast-food joints, amusement arcades, ugly modern buildings, billboards and signs cannot quite obscure its inherent grandeur. It was planned (as Sackville Street) in the mid-1700s by the first Viscount Mountjoy, Luke Gardiner, who widened

TIP

Book well ahead for Abbey performances. Tel: Dublin 878 7222.

BELOW: O'Connell Street Bridge.

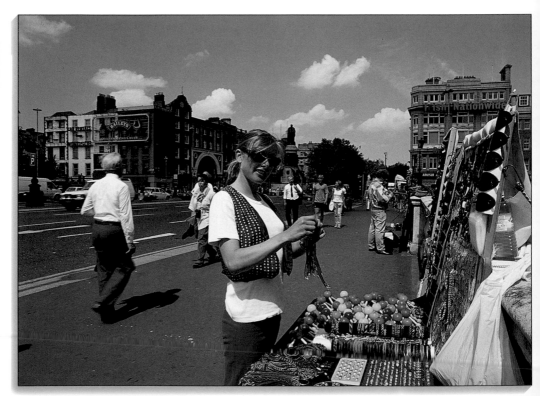

the existing narrow roadway, Drogheda Street, and planted trees on a central mall. In 1794, the construction of Carlisle Bridge turned it from a fashionable residential promenade into the city's main north-south artery. A tall column surmounted by a statue of Horatio Nelson, like that in London's Trafalgar Square, was erected in 1815 to mark the famous sea victory over Napoleon; republicans blew it up, neatly, by an explosion one night in 1966 to mark the 50th anniversary of the Easter Rising.

Map, page 138

The **statues** still lining the centre of the street are (from the bridge end): Daniel O'Connell (1775–1847), a great leader of constitutional nationalism; William Smith O'Brien (1803–64), leader of the Young Ireland Party; Sir John Gay (1816–75), proprietor of the *Freeman's Journal* and organiser of the city's water supply; James Larkin (1876–1947), a great trade union leader; Father Theobald Mathew (1790–1856), the "Apostle of Temperance"; and Charles Stewart Parnell (1846–91), inspiration of the Home Rule movement and a tragic victim of intolerance whose career was ruined by the outcry over his union with Kitty O'Shea, who happened to be married to another Irish politican.

Daniel O'Connell, presiding over the street named after him, fought for an Irish parliament but not a break with Britain.

The large **aquatic sculpture** in the central promenade was installed as part of the city's millennium celebrations in 1988 (the date was somewhat arbitrary, chosen more to boost tourism than to mark any historical event). The female figure is Anna Livia, the river goddess of the Liffey who featured in James Joyce's *Finnegans Wake*. However, she was instantly rechristened, with typical Dublin wit, "the floozy in the Jacuzzi."

Centrepiece of the street is the imposing Ionic portico of the **General Post Office ㉘** (1815), headquarters of the 1916 Rising and the place where the rebels proclaimed the republic in ringing terms, to the initial bemusement of Dubliners

BELOW: "the floozy in the jacuzzi"; pause for a pint.

– a reaction, in Yeats's words, "changed utterly" by the subsequent execution, one by one, of 15 captured leaders. The GPO's pillars are still pock-marked by bullets; although the building survived the fighting, much of the street was wrecked by British artillery and it suffered further in 1922 in the Civil War.

But those struggles are not the principal cause of O'Connell Street's fall from grace: it was rebuilt well enough in the 1920s but, as the journalist Frank McDonald wrote in *The Destruction of Dublin*, "the dignified and noble facades... got scant attention from the developers who descended on the street during the late 1960s and early 1970s." In McDonald's angry words: "This magnificent thoroughfare could have become Dublin's answer to the Champs Elysées, lined with fashionable shops and terrace cafés where people could sit and watch the world go by. Instead, the capital's main street was transformed into a honky-tonk freeway, cluttered with fast-food joints, slot-machine casinos, ugly modern office blocks, vacant buildings and even the odd derelict site."

Moore Street market

Off O'Connell Street, just past the GPO, **Henry Street** is the northside's main shopping street. Its tributary, **Moore Street**, is filled with fruit and vegetable stalls staffed by colourful and vociferous women, and with a remarkable battery of butchers' shops. It is well worth visiting for a dose of down-to-earth Dublin. On the opposite side of O'Connell Street, walk down Earl Street and turn left into Marlborough Street to visit **St Mary's Pro-Cathedral** ㉙ (1816–25), the city's main Catholic Church. John Henry Newman first publicly professed Catholicism here in 1851. John McCormack, the great tenor (1884–1945) was a member of the church's Palestrina Choir. The area was once

Inside the GPO (open Mon–Sat 8am–8pm, Sun 10.30am–6pm) is a fine bronze statue of the ancient Irish hero Cuchulainn, with the Proclamation of the Republic on its base.

BELOW: Moore Street market.

a notorious red-light district, known as "Monto" (James Joyce's "Nighttown").

At the north end of O'Connell Street are the late 18th-century **Rotunda Rooms**, occupied in recent years by a cinema. The **Rotunda Hospital** to the left (Europe's first maternity hospital) was financed by concerts in the Rooms. Built in conjunction with the hospital, the **Gate Theatre** at the bottom of Parnell Square East was founded in 1928 by Micheál MacLiammóir and Hilton Edwards; the teenage Orson Welles made his first professional appearance here.

A few yards past the Gate, the **Garden of Remembrance** (1966) commemorates Ireland's martyrs. The sculpture by Oisin Kelly, beyond the central lake, is based on the myth of the Children of Lir, who were changed to swans.

On the northside of Parnell Square is the **Municipal Gallery of Modern Art** ❸⓿. Its nucleus is formed by the mainly Impressionist collection of Sir Hugh Lane, who died when the liner *Lusitania* was torpedoed in 1915. As a result of a wrangle over his will, the collection was split, each half being alternated every five years between Dublin and London's Tate Gallery. In 1998 the gallery painstakingly dismantled the London studio of the Dublin-born artist Francis Bacon and is faithfully reconstructing it here as part of new exhibition area to be opened in 2001.

At 18–19 Parnell Square North, the **Dublin Writers Museum** ❸⓵ displays photographs, paintings, busts, letters, manuscripts, first editions and other memorabilia relating to celebrated writers such as Swift, Shaw, Yeats, O'Casey, Joyce, Beckett and Behan, though it's rather short of material on more recent authors. The first-floor **Gallery of Writers** is splendidly decorated.

The **National Wax Museum** (Mon–Sat 10am–5.30pm, Sun noon–5.30pm), around the corner in Granby Row, caters for eclectic tastes, mixing Charles Stewart Parnell, Elvis Presley and Pope John Paul II.

Map, page 138

ABOVE: Yeats painting in Dublin Writers Museum. **BELOW:** an exhibit at the Municipal Gallery of Modern Art.

Return to Parnell Square East, turn left and then right into Great Denmark Street. On the left is **Belvedere House** ㉜, a fine 18th-century mansion which has been the Jesuit Belvedere College since 1841. James Joyce, who was a pupil here, described its atmosphere in *Portrait of the Artist as a Young Man.*

Turn into **North Great George's Street,** an address which is regaining its cachet as many of its grand Georgian houses are rescued from decades of decrepitude. At number 35 is the **James Joyce Centre** ㉝ (year-round Mon–Sat 9.30am–5pm, Sun 12.30–5pm; tel: 8788547). This recent addition to the literary tourist trail is located in a beautifully restored late 18th-century townhouse which features in *Ulysses* as the venue for dancing classes run by a character named Denis J. Maginni. The centre's most interesting exhibit is a set of biographies of real Dublin people fictionalised in Joyce's masterpiece (Maginni's real name was Maginnis). There are also photographs and storyboards about Joyce's family and the many different homes they inhabited. And, in a suitably Joycean collision of fact and fiction, you can view the front door of No. 7 Eccles Street, home of Leopold Bloom and his wife Molly, the central characters of *Ulysses* (the house itself was demolished). The centre's interior has splendid stucco ceilings, the work of Michael Stapleton.

Returning past the Municipal Gallery to Parnell Square West, turn right, then left into Bolton Street, then right again at **Henrietta Street**, the oldest and once, it is said, the finest of the city's Georgian streets, the home of archbishops, peers and Members of Parliament. It is now mostly decrepit. At its far end are the **King's Inns** ㉞, the Dublin inns of court, where, in the English tradition, newly qualified barristers must eat a prescribed number of meals. The building was designed by Gandon and built at the turn of the 19th century.

The main James Joyce commemorations centre on Bloomsday, hed on 16 June.

BELOW: convent in Henrietta Street.

Continue now down Bolton Street bearing left into **Capel Street**, which contains some interesting old shops. To the left in Mary Street is **St Mary's Church** ❸❺, built from 1697 by Thomas Burgh, architect of Trinity College library. Here, in 1747, John Wesley preached his first sermon in Ireland. Theobald Wolfe Tone (1763–98), founder of the United Irishmen and father of Irish republicanism, was born nearby in a street now named after him.

To the other side of Capel Street, Mary Street leads via Mary's Lane to Church Street, where you find **St Michan's Church** ❸❻, founded in 1095 as a Viking parish church. The present structure dates from the late 1600s, but it was much restored in 1821 and again after the Civil War. Handel is said to have played on its organ. In the vaults are 17th-century mummified bodies, preserved because the limestone walls absorb moisture from the air.

Leaving the church, walk south to the quays and turn left to end this section of the tour as you began it: with a look at a Gandon masterpiece. The **Four Courts** ❸❼ was built between 1786 and 1802. The dominant lantern-dome is fronted by a six-columned Corinthian portico surmounted by the statues of Moses, Justice and Mercy, and flanked by two wings enclosing courtyards. In 1922, after the building was barricaded by anti-Treaty republicans, troops of Michael Collins's new government shelled it from across the river (so beginning the Civil War). In the ensuing fire, the Record Office was burnt, destroying many priceless documents. Restoration of the building was completed in 1932.

West Dublin

On the south bank of the river about 1½ miles (2.5 km) west of O'Connell Bridge, and just past the Guinness Brewery, is **Kilmainham Jail** ❸❽ (closed Sat,

Map, page 138

Unlike many English architects, James Gandon liked Dublin and chose to live in Ireland. He finally retired there and died in 1823.

BELOW: St Michan's Church vaults; the Four Courts.

A Kilmainham Jail plaque lists the executions in 1916 that turned many apathetic Dubliners into fervent supporters of Irish independence.

Oct–Mar), intimately connected with Ireland's struggle for independence from its construction in the 1790s until it ceased to function as a prison in the 1920s. Visitors are first invited to browse in the museum, which explores 19th-century notions of crime, punishment and reform through a series of imaginative and well-captioned displays. The upstairs section is devoted to the nationalist figures, some famous, some obscure, who were imprisoned here, many awaiting their execution. A guide then leads visitors into the vaulted east wing of the gaol, with its tiers of cells and overhead catwalks, and upstairs to the prison chapel, where an excellent audiovisual summary of the nationalist struggle is shown. Visitors are then brought to the "1916 corridor", containing the cells that housed the captured leaders of the Rising, and finally led to the stone-breakers' yard where 14 of them were shot between 3 and 12 May of that year.

To the east, across South Circular Road, stands **Kilmainham Royal Hospital,** (1680–84), founded by Charles II "for the reception and entertainment of antient (*sic*) maimed, and infirm officers and soldiers." The building has been painstakingly restored and is used for concerts and exhibitions.

It also houses the **Irish Museum of Modern Art** (Tues–Sat 10am–5.30pm; Sun noon–5.30pm), which combines Irish and international 20th-century art with associated educational and community programmes. Performance, theatre and music figure in its work, with emphasis on the overlap between the visual and performing arts. The permanent collection is rather patchy, but the temporary exhibitions are often interesting.

You can now go down **Steeven's Lane** past Heuston Station and cross the river to visit the **Phoenix Park** ❸❾, whose southern boundary extends west on the Liffey's north bank for about 3 miles (5 km). At 1,760 acres (712 hectares), it is more than five times as large as Hyde Park, London. Its name does not derive from the reincarnatory bird but is a corruption of the Gaelic *fionn uisce* ("clear water").

Among its features, all signposted, are: the **Wellington Monument**, an obelisk 60 metres high, erected after Waterloo; the **Zoological Gardens**, the third oldest public zoo in the world (1830), well known for the breeding of lions (it supplied the MGM announcer); the President's residence, **Aras an Uachtaráin**, formerly the Viceregal Lodge (1751–54); the US Ambassador's residence, formerly the Chief Secretary's Lodge; and the "15 acres", an open space actually of 200 acres containing paths and playing fields, the duelling ground of 18th-century Dublin gentlemen.

On the way back to the city, on the north side of the quays, is the former **Collins Barracks**, now the **National Museum extension** displaying collections of Irish silver, glassware, musical instruments and Japanese art.

BELOW: interior of Kilmainham Jail.

Southside suburbs

Most places mentioned in this section are served by various buses departing from **Eden Quay**, beside O'Connell Bridge, and by the excellent DART suburban trains.

Travelling out through Merrion Square North, along Northumberland Road past the squat, circular block of the **American Embassy** (1964), you reach the prestigious suburb of **Ballsbridge** ❹❶, named after the bridge over the River Dodder. The large greystone buildings to the right on Merrion Road, just past the bridge, are the headquarters of the **Royal Dublin Society** ("the RDS"), the traditional sponsor of improvements in agriculture and stock breeding and the venue for the **Dublin Horse Show** (in August). The RDS's Simmonscourt Extension is used for exhibitions and concerts.

The **Chester Beatty Library and Gallery of Oriental Art** is a little further out, at 20 Shrewsbury Road. Founded by an American mining tycoon, Sir Alfred Chester Beatty, it has a fine collection of Chinese, Japanese, Persian, Indian and Middle Eastern manuscripts, paintings and ornaments.

The main road south soon skirts the coast, affording fine views of the bay, and passes through **Blackrock ④**, where Eamon de Valera studied and later taught at the boys' college. A couple of miles further on is the town and port of **Dun Laoghaire ④** (pronounced *Dunleery*), departure point for ferries to Britain. The harbour, with its long, granite piers, was built between 1817 and 1859.

The next promontory, within easy walking distance, is that of **Sandycove ④**, with its **Martello tower** where Joyce lived for a short time in 1904. He used it as the setting for the opening scene of *Ulysses* and it is now a **Joyce Museum**. The nearby **Forty Foot** bathing place has been for generations a spartan haven of nude bathing for men, though feminists have made incursions.

About a mile further on is **Dalkey ④**, a meandering old village of great charm and some *cachet*; from nearby **Coliemore Harbour** there are boat trips in summer to **Dalkey Island**, a stone's throw offshore; it contains another Martello tower and the ruins of a Benedictine church. The island is a bird sanctuary. From Vico Road, which continues along the coast, you can enter **Killiney Hill Park**; motorists should drive instead up Dalkey Avenue, to the public car-park.

At the summit of the park is a Victorian obelisk commanding splendid views

The Round Room at the Joyce Museum. Tel: Dublin 280 9265.

Map, page 161

of the broad sweep of **Killiney Bay** (often likened to the Bay of Naples), **Bray Head** (the hump-backed promontory at its far side) and the two **Sugar Loaf Mountains**. DART travellers can easily continue on to **Bray** ㊺; as a seaside resort it has seen better days, but the seascapes *en route* are impressive and Bray Head offers bracing walks and fine views further southwards.

Northern suburbs

The attractions of the northside are more diffuse, but it is worth making the trip to the north-central suburb of **Glasnevin** ㊻ (buses 13 and 34) to see the beautifully arranged **Botanic Gardens**, which occupy the former demesne of Joseph Addison, the English essayist and founder of *The Spectator* magazine, who lived in Dublin as secretary to the Earl of Sutherland.

The coastal route northeast by the Custom House leads past **Fairview Park** to the middle-class enclave of **Clontarf** ㊼, site of the battle in 1014 in which Brian Ború defeated the Danes. **Malahide Road** branches off to the left and to the left again is the recently restored **Casino**, once part of the seaside estate of Lord Charlemont, whose town house is now the Municipal Gallery. It is a small Palladian building, a gem of its kind, with several unusual features: the roof urns are actually chimneys and the columns are hollow, serving as drains.

ABOVE: Cyril Fry Model Railway Museum. **BELOW:** quayside meeting. **RIGHT:** relaxing at Malahide.

Beyond **Clontarf** the coast road passes the **North Bull Island**, a huge sandbank growing from the North Wall of Dublin Port and containing two golf courses: St Anne's and the famous **Royal Dublin**. It is also an important sanctuary for winter migrant birds.

Carrying on via the isthmus at the suburb of **Sutton** you reach **Howth Head** (also accessible by DART and bus), whose rugged brow overlooks the northern

entrance to Dublin Bay. You can go directly to the village of **Howth** ㊽ or start instead at The Summit and walk to the village around the nose of the promontory by a splendidly scenic cliff path, which descends steeply to the fishing harbour. The novelist H.G. Wells called the view from the head "one of the most beautiful in the world." The offshore island of **Ireland's Eye** was the site of a 6th-century monastery and is now a bird sanctuary. Howth is the most fashionable place to live on the northside, and it is easy to see why. The gardens at nearby **Howth Castle** are beautiful, especially if you like rhododendrons.

Five miles (8 km) north of Howth lies the resort of **Portmarnock** ㊾, which has fine beaches and a championship golf course. From here, a turn west leads to **St Doulagh's Church**, claimed to be the oldest still in use in Ireland; its high-pitched stone roof is 12th-century. **Doulagh Lodge**, nearby, was the home of the great landscape painter, Nathaniel Hone (1831–1917).

At **Malahide** ㊿, a pleasant resort and dormitory town 7 miles (11 km) north of Howth, is **Malahide Castle**, which was inhabited continuously by the Talbot family from 1185 until 1976, except for a short period when Oliver Cromwell was around. The castle, now owned by Dublin County Council, houses many portraits from the collection of the National Gallery. In its gardens is the **Cyril Fry Model Railway Museum**; the models of trains and stations are meticulous.

NO
THROUGH
ROAD

DAY TRIPS FROM DUBLIN

*To the south lie the Wicklow Mountains, to the north the
remarkable prehistorical burial chambers of Newgrange,
and to the west some of the world's best racehorse country*

I t is easy for Dublin dwellers to take for granted the wild beauty of the **Wicklow Mountains**, just a few miles to the south. As one writer has pointed out, it is, for a Londoner, as if the Lake District began at Golders Green. The "hills" are great outcrops of granite thrown up by ancient earth movements. In the Ice Age, glaciers smoothed and rounded their peaks and carved deep, dark, steep-sided glens whose wide floors glitter with rivers and lakes. The region is sparsely inhabited – just a few villages, scattered farms and cottages, and the occasional great house.

The chief attractions of Wicklow are well served by coach tours from Dublin. If you are driving, take the N81 southwest, through the bleak new suburb of **Tallaght**, to **Blessington**, a 17th-century village consisting mainly of one long, broad street. Just past the village, the large artificial lake of **Poulaphouca** lies to the left of the road. It supplies Dublin with its water supply and is part of the Liffey hydroelectric scheme. A popular scenic road encircles the lake.

Two miles (3 km) on is **Russborough ❶**, a Palladian house built in the 1740s by Richard Castle for the Earl of Miltown. Its 700-ft (210-metre) frontage is the longest in Ireland; inside is the Alfred Beit art collection, with works by Vermeer, Goya, Reubens and Velasquez.

BELOW: the Wicklow
Mountains.

Four miles (6 km) south at Hollywood, a left turn leads into the wild heart of the mountains through the Wicklow Gap to **Glendalough ❷**, a secluded, seductive valley, steep-sided and well-wooded, where in 545 St Kevin founded a great monastic settlement between two lakes. The sight of the ruins – a cathedral and several churches, dominated by a 110-ft (33-metre) round tower – evokes that deep longing for peace and solitude central to the monk's idea of sanctity.

Driving south through **Rathdrum** you reach **Avondale**, the beautiful Georgian home of the politician Charles Stewart Parnell (1846–91); it is now a museum surrounded by public parklands. A couple of miles further south is the celebrated **Vale of Avoca**, where the Avonmore and Avonbeg rivers join, supposedly described in Thomas Moore's song, *The Meeting of the Waters*. At Avoca village you can turn northwards again and drive, via the unremarkable county town of **Wicklow ❸**, to the village of **Ashford**, near which there are two spots of great beauty: to the south, the **Mount Usher Gardens**, a lush display of trees, sub-tropical plants and shrubs; to the northwest, the **Devil's Glen**, a deep chasm with spectacular walks above the rushing Vartry river.

Return to Dublin via **Roundwood** and **Enniskerry**, where you can divert to visit the magnificent landscaped gardens at **Powerscourt ❹**, the 18th-century mansion that was destroyed by fire in 1974, and the nearby **Powerscourt Waterfall**, the highest in these islands (90 metres). You now drive directly back to Dublin or divert again through the magnificent valley of **Glencree**; the gaunt old military barracks there is now a "reconciliation centre" to promote understanding between the divided communities in Northern Ireland; nearby is a small German cemetery for servicemen (mainly airmen and sailors) who died in or near Ireland in the world wars.

Map, page 166

ABOVE: catering for visitors to the Glendalough ruins. **BELOW:** the 11th-century round tower, Glendalough.

Excursions north

A half-hour's driving on the N2 road across the rolling fields of Meath takes you to the beautiful old village of **Slane** ⑤, built on a steep hill above a bridge on the **River Boyne**. The grounds of the nearby castle have been used to stage concerts by such stars as Bob Dylan and the Rolling Stones.

The **Hill of Slane**, where St Patrick proclaimed Christianity in Ireland by lighting a paschal fire in 433, is on the northern outskirts of the village. The ruins of a 16th-century church stand on the site of the church he founded. The view over the plain is striking.

A few miles east along the north bank of the Boyne is one of Europe's most remarkable prehistoric sites: the burial chambers of **Newgrange** ⑥, **Knowth** and **Dowth**. Although the Dowth burial mound is inaccessible, conducted tours of the other two chambers provide fascinating insight into the 5,000-year-old Boyne Valley culture. At Newgrange, a

20-metre passage leads into the central burial chamber. A small aperture over the entrance is aligned so that the sun's rays penetrate to illuminate the chamber only at the winter solstice – a powerful symbol of rebirth and renewal. The chamber is older than the Pyramids of Egypt, but keeps out the water even today. The road on to Drogheda passes the site of the Battle of the Boyne (1690).

Drogheda ❼ is a large town and port dating from Viking and Norman times and was a frontier outpost of the Pale. The name of Cromwell is still an accursed one here: during his campaign of suppression in 1649 he captured the town and slaughtered 2,000 people – "a righteous judgment of God upon those barbarous wretches".

The main features of the town are: the **Millmount**, a prehistoric mound surmounted by an 18th-century barracks, now including a museum; **St Lawrence's Gate**, one of the best-preserved town gates in Ireland; the ruins of several medieval churches; the 18th-century **Tholsel**, or town hall, now a bank; and the 19th-century high Gothic **St Peter's Church**, erected in memory of Oliver Plunkett, a Meath man who became Catholic Archbishop of Armagh. He was martyred in London at Tyburn (now Marble Arch) in 1681, and canonised in 1975. His head is preserved in a shrine at the church.

You have now crossed into **Louth**, Ireland's smallest county. Six miles (10 km) northwest of Drogheda, by the River Mattock, stand the ruins of **Mellifont Abbey** ❽ (1142), Ireland's first Cistercian foundation. Remains include those of a square tower, a large church, and a lavabo, an octagonal building where the monks used to wash. At **Monasterboice** ❾, a few miles northeast, are the remnants of a 5th-century monastic settlement founded by St Buithe: a round tower, two churches, three sculptured crosses, two early grave-slabs and a sundial.

Map, page 166

The head of the martyred Oliver Plunkett is preserved in St Peter's Church.

LEFT: the Neolithic passage grave at Newgrange. **BELOW:** Drogheda.

*The coastal strip
north of Dublin now
promotes itself as
"Fair Fingal", and
claims to be Ireland's
most populated golf
area (28 courses).*

You can now join the main N1 route north to **Dundalk** , a busy border town and a good centre for exploring the picturesque **Cooley Peninsula**. This area features prominently in the great epic legends of ancient Ireland, particularly those concerning Cuchulainn, hero of the Red Branch Knights. At **Carlingford** village, a fine Norman castle commands the entrance to the sea inlet, Carlingford Lough. A corkscrew road through the nearby forest park climbs to a viewing point near the summit of **Carlingford Mountain**, providing splendid views of the Mournes to the north. **Greenore** and **Omeath** are small resorts.

The N52 road southwest from Dundalk leads to **Ardee** ⓫, or Irish *Baile Atha Fhirdiadh*, "The Town of Ferdia's Ford". It is here that Cuchulainn slew his friend Ferdia, the champion of Queen Maeve, in the great epic story of the Cattle Raid of Cooley. Continuing through Meath's county town of **Navan**, you reach **Kells**, where St Colmcille founded a monastery in the 6th century. The extant remains are more recent: a round tower and a high-roofed 9th-century building known as **St Colmcille's house** are the most interesting.

Trim, another pleasant town 16 miles (26 km) further southwest, can claim the largest Anglo-Norman fortress in Ireland: its complex and well-preserved remains cover two acres and the surrounding moat could be filled from the River Boyne. The ragged outline of the so-called **Yellow Steeple** (1358), part of a collapsed abbey, stands on a ridge opposite the castle.

Return now to Navan and take the main Dublin road, which passes near the **Hill of Tara** ⓬, the cultural and religious headquarters of ancient Ireland. A great assembly or *feis* was held there every three years to pass laws and settle disputes. By the 6th century, when Niall of the Nine Hostages founded the house of O'Neill that was to rule Ulster until the Plantations, Tara had become pre-

BELOW: Hill of Tara.

eminent among Ireland's five kingdoms, but its influence declined soon after as Christianity took root in the country.

It has remained a powerful symbol of Irish unity, expressed in the Thomas Moore (1779–1825) song, *The harp that Once through Tara's Halls*, and Daniel O'Connell chose it in 1843 as the venue for one of his "monster meetings" to demand repeal of the Corn Laws. A million people attended, according to *The Times*. On top of the hill is a modern statue of St Patrick and a pillar-stone said to have been used in the coronation of the ancient kings.

Excursions west

Kildare, the county to the west of Dublin, is the "horsiest" part of Ireland, but there are many charms even for those whose blood does not rise at the sound of hoof-beats. **Naas**, the county town, is a handy centre for touring the county.

You can drive there quickly over one of the Republic's few modern highways, or via **Celbridge** ⓭, an attractive village which was the home of Esther Van-homrigh, the "Vanessa" who competed with "Stella" (Esther Johnson) for the affections of Jonathan Swift. He often came here to visit her and you can see the seat by the river where they sat and talked. Nearby is the magnificent Palladian mansion of **Castletown House** (1722), the largest private house in Ireland, now the headquarters of the Irish Georgian Society.

Drive west from Naas through Newbridge to reach the great expanses of the **Curragh**. Apart from the race-course and many training stables, it has contained an important military camp, established in 1646. This was the scene of the "Curragh Mutiny" of 1914, when British officers threatened to refuse orders to fire on Edward Carson's Ulster Volunteers, who had armed to oppose Home Rule.

Near the road south to Kilcullen is a depression, **Donnelly's Hollow**, where a small obelisk commemorates an 1815 prize fight in which Dan Donnelly, the giant Irish champ, beat England's George Cooper.

Kildare town, 6 miles (10 km) from Newbridge, was the site of a monastery founded by St Brigid (*circa* 450–520), the most revered Irish saint after Patrick. Her attributes have been reinforced by others borrowed from the great goddess of the same name, who was venerated also in Britain and Europe. The **Cathedral of St Brigid**, begun in 1229, has been rebuilt many times, most substantially in 1875. A mile from the town, at **Tully House**, is the **National Stud** (*see also page 182*).

At **Athy**, 16 miles (26 km) south of Kildare, a 16th-century town, now a private house, overlooks a fine old bridge over the **River Barrow**, once an important commercial waterway to Dublin. But the town's main attraction is the striking, fan-shaped **Dominican Church** (1963–65). The painter George Campbell designed the stained glass and the stations of the cross.

Returning to Dublin from Naas, it is worth diverting via **Maynooth** ⓮, where Ireland's Catholic diocesan clergy are trained at **St Patrick's College**. It was founded in 1795, when the British acknowledged that it was not in their interests that all Irish priests were trained abroad, and became a college of the National University in 1908. An ecclesiastical museum can be seen by prior arrangement.

Map, page 166

For more about Kildare's horse culture, see the feature on pages 105–8.

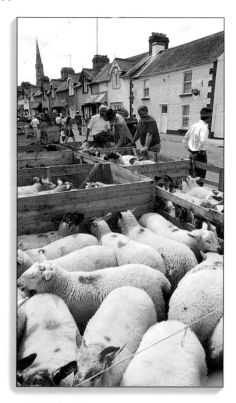

BELOW: market in Trim, Co. Meath.

Southern Region

0   20 km

0   20 miles

ATLANTIC

OCEAN

THE SOUTHEAST

Map,
page 170

*Between Dublin and Cork, you can find opera in Wexford,
crystal glass in Waterford, horse-racing at the Curragh,
and ancient historical sites at Kilkenny and Cashel*

The southeast is the least typical region of Ireland. Its climate is mild and sunny, and it has the lowest average rainfall in the whole island. In contrast to the wild and rugged west, the coast of south county Wicklow, county Wexford and county Waterford is mainly flat and sandy, with small, hilly dunes. Inland counties Carlow, Tipperary and Kilkenny consist of undramatic, restful country – rich farmland and low hills intersected by winding rivers.

Because of its proximity to mainland Europe, the history of the southeast is marked by invasions. Inland, the Rock of Cashel was an important ceremonial centre from the 7th century, while other monasteries thrived at Lismore, Ardmore and Kilkenny.

The Vikings, who regularly raided Ireland's coastal monasteries, began to settle here in the 9th century, founding the towns of Waterford and Wexford. Two hundred years later the same cities were among the first to be conquered by the Normans. Most of the region's churches were ruined during Oliver Cromwell's Irish campaign in 1650.

It is now 200 years since the 1798 Rebellion, whose decisive battle took place at Vinegar Hill near Enniscorthy, when 20,000 rebels armed only with pikes were cut down by British cannon fire. However, this unsuccessful bid for a united Ireland, inspired by the French Revolution of 1789, remains vividly alive in folk memory, and is commemorated by numerous monuments in the region.

OPTION 1: Dublin to Cork via the coast

The first tour travels from Dublin to Cork, through Wexford, Waterford, Dungarvan and Youghal. This route takes 4½ hours – about an hour longer than the main N7/N8 route, but it is far more scenic, with frequent sea views, and far less congested. Take a full day for the drive, or plan one or two overnight stops.

Leave Dublin on the N11 Bray road, and follow this through Rathnew to **Arklow ❶**. This is a small but lively fishing port and seaside resort on the estuary of the River Avoca known for boat building and for its pottery that makes everyday tableware.

Gorey, the first town in county Wexford, has a more genteel ambience than Arklow. It is not actually on the sea, but nevertheless is chiefly a holiday resort. The seaside cottages will be found by turning left in Gorey on to the R742, a pleasant alternative route to Wexford.

The R742 passes **Curracloe Strand** 7 miles (11 km) northwest of Wexford Harbour. Curracloe is the prettiest of the seaside villages on this stretch, with thatched and whitewashed cottages. The totally unspoilt strand is backed by dunes, and stretches for 6 miles (9 km). In winter it is home to numerous Canada geese. Information on the birds of the region can be found at the **Wex-**

PRECEDING PAGES:
Cashel Abbey.
LEFT: the approach
to Kilkenny.
BELOW: pub singer
in Wexford town.

ford Wildfowl Reserve (tel: 053-23129, admission free.) which is signposted off the R741 just outside Wexford. The harbour is partly silted up, and its mud flats attract a variety of ducks, geese and swans.

Wexford: opera and heritage

Wexford was founded by the Norsemen, who used the inlet as a good base from which to plunder the area. Later they turned to trading.

Wexford ❷ is a small, easy-to-explore town consisting of a series of quays parallel to the water, with a compact network of smaller streets parallel to the quays. Head for the **Westgate Tower** which is a short walk inland from the main bridge. This red sandstone building is the only remaining of five fortified gateways in the Norman town walls. It now houses the **Wexford Experience** (tel: 053-46506, admission fee), a 30-minute audio-visual display.

Wexford, which has an interesting selection of small, old-fashioned shops and pubs, is at its best in October during the three-week run of the **Wexford Opera Festival** (tel: 053-22141). Three full-length operas are performed at the **Theatre Royal** with an international cast of up-and-coming stars. The tradition is to choose little-known works, with consistently interesting results. A series of fringe events guarantee musical entertainment from 11am to midnight.

The **Irish National Heritage Park** (tel: 053-20733, admission fee, open mid-Mar–Oct) at Ferrycarrig, 3 miles (5 km) northwest of Wexford on the N11 Enniscorthy road, is an open air theme park on the banks of the River Slaney. A couple of hours among its life-size replicas of typical dwelling places will make you an expert on Irish history and architecture, from Stone Age man, around 6000BC, up to the 12th-century Norman settlements.

BELOW: the Irish National Heritage Park, Wexford.

Follow the N25 for 3 miles (5 km) in the Rosslare direction to visit **Johnstown Castle Gardens**. The castle itself, a grandiose grey stone Gothic building dating from the mid-19th century is now an agricultural college, but the attractively landscaped gardens can be visited. The **Irish Agricultural Museum** (tel: 053-42888, admission fee) is in the stable yards. It has extensive displays of artefacts from Ireland's rural past, and a collection of Irish country furniture.

Map, page 170

The scenic way to Waterford

The N25 travels to Waterford via New Ross, but we suggest this scenic alternative route to Waterford. Take the N25 in the Rosslare direction and turn off at Piercetown for **Kilmore Quay** ❸. This is a really quaint little fishing village of thatched, whitewashed cottages and small, friendly pubs that seems to be caught in a time warp somewhere around 1920. The village is built between the dunes and a stone harbour wall, and looks out to the uninhabited **Saltee Islands**, Ireland's most important bird sanctuaries. In late spring to early summer, 3 million birds from 47 species stop here, and can be observed from local boats.

Heading west, the R736/R733 will take you to the **Hook Head Peninsula** which forms the eastern side of Waterford harbour. Beyond Arthurstown is **Ballyhack**, where you can catch the five-minute car ferry to the Waterford side. Ballyhack is a picture-book-pretty waterside village, dominated by **Ballyhack Castle**, a 16th-century tower house.

Waterford ❹, a city of 51,000 inhabitants, has a proud past as an important European port but nowadays its wide, stone quays look rather grim. Its heyday as a port was in the 18th century, and it was then that the famous glass-manufacturing industry was established.

The Tourist Office is on the quays at No. 41. From here you can see the distinctive landmark **Reginald's Tower** (tel: 051-73501, admission fee), a mas-

BELOW: Kilmore Quay, Co. Wexford.

ABOVE: Reginald's Tower, built in 1003 by Reginald the Norseman, is now a civic museum.

BELOW: Waterford's crystal glass plant, open to visitors.

sive, cylindrical tower built by the Vikings in 1003 for the city's defence. It is said that when the Norman Strongbow married the daughter of Dermot McMurrough, thus peacefully uniting the Norman invaders and the native Irish, the wedding took place here.

The **Waterford Heritage Centre** (tel: 051-71227, admission fee) is nearby in Greyfriar's Street. This attractive new museum displays artefacts from Waterford's Norman and Viking past (mainly 10th and 11th-century) excavated in the 1980s. These include jewellery, wooden and ceramic bowls and weaponry.

Georgian Waterford is only a short walk from Reginald's Tower, up **The Mall**. The **City Hall** (open office hours, admission free) is a neo-classical building dating from 1788, which contains some good examples of early Waterford crystal, including a huge chandelier. Just beyond it is **Bishop Foy Palace,** originally an imposing town house, which is also used by the Corporation as offices. Behind the palace is **Christ Church Cathedral** which replaced an older church in 1773.

Waterford Crystal Factory (tel: 051-73311, admission fee) offers tours of its glass-cutting and glass-blowing workshops which most first-time visitors seem compelled to take. Tours last 40 minutes and include an audio-visual display and a chance to buy crystal. The factory is a mile from the town centre on the N25 Cork road. In high season you should book in advance.

The main N25 takes a fast inland route to Dungarvan. If you have time, take the coastal route leaving Waterford on the R684 for **Dunmore East**. This pretty cliff-side fishing village and holiday resort of thatched cottages is on the open sea at the head of Waterford Harbour.

Tramore is a total contrast, with a long flat sandy beach, a fun fair, caravan parks and other facilities aimed at the budget holiday market. The coast road continues through a series of villages with good beaches – **Annestown, Bunmahon** and **Clonea**. Elsewhere in the sandstone cliffs secluded coves can be reached by foot. **Dungarvan ❺**, situated on Dungarvan Harbour and backed by wooded hills, is the county town of Waterford. It has some lively waterside pubs, and is increasingly popular as a centre for activity holidays.

If you're headed for Cork, skip to Ardmore below. Those heading for Killarney, or with time for a scenic detour into the **Blackwater Valley**, should pick up the N72 Cappoquin road outside Dungarvan.

Map, page 170

Vee Gap: the scenic route to Lismore Castle

Cappoquin ❻ is a quiet village nicely situated on a wooded hillside on the River Blackwater, a beautiful salmon and trout river. About 3 miles (5 km) north of the village is **Mount Melleray** (tel; 058-54404), a Cistercian abbey dating from the mid-19th century that welcomes visitors in search of solitude. The Vee Gap route is signposted form here, going north on the R669 into the Knockmealdown Mountains. The Vee Gap is at the summit, from which you can see the Galtee Mountains in the northwest, and in good visibility the Rock of Cashel due north, rising out of the Tipperary Plain. Turn back here, and take the R668 to Lismore.

Lismore ❼, a pretty wooded village of 900 inhabitants approached over a stone bridge, was an important monastic centre from the 7th to the 12th centuries, which is why it has two cathedrals. **St Carthage's** dates from 1633 and has some interesting effigies. Nowadays the village is dominated by the grey stone turrets of **Lismore Castle** (tel: 058-54424, admission fee; gardens open

The Cistercians, a Roman Catholic monastic order founded in 1098 in France, were introduced to Ireland by St Malachy in 1142.

BELOW: peckish ponies.

May–Sept). Built on a rock overhanging the river in the mid-18th century, it is an unusually dramatic and imposing building. The castle is used as a summer residence by the Duke of Devonshire, and is not open to the public. The gardens, which are, include an 800-year-old yew walk.

If you are heading for Killarney, follow the Blackwater valley on the N72 from Lismore to Fermoy to Mallow,and on to Killarney, a journey time of about two hours.

Beyond Dungarvan the main tour joins the N25, which climbs the **Drum Hills** giving good views back across Dungarvan harbour. **Ardmore** involves a 5-mile (8-km) detour, but is well worth the effort. St Declan established a monastery here in the 5th century. Today the remains of a medieval cathedral and round tower stand on the site of the original foundation, a cliff top with stunning views over Ardmore Bay. The 12th-century cathedral with its sturdy, rounded arches is a prime example of the Hiberno-Romanesque style, while the slender round tower with its conical roof is an elegant contrast. There are also interesting stone and carvings. The tiny village is at the bottom of the cliff, and is a lively, pleasant place with good sandy beaches.

Youghal ❽ (pronounced *yawl*), famous for its long sandy beaches, peaked as a holiday resort in the 1950s when John Huston filmed the New Bedford scenes of *Moby Dick* here. It is currently undergoing a refurbishment. The **Youghal Heritage Centre** (Market Square, tel: 024-92390, admission fee) provides an audio-visual introduction to the town's history and guided tours on request. The **Clock Tower** is a distinctive landmark built in 1776 as a jail, that straddles the main road in the town centre. The steps beside it lead to a street with excellent harbour views, and to the 13th-century **St. Mary's Collegiate Church**. Sir Walter Raleigh lived next door, where he smoked the first tobacco and planted the first the potato plant in Ireland – a claim disputed by several other places.

Quaker connections

Turn left off the N25 in Castlemartyr for **Shanagarry** ❾, a tidy village built of grey stone with many Quaker connections. To the east of the village is the famous hotel, **Ballymaloe House**. The **Ballymaloe Cookery School Gardens** (tel: 021-646785, closed Nov–Mar) in the village centre feature a geometric potager, a formal fruit garden, a Celtic maze and a shell house. The gardens of **Shanagarry Castle** are also undergoing restoration. Next door is **The Emporium**, a large factory outlet for Stephen Pearce's pottery which also stocks hand-made crafts from around the world. **Shanagarry House** where William Penn, the founder of Pennsylvania, grew up, is opposite the Emporium.

Ballycotton, 3 miles (5 km) beyond Shanagarry is a fishing village built on a cliff top overlooking a small island and lighthouse. There are good cliff walks, and numerous nesting seabirds can be seen in early summer. The brightly-coloured fishing fleet supplies much of Cork city's fish.

Midleton ❿, a pleasant market town, is the home of Ireland's largest distillery. A new distilling complex was built in 1966, and the old Midleton distillery is now the

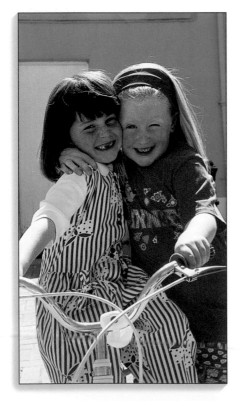

ABOVE: Youghal has some distinctive architecture.
BELOW: Youghal's younger generation.

Jameson Heritage Centre (tel: 021-613594, admission fee). An audio-visual display and an optional guided tour will explain the distilling process of Irish whiskey. Afterwards you can sample a drop of the famous product in a traditional Irish pub. Admirers of industrial architecture will enjoy the carefully restored 11-acre (4.5-hectare) 18th-century site. Most of the buildings are of cut stone, and the original waterwheel still functions.

The N25 continues for 15 miles (24 km) into Cork City.

OPTION 2: Kildare to Cashel via Kilkenny

This is an alternative, inland route from Dublin to Cork, visiting some of the southeast's most interesting historical sites. Kildare, with its Japanese Gardens and National Stud, has a 16th-century Cathedral and a 12th-century Round Tower associated with St Brigid. The historic medieval town of black marble, Kilkenny, lies 23 miles (37 km) south of Kildare, and has a magnificently restored castle.

You can linger in the Kilkenny area exploring the pretty riverside villages of the Nore and the Barrow, or continue to Clonmel, a compact market town on the River Suir, and head into the Nire Valley for a taste of unspoilt hill and bogland. Both options lead to Tipperary, and the spectacular ecclesiastical ruins on the Rock of Cashel. At Caher, there is a massive castle to visit, and quiet woodland walks in the relatively unfrequented Glen of Aherlow.

Leave Dublin on the main N7 Limerick road. At the end of the motorway, the road cuts through **The Curragh ⑪**, a broad plain of 6,000 acres (2,400 hectares). The **Curragh Racecourse** is the heart of the Irish racing world, and the Irish Derby is held here every June. If you are lucky, you might see a string of

Map,
page 170

The Curragh means The Racecourse in Gaelic (An Currach) It was once known as St Brigid's Pasture Land.

BELOW: a race at The Curragh.

race horses galloping by. Otherwise, the plain is used for exercises by the Irish Army who have a large camp here.

St Brigid founded a religious settlement in **Kildare** in the 5th century. The present **Cathedral** dates partly from the late 17th century and partly from the 19th century. The 108-ft (33-metre) **Round Tower** beside the cathedral belongs to a 12th-century monastery. You can climb to the top for excellent views of the surrounding country.

Nowadays Kildare is a prosperous town, closely associated with the horse racing business, with dozens of small studs in the area. Admission to the most prestigious of them all, the **National Stud**, where top-class breeding stallions are stabled, and the **Irish Horse Museum** (tel: 045-21617, admission fee, closed Nov–Feb.) also allows you to visit the rather strange **Japanese Gardens** that were laid out here in the early 20th century by the Japanese landscape artist Eida. The gardens trace a symbolic journey through life, and are considered by experts to be among the finest in Europe.

To see the most interesting part of **Monasterevin**, turn right at the traffic lights in the centre of town. Immediately ahead, the 18th-century **Grand Canal** crosses the River Barrow on an aqueduct in an interesting feat of industrial engineering. There are a couple of very pleasant, old-fashioned little pubs with waterside gardens hidden away on this side road.

Return to the traffic lights and turn left, back towards Dublin, keeping an eye out for a right-hand turn, the R417 Athy road. If you look hard enough, you'll find the remnants of a fine Georgian town in **Athy** (pronounced a-*thigh*), which was once an important fording place on the River Barrow. There's also a striking, fan-shaped Dominican church (1963–65).

For more about the National Stud, see the feature on horses on pages 105–8.

BELOW: the Japanese Gardens at Kildare.

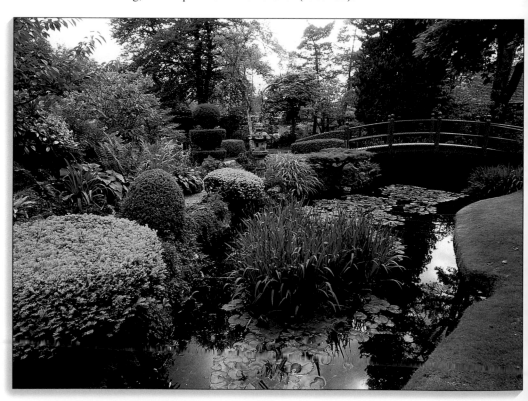

Medieval Kilkenny

Kilkenny **⑬** was founded as a monastic settlement by St Canice in the 6th century. In 1641 a Catholic parliament, the Confederation of Kilkenny, attempted to organise resistance to the persecution of Catholics. Cromwell's destructive 1650 campaign put a brutal end to such aspirations. While **Kilkenny** likes to promote itself as "Ireland's medieval capital", its rich heritage is not immediately obvious. Start at the Tourist Information Office in **Shee Alms House**, Rose Inn Street (tel: 056-51500) where you can equip yourself with free maps. This charming stone house with mullioned windows was built in the mid-17th century as a hospital for the poor. Frequent walking tours leave from here daily between March and October.

The sites of medieval Kilkenny start with St Canice's Cathedral at one extreme and end with the Castle at the other. Between them is a **Tholsel** (town hall) dating from 1761, the ruins of a 13th-century friary, the **Black Abbey**, and **Rothe House**, a 16th-century merchant's townhouse.

Kilkenny Castle (tel: 056-21450, admission fee; guided tours only) has recently been sumptuously restored. The grey stone, turreted landmark towers over the River Barrow which serves as its moat. It dates from 1820, but there has been a Butler family castle here for over 500 years. The furnishings are mainly 19th-century. The stableyard of the castle is occupied by the **Kilkenny Design Centre** which has a big display of local and national crafts and several workshops.

St Canice's Cathedral dates from the 13th century and is built in the Early English style. The Gothic interior is remarkable for its wealth of medieval monuments and life-size effigies, many of them carved from a locally quarried black

Map, page 170

ABOVE: Kilkenny's Design Centre.
BELOW: Kilkenny Castle; shop fronts in Kilkenny town.

marble. The 6th-century **Round Tower** in the Cathedral grounds is the only remnant of St Canice's monastery.

Riverside villages and craft trail

If you have time for a day-long drive around the Kilkenny area, we recommend you explore of the pretty villages on the rivers **Nore** and **Barrow**. The rivers meander through rich countryside with gently sloping wooded hills dotted with old villages of grey stone buildings, until they meet in New Ross and flow into the sea at Waterford.

ABOVE: statues at Jerpoint Abbey.
BELOW: Inistioge, a pretty Kilkenny town on the banks of the River Nore.

Leave Kilkenny on the R700 south for **Bennettsbridge** ⓮. Some of Kilkenny's best craft makers live and work in this old-world village which straddles the River Nore, and have created their own craft trail. You can visit **Chesneau Leather Goods** (tel: 056-27456), makers of handbags and belts, the **Nicholas Mosse Pottery** (056-27126), which makes painted spongeware and also has a pottery museum, and the **Stoneware Jackson Pottery** (tel: 056-27175). Another Kilkenny craft maker, **Jerpoint Glass** (tel: 056-243350), where you can watch heavy, uncut glass being shaped by hand into modern designs, can be visited in **Thomastown**. This is now a small market town (pop. 1,300) with a couple of good pubs, but in the 13th century it was walled and fortified. Its 18th-century stone-arched bridge over the Nore indicates its former importance.

Cross the bridge for a short (1½ miles/3 km) detour to **Jerpoint Abbey** (tel: 056-24623, admission fee), one of the most attractive monastic sites in Ireland. The ruined Cistercian monastery dates from the 12th century. The cloisters are especially fine, and there are many interesting carvings and effigies.

Return to Thomastown and cross the Nore again to reach **Inistioge**. The vil-

Map, page 170

lage is on a bend of the river and has a tree-lined square beside a 10-arched stone bridge. Its narrow, sloping streets of small stone houses make it a popular location for filming period movies such as the 1994 comedy-drama *Widow's Peak* with Mia Farrow and Joan Plowright. The parkland of **Woodstock Estate Forest Park** which was laid out in the 19th century with interesting shrubs from the Far East, is open to the public, but the house itself was burnt down in 1922.

Seven miles (11 km) south of Inistioge, turn left off the N700 to **The Rower**. This little village marks the start of an especially scenic stretch of road, with views over the River Barrow on the right hand side, and the Blackstairs Mountains beyond the river.

Graiguenamanagh ⓯ was an important commercial centre in the 19th century, when the River Barrow was used to transport coal and grain. Nowadays herons fish along its weir, and one of its stone-built warehouses has been turned into a stylish waterside B&B and restaurant.

There is a genuinely nostalgic stretch of old-fashioned pubs on the hill to the west of the bridge, in whose dark interiors you can buy groceries as well as pints. At the top of this hill on the right is **Duiske Abbey**, a Cistercian Abbey founded in 1204, but much added to since. The exterior is pebble-dashed and does not look very promising. However, the main nave of the abbey was adapted in 1983 to serve as the parish church. Its combination of modern and ancient features is much praised by some, and lamented by others. Whatever your opinion, it is certainly worth a look at its light-filled interior. Look out for the **Knight Of Duiske**, an effigy in chain mail, the hammer-beam roof in Irish oak, and the magnificent Romanesque processional door in the south transept.

Return to Thomastown on the R703, and from there to Kilkenny.

Gráig na Manach, the Gaelic name for the town in which Duiske Abbey (above) was built, means The Village of the Monks.

BELOW: the harbour, Graiguenamanagh.

Clonmel and Cashel

From Kilkenny, follow the N76 south to **Clonmel** ⓰, a busy county Tipperary market town on the River Suir. The area to the north and east of the town is known for its apple orchards, and Clonmel is the centre of the Irish cider-making industry. However, travel to the south, and you will find another kind of scenery altogether.

The **Nire Valley Drive** is a sign-posted circular route of about 23 miles (37 km) that travels along the edge of the **Comeragh Mountains** to **Ballymacarbry**, and the **Nire Valley**, and returns to Clonmel through **Clogheen** and **Ballybeg**. This is not for the faint-hearted; the roads are narrow, sometimes steep, and there are several hair-pin bends. However, it is an extraordinary experience to leave the tranquil apple-growing plains of Clonmel and, after only a few miles, find yourself in a wilderness area consisting mainly of pine forest and, above the tree line, uninhabited boglands. If you are interested in walking, **Ballymacarbery** village is a good base from which to follow the various way-marked trails in the area.

From Clonmel, head northwest on the R688 to **Cashel** ⓱. A cluster of romantic-looking, grey, turreted buildings stands on a limestone outcrop rising 60 metres (200 ft) above the Tipperary plain, and absolutely every tour bus stops here. It will greatly enhance your visit if you can avoid the crowds by visiting the rock at lunch time or in the late afternoon.

The **Rock of Cashel** (tel: 062-61437, admission fee) was probably once a centre of Druidic worship. By the 4th century AD Cashel was the ceremonial centre of the Kings of Munster. According to legend, it was here that St Patrick baptised King Aengus.

The reason so many Irish place-names start with Bally- is that the word Baile in Irish means "town". So Ballmacarbery means Town of the Mac Cairbre Family.

BELOW: Cashel.

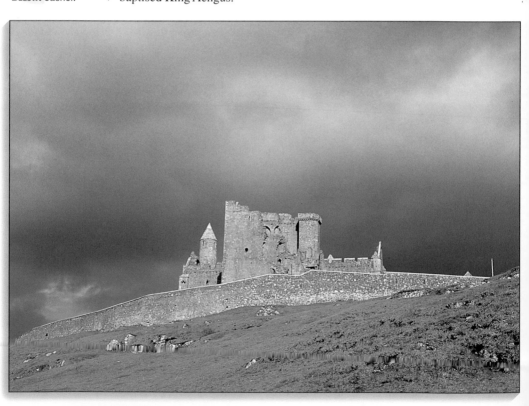

The largest building on the rock, the shell of **St Patrick's Cathedral**, built in the Hiberno-Romanesque style, was in use from the 13th to the mid-16th centuries when it was desecrated in Oliver Cromwell's campaign. The octagonal staircase leads to the top of the tower, and a wonderful view of the Tipperary plain. **Cormac's Chapel** is a simpler building dating from 1127, with a high, corbelled roof similar to those found in early saint's cells in Glendalough and Dingle.

Map, page 170

Spend some time lingering among the carvings and stones of Cashel, absorbing its unique atmosphere. Rather than spending time and money on the various heritage centres in Cashel town, concentrate on the Rock. As a town, Cashel suffers because its high street is also the main Dublin-Cork road. Take a quick look and maybe a light snack at the **Cashel Palace Hotel,** a red-brick, Queen Anne-style bishop's palace built in 1730. A path leads to the rock from its back garden. Note also the well-preserved wooden Victorian shop fronts across the road.

Stone carvings on Cashel's cathedral. When Henry VII asked Gerald, Earl of Kildare, why he had burned the cathedral in 1495, Gerald said he had thought the archbishop was inside. The king was amused.

Caher ⑱ (pronounced *Care*) has improved enormously since it was bypassed by the main Dublin-Cork road. **Caher Castle** (tel: 052-41011, admission fee) is a massive limestone fortress dating from the mid-12th century set on a rock in the River Suir. There is an informative guided tour, but avoid the audio-visual display. Walk up the hill beside the castle to have a look at Caher's main square which has some good Georgian buildings and several serious antique shops. About a mile outside Caher on the Clonmel road is the **Swiss Cottage** (tel: 052-41144, admission fee, closed Dec–mid-March), a thatched *cottage orné* built in 1810 to amuse the Earls of Glengall.

Walkers might like to detour northwest on the N24 for 14 miles (22 km) to **Bansha**, and on to Tipperary town and the **Glen of Aherlow**, an excellent area for hiking with marked trails of various lengths. The Glen, which is partly wooded and runs alongside the Aherlow River, has great views of the Galtee mountains (sometimes spelt Galty), and is a good base for getting off the beaten track.

BELOW: Caher Castle.

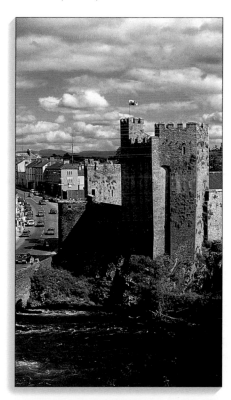

The Glen of Aherlow leads to **Kilfinane ⑲**, at the heart of the Galtee and Ballyhoura Mountains. Its main feature, the Kilfinane Moat, is an ancient, flat-top mound encircled by three ramparts. The 56-mile (90-km) **Ballyhoura Way** is a marked footpath that travels through north Cork and county Limerick to Tipperary town. More than 930 miles (1,500 km) of way-marked loop walks varying in length from 2 miles (3 km) to 12 miles (20 km) have been laid out in the Ballyhouras, with a map board at the starting point of each walk. This is beautiful, unspoilt country, a mixture of pasture and woodland, with several medieval and megalithic monuments, well worth exploring on foot.

You will see the south side of the Galtee mountains from the main N8 Cork road between Caher and **Mitchelstown**. If the open-air market is on, stop for a walk around Mitchelstown's main square. This will give you a taste of life as lived by the local farmers and their families, who travel perhaps once a week to this small market town.

From Mitchelstown it is less than an hour's drive to Cork city.

THE TRAVELLING PEOPLE

Ireland's 30,000 nomads belong to an ancient and romantic tradition – but the conditions under which they often live these days are far from romantic

Among the vacations on offer to tourists in Ireland are trips in horse-drawn caravans. It is something of a bad joke that, while tourists enjoy the freedom and leisure of a make-believe nomadic life, the country's real nomads subsist for the most part in poverty and squalor.

There are over 3,500 families of travelling people in Ireland, North and South, adding up to more than 30,000 people. About a third of these families are living in illegal campsites – by the road sides, on waste ground, on land cleared for development. They are a tiny minority: less than 1 per cent of the population. But even the casual visitor is likely to see some of them: bedraggled women and children begging in Dublin or a jumble of caravans, trailers, dogs and children glimpsed by the roadside.

PREJUDICE REMAINS

They are frequently moved on. Temporary sites provided by local councils often resemble refugee camps, and are resisted by communities, though a 1995 law forbade discrimination. Yet Travellers are no more drunken or lawless than other people.

"Tinkers", a word deriving from the days of the roving menders of tin kettles and pots, has become a term of abuse. "Itinerants" is intended to be polite but smacks of condescension. The travelling people hate it. "Travellers" is the word they prefer.

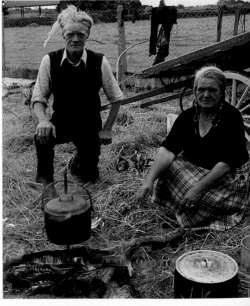

◁ **WHY DO THEY CLING TO THIS WAY OF LIFE?** "Being a Traveller." says one man, "is the feeling of belonging to a group of people. Knowing through thick and thin they are there for you, having the support of family systems. Having an identity."

◁ LIFE ON THE OPEN ROAD

Until the early 1960s, almost all travellers lived in brightly painted horse-drawn caravans or in tents. They dressed differently from other people – especially the women, with plaid shawls wrapped around their heads and shoulders. Then they began drifting to urban areas such as Dublin.

▽ FAMILY LIFE

Travellers traditionally have had large families, until recently averaging eight children. The birth rate has been falling, however, and many children are now more attracted to settled urban life than to the tradition of travelling. But it's not an easy tradition for families to make.

◁ REDUNDANT SKILLS

Travellers played a particular economic role for a society that was still mainly rural: mending utensils, making baskets and sieves, peddling ornaments and knick-knacks, dealing in horses and donkeys, and selling scrap.

△ LIVING CONDITIONS

The infant mortality rate for Travellers is twice that of the settled population. Most do not have electricity, and many do not have adequate toilet or washing facilities. But children have the security of having an extended family.

THEY'RE PART OF AN ANCIENT TRADITION

Although Ireland's Travellers share similar traditions to the 500,000 Gypsies in France and Spain and the 3 million in Romania, they are completely Irish in their ethnic origins. The true Romanies, like the Romans, never reached Ireland.

Like their counterparts in the rest of Europe, however, they have no tradition of written history and therefore it is hard to trace their origins with any degree of certainty. Some sociologists believe they are descended from various groups who took to the roads in the past few hundred years: families dispossessed or evicted from their homes, tradesmen who had to travel to make a living, individuals who "dropped out" from settled society, as some still do.

It has also been suggested that today's travellers may be descended from the roving bards referred to in Irish literature or from a particular caste in ancient Gaelic society.

The word *tynker* appears in 12th-century records as a term for an itinerant trades-man and Travellers are still occasionally called tinkers. In the days before recycling became fashionable, they were great recyclers of farm and household scrap metal. But the relentless erosion of Ireland's agrarian economy in the 20th century destroyed their economic base.

CORK CITY AND SURROUNDINGS

Map, page 194

After experiencing Cork's gentle charms, you can explore the port of Cobh, visit an innovative wildlife park and hope to acquire eloquence by kissing the Blarney Stone

The inhabitants of Cork, Ireland's second city with a population of 134,000, are known for their strong sense of civic pride. While visitors from Dublin and other European capitals might find Cork a small, drowsy city, to Corkonians it is a place of enormous importance.

The old city of Cork was founded by St Finbar in the 6th century. The name *Corcaigh* means "marshy place" in Irish. While the marshes are long gone, the city is still well-endowed with waterways. The city centre stands on a island between two branches of the River Lee. First impressions are of a confusing number of bridges and quays. Its medieval buildings have long gone, and the fabric of today's Cork dates mainly from the 18th and 19th centuries. The centre is flat, but to the north of the River Lee an escarpment rises up so steeply that many streets have steps cut into their pavements.

Cork was at its most affluent in the 18th century, when its butter market was a source of vast wealth. Much of the best domestic architecture as seen in the South Mall, Grand Parade and the North Mall dates from this period. Cork has retained the sober air of a merchants' city, and new industry in the form of multinational chemical plants and other high-tech industries have replaced heavier industries, such as car assembly and shipbuilding. Cork may lack the youthful energy that characterises Galway City and Dublin's Temple Bar, but it has a gentle, old-fashioned charm of its own.

PRECEDING PAGES: Blarney Castle. **BELOW:** Cornmarket Street, Cork. **BELOW:** strolling in Cork.

A walking tour of the city centre

The centre of Cork is best explored by foot. The highlights can be comfortably covered in half a day. Start at the **Tourist Information Office ❹** (tel. 021-273251) on **Grand Parade**. Take a look across the street in front of the TIO at a terrace of three elegant Georgian houses with slate-hung, bow-fronted windows, typical of Cork's 18th-century prime. In the west, across the south channel of the River Lee, you can see the spires of **St Finn Barr's Cathedral ❺**, where the city began as a monastic school in about AD650. Both the Gothic, late 19th-century cathedral, and the bridge across the Lee are built of characteristic white limestone.

Washington Street, which reaches Grand Parade in a T-junction opposite the multiplex cinema, leads, after a 10-minute walk, to the campus of **University College, Cork ❻** (tel: 021-276871). Known locally as UCC, the college has about 10,000 students. Guided tours of the campus, which has a 19th-century Tudor-Gothic style quadrangle and an interesting Hiberno-Romanesque chapel dating from 1916, are available on request. Walk a few steps to the left of the TIO for a look at **South**

Pavement artists like this one in Cork are popular in Irish cities – surprisingly in view of the island's reputation for year-round rainfall.

Mall, Cork's most fashionable residential area in the city's 18th-century prime. It is now the legal and banking district.

Leaving the river to your back, walk along the Grand Parade to Cork's indoor food market, the **Princes Street Market ⓓ**, also known as the English Market, which extends across a whole city block. Recent refurbishment work has revealed an ornate Victorian cast-iron frame. At the far (Princes Street) end of the market there is a top-lit piazza with a central fountain. Some 150 stalls sell a wide variety of fresh food, ranging from traditional meat and seafood to organic vegetables and hand-made Irish cheeses. Note the stall at the door with a display of tripe (cows' intestines) and drisheen (blood sausage). This, and more tempting local specialities can be sampled at the fountain end of the market in its first-floor **Farmgate Café** (inexpensive), one of the city's liveliest lunch spots.

Shopping for Irish glass

Follow the Grand Parade into the graceful curve of **St Patrick Street**, Cork's main shopping street. The major department store, **Cash's**, is halfway down the street on the right-hand side, and has a good stock of Irish crystal, including Waterford Glass. Be sure to look up, because many of the buildings on St Patrick Street have retained 18th- and 19th-century features. If it's after lunch, you'll hear a uniquely Cork phenomenon – cries of "Eeechoooo!" from vendors of Cork's evening paper, *The Echo*. A bronze statue of this beloved Cork symbol, "the Echo boy", stands at the junction of Patrick Street and Cook Street.

About 20 metres along St Patrick Street on the left-hand side, a pedestrian alleyway next to the Body Shop leads to **Paul Street Piazza ⓔ**, a small pedestrianised square popular with buskers. This is where an old part of Cork known as the **Huguenot Quarter**, named after the French Protestants who settled here in the 18th century, meets a new shopping development. This is the closest Cork gets to a "left bank", with a cluster of antique shops, bookstores, design-conscious home furnishing stores, fashion boutiques and trendy restaurants.

Turn right on to Paul Street for the **Crawford Municipal Gallery** (tel: 021-273377). If you have time to look at only one museum in the southwest, this stately, red-brick Victorian edifice is the one to choose. Its collection is unusually good for a small municipal gallery, and it also mounts exciting contemporary exhibitions. A collection of classical casts is housed in its ground-floor sculpture galleries, which is also where contemporary exhibitions are held. Most major 20th-century Irish artists are represented in the Crawford's permanent collection. To get a vivid idea of the charms of Cork and Cobh in the 18th and 19th centuries, look out for topographical landscapes and seascapes by Nathaniel Grogan and George Atkinson.

The **Opera House** **G**, just around the corner in the direction of the river, is an unattractive concrete landmark dating from 1965, replacing one burnt down in 1955. To your right is St Patrick's Bridge, and straight ahead is the modern Christy Ring Bridge. Both lead from the central island of Cork to the northside.

Cross the Christy Ring Bridge, and climb the hill to the **Firkin Crane Centre**. Part of the Firkin Crane, a classical rotunda attractively built in cut limestone, is used for dance performances, and part of it houses the **Shandon Craft Market**. The Firkin Crane dates from the 18th century when much of Cork's wealth derived from the exporting of butter. Butter was packed in wooden barrels known as firkins, which were weighed here by a crane.

Across the road is **St Anne's Church**, whose Shandon Steeple is topped by a

Map, page 194

TIP

The Crawford Café in the Municipal Gallery is a popular meeting place serving light lunches and cakes, and often has smaller exhibitions on its walls.

BELOW: Cork City.

The bells in St Anne's Church were made famous by the ballad:
'Tis the bells of
Shandon
That sound so
grand on
The pleasant waters
of the River Lee.

BELOW: kissing the Blarney Stone.

large salmon-shaped weather vane and has a four-sided clock. This is a famous landmark, that can be seen from most of the inner city. It is also known as the four-faced liar, as the clock often tells a different time on each side. For a small fee, you can climb the tower and attempt to ring a tune on the bells.

Blarney Castle

A visit to Blarney Castle makes a pleasant half-day outing. Don't be put off by Blarney's reputation as a tourist trap. The castle is surrounded by well-tended gardens, and is well worth seeing. **Blarney Castle ⑳** (tel: 021-385252, admission fee) is not furnished, but nor, like many castles of its age, is it a ruin. Blarney, one of the largest castles in Ireland, was built in the mid-15th century. It is basically a fortified home. Above the narrow entrance lobby is a removable stone, known as a murder hole, which enabled the residents to pour boiling oil on to intruders. The staircase is narrow so that it can be defended by one man holding a sword. While there is only one slit-window at ground level, the windows get larger as you climb higher, and they become less vulnerable to attack.

Kissing the **Blarney Stone** is supposed to bestow the gift of eloquence. The word Blarney has entered the English language to mean "smoothly flattering or cajoling talk", but the origins of the tradition are obscure. The stone (which is actually the sill of an opening through which boiling liquids could be poured on invaders in the old days) is located right at the top of the castle, on a parapet which is open to the sky. To kiss the stone you must lie on your back while an attendant holds on to you, and drop your head backwards and downwards. There is no charge, but most people who play along with this preposterous legend are so happy to survive the ordeal that they tip £1.

Fota Wildlife Park and Arboretum

The east side of Cork Harbour is formed by three islands, **Little Island**, **Fota Island** and **Great Island**, all of which are connected by causeways. The road from Cork to Cobh brings you past the walls of the 780-acre (315-hectare) **Fota Estate**. **Fota Wildlife Park** ㉑ (tel: 021-812678, admission fee, closed Nov–mid-March) aims to breed certain species that are under threat in the wild. Giraffe, zebras, ostrich, oryx and antelope roam freely in grassland, monkeys swing through trees on lake islands, while kangaroos, wallabies, lemurs and peacocks have complete freedom of the park. Fota is the world's leading breeder of cheetahs, one of the few animals here that must be caged.

The **Fota Arboretum** (freely accessible) is beside the Wildlife Park, behind Fota House. The house, currently closed, was built as a shooting lodge for the Barrymore family and enlarged in 1820 to a symmetrical neo-classical design. The arboretum has a beautiful collection of mature trees from all over the world.

The Cove of Cork

Cobh ㉒ (pronounced *Cove*) was a small fishing village, referred to as the Cove of Cork, and virtually unknown until the early 1800s. It grew in importance as a British naval base during the American Civil War, when its value as a natural deep-water harbour was first recognised. It grew again during the French Revolutionary and Napoleonic Wars (1792–1815), when it was a refuelling and assembly point. The fine cut-stone buildings on the two main islands in its harbour date from this period. In Victorian times it became Queenstown.

Cobh today is an interesting and highly atmospheric town. Most of its buildings are solid and Victorian in style, dating from about 1830 to 1900. In the mid-19th century there were plans to promote Cobh as a spa, hence the nicely laid-out promenade behind its quays. But instead, its heyday came when its strategic position with regard to transatlantic traffic was recognised. Instead of tall ships carrying convicts to Australia, Cobh became the last – and first – European port of call for transatlantic traffic.

Between 1848 and 1950 about 2½ million adults and children emigrated through the port. Their transport ranged from the notorious "coffin ships" of the famine years, overcrowded and unseaworthy, to the luxury of liners belonging to the White Star and the Cunard lines. Cobh was the last port of call of the supposedly unsinkable *Titanic* in 1912, and it was to Cobh that most of the bodies recovered from the torpedoing of the *Lusitania* in 1915 were brought. These, and other happier events in Cobh's history, are enlarged on in **The Queenstown Story** (tel:021-813591, admission fee), a lively and imaginative visitor centre at the entrance to Cobh. Allow at least an hour.

A large, Gothic-revival church, **St Colman's Cathedral**, was built in granite between 1868 and 1915. Spend some time on the cathedral parapet enjoying the view of the harbour and its islands. In the south you can see Roches Point, which marks the harbour entrance, and the open sea beyond it. The Cathedral's spire has a carillon of 47 bells which rings out over the harbour at 9am, 12 noon, 4pm and 6pm daily.

Map, page 170

ABOVE: tree-ranging in Fota Wildlife Park.
BELOW: Cobh Harbour, departure point for emigrants.

THE SOUTHWEST

This is where the Atlantic first touches Europe, and the mild climate enhances the spectacular scenery of Bantry Bay, Killarney, the Ring of Kerry and the Dingle Peninsula

Map, page 170

This is as far as you can get from Dublin, both physically and mentally. The pace of life really is slower, people have time to stop and talk, and a friendly informality prevails. Leave your formal clothes at home; bring strong walking shoes, waterproof jackets, casual evening wear, and buy a hand-knitted sweater at the first craft shop you visit. For many visitors Cork and Kerry are the essence of Ireland, combining wild, rugged landscape and, where the coastal waters are warmed by the Gulf Stream, a mild, frost-free climate.

The pleasures of the southwest are chiefly rural. Most people who visit the area are here for the outdoors and the scenery. The lakes and mountains of Killarney can compete with the best Europe has to offer, while the Ring of Kerry presents a succession of spectacular seascapes. The less-frequented Beara Peninsula is preferred by walkers and cyclists who enjoy the relative lack of traffic and the simple B&B accommodation. The coast of West Cork also has its champions, people who like the relatively small scale of its cliffs and hills, the miles of fuchsia hedges, dripping with dark red, honey-scented flowers, clashing exuberantly with great swathes of purple heather.

The most popular part of the west among visitors from both Europe and America is the tip of the Dingle Peninsula, a largely Irish-speaking area rich in prehistoric and early Christian remains, with some of the world's best coastal scenery and arguably the country's best traditional music.

PRECEDING PAGES: west coast vista near Caherdaniel. **LEFT:** Slea Head, the Dingle Peninsula. **BELOW:** Charles Fort, Kinsale.

Kinsale – Ireland's gourmet capital

Kinsale ㉓, 12 miles (19 km) south of Cork Airport on the R600, is the big success story of Irish tourism. Once a run-down fishing port, it is now a wealthy resort with so many restaurants that it's known as "the gourmet capital of Ireland". It is situated at the top of a fjord-like harbour where the River Bandon runs into the sea. Craft shops, galleries, restaurants and antique shops abound.

The **Old Courthouse** in Market Square dates from 1600. In 1706 a Dutch-style gabled frontage and octagonal clock tower were added. The Courthouse now contains the **Kinsale Regional Museum** (tel: 021-772044, admission fee) whose exhibits include mementoes of the *Lusitania*, which was sunk 14 miles (23 km) off the coast of the Old Head of Kinsale in 1915 by a German submarine. The action, in which 1,198 passengers and crew were killed, was responsible for bringing the United States into the Great War. Also of interest nearby are the 12th-century **St Multose Church** and the 16th-century **Desmond Castle**.

Charles Fort (tel: 021-772684), a five-minute drive down Kinsale Harbour, is a star-shaped fort enclosing 9 acres (3.5 hectares) of ground, and was built in 1677. Because it is overlooked by high ground, it wasn't a

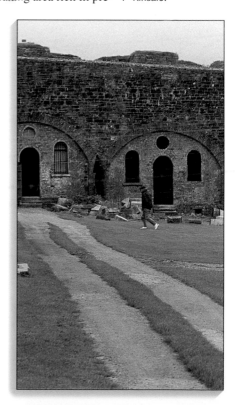

great success militarily. There is good cut-stone work on many buildings, and wonderful sea views.

Leave Kinsale by crossing the River Bandon to the west. The land at the extremity of the **Old Head of Kinsale** became a private golf club in 1997, and you may be asked to pay a fee to walk to the lighthouse. Allow about 40 minutes each way. The R600 then runs along the edge of the **Courtmacsherry Estuary** which in winter months is home to great flocks of plover, oyster catchers and curlew. In the summer cormorants and herons should be easy to spot.

The distant view of **Timoleague** ❷ is dominated by the grey stone ruins of a waterside 12th-century **Franciscan Friary**. Until the 16th century the monks were wine importers. The ruins are freely accessible. There are some garish modern graves inside, but the tall Gothic windows framing views of the estuary offer an irresistible photo-opportunity. The interior walls of Timoleague's tiny 19th-century **Church of Ireland** are entirely covered by a mosaic mural in the decorative style favoured by the Oxford Movement. The replica Hiberno-Romanesque-style **Church of Our Lady's Nativity** contains some fine stained-glass windows by the acclaimed Dublin artist, Harry Clarke (1889–1931).

Clonakilty and Environs

Turn left off the main road in **Clonakilty** ❷ at the large Catholic church and park. **Emmet Square** is lined by tall Georgian houses. The **General Post Office** is in a small 19th-century church. Note the hand-painted shop signs above wooden shop fronts which have been revived in recent years. Historians will like the eclectic **West Cork Regional Museum** which features memorabilia of the controversial patriot Michael Collins among its extensive collection.

BELOW:
Kinsale Harbour.

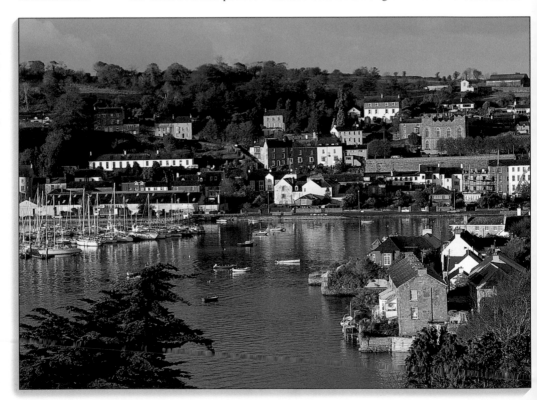

Collins's birthplace is signposted 4 miles (6.5 km) west of Clonakilty just beyond **Pike Cross**.

Continue west on the N71. After running through a cutting of exposed slate, the same material you see on most roofs in the southwest, the road crosses a wide sea inlet at **Rosscarbery ㉖**. This was an important monastic centre from the 6th to the 12th centuries. The small Protestant Cathedral (1612) is no bigger than most churches. It has been extensively and attractively renovated.

Turn left just beyond Rosscarbery on to the R597 Glandore road. From June to September this little road, and many others like it around west Cork, are lined by tall hedges of *fuchsia magellanica*, a shrub with bright red bell-shaped flowers imported from Chile in the 19th century. It has adapted so well to the climate that it grows wild in profusion.

About 2 miles (3.5 km) along is the road to the **Drombeg Stone Circle**, one of the most complete and most impressively situated of the region's early Iron Age remains. The circle is oriented to the winter solstice. If it's cloudless on 21 December, it's an impressive sight as the last rays of the sun travel through a cut in the distant mountains and land on the flat stone at the far side of the circle.

In winter **Glandore ㉗**, a tiny village built on the south-facing slope of a protected harbour, with a year-round population well below 100, will be virtually empty, while in summer it will be teeming with wealthy visitors and their yachts. This lovely spot is known locally as Millionaire's Row. **Union Hall**, on the opposite side of Glandore Harbour, is not a hall but a small fishing village. Note the multi-coloured houses which are such a feature of the area. It is said this tradition originated because fishermen used whatever was left over from the annual painting of their boats, to brighten up their houses.

Map, page 170

Michael Collins bust at his Pike Cross birthplace. He was gunned down on the Macroom to Bandon Road in Co. Cork in 1922 during Ireland's civil war.

BELOW: Drombeg Stone Circle.

ABOVE: Sailing on Lough Ine.

Castletownshend is signposted from Union Hall on an attractive back road which passes through **Rineen**. Castletownshend may be the prettiest village in west Cork, but it is also the least typical. Wander along its two streets, noting its large, well-designed three- and four-storey houses, often stone-built and neoclassical. These belonged to "planter" families – Protestant English ex-soldiers – who were given lands in the area in the late 17th century.

A wall plaque in **St Barrahane's Church** enlarges on their history. Behind the church are the graves of Edith Somerville (1858–1949) and her writing partner, Violet Martin (1862–1915). As Somerville and Ross, they are best known for a series of comic sketches of Irish country life, *Some Experiences of an Irish RM* (Resident Magistrate).They also wrote a well-received novel, *The Real Charlotte*. There's a wonderful view of the sheltered anchorage from their graves.

Skibbereen ㉘ is a traffic-choked market town built in a solid bourgeois style in the 19th and early 20th centuries. **Lough Ine** (also spelt Hyne) is just off the Baltimore road. The land-locked salt water lake is a marine reserve with many unusual species. Its high wooded shores and sheltered location give it a very special atmosphere. Walk around the path on the west side of the lake to discover the narrow passage where sea water rushes in at high tide.

Baltimore,19 km (12 miles) south of Skibbereen, is another popular sailing and holiday village, the most easily accessible port on **Roaringwater Bay**. Baltimore can be hectic in July and August. The bay covers an area between the Mizen Head in the west and Baltimore in the east which is known for its numerous rocks and islands. In good visibility, the **Fastnet Rock Lighthouse**, can be seen on the horizon some 14 miles (23 km) to the south.

BELOW: Skibbereen.

Baltimore is also the base for the mail boats and ferries servicing Roaring

Water Bay's two largest inhabited islands, Clear and Sherkin. **Sherkin Island** is only a quick hop (tel: 028-20187 for ferry details; services half-hourly in summer). There is one pub, The Jolly Roger, and the ruins of a 15th-century Franciscan Friary. Sherkin's marine life is explained in the small museum at **Sherkin Island Marine Station** (tel: 028-20187, admission fee).

Birdwatching centre

Clear Island is reached by a thrilling 45-minute boat ride through the rocks of Roaringwater Bay (tel: 028-39119 for ferry details. There is usually a boat out at 11am, returning at 5.30pm, weather permitting). Cape Clear (pop. 170) is an Irish-speaking island about 3 miles (5 km) long by 1 mile (2 km). There is one pub, a youth hostel, a bird observatory, a heritage centre and about 20 B&Bs. Because of its southerly position, Cape Clear's Bird Observatory often reports landings of rare migratory birds, and the appearance of large flocks.

The N71 west leaves Skibbereen beside the banks of the **River Ilen**. About 6 miles (9 km) out of town, keep an eye out to the left for your first panoramic view of Roaringwater Bay and its numerous islands.

Ballydehob ㉙ is a lively, brightly-painted village built on a hillside, apparently in the middle of nowhere. Although it appears to be inland, Ballydehob has a harbour. Before the harbour silted up, the village was the marketing centre for the islanders of Roaringwater Bay. Now it's a popular retreat for city folk – English, Dutch, German and even Irish – seeking a better quality of life.

Continue on the R592 towards Schull. In good weather you will see **Mount Gabriel** (1335 ft/407 metres) on your right. The two white balls on its summit guide transatlantic air traffic. If you wake early in west Cork, you can often hear

Map, page 170

Cape Clear is Ireland's most southerly point. The Fastnet Rock and lighthouse, 4 miles (6km) to its southwest, are familiar navigation points to sailors.

BELOW: mermaid sculpture by the river at Ballydehob.

Altar Rock. For more information about megalithic tombs, see page 227.

a stream of jumbo jets high above, heading for the airports of Europe. While Ballydehob has a reputation for being arty, **Schull**, 3 miles (5 km) down the R592, is the heart of fashionable west Cork, a summer resort for wealthy Dubliners. Walk down to the pier for another look at Roaringwater Bay, then explore its one main street, checking out its restaurants, bookshops and craft boutiques.

Leave Schull on the R592 to travel to the tip of the **Mizen Peninsula**. The road passes rocky, rugged bits of low-lying coast. About 4 miles (7 km) west at **Altar**, there is a megalithic tomb on the left, known locally as the Altar Rock. The **Mizen Head** is a dramatic spot with wild Atlantic waves pounding the rocks even in the calmest weather. The lighthouse signal has been automatic, and the station unstaffed since 1993. The **Mizen Vision** (tel: 028-35225, admission fee) is located in the lighthouse keeper's house on an island at the tip of the peninsula. To reach it you must cross a concrete suspension bridge while the waves swirl around 150 ft (45 metres) below. Don't forget your camera.

The shores of Bantry Bay

The town of **Bantry** ③ is distinguished only by its setting on the shores of **Bantry Bay**. **Bantry House** (tel: 027-50047), a short walk from the town centre, is a large, mid-18th century mansion with a magnificent setting overlooking the famous bay (which is 4 miles/6.5 km wide), and the mountains on the opposite shore. The interior is either under-restored, verging on the shabby, or full of atmosphere depending on your taste.

There is a fine collection of treasures, including Aubusson carpets, Gobelin tapestries, Russian icons, Chinese lacquer and a mixture of French and Irish 18th-century furniture. In the yard the **Bantry 1796 French Armada Exhibition Centre** is a small museum commemorating the failed attempt by Wolfe Tone and his French allies to land 14,000 troops in Bantry Bay just over 200 years ago. The landing was impeded by bad weather.

BELOW: St Finbar's Oratory.

Head inland from Bantry via **Kealkil** to visit **Gougane Barra**, a deep tarn which is the source of the River Lee. The lake is walled in on three sides by steep precipices which run with cataracts after heavy rain. **St Finbar's Oratory**, a small stone-built chapel on an island in the lake, can be reached by a causeway. The existing building is a 20th-century replica, built on the site where St Finbar supposedly lived and prayed in the 6th century before founding his monastery downstream in the place that is now Cork city. A pilgrimage is still held on the first Sunday after St Finbar's Feast Day, 25 September. There's certainly something special about the place, particularly if you arrive early, before the majority of day trippers.

The N71 climbs above Bantry Bay into open, more rugged country, offering ever-changing views across the bay. **Glengarriff** ③, a wooded glen with a sheltered harbour warmed by the Gulf Stream, has an especially mild climate, with an average annual temperature of 11°C (52°F). Azaleas, rhododendrons, magnolia, and camellias grow in abundance. Glengarriff village is teeming with craft shops and coach parks, but the gardens on the island of **Ilnacullin** (tel: 027-63040, admission fee, closed Nov–Feb) five minutes offshore are well worth a visit. An added bonus in sunny weather is the sight of basking seals on the rocks between the mainland and the island. Allow about an hour and a half. Don't miss the Italian Garden, a formal garden with colonnades and a terrace from which the contrast between the classical man-made beauty of the garden, and the wild mountain scenery that surrounds it, is at its greatest.

Map,
page 170

The Ring of Beara

The Ring of Beara is less well known than its neighbour to the north, the Ring of Kerry, yet it also offers impressive scenery. It is a favourite haunt of walkers, cyclists, bird watchers and people who enjoy natural beauty. Although the drive covers only about 68 miles (110 km), much of it is on narrow, winding roads, so allow a full day. The **Beara Peninsula** stretches for about 30 miles (48 km) southwest from Glengarriff, forming the north side of Bantry Bay. The **Caha** and **Slieve Miskish** mountains run down the centre of the peninsula, and the road around it is mainly on a narrow coastal plain.

Many would consider **Castletownbere ㉜**, with a population of about 850, little more than a village. However, it is a busy working port, home to Ireland's largest white fish trawling fleet. Large Russian factory ships are often anchored for months between the town and Bere Island. Get a feel for the place by walking along the quays and admiring the brightly coloured fishing fleet.

Leave town on the R575 for **Allihies**. This straggling line of brightly coloured cottages set between sea and hills, was originally built for the copper miners working in the hills behind it. The sandy beach at **Ballydonegan** was formed of spoil from the mines. Walk up to the abandoned mines (marked by tall brick chimneys) and enjoy the views of sea and wild hillside. You can walk from here

TIP

There are good opportunities for bathing in the area around Allihies.

BELOW: digging for sea urchins at Bantry Bay.

to the next village, Eyeries (7 miles/11 km), on a footpath that forms part of the Beara Way. Even if you only walk a few miles of it, the peace and isolation will be unforgettable.

The road between Allihies and **Eyeries**, another village of small, brightly coloured houses, is one of the highlights of the Ring of Beara. In good weather the **Iveragh Peninsula** is clearly visible to the north, across the **Kenmare River**, as are the conical shaped **Skellig Rocks** off its tip. You will get a closer look at these rocky islands from the Ring of Kerry.

Derreen Gardens (tel: 027-70054) were planted 100 years ago beside Kilmakilloge Harbour, a sheltered inlet on the south shore of the Kenmare River. The woodland gardens run down to the water's edge and contain many azaleas and rhododendrons, massive stands of bamboo and a grove of New Zealand tree ferns – all of which thrive in the mild air warmed by the Gulf Stream.

The first Marquess of Lansdowne, the local landowner, was responsible for the layout of **Kenmare ③③**, an attractive market town at the head of the Kenmare River (which is in fact a sea inlet). The two principal streets intersect each other to form an X. Kenmare, with its background of mountains, is a popular stop on the Ring of Kerry, and has a better than average selection of shops. The **Kenmare Heritage Centre** (tel: 064-41233, admission fee, closed Nov–Mar) explores themes of local interest. There is a Kenmare lace showroom above it.

Killarney's lakes and mountains

Killarney ③④ may be the most commercialised area in the Southwest, but it is still possible to avoid the crowds and enjoy the lakes and hills. The romantic scenery of boulder-strewn, heather-clad mountains, deep blue lakes dotted with

BELOW: jaunting cars are popular with tourists.

Map,
page 209

wooded islands, and wild woodland has been preserved within a large National Park. Avoid the town by day. Killarney isn't a good place to shop for crafts in spite of (or because of) its large number of visitors. Kenmare and Blarney are better shopping destinations. The town is chiefly remarkable in high season for its traffic jams. However, there are several good restaurants open in the evening, and the singing bars can be enjoyable if you don't mind organised fun.

Enjoying a visit to Killarney is largely a matter of attitude. You won't appreciate Killarney from the inside of a car. One great pleasure here is the damp woodland aroma that permeates the mild air. As in the rest of Kerry, it is important not to be put off by rain. Any weather, good or bad, tends not to last long around here. In fact, the lakes of Killarney look especially good when seen through a light drizzle.

Rather than regarding Killarney as a series of sights to be ticked off a list, it is more satisfying to do only one or two things in a leisurely way. Arriving from Kenmare, you may decide to stop on the N71 and climb the path beside the **Torc Waterfall** to enjoy the view – and plan your next move.

A nice contrast to the wildness of Torc can be found across the road in **Muckross Park**, a neatly trimmed lakeside area with gravel paths that forms the nucleus of the **Killarney National Park** Ⓐ. This is a car-free zone, and it is a good place to take a ride on one of Killarney's famous jaunting cars (open horse-drawn carriages). The drivers, who are called jarveys, are traditionally great talkers. Don't be surprised if you hear a phone ring during your quaint jaunting car ride; most drivers carry mobile phones to help locate their next fare.

Muckross House Ⓑ (tel: 064-31440, admission fee, closed Nov–mid-Mar) was built in the 19th century in the Elizabethan style, and houses a folklore and

ABOVE:
Muckross House.

Map,
page 209

farming museum. You can admire the formal gardens without an entrance fee.

Ross Castle is a 14th-century castle keep that has recently been fully restored. You can hire a rowing boat here, and take a picnic over to **Innisfallen Island** about 1 mile (1.5 km) offshore. The wooded island has the remains of an abbey founded about AD 600, which is famous for the *Annals of Innisfallen*, a chronicle of world and Irish history written in this remote and beautiful spot up to 1320 by a succession of monastic scribes.

Consider taking an organised half-day coach-horse-and-boat trip through the **Gap of Dunloe** , a narrow mountain pass formed by glacial action. The organised trip has the advantage of allowing you to travel through the Gap on foot or horseback and then go back to town by boat without having to retrieve your car. The Gap itself is an unpaved path that stretches for 4 miles (6.5 km) between the **Macgillicuddy's Reeks** and the **Purple Mountain** , which gets its name from the heather that covers it in the autumn. There is no motor traffic, but in summer there is a constant stream of ponies, jaunting cars and pedestrians. The scenery is first-rate, with a chain of five small lakes beside the road, and massive glacial boulders, but don't expect solitude.

The Macgillicuddy's Reeks (peaks) include Carantuohill, Ireland's highest summit at 3,414 ft (1,041 metres).

The Ring of Kerry

You can drive non-stop around the 118 miles (190 km) of the Ring of Kerry in about four hours, but allow a full day as you will want to make several stops. The Ring of Kerry is justifiably famous for its combination of lush, sub-tropical vegetation and rugged seascapes. In July and August the narrow two-lane road can be clogged by a slow procession of tour buses and RVs. If traffic and commercialism bother you, do the Ring of Beara instead, or go straight to Dingle.

BELOW: the alluring Ring of Kerry.

Killorglin ㉟ is a busy village which makes the most of its strategic position on the road between Killarney and Dingle. It is famous for Puck Fair which takes place on the 10–12 August. On the first day a mountain goat is crowned King Puck and installed on a tall throne overlooking the town, until the evening of the third day. There are various explanations of its origin, but nowadays it is chiefly a drinking festival, and can get rowdy. A short drive inland from the road to Glenbeigh, **Caragh Lake** is a delightful, sheltered spot, popular with game anglers. The lake shore is discreetly dotted with luxury hotels and holiday homes, mostly 19th-century. A scenic drive encircles the lake.

Glenbeigh is a popular touring base, convenient for both sea and hills. Nearby **Rossbeigh** is a 3-mile (5-km) long sandy beach facing west over Dingle Bay, backed by dunes. There are good walks here in **Rossbeigh Woods**.

Cahersiveen ㊱ (pronounced Cah-her-sigh-*veen*) is the chief market town for the Iveragh peninsula, but don't expect a buzzing metropolis. At its best it has a certain dilapidated charm. Don't miss the community-funded visitor centre, **The Barracks** (tel: 066-72777, admission fee.). This is an exotic-looking, white-turreted building. The story goes that it should have been built in India, on the Northwest Frontier, but the plans were mistakenly sent to Ireland. In fact its architect, Enoch Trevor Owen, habitually built in what he called the Schloss style, and looked at from another angle, his design suits the hill-backed location very well. But why spoil a good story? Nowadays it houses an amusing and informative series of exhibitions. Follow the sign outside The Barracks to the pier. The prettiest part of Cahersiveen is its backside which overlooks the wide estuary of the River Ferta and the green hills beyond.

Look out for signs to the Valentia Island car ferry about 3 miles (5km) west of

Map, page 170

The Barracks: destined, some say, for India and built in Ireland as a result of clerical error.

BELOW: horse for sale at Killorglin's Puck's Fair.

Cahersiveen. This lands you in **Knightstown** at the eastern tip of **Valentia**, a sleepy place, eerily quiet, its one hotel semi-derelict. The island is 6¾ miles (11 km) long and 1¾ miles (3 km) broad, a quiet place with a population of about 700. The original transatlantic cable connecting Europe with Newfoundland was laid from here between 1857 and 1865. Valentia is connected to the mainland by a causeway at **Portmagee**.

The Skellig Experience (tel: 066-76306, admission fee, closed Oct–Mar), beside the causeway, is a dull and portentous visitor centre, chiefly useful for its two-hour cruise around the islands. Bear in mind that all the boats are open, the water can be rough, and bad weather leads to frequent cruise cancellations.

Skellig Michael was popular for centuries with pilgrims, who performed penances on the island. Extra penances were to endure the rough seas and steep slopes.

Skellig Michael, the largest of the three islands, was inhabited by monks from the 7th until the 12th centuries. It rises in a cone shape to a double peak 712 ft (217 metres) high. A flight of over 500 steps lead to the monastery which is built of dry stone with no mortar. It has undergone major restoration work to enable it to cope with increased visitor numbers, but there are still fears about unexplained changes in its plant life. Boats that land visitors can be found locally, but unless you have a very special interest, take a non-landing cruise.

A scenic drive

If the weather is good, take the scenic road from Portmagee to Waterville through **Ballynahow**. The road climbs the **Coomanaspig Pass**, revealing an impressive arc of coast and mountains. It then travels through **The Glen**, offering the best views so far of the Skelligs. Drive through **Ballinskelligs**, a small, Irish-speaking village, and rejoin the main Ring road just before Waterville. **Waterville** ❸❼ is a popular base for golfers, who enjoy the famous links, and anglers who have

BELOW: the lure of the Atlantic.

a choice of deep-sea fishing in Ballinskelligs Bay or angling on Lough Currane.

The next stretch of road which winds along the edge of **Ballinskelligs Bay** through the **Commakesta Pass**, then crosses **Lamb's Head**, has some of the best views on the Ring, with rocky coastline backed by rugged green hills. **Derrynane House** (tel: 066-75113, admission fee) is a mile beyond **Caherdaniel**. The house belonged to Daniel O'Connell (1775–1847), also known as The Liberator, who is remembered chiefly for his campaign for Catholic emancipation (granting civil rights to Catholics), which was won in 1829. O'Connell is still a great hero in this part of the world, and the house contains a greatly respected collection of his personal possessions and furniture. These range from a magnificent throne-like carved chair, to the pistol with which O'Connell killed a man in a duel in 1815. The 320 acres (130 hectares) of woods surrounding the house have pleasant walks, and access to an attractive sandy beach.

Castlecove is a small, friendly place with several good sandy beaches. A narrow lane beyond the church climbs 1¾ miles (3 km) to **Staigue Fort**. This is a well-preserved example of a prehistoric stone fortress, dating from 1500 BC. It consists of a circular dry-stone wall, 115 ft (35 metres) in diameter, varying in thickness from 13 ft to 5 ft (4–1.5 metres). A series of steps in the walls lead to a platform with good sea views. A small donation is requested by the landowner.

Sneem ㉘ is another pretty but untypical village, laid out English-style around a village green beneath a semi-circle of low mountains A variety of indifferent modern sculpture is dotted around. Ignore this, and look for "the pyramids" as they are called locally, beside the Catholic parish church. These small stone-built beehive huts inlaid with stained-glass panels look ancient. In fact, they were built in 1990 with local labour, and designed by Cork artist James Scanlon.

ABOVE: a kingly tree sculpture at Derrynane House.

BELOW: Sneem.

Map, page 170

ABOVE: one of
Dingle's local crafts.

BELOW: on the road
at Dingle in a self-
drive caravan.

Sneem marks the start of the most sheltered part of the Ring of Kerry's coast. In contrast to the dramatic rocky scenery of Lamb's Head, you will see lush, subtropical growth – wild rhododendrons, azaleas, camellias and bamboo – evidence of the benign effect of the Gulf Stream.

The N70 continues on to Kenmare, where the N71 leads to either Killarney or Glengarriff. If you are heading for Dingle, turn left at **Blackwater Bridge** to drive through the **Ballaghbeama Gap** and **Glencar**, a popular base for climbers and walkers, to Killorglin. This is a narrow, twisty road, not recommended for nervous drivers, but it offers some wonderful unspoilt bogland scenery.

The Dingle Peninsula

The weather can make or break a visit to Dingle. If the sea mist is down, consider postponing your trip. At Killorglin take the N70 to Castlemaine, and in Castlemaine take the R561, which gives good views of the coast of the Iveragh peninsula. **Inch** has 4 miles (6.5 km) of sandy beach backed by dunes.

Dingle ㊴, the chief town of the peninsula, has a population of about 1,500, which can be doubled and trebled in the summer. Backed by mountains, it faces on to a sheltered harbour. Until the 16th century, Dingle was a walled town, and the chief port of Kerry, and had regular trade with France and Spain. It is in an Irish-speaking area, as is all the peninsula west of Annascaul.

Dingle's popularity as a tourist destination increased dramatically after the filming nearby of *Ryan's Daughter* in 1969. A further boost occurred in 1985 with the arrival from the wild of a friendly bottle-nosed dolphin known as Fungi who will play with swimmers, and follows boats in and out of the harbour.

Dingle offers an appealing combination of the bucolic – farmers regularly come to town on their tractors, perhaps with a few sheep in the trailer behind – and the sophisticated, with a choice of serious restaurants and craft shops. There is a triangular walk from the pier area, up Green Street, down Main Street and back along the Mall to the pier that takes you past the best shops, pubs and restaurants.

Continue west on the R559. Between **Ventry** and Slea Head there are over 400 *clocháns* ("beehive" huts). The farmers may charge you a nominal sum to visit them. These small conical huts of unmortared stone are not in fact prehistoric, as the farmers claim; the oldest date from the early Christian period, the 5th to 8th centuries, and were used by hermit monks. Others were built as recently as the 19th century to house farm implements. The road climbs westward around Eagle Mountain to **Slea Head,** and you will want to stop at one of the viewing points to take in the panorama.

The Blasket Islands

The group of seven rocky islands offshore are the **Blasket Islands**. **Great Blasket,** the largest one, is about 4 miles (7 km) long and ¾ mile (1.5 km) wide. It was inhabited until 1953. The islanders were great storytellers, and have made a lasting contribution to Irish literature. Below Mount Eagle is the village of **Dunquin**, a scattered settlement whose harbour was once the landing point for the islanders. Stop at Dunquin Pier, and walk down the steep, concrete path to a tiny landing place. The islanders landed here in curraghs, open fishing boats made of tarred animal hide stretched over wood.

Boats go to the island regularly in the summer, weather permitting. The **Great Blasket Centre** (tel: 066-56371, admission fee, closed Oct–Easter) is a labyrinthine interpretative centre with many old records and photographs.

Map, page 170

On towards Tralee

Gallarus Oratory (well signposted) is an extraordinary little building of unmortared "dry" stone, probably dating from the 8th century. It is in the shape of an inverted boat, with a door at the west and a window in the east wall. It remains as dry and solid as the day it was built, and is very dark inside.

There is no point in negotiating the **Connor Pass** in bad weather – take the N78 through Anascaul instead. The drive is hair-raising in all weathers as you climb steeply to 1,496 ft (456 metres) above sea level. A section of the narrow-gauge **Tralee and Dingle Light Railway**, which ran from Dingle to Tralee until 1963, has been restored at **Blennerville**. A nostalgic half-hour steam journey can be taken into Tralee (tel: 066-21064, admission fee, closed Nov–Apr).

Tralee ⑩ is the county town of Kerry, and its chief shopping centre (but don't expect a lot). While it may seem like a booming metropolis after a few days in Dingle, Tralee is generally a dull place. The exception is in August when Tralee's **Race Week** is followed by the **Rose of Tralee Festival**, a beauty and personality pageant, and the whole town parties for a week. The most attractive area is the Denny Street area near the museum, with its nicely proportioned Georgian houses. The enjoyable **Kerry County Museum** (tel: 066-27777, admission fee) is in a neo-classical building at the top of the street.

ABOVE:
Gallarus Oratory.

BELOW: The oddly shaped "Dead Man", one of the Blasket Islands off Slea Head.

THE SHANNON REGION

Map, page 170

Within easy reach of Limerick is a region of ruined castles, a dramatic coastline, spectacular caves and the eerie moon-like landscape of the Burren

Shannon Airport is on the estuary of the mighty River Shannon, the longest river in Britain or Ireland, which flows through Lough Derg, the last and the largest of its lakes, emerging into the Atlantic through a wide estuary. Limerick city, Ireland's fourth largest town sits on a bend in the river. When Shannon Airport opened in 1945 it attracted many foreign companies to its surrounding estates, and revived a region that had been in decline for most of the 20th century. Since the 1960s, high-tech multinationals have been setting up bases in the area. Limerick and its hinterland is now a prosperous region with well-developed facilities for visitors, including Bunratty Castle and Folk Park.

In the far west of the region, the coast of County Clare is a popular holiday destination among the Irish, offering a combination of Atlantic rollers, sandy beaches and imposing cliffs. The Cliffs of Moher rise almost vertically out of the sea to a height of 650 ft (200 metres). From the top you can see the Aran Islands and, to the north, across Galway Bay, the shores of Connemara. The Burren, in north Clare, consists of huge pavements of exposed grey limestone topped with massive boulders, and is often said to resemble a lunar landscape. An amazing variety of wild flowers, both Mediterranean and Alpine, grow in the crevices of the rocks.

PRECEDING PAGES: on the road to Limerick. **LEFT:** the mighty Cliffs of Moher. **BELOW:** a memorial in Limerick city to the 1916 Rising.

Limerick City

Limerick ④ (pop. 60,000) is probably Ireland's least loved city. It's a staunchly Roman Catholic and conservative place, with innumerable but not very distinguished churches. In the 17th century Limerick supported the Jacobite cause for a whole year after the defeat of James II at the Battle of the Boyne. When the Irish leader, Patrick Sarsfield, finally surrendered in 1691, the Treaty of Limerick marked the start of the denial of religious and property rights to Catholics which lasted until Daniel O'Connell's Catholic Emancipation Bill in 1829.

The bulk of the city lies to the east of the River Shannon, and until recently Limerick's city centre resolutely turned its back on the river, its best asset. New developments have concentrated on revealing attractive stretches of river, and one's spirit is less inclined to sink at the prospect of having to spend time in Limerick. A good example of this focus on the river is the **Tourist Information Office** at **Arthur's Quay** in a stylish new shopping mall, built beside a small park on the banks of the Shannon. The inland side of the TIO leads to **O'Connell Street,** Limerick's main shopping area, a mass of neon and plate glass. The liveliest part of the shopping district is the pedestrianised **Cruises Street** area.

Head north of Arthur's Quay for **The Custom**

House to view the **Hunt Museum** (tel: 061-312833, admission fee). This magnificent collection of treasures ranges from the 9th-century enamel Antrim Cross, to Egyptian, Roman and Etruscan pieces, Chinese porcelain, and even a drawing by Picasso. The collection was privately assembled by John Hunt, who was chiefly a medievalist, and his wife Gertrude, and left to the nation on his death in 1976.

The old, chiefly Georgian part of Limerick lies to the north of Arthur's Quay. **St Mary's Cathedral** dates from the 12th century when it was built in the form of a cross by Donal O'Brien, King of Munster. Not much of the original remains, but the most interesting current feature is the black oak seats of its misericords which are carved with animal figures.

King John's Castle (tel: 061-411201, admission fee) was built by the Normans in the 13th century. A recently added glass entrance hall spoils the first impressions of this imposing Anglo-Norman castle. Climb one of its round towers for a good view of the town. An audiovisual display introduces Limerick's history since its founding by the Vikings in AD922.

Also worth a visit is the **Beltable Arts Centre** (tel: 061-319866) at 69 O'Connell Street which has contemporary exhibitions and a small theatre, and the small but very pleasant **City Gallery** (tel: 061-310633) in a neo-classical building in **Pery Square** beside the **People's Park**, on the opposite side to the railway station. There is a small collection of Irish art and visiting contemporary exhibitions.

The best thing in Limerick's suburbs is the campus of the newly created (1989) **Limerick University** at **Plassey** which is a successful showcase for contemporary Irish architecture.

Limerick claims the origin of the five-line verse, known worldwide as the limerick and all too often beginning "There was a young lady from..." The genre, originally oral, was most famously adopted by the English painter and humorist Edward Lear.

BELOW: King John's Castle, Limerick.

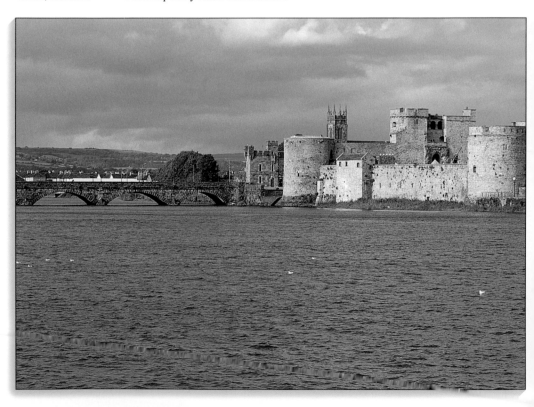

North of Limerick City

This is castle country, with ruined stumps of crumbling tower houses dotted around the place. There were once over 420 tower houses in the Limerick area. Few are as imposing nor as carefully restored as Bunratty, whose rectangular 15th-century keep is surrounded by four corner turrets, each topped with battlements and a set of flags.

Map, page 170

Bunratty Castle and Folk Park ❷ (tel: 061-360788, admission fee) is strategically placed on the road between Shannon Airport and Limerick City. It contains an interesting collection of furniture and paintings from the 15th and 16th centuries. The Folk Park behind it consists of 25 acres (10 hectares) of reconstructed and fully furnished farmhouses, cottages and shops, as they would have appeared to a visitor to mid-western Ireland in the late 19th century. There is even a village street with blacksmith, pub, drapery, print works and post office. It is aimed firmly at the first-time visitor, but is so carefully detailed that it is hard to resist getting involved. Don't miss **Durty Nelly's**, an old-world Irish pub next door to the village, which has been copied all over the world.

Another corny but enjoyable experience is the medieval Irish banquet, a purely tourist-oriented but good-natured event – essentially a meal with Irish cabaret in which the guests are serenaded by Irish colleens – which takes place twice nightly at Bunratty and also at the nearby **Knappogue Castle** (tel: 061-368103, admission fee) at **Quin** to the north of Bunratty. Knappogue is a 15th-century Macnamara stronghold that has also been fully restored and furnished in period.

The **Craggaunowen Project** (tel: 061-367178, admission fee) is built in

ABOVE: Bunratty Castle interior.
BELOW: by the River Shannon in the city.

the grounds of another castle, a 16th-century tower house. The project has reconstructed authentic replicas of dwelling places in prehistoric and pre-Christian Ireland. On an island in the lake, reached by means of a footbridge, is a *cranndg*, a fortified dwelling of clay and wattle. A small ring fort which shows how a farmer would have lived in the 5th or 6th centuries has been built. Also at Craggaunowen is the traditionally-built boat in which the writer and adventurer Tim Severin sailed to Nova Scotia in 1976, retracing the legendary 6th-century voyage of St Brendan, and making a plausible case for its historical reality.

To escape from the beaten path of the castle trail, consider an outing to **Scarriff** ❸, a quiet little town set on high ground overlooking Lough Derg. It is a true rural backwater, popular with visitors in summer and totally sleepy in the winter, which has a reputation for good traditional music. **Drewsborough House** near **Tuamgraney**, to the south of Scarriff, is the birthplace of the 20th-century novelist Edna O'Brien who has written scathing descriptions of the narrow-minded inhabitants of this area which was considered relatively remote 50 years ago.

Both Scarriff and Tuamgraney are on the scenic drive that goes all the way around **Lough Derg**, a wide, almost sea-like part of the Shannon River which is popular with watersports enthusiasts and other outdoor types. It is worth taking in at least the 5-mile (8-km) stretch northeast to **Mountshannon**, a neat 18th-century village.

Offshore you can visit **Holy Island**, an uninhabited 49-acre (20-hectare) island which had a 7th-century Christian settlement. There are the remains of five churches and a 79-ft (24-metre) high round tower.

Ennis ❹ is the county town of County Clare, a busy place with narrow streets. Its recently refurbished market area is a cheerful, brightly painted, partly pedestrianised area with numerous small shops. **Ennis Friary** (tel: 0615-21900, admission fee) beside the fast-flowing **River Fergus**, was once next to an important school with 350 friars and over 600 pupils. The remains date chiefly from the 14th century and include cloisters and a roofless church with interesting medieval stone carvings.

South of Limerick City

Lough Gur ❹ (tel: 061-85186, admission fee, closed Oct–Apr), 12 miles (19 km) due south of Limerick on the R512–R514, is one of Europe's most complete Stone Age and Bronze Age sites. It is a lovely quiet lake, rich in bird life. The **Grange Stone Circle** is 150ft (45 metres) across and contains about 100 boulders. More than 20 other stone circles, tombs, hut foundations, lakeside dwellings and ring forts have been excavated beside Lough Gur. An interpretative centre built in the form of Neolithic huts houses a collection of artefacts and has an audio-visual presentation introducing the site.

Adare ❹, 10½ miles (17 km) southwest of Limerick, is generally considered one of Ireland's prettiest villages. Several of its stone-built cottages are thatched, and they all have colourful front gardens.

Edna O'Brien's "The Country Girls" (1960) was the first of a trilogy of novels tracing the fortunes of two ex-convent girls as they escaped from rural Ireland to the bright lights of Dublin and later London.

BELOW: pasture near Lough Gur.

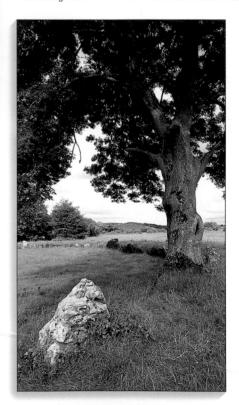

Adare is noted for its antique dealers, but don't expect great bargains. Opposite the Dunraven Arms Hotel is the entrance to **Adare Manor**. This was the seat of the Earls of Dunraven, who built the picturesque cottages that line the village for their workers. It is now an American-owned luxury hotel. The original 18th-century manor was enlarged in the Gothic Revival style in the mid-19th century. The architect Augustus Pugin, who was also responsible for London's Houses of Parliament, did some of the work. The splendidly grandiose result makes it worth going in for a coffee and a look. Don't miss the Great Hall with its massive stone chimney piece.

Rathkeale **47** is more of a typical Irish village – its long main street of small shops and bleak-looking houses straggling along the road. It is worth going there to visit **Castle Matrix** (tel: 069-64284, admission fee, closed mid-Sept to mid-May), a 15th-century tower house that was rescued and restored by an American architect and military historian, the late Seán O'Driscoll. The castle is sumptuously furnished with interesting objects. It has a tiny chapel on its top floor, and a medieval bedroom. Its library contains a collection of documents relating to the Wild Geese, Irishmen who served in European armies in the 17th and 18th centuries. There is also a collection of weaponry from the Middle Ages and earlier. It is said that Sir Walter Raleigh and the poet Edmund Spenser met here while they were both serving in Ireland.

Situated on the south bank of the Shannon Estuary, **Foynes 48** played an important part in aviation history. In the late 1930s flying boats would land on the sheltered stretch of the Shannon between Foynes Island and the shore, having made the transatlantic crossing from Newfoundland. **Foynes Museum** (tel: 069-65416, admission fee, closed Nov–Feb except by appointment) com-

Map, page 170

Rathkeale's ancient origins are underlined by its Gaelic name, Ráth Caola, meaning Caola's Ring-fort.

BELOW: slowly through the lanes of Limerick.

memorates those days with models and photographs, and includes the original terminal building, radio room and weather forecasting equipment. It was at Foynes during the flying boat days that Irish Coffee – coffee and whiskey topped with whipped cream – was invented by an enterprising barman who wanted to cheer up a group of cold, travel-weary passengers who had been forced back by bad weather.

Glin derives from the Gaelic An Gleann, meaning The Valley. It is an important centre for the dairy industry.

There is a pleasant drive along the wooded shores of the estuary to **Glin Castle** 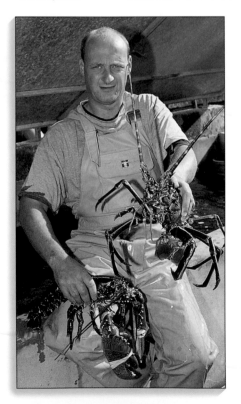 (tel: 068-34173, admission fee. By appointment outside May and June). There has been a Fitzgerald castle on this site, right on the banks of the Shannon, for over 700 years. The present house, which is surrounded by formal gardens and parkland, is an 18th-century building. The crennelations and Gothic details which make it look like a fairy-tale castle were added in the mid-19th century. There is an amazing "flying staircase" in its entrance hall with delicate balustrades and a mahogany handrail. The hall also has a superb plaster work ceiling. The head of the Fitzgerald clan is known as the Knight of Glin. The present (29th) Knight, Desmond Fitzgerald, is a keen campaigner for Irish heritage, and a former curator at London's Victoria and Albert Museum. The interior of the house is impeccable, and houses an impressive collection of 18th-century furniture, ceramic and paintings.

From Glin it is only 7 km (4 miles) to **Tarbert** where a car ferry will take you across the Shannon Estuary in 20 minutes to County Clare.

The coast of West Clare

BELOW: a fresh catch at Carrigaholt.

From Ennis take the N68 to Kilrush. Kilrush is 5½ miles (9 km) west of Killimer, where the car ferry from north Kerry docks. **Kilrush** ⑤, with a population of 2740, is the biggest town, or village if you prefer, on the coast of west Clare. Like Adare, Kilrush was designed by a local landlord in the 18th century to complement his estate. Unlike Adare's cottagey English pastiche, the style chosen for Kilrush is pleasantly neo-classical, with wide streets and a main square big enough to accommodate horse fairs which are still held there regularly. Kilrush, which has good sandy beaches nearby, became popular with the people of Limerick as a holiday resort in the 19th century. This and other local lore is explained in the **Kilrush Heritage Centre** (tel: 065-51577, admission fee, closed Oct–Apr) in the main square.

The ruins of the Vandeleur family mansion, which was destroyed by fire in 1897, are at the centre of the 420-acre (170-hectare) **Kilrush Forest Park** (freely accessible). Kilrush recently acquired a 120-berth marina. A 15-minute boat ride from the marina will take you to **Scattery Island** which has a 6th-century monastery founded by St Senan, the remains of five churches and a round tower. **Scattery Island Visitor Centre** (tel: 065-52139, closed mid-Sept to mid-June) explains the history of the island.

Kilkee, 8½ miles (13 km) to the west, is on the Atlantic coast of Clare, as opposed to the banks of the Shannon Estuary, and has a good sandy beach. There is a scenic drive from there south to **Loop Head** lighthouse, a round trip of about 34 miles (55km). At

Carrigaholt there is a 16th-century tower house beside the pier with good views from its top floor across the Shannon Estuary to north Kerry. A **dolphin watching cruise** (tel: 065-584711, booking essential) operates from Carrigaholt daily in summer, weather permitting, to watch families of bottle-nosed dolphins playing in the estuary.

There are good sandy beaches, popular with surfers, wind surfers and families, all the way up the coast to Lahinch. **Lahinch** is chiefly famous for its golf links. **Ennistymon**, 2½ miles (4 km) inland is a charming, old-fashioned resort town on the **Cullenagh River** which has retained many original wooden shop fronts. The river has a series of waterfalls visible from its seven-arched bridge.

A short (5½-mile/9-km) drive inland from Ennistymon will allow you to visit the **Burren Centre** (tel:065-88030, admission fee, closed Dec to mid-Mar) at **Kilfenora** ⑤. The small, low-tech visitor centre provides a good introduction to this unusual region. This tiny village also has the remains of a 12th-century cathedral and three 12th-century high crosses with weathered but still decipherable carvings.

All roads around here lead to the **Cliffs of Moher** ㉒, or so it seems from the innumerable signposts. Park at the **Visitor Centre** (tel: 061-360788, closed Nov–Feb) which will introduce you to the flora and fauna of the area, and explain the local bird life. Don't be put off by the crowds and the buskers at the bottom of the hill – the razzmatazz is easy to escape by simply walking up to the cliffs themselves. The great, dark shale and sandstone cliffs are magnificent, rising 650 ft (200 metres) sheer above the Atlantic and stretching for about 5 miles (8km). At their base the Atlantic waves throw white spume on

Map, page 170

ABOVE: the Sea Life Centre at Lahinch. **BELOW:** pitch and putt at Lahinch.

ABOVE:
fresh produce on
sale at Ailwee Cave.

BELOW: a waterfall
in Ailwee Cave.

to jagged stacks. In summer you can spot comical-looking puffins nesting on the ledges, while numerous other seabirds wheel around in the up-currents.

Doolin (also called Roadford on some maps) is a tiny village consisting of numerous B&Bs and hostels, several restaurants and three pubs. The pubs are renowned for traditional music. Some young musicians spend the whole summer camping here, learning from their elders.

There is a 45-minute open-boat ferry from Doolin pier to **Inisheer**, the smallest of the bleak but romantic **Aran Islands**, which makes an interesting day trip (*see pages 253–4*).

The Burren

You will have noticed an absence of trees on driving up the coast. The Atlantic wind means that trees grow very slowly here, and seldom reach any great height. Many were cut down for fuel in the past 150 years when times were hard, and there is no tradition of replacing them.

Beyond Doolin the deeply fissured limestone plateau of the **Burren** dominates. The limestone is revealed in great irregular slabs known as pavements, with deep cracks between them. Their geological name is karst, from an area in Yugoslavia with similar terrain. Turloughs, seasonal lakes which disappear underground in dry weather, appear at times on the plateau's surface. As far as the eye can see the landscape is grey, which comes as quite a shock after the predominant green of the rest of Ireland. So barren did it look to Oliver Cromwell's troops in the 17th century that they declared that here was neither wood to hang a man, water to drown him nor earth to bury him. The Burren is of immense botanical interest (*see feature on pages 226–7*).

The best Burren drive goes inland through **Lisdoonvarna ㊾**, an odd little spa town with hot water springs, where Ireland's bachelor farmers congregate in September for the Matchmaking Festival at which they attempt, usually half-heartedly, to find a wife. Continue down the switchback **Corkscrew Hill** to **Ballyvaughan**, a lively little seaside village, and back to Lisdoonvarna around **Black Head**. Scattered throughout the region are tombs, chambers and dolmens of the Stone Age, notably near Corkscrew Hill, the Poulnabrone Dolmen, 2500BC. Beyond Black Head the three **Aran Islands**, are visible in the west. In some weathers they appear to be floating and drifting, due to tricks of light.

If you are keen to see the Burren from the inside, stop at Ballyvaughan to visit **Ailwee Cave** (tel: 065-77036, admission fee, closed Dec–mid-Mar). The guided tour takes you through a tunnel stretching for ¾ mile (1 km) into the Burren which contains stalactites and stalagmites, and ends at a waterfall which is floodlit from below.

There is a pleasant scenic drive from Ballyvaughan along the south shore of Galway Bay to **Kinvara**, a charming little fishing village at the head of Galway Bay, with a grassy quayside. Kinvara is increasingly popular with visitors, who enjoy its old-fashioned pubs and more up-to-the-minute restaurants. The highlight of the year is the annual *Cruinniú na mBád* in mid-August, literally "the gathering of the boats". This is a festive regatta in which traditional Connemara sailing craft – the famous brown-sailed Galway Hookers – which were once used to carry turf across the bay, race against each other in a grand spectacle.

The other sight to see in Kinvara is the floodlit **Dunguaire Castle** (tel: 091-371108, admission fee, closed Nov–Apr), a four-storey tower house built by the shore in 1520. At night this lonely sentinel is used for medieval banqueting, hence the floodlighting.

The easiest way back to the N18 from Kinvara is the R347 Ardrahan road. Turn right at the N18 in the Gort direction to visit **Thoor Ballylee** ⑤ (tel: 091-31436, admission fee, closed Oct–Easter), a 16th-century tower house which was the summer home of the Nobel prize-winning poet W. B. Yeats from 1917 to 1928. The tower is carefully restored with much of Yeats's original furniture, and beautifully situated in a wooded area near a stream, but the incessant audio commentary that follows you around the interior is unnecessarily intrusive.

The tower house was discovered for the poet by his benefactor, Lady Gregory (1852–1932), herself a playwright and collector of folklore. Her house at **Coole Park** ⑤ just off the Gort road was demolished in 1947, but its grounds are now a national park with a deer enclosure, forest walks and a lake whose petrified trees stick out of the water. In the walled garden is a great copper beech tree on which Lady Gregory's guests – Yeats, the playwrights George Bernard Shaw, J. M. Synge and Sean O'Casey, the poet John Masefield and the painter Augustus John – carved their initials.

The N18 continues south to Ennis and north to Galway.

Map, page 170

ABOVE: the autograph tree at Coole Park. **BELOW:** Dunguaire Castle, Kinvara.

THE BURREN

North Clare contains one of Ireland's strangest landscapes, a treeless limestone plateau which is a place of pilgrimage for botanists and geologists

A frustrated general serving Oliver Cromwell, one of the many ruthless invaders from across the Irish Sea, famously condemned this bleak place as having "not enough wood to hang a man, not enough water to drown him, not enough clay to cover his corpse." The view probably hasn't changed much in 350 years, but now the Burren (meaning great rock) is a national park. It covers 500 sq. km (200 sq. miles) of lunar-like limestone formation with delicate flora and fauna of Arctic, Alpine and Mediterranean origin, brought to the area by migrating birds. Here you will find, in seasonal abundance – but protected by the State – orchids, the purple bloddy cranesbill and azeleas. The Burren is also an area of potholes, seasonal lakes, caves and streams.

THE VIEW FROM CORKSCREW HILL

Properly appreciating the extraordinary nature of the place requires some study. The Burren Experience, on the northside of Ballyvaughan village, on the Kinvara road, gives an introduction, but a finer overview can be had at the original Burren Centre, to the south in Kilfenora village. A good overall view of this "stony district" can be had from the so-called "Corkscrew" Hill on the road lining Ballyvaughan with Lisdoonvarna, but by far the best way to explore the fissured terrain is on foot.

Scattered throughout the region are tombs, chambers and dolmens of the Stone Age – notably, near Corkscrew Hill, the famous Poulnabrone Dolmen, 2500BC.

▽ OCEAN FURY
Co. Clare is very much part of the western seaboard, from its natural boundary of the Shannon estuary to its northern border with Galway. The full force of the Atlantic can be felt here and lighthouses played a vital part in warning ships clear of the treacherous coastline.

◁ A HARDY BREED
It is surprising to find, in such a stony landscape, pockets of small green fields. But sheep farmers need to be a determined breed to survive the bleak winters in the west of Ireland. Animal farming has always flourished, though, because of the Burren's natural mineral wealth, which has proved particularly beneficial for horse breeding.

THE TOMBS THAT HAVE DEFIED TIME

Poulnabrone Dolmen (above) dates from 2500BC and is a striking example of the many ancient monuments which are particularly common in this part of Ireland because of the ready availability of limestone slabs. Its name means "pool of sorrows". Because its massive cap-stone is set at an angle, it has been fancifully called a launching-pad for a Stone Age missile.

Such single-chambered portal graves were originally covered with a mound of earth and stones, and are a testament to the great reverence the Neolithic people had for their dead.

Passage-graves, in which the burial chamber was reached through a passage, reveal sophisticated building techniques and often intricate abstract carvings. Some of Europe's most spectacular examples can be seen at Newgrange, west of Drogheda in Co. Louth.

Stone circles, which served as prehistoric temples, are probably related to the megalithic tombs. Some of the most impressive can be found at Lough Gur in Co. Limerick and near Hollywood in Co. Wicklow.

The commonest monument is the ring fort – about 30,000 survive. These were circular stone defences surrounding dwellings or royal seats.

◁ BRONZE AGE SECRETS

Carran, to the east of the Burren, means the Cairn and has yielded up some of the most useful archaeological evidence of Bronze Age life. The stones that today form walls to keep the wind at bay were then used to construct a great cairn of stones 8ft high and 50ft in diameter (2.4 by 15 metres) which protected the bodies in the burial mound. At Kilnaboy, in the upland part of the Burren, the magnificent stone fort of Cahercommaun, dating from the 7th to the 10th centuries. The outermost of its three massive walls was 450ft (140 metres) in diameter.

△ AN ANCIENT RUIN

Lemaneagh Castle, on route R476 from Kilfenora through Killinaboy, dates from 1480. It was once owned by a formidable woman, Máire Rua McMahon (Red-haired Mary), who saw off two husbands, including one of Oliver Cromwell's officers, but she held on to Lemaneagh.

▽ PLETHORA OF PLANTS

Pictured below is bird's-foot trefoil (Lotus corniculatus), one of the many plants which flourish in the apparently inhospitable landscape of the Burren. They are nurtured by a unique combination of soil, heat and moisture.

◁ LUNAR LANDSCAPE

This bleak limestone terrain had its origins 70 million years ago when shells of marine animals were compacted on the seabed and later pushed above the waves by geological shifts. A soft rock, the limestone has been eroded by wind and rain, creating cracks and crevices which both drain off rainwater and provide shelter for the remarkable variety of fauna.

Midlands and Far West Region

THE MIDLANDS

*Water, in the form of bogs, lakes and rivers, dominates
this often overlooked region. Fishing and boating are
the big attractions, and the landscapes are seductive*

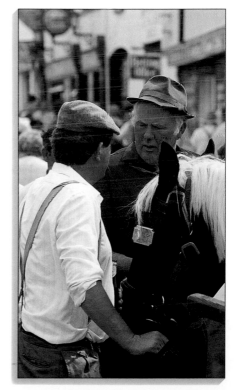

Map,
page 230

Irish schoolchildren used to be taught that Ireland could be visualis   s a
saucer, the raised rim standing for the hilly coastal regions, and the flat base
representing the low-lying Midlands. Not only are the Midlands low-lying; a
high proportion of the so-called land is in fact water of one kind or another, and
if not water, then it is bog. The tract of country running north from County I ois
through Offaly, Westmeath, Longford and Roscommon consists of bog pasture
and water: canals, scores of rivers, hundreds of lakes and streams, thousa of
ditches, all of them feeding into the River Shannon which bisects the region.
Little wonder that many of the visitors to the region are keen anglers.

Most visitors to Ireland who venture beyond Dublin go either to the coastal
areas or the mountain and wilderness areas. The Midlands of Ireland have to
work harder to attract visitors than naturally spectacular places like Killarney
or Connemara. Vast improvements have taken place over the past 10 years to
ensure that visitors will be entertained and looked after. Hotels, restaurants
and B&Bs have improved greatly, while major heritage attractions like
Strokestown House and Famine Museum, Carriglas Manor, Birr Castle
Gardens and Emo Court are being enthusiastically discovered by independent
travellers, and are even tempting the occasional tour bus away from the beat-
en track.

PRECEDING PAGES:
Lough Key.
LEFT: fresh fruit at
the fete.
BELOW: farmers
confer at market.

The towns of the Midlands are not especially exciting. While it's one thing to pass through and admire
their old-fashioned charm, most visitors are probably
very glad that they don't have to live full-time in these
small, architecturally undistinguished, often culturally dormant communities. Nevertheless, their shops
and pubs can be enjoyable if you are susceptible to
antiquated ways of doing things. Readers of William
Trevor's Irish short stories will feel at home in the
Midlands. "Time warp" is the expression that comes
to mind. You are far more likely to find a bar with groceries on one side and tall stools, whiskey and
Guinness on the other in the Midlands than you are in
the more picturesque and fashionable Connemara or
West Cork.

Bog Rail Tour

Ballinasloe , the chief town of east County Galway,
has long been an important crossing place of the
River Suck, and marks a kind of border, more psychological than physical between the west of Ireland
and the Midlands.

Take the R357 to **Shannonbridge** ❷. This is the
point where county Galway meets counties Offaly and
Roscommon, and the River Suck flows into the River
Shannon. You will see a lot of bog in the Midlands, in
various stages of development, and the **Clonmacnois**

The 13-ft (4-metre) Cross of the Scriptures at Clonmacnois dates from the 10th century and has scenes from the Last Judgment and the Crucifixion.

BELOW: roadside sales; O'Rourke's Tower, Clanmacnois, dating from 1124.

and West Offaly Railway (tel: 0905-74114, admission fee, closed Nov–Mar) just outside Shannonbridge on the R357, provides an excellent introduction to its flora and fauna. The narrow-gauge railway takes a slow 5-mile (8-km) circular tour across the **Blackwater Bog**. Ironically, it is run by **Bord na Mona**, the state-run Irish Peat Board, who also run the nearby **Blackwater Power Station**, which is powered by peat, as the brown smoke belching from its chimneys confirms. The tour includes a view of the various stages in harvesting the peat, and you can have a go yourself with a special sharp spade called a slane. The tour also gives you a close-up view of the plants that thrive in this intensely acid environment.

Clonmacnois ❸ (tel: 0905-74134, admission fee) is one of Ireland's most important monastic sites, superbly located on a bend in the River Shannon. It was built on an esker, or natural gravel ridge, that overlooks a large marshy area. The monastery was founded in AD545 by St Kieran and was the burial place of the Kings of Connaught and Tara. While it may appear remote today, in earlier centuries transport for pilgrims was easier by water than over land.

The earliest of the surviving ruins dates from the 9th century. The monastery was regularly plundered from then onwards by the Irish, the Vikings and the Anglo-Normans until it was destroyed in the Elizabethan wars of the mid-16th century by the English garrison from Athlone. Nevertheless, there is still plenty to be seen. The Visitor Centre has a collection of carved grave slabs dating from the 9th to the 12th centuries, as well as a helpful audio-visual presentation.

Among the older surviving buildings is the shell of a small cathedral, two round towers, the remains of eight smaller churches and several high crosses.

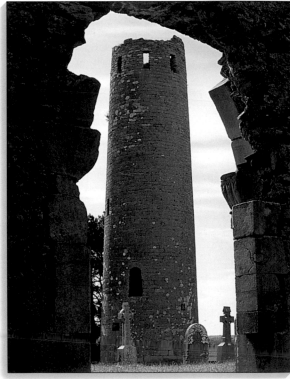

There are various doorways and chancel arches in the Irish Romanesque style. One of the churches, Temple Connor, was restored by the Church of Ireland in 1911 and is used for services.

**Map,
page 230**

Around Lough Derg

Head south for **Shannon Harbour**, the junction of the Grand Canal and the River Shannon which is a popular mooring place for river cruisers. About 5 miles (8 km) further south is **Banagher ❹**, another popular boating centre with a new marina. This pretty, one-street village will be eerie and empty in winter, and bustling with river enthusiasts in summer.

Birr ❺ is an attractive Georgian town, more or less in the centre of Ireland, dominated by **Birr Castle and Demesne** (tel: 0509-20336, admission fee). The gardens of Birr Castle cover 100 acres (40 hectares) and have more than 1,000 species of trees and shrubs with an especially strong Chinese and Himalayan collection. In spring, magnolias, crab apples and cherries will be in flower; in the autumn, maples, chestnut and weeping beech supply colour. The box hedges which subdivide the formal gardens are in the *Guinness Book of Records* as the highest in the world.

The 17th-century castle is private, but its stable block now houses **Ireland's Historic Science Centre** (tel. as above). The owners of Birr Castle, the Parsons family, later ennobled as the Earls of Rosse, have manifested a scientific bent for several generations. In the 1840s the 3rd Earl of Rosse built the Great Telescope which enabled him to see further into space than any of his contemporaries. The telescope, which has a 56-ft (17-metre) tube and a 6-ft (1.8-metre) mirror, was in use until 1908. It has now been rebuilt and

TIP

Fans of Georgian houses can find some good examples in Birr, in John's Mall and Oxmantown Mall.

BELOW: Birr Castle.

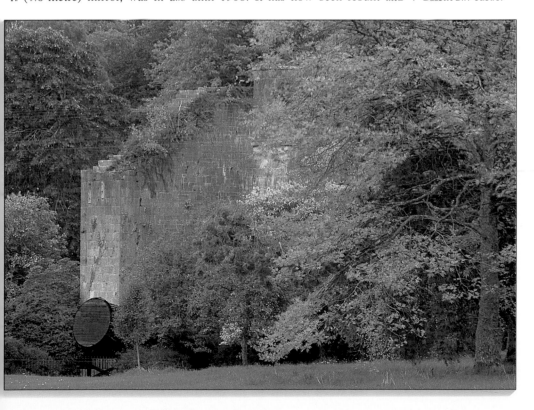

restored to working order. Astronomy, photography, and engineering are the main themes of the science centre.

Walk into town along **Oxmanton Mall**, a tree-lined thoroughfare which leads from the gates of the castle past a row of elegant Georgian houses. **Emmet Square** in the town centre is the location of **Dooly's Hotel** (1740) which gave its name to the Galway Blazers when they set fire to it after a Hunt Ball in 1809, almost but not quite destroying the building.

From Birr, head to **Borrisokane** and the western shores of **Lough Derg ❻**. At Lough Derg the Shannon widens into a 50 sq. mile (130 sq. km) lake that is about 10 miles (16km) across at its widest point. This side is in County Tipperary and the west of the lake is in County Clare. The circular **Lough Derg Drive** (about 50 miles/90km) passes through a succession of pretty villages, but the lake itself is not always visible. The villages on this side of Lough Derg are peaceful, out-of-the-way places to stay that have recently been gaining in popularity. Most visitors either have a boat of some kind or are interested in fishing – mainly coarse angling – on the lake. Others enjoy walking, both near the lake and on the other side of Birr in the way-marked trails of the **Slieve Bloom Mountains**.

Terryglass is one of the prettiest villages, although you have to leave the main road to find the lake. **Dromineer** on the other hand is right on the water, and has a ruined castle on its pier. Many of the people you meet in the pubs will be temporarily living on river cruisers which they own or have hired.

Nenagh ❼ is a Tipperary market town with the disadvantage of being on the busy Dublin-Limerick main road. All that remains of the original Norman settlement is the **Nenagh Castle Keep**, or donjon, with walls 20 ft (6 metres)

ABOVE: good country for walkers.

BELOW: Nenagh.

thick. It reaches to a height of 100 ft (30 metres). Across the road in the **Governor's House** of the old town gaol is the **Nenagh Heritage Centre** (tel: 067-326633, admission fee) which includes the condemned cells and execution room of the gaol, and a museum of rural life

Roscrea ❽, further up the N7 in the Dublin direction, is also plagued by traffic. In fact, the Dublin–Limerick road actually cuts through the remains of the 12th-century **St Cronan's Abbey**. As you sit in a traffic jam on a bend in the road, you will probably see the west facade, which is all that remains, with a round-arched doorway containing a moulded figure of St Cronan. Roscrea is worth visiting to see its Norman castle which contains an 18th-century town house, Damer House, within its walls. The 13th-century castle is a polygonal structure with two D-shaped towers. The gate house is topped by 18th-century gables and chimneys. It now houses the **Roscrea Heritage Centre** (tel: 0505 21850, admission fee includes Damer House) which has an interesting exhibit on Norman castles.

Damer House, which stand inside the castle walls, is an elegant, three-storied house dating from the 18th century with a plain, symmetrical facade and a handsome pine staircase. It was completed in the 1720s and became a Bishop's Palace before being converted to a military barracks in 1798. It was very nearly demolished in the 1970s to make room for a car park but was saved through the vigilance of the Irish Georgian Society.

Great Irish houses
Travel east again, by-passing **Portlaoise**, to visit **Emo Court** (tel: 0502-26573, admission fee; house closed mid-Sept–May). This fine Georgian man-

Map, page 230

The 8th-century Book of Dimma, which once belonged to Roscrea monastery, can now be seen in Trinity College, Dublin. It includes a copy of the Gospels.

BELOW: tranquillity on the borders of Co. Meath and Co. Cavan.

sion was built in 1792 for the Earl of Portarlington in the Classical style by James Gandon, best known for Dublin's Four Courts and Custom House. It was restored and donated to the nation in 1996 by a private benefactor. The interior has some fine plaster work. The gardens were created in two parts. The Clucker, named because it was once the site of the nun's quarters of an ancient abbey, is planted with azaleas, rhododendrons and Japanese maples. The Grapery is planted with trees and shrubs and leads down to the lakeside walk.

Half a mile west of Tullamore is Shrah Castle, built in 1588. It is a good example of the small fortified house that Elizabethan settlers constructed.

There is another interesting recently restored house in an entirely different style to the north near **Tullamore** ❾, **Charleville Forest Castle** (tel: 0506-21279, admission fee; appointment required Oct–Mar). The house was designed by Francis Johnston in 1798 in the neo-Gothic style. It is built of grey limestone. An internal gallery extends the full length of the garden front, and is decorated with plaster work. The morning room, music room and dining room are also of impressive size and proportion, and are decorated in the William Morris style. Five avenues lined by Irish yew trees radiate from the house. The grounds include many impressive trees including an oak which is believed to be 700 years old.

Around Lough Ennel

BELOW: Lough Ennel; at play in Bantry Golf Club.

Follow the N52 from Tullamore for 7½ miles (12 km) north to **Kilbeggan** ❿. **Locke's Distillery** (tel: 0506-32134, admission fee), advertised for miles around, is on the banks of the River Brosna which is fed by springs from nearby Lough Ennel. It is said that all good whiskey depends on the water that goes into the distillation process. The distillery was in use from 1757 to 1953,

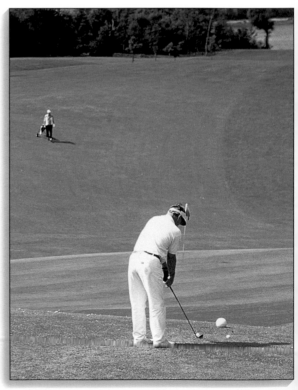

and much of the original equipment is still in place. Although there are enticing smells of malt and oak as you view the equipment, unfortunately there is
no end product to taste as you leave, an omission which may disappoint some
thirsty visitors.

The low-lying **Lough Ennel** can be seen from the N6 between Kilbeggan
and Mullingar. It is a popular place for swimming, boating and fishing.
Belvedere House and Gardens (tel: 044-42820, admission fee, closed
Nov–Mar) is remarkable for its beautiful setting, with terraced gardens
descending in three stages to the shores of the lake. The house is currently
under renovation and will eventually open to the public. The family history
behind Belvedere House is far from edifying – the first Earl of Belvedere,
who built the house as a fishing lodge in 1740, spent his life fighting with his
younger brothers, and imprisoned his wife for 31 years in another house on
suspicion of an adulterous affair with one of them. He actually built a ruin, in
a part of the world where you will have noticed that ruins abound, in order to
block his view of the house where his brother lived. This large and oddly
attractive Gothic folly is known as the **Jealous Wall**.

Mullingar , the chief town of County Westmeath, is an important cattle-
dealing centre which is also popular with anglers. If things military appeal,
the **Military Museum** (tel: 044-48391, phone in advance for appointment)
should not be missed. It contains weaponry from both world wars, uniforms
and flags from all over the world and a section dedicated to the old IRA (as
distinct from the current incarnation). The museum is run by the army, curat-
ed by an army captain who will show you around, and is actually in the
Columb Barracks.

Map,
page 230

*Fishermen like Irish
trout because most are
wild – a rarity in
Europe. Some lakes
are stocked with fully
grown fish, but finger-
lings reared from wild
stock are more usual.
There are also some
lakes stocked with
rainbow trout.*

BELOW: brown trout
can be found in
Lough Ennel.

*Lady Antonia Fraser,
part of the Longford
clan, is famous as the
biographer of Mary
Queen of Scots and
Oliver Cromwell. She
is married to the play-
wright Harold Pinter.*

BELOW: Lough
Derravaragh.

Around Lough Derravaragh

Tullynally Castle (tel: 044-61159, admission fee; house open mid-June to mid-Aug), to the north of Mullingar, just beyond **Castlepollard** , used to be known as Pakenham Hall. This massive, grey stone, turreted house overlooking **Lough Derravaragh** is well worth a visit. It has been the seat of the Pakenham family, now the Earls of Longford, since 1655. The current family includes the Socialist peer, Lord Longford, his biographer wife Elizabeth, his historian son Thomas, and their daughters, biographer Antonia Fraser and novelist Rachel Billington. The castle is the home of Thomas Pakenham.

The original fort was converted into a two-storey house in the 18th century. A Gothic facade was added in the early 19th century, and in the mid-19th century Sir Richard Morrison designed the central tower and two wings. There is an entertaining upstairs-downstairs guided tour, which includes the Great Hall, the library (which is one of Ireland's largest private collections with over 8,000 volumes), the drawing room and also the kitchen and laundry, fully equipped as in Victorian times. The landscaped gardens, which include a grotto, have spectacular views of Lough Derravaragh.

Multyfarnham, a 2-mile (3-km) detour off the N4 Longford road, is a one-street town with some pleasantly old-fashioned pubs. Multyfarnham's **Cistercian monastery**, founded in 1306, has an attractive slender tower 88 ft (27 metres) high. The abbey was restored by the Franciscans in 1973. Its new stained-glass windows show the legend of the Children of Lir who were turned into swans and lived nearby on Lough Derravaragh. The Franciscans have built a life-size Stations of the Cross in a grove of evergreens beside a fast-flowing stream.

Just to the north of Longford, **Carriglas Manor** (tel: 043-45165, admission fee; tour by appointment only) has been the home of the Lefroy family, who are of Huguenot descent, since the late 18th century. Jeffry and Tessa Lefroy offer a lively guided tour full of family anecdotes. They will show you ancestral portraits, Victorian costumes and 18th-century furniture, and tell you about the ancestor who nearly married Jane Austen. Oddly enough, the stables are considered more interesting architecturally than the house. They were designed by James Gandon, architect of the Dublin Custom House. The stables are now converted for self-catering accommodation.

If you can only visit one stately home in the Midlands, then follow the N5 for 25 miles (40 km) west of Longford to **Strokestown Park House and Famine Museum** ⓭ (tel: 078-33013, admission fee, closed Oct–April and Mondays). The village leads you to an imposing Georgian-Gothic arch which leads to the house. The village, with its exceptionally broad main street, was laid out in the early 19th century to complement the new entrance. The house itself is a fine Palladian mansion designed by Sir Richard Cassels in the 1730s. The central block was the family's residence while the wings either side contained the stables and the kitchen areas. The kitchen is especially interesting. A gallery runs above it from which the lady of the house could oversee the staff without entering the kitchen itself. Each Monday morning she would drop a menu with instructions for the week's meals. Tunnels to hide the movements of tradesmen and servants link the main block of the house to the kitchens and stables. The walled garden is also being restored, but needs more time to mature.

The house, which is accessible by guided tour only (40 minutes) was at the

The great period of country house building in Ireland began in the early 1720s. English architects who had studied in Italy introduced Palladianism and soon a diluted version of the style appeared everywhere, from village churches to farmhouses.

BELOW: traditional piper.

Map,
page 230

In Roscommon town itself, the ruins of a Dominican priory contain the tomb of the priory's 13th-century founder, Felim O Connor. The carved tomb vividly displays the clothes and armour worn at that time.

BELOW: an Athlone shopkeeper. **RIGHT:** where freedom is a cabin cruiser.

centre of a large estate. It stayed in the Mahon family until 1979 when it was bought by a local businessman and restored. Allow another hour to do justice to the **Famine Museum**, which is housed in the stable yard. This presents a vivid and comprehensive display which traces the history of the family and the estate and links this to the national events in the mid-19th century which led to the Great Famine and the subsequent mass emigration. Parallels are drawn between economic conditions in Ireland in the 19th century and in the Third World in the 20th century.

Roscommon ⓮, to the south of Strokestown, is a pleasant market town built on a low hill in the midst of rich cattle and sheep country. **Roscommon Castle** (freely accessible), to the north of the town, is an impressive ruin on a green field site. It was originally a 13th-century Norman stronghold. It has massive walls defended by round bastions at each corner, and the mullioned windows can still be seen in some of the remaining walls.

Around Lough Ree

Thanks to the new ring road around Athlone, it is possible to drive from Roscommon to **Glassan** which is about 6 miles (10 km) outside Athlone, without going through Athlone's often traffic-clogged centre. Glassan is one of a series of pretty villages on the eastern shore of **Lough Ree**, which is part of the **River Shannon**. There are good amenities for watersports, attractive country pubs and restaurants, and a series of lakeshore and forest walks.

The poet and dramatist Oliver Goldsmith (1730–74), best known for his 1773 comedy *She Stoops to Conquer*, is associated with this area. The house where he grew up, now in ruins, **Lissoy Parsonage**, can be visited near the village called **The Pigeons**.

Athlone ⓯, which straddles the **River Shannon** at an important strategic point to the south of Lough Ree, has the distinction of being half in County Westmeath and half in County Roscommon. It is now an important commercial centre, and the busiest town in the Midlands. **Athlone Castle** (tel: 0902-92912, admission fee, closed Nov–Mar) is a squat, 13th-century building, which was badly damaged in 1690 when the Irish made a stand here against the advance of Oliver Cromwell's forces. The castle keep now houses a **Folk Museum** which includes souvenirs of the tenor John McCormack, who was born in Athlone in 1884. The area behind the castle is being promoted as Athlone's "Left Bank". There are some nice old town houses dating from the 18th and 19th centuries, several good restaurants and bars, but the project has a way to go yet.

You will notice that even relatively modest restaurants in Athlone tend to have trilingual menus. This is because the town is very popular with people holidaying on Shannon cruisers, most of whom eat ashore as often as they can.

The nicest thing to do in Athlone is to take a boat trip up the Shannon to Lough Ree. Boats leave regularly between June and August for a 90 minute cruise from the **Jolly Mariner Marina** (tel: 0902-72892) on the Shannon's Right (west) Bank.

THE FAR WEST

Beyond Galway city lies a wild, romantic landscape at the very edge of Europe where Irish is still spoken. But can the increasing number of visitors still find solitude?

Galway city ⓰ stands at the mouth of the salmon-filled river that flows between **Lough Corrib** and the sea. It began as a fishing village, but by the 13th century had become a walled and fortified town in the most sheltered corner of **Galway Bay**. The fishing village survived until the mid-1930s as a neat collection of picturesque thatched cottages. They were demolished, for sanitary reasons, and replaced by the present-day Claddagh, a cluster of grey, slated cottages. The place has given its name to the distinctive Claddagh finger-ring, carrying a crowned heart motif between two hands.

The city developed as a Norman-English settlement surrounded by hostile natives. Its governors were very loyal to the English crown and the city gained its Royal Charter, as an independent city state, from Richard III in 1484. This led to a long period of political stability, material prosperity and increased trade with England and the Continent. During this period the city was ruled by the representatives of the 14 most prominent families, or Tribes, and Galway is still known as the City of the Tribes.

The style in which they lived can be judged by what remains of their architecture. The **Church of St Nicholas**, on the market place, is the largest parish church of the medieval period in Ireland and has been the Anglican Cathedral since the Reformation. Lynch's Castle, town house of the premier Tribe, is now a bank on the main street, and **Browne's Gateway**, which was the entrance to the town house of another great merchant family, has been erected at **Eyre Square**, near the **John F. Kennedy Memorial Garden**.

Myth makers

In a country where myth is often as potent as history, and in a city much given to creative folklore, the visitor will hear much that must be taken with a grain of salt. One of the main tourist "sights" in Galway is **Lynch's Window** where, in 1493, Walter Lynch, mayor of the city, hanged his own son for the murder of a Spanish guest. It was a crime of passion and such was the son's popularity with the people that the mayor feared a mob would release him from jail. He then decided to perform the hangman's task himself. Some writers have speculated that this event originated the term "lynch law". However, historians have found no basis for the story in any of the contemporary records. But the window is worth seeing and is only around the corner from the Church of St Nicholas, where Christopher Columbus is reputed to have heard Mass before leaving to discover America. The "evidence" for this is that one of his crew was known as William of Galway.

Much more of the architectural excellence of this period in Galway's history would have survived had the

PRECEDING PAGES: Clifden, Connemara. **LEFT** and **BELOW:** turf is big business in the boggy Far West.

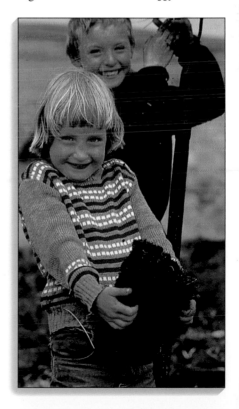

city fathers not backed the wrong political horse in the middle of the 17th century. But they staunchly backed England's Royalist forces against Cromwell's invading army and paid the price. When the city was forced to surrender in 1652, the Roundheads pillaged, plundered and burnt, destroying many of the finest stately homes. All that remains of the elaborate city walls is the portion known as the **Spanish Arch** across the river from Claddagh.

Although this military defeat resulted in the decline of Galway as a major port and commercial centre, it also began a new relationship between the city and its hinterland. Today, Galway is the only city or town in Ireland where two languages, English and Irish, can be heard spoken daily in the streets. In summer many other languages can be heard as the city has become one of the country's busiest tourist centres: the gateway to the Aran Islands, Connemara and Mayo.

Galway's gatherings

Galway today is a prosperous place. In 1986 it became Ireland's first newly created borough since independence was achieved, with a population of over 50,000. Alone among Irish cities it has managed to retain, virtually intact, the maze of narrow, winding streets that comprise its commercial centre. This extends from **Eyre Square**, through **Williamsgate Street**, **Shop Street** and **Mainguard Street** as far as **O'Brien's Bridge**, including the many streets that meander away toward the Corrib and the docks.

Although busier in summer than in winter, because of the influx of tourists, Galway is always a bustling place. It has a growing university (the original limestone building and quadrangle dates from 1849) as well as a College of Technology, two large hospitals, docks and a thriving industrial complex on the

ABOVE: Galway's slogan. **BELOW:** the city's High Street.

outskirts of the city. There are two theatres: **An Taibhdhearc** (pronounced *thive ark*), which stages plays in the Irish language; and the **Druid Theatre**, which has created a reputation that extends to the West End of London.

Kenny's bookshop (9am–6pm, Mon–Sat) is on High Street. This four-storey cramped building, part of which dates from 1472, became a bookshop in 1942. It holds an unbelievable collection of books of antiquity as well as contemporary titles, old and new paintings and pieces of sculpture. It encourages browsing with a cup of tea and a chat with the Kenny family, who so obviously enjoy search, research and book queries. It's on the World Wide Web, too.

The highlight of the year is the summer **Race Week**, which begins during the last week in July. The racecourse is situated on the slope of a hill at **Ballybrit**, about 4 miles (6 km) from the city centre and overlooking Galway Bay and the Aran Islands. It is as much a carnival as a race meeting and, although over £1 million is wagered daily, many of those attending remain in the popular enclosure and rarely see a horse, such is the variety of side-shows: hawkers, musicians, fortune-tellers, three-card-trick operators and travelling people who converge from all parts of Ireland. Such is the fun to be had at Ballybrit that the city closes down every afternoon to enable everyone to get there.

A breath of sea air

To recover from the excesses of a day at the races – not to mention the hectic nightlife that follows – victims would be well advised to head for the nearby seaside resort of **Salthill** ⑰ It is within pleasant walking distance from the city centre and, although it is not a particularly beautiful place – consisting mainly of functional tourist hotels, pubs, clubs and casinos, it has a magnificent 2-mile

Map, page 230

BELOW: Sunday lunchtime jazz in Galway's "Latin Quarter".

(3-km) stretch of promenade that skirts the sea, with an uninterrupted view of the bay and the Burren beyond. It is said locally that an early morning walk from one end of it to the other has the curative powers of two gins and tonics. **Leisureland** has water-based amusement for the family with a 213-ft (65-metre) waterslide and tropical beach pool and treasure trove; an 80-ft (25-metre) swimming pool and an outdoor amusement park.

But gentler pleasures are also on hand. One could stand for hours on the **Salmon Weir Bridge**, which spans the river at the point where it flows out of Lough Corrib. Here the salmon lie in ever-shifting ranks waiting to assault the weir on their way upstream. The bridge leads to what was once Galway Jail, now the site of Ireland's newest cathedral. This is the **Catholic Cathedral of St Nicholas and Our Lady Assumed into Heaven**. Consecrated in 1965, it is constructed in an amazing variety of architectural styles in local limestone and Connemara marble. It also contains some unusual mosaics in its side-chapels; particularly the mortuary chapel where the lately-departed are presided over by images of John F. Kennedy and Pádraic Pearse, one of the leaders of the 1916 Easter Rising.

American connections

President Reagan visited Galway during its quincentennial celebrations in 1984 and, like President Kennedy, who visited in 1963, is enrolled as a Freeman. The Kennedy visit is marked by a stone tablet in the garden named in his honour at **Eyre Square**.

At one of its corners stands a beautiful limestone statue of the writer, Pádraic O'Conaire. Although born in the city, he was reared in Connemara and wrote exclusively in Irish until his death at an early age in 1927. As he was as famous

ABOVE: a stained-glass window in the cathedral. **BELOW:** Pádraic O'Conaire's statue, Eyre Square.

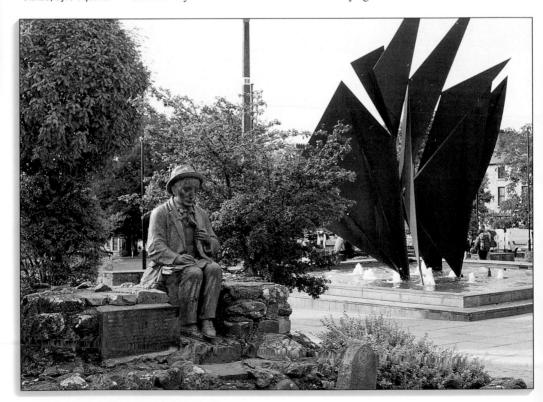

for his nomadic life-style as he was for his writings and was very partial to the bottle when he had the price of it, some of the more respectable citizens were scandalised when it was proposed to erect this statue in his honour. It has long since become one of the country's showpieces, as most of the country's recently erected statuary is quite hideous, and Galway has the distinction of being the first town in Ireland to erect a memorial to a contemporary artist.

The striking fountain, with its triangular brown centrepieces, which stands behind **Browne's Gateway**, was erected to commemorate the city's quin-centennial. The motif is the sails used on the traditional Claddagh fishing boats, known as hookers. They no longer exist in Claddagh but many of the surviving boats have been restored along the Connemara coast for use as pleasure craft.

Before venturing west from Galway it is necessary to know that without the benefit of a car (or a conducted coach tour) it is difficult, if not impossible, to explore Connemara and Mayo with the aid of public transport. Railways have almost vanished and buses are few and far between. But the main roads are good and the secondary ones reasonably so, if only because most people who use them also travel by car.

The Aran Islands

Before moving out of the city, though, it is worth casting an eye at the three **Aran Islands** ⑱ that straddle the mouth of the bay, like three limestone whales at rest on the surface of the Atlantic. Without the benefit of this natural break-water, Galway Bay would be a very exposed harbour and it is from Galway that the regular ferry boats to Aran sail all through the year. There is also a daily plane service to the three islands run by Aer Arann (Aran Air) from Minna, near

Map, page 230

ABOVE: busking in the High Street.
BELOW: stone walls breaking the wind on the Aran Islands.

Inverin, about 13 miles (20 km) west of Galway. The air journey takes only 15 minutes; the sea journey three hours. However, the air journey costs much more. In summer (Jun–Sept) many small ferries run between **Ros a' Mhíl (Rosaveel)** on the Connemara coast and Inishmore. This journey takes about an hour.

The three Aran Islands, **Inishmore**, **Inishmaan** and **Inisheer**, have been inhabited long before recorded history and contain many pre-Christian and early-Christian remains. Most noteworthy is **Dún Aengus** stone fort on Inishmore, one of Europe's finest prehistoric monuments. Perched on the edge of a vertical 200-ft (60-metre) cliff, it consists of four semi-circular defensive walls.

The experts have failed to date Dún Aengus with any accuracy: some say 4,000BC and others 1,000 BC. But apart from its striking aspect and historic interest, the view from its ramparts is one of the most striking imaginable. On a clear day one can follow the sweep of coastline from Kerry and Clare to the south, as well as the length of Galway to the western extremity of Connemara.

The islands have long attracted artists, writers, philologists, antiquarians and film makers. Robert Flaherty's film *Man of Aran* (1934) made the islands known to a worldwide audience. The playwright John Millington Synge wrote his book *The Aran Islands* while living on Inishmaan, where he also heard the plot of his most famous play, *The Playboy of the Western World*. Inishmore has produced one internationally known writer, Liam O'Flaherty. Born in the shadow of Dún Aengus, he is famous for his nature stories and as author of the novel *The Informer* (filmed by John Ford in 1935).

Irish is the daily language of the people of Aran, but most are equally fluent in English. This is also true of the people living on the southern shore of the Connemara coast, across the bay. Both areas are part of what is known as the Gaeltacht. About 65,000 native speakers of Irish live in areas of varying sizes in Waterford, Cork, Kerry, Galway, Mayo and Donegal (though perhaps only 10,000 speak it regularly in the home).

The Gaeltacht

The Connemara Gaeltacht begins on the outskirts of Galway, on the coast road through **An Spidéal (Spiddal)** ⑲. This is obvious to the tourist for, suddenly, the signposts are in Irish only instead of being bilingual. This is a recent innovation, brought about by public agitation in the 1970s as part of an effort to strengthen the role of Irish in everyday life. It also resulted in the setting-up of a special radio service for all the Gaeltacht areas with its headquarters in Connemara. (Because most existing road-maps still carry anglicised place-names, these forms are also given in brackets here).

Connemara is one of the most beautiful regions in Ireland and also one of the most barren. To travel through it is to understand why so many of its people are to be found in Boston, Birmingham and London. The amazing thing is that so many remained to eke out a precarious existence on the rugged, marshy land and on the sea. They are a hardy and resourceful people and one of the ways by which they supplement their income is through the illegal distillation of a white spirit called poteen: from the Irish *poitín*, a little pot.

The tourist is bound to hear of it, and may even be

BELOW: the Aran island of Inishmore.

offered some to drink or to buy, as it is now made in even greater quantities among the hills and on the remote lake and sea islands that abound in Connemara. It is made from a mixture of barley, sugar, yeast and water. The resulting liquid, or "wash", is then boiled over a constant flame and the steam run through a home-made still: usually a coil of narrow copper piping in a barrel through which cold water flows.

Before bottled gas was invented, the police were always on the look-out for the spiral of peat-smoke in isolated places. The pungent smell of the boiling "wash" made isolation necessary and the penalty for being caught in the act meant a heavy fine. Now the odds are in favour of the makers, and poteen costs about half the price of legal whiskey. If the liquid is run through the still three times the poteen is perfectly safe, if exceedingly fiery, to drink. One-run poteen, or poteen to which some unscrupulous distillers add commercial alcohol, can be very dangerous. Beware. For the benefit of those who like to live dangerously, the greatest centres of poteen-making in Connemara are **Leitir Móir (Lettermore)**, **Leitir Mealláin (Lettermullan)** and **Ros Muc (Rosmuck)**.

Bays and hills

By following the coast road to **Casla (Costelloe)**, then turning right to **Scrib (Screeb)** and then left again along the much-indented coast road through **Cill Chiaráin (Kilkieran), Caiseal (Cashel), Roundstone ㉒** – where one re-enters the non-Gaeltacht part of Connemara – and on to Clifden, one sees all that typifies coastal Connemara. The land is painfully poor, with tracts of lake, mountain and moorland stretching as far as the eye can see to the north. To the south lie the deep, curling bays filled with islands and fringed by black, red and orange sea-

Map, page 230

ABOVE:
BELOW: a cottage on Inisheer. **BELOW:** a tour by horse and trap on Inishmore.

ABOVE: crosses made locally from Connemara marble.

weed. Along the road, and away in the hills, are clusters of white-washed cottages and modern bungalows. The village of Roundstone is outstanding, with a lovely bay and a lively harbour area. It contains no-frills restaurants and pubs and is a venue for deep-sea anglers. Here are small-scale craft industries, including a *bodhrán*-making business, open to visitors seven days a week. This one-sided drum is made of stretched goat skin and gives a variety of sounds, depending on the skill of the player.

A little-known gem is **St Macdara's Island**, lying a few miles off Connemara's coast near Roundstone. Although only 60 acres (24 hectares), it has an exquisite 6th-century oratory. It was named after St Macdara, a protector of sailors and the first recorded Irish saint to have a surname. There is no regular ferry service to the island, but local fishermen will transport visitors for a fee.

A lure for fishermen

Clifden ㉑ is the region's principal town and one of the best places to buy traditional tweed. If time permits, it would be worth doubling back towards Galway, through **Recess**, **Maam Cross** and **Oughterard**. This road affords a fine view of the **Twelve Pins** mountain range and the islands on Lough Corrib. Those who come to Ireland with a view to fishing for salmon, trout, and a variety of coarse fish would find an agreeable and rewarding base in any of the many hotels and guest-houses along this road. About 2 miles (3km) east of Oughterard is **Aughnanure Castle** (mid-Jun–Sept, admission fee). Built by an O'Flaherty in the 16th century, it is picturesque and well preserved, an example of a tower house with two fortified enclosures and watch tower and a banqueting hall. It stands on a natural but drying-up moat on the shores of Lough Corrib.

BELOW: fresh lobsters on offer at the Oughterard House Hotel.

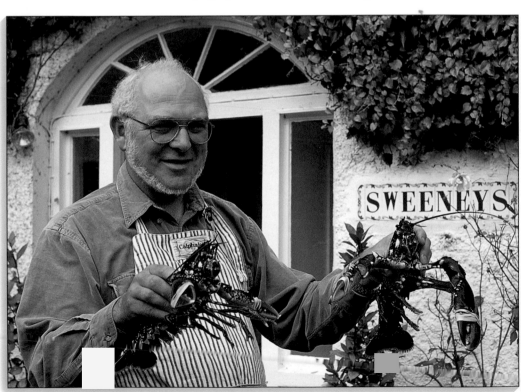

From Clifden one can also enter **Mayo** by a most pleasant route. It goes by **Kylemore Abbey**, one of the country's most-photographed buildings, which looks even better in reality. It is a late 19th-century limestone and granite building erected by a Liverpool merchant as a gift to his son, and is now run by the Benedictine nuns as a boarding-school for girls. The hall, Gothic chapel and three reception rooms are open to visitors (daily 9.30am–6.30pm).

Mayo is Ireland's third largest county but most of its interesting features are in the western half, particularly along its varied coastline.

The road from Kylemore Abbey leads to **Leenane**, where the **Leenane Cultural Centre** (Mar–October), on the Clifden-Westport road, deals interestingly with sheep rearing, wool production and products. It is functioning with 20 breeds of sheep grazing locally. Further on is **Killary Harbour**, Ireland's only fjord – so deep and sheltered that it could accommodate the entire navy of any world power – and a left turn takes you to **Louisburgh**, a small town at the back of **Croagh Patrick** ㉒, Ireland's holy mountain. It is a place of pilgrimage for thousands on the last Sunday of July, but a climb to its summit, on a clear day, is rewarding for even the greatest unbeliever.

It affords one of the finest panoramic views in Ireland: out over the Atlantic and the offshore islands, to the west; south over the mountain fastnesses of Mayo and Connemara; the rolling plains of central Mayo to the east; the island-studded **Clew Bay** to the north with **Achill Island** looming in the distance. The English writer William Makepeace Thackeray, who visited the west in 1842, described the scenery around Clew Bay as the "most beautiful in the world".

Westport ㉓ (pop. 4,000) lies on an arm of Clew Bay and is unique among Irish towns in that it was designed to the plan of the well-known architect of the

Map, page 230

The bodhran, made locally, is a round goatskin tambourine or drum, and is played with a small stick.

BELOW: the much photographed Kylemore Abbey.

ABOVE: trying a fireman's hat for size at Westport.

BELOW: a typical quiet Mayo high street – this one is in Castlebar.

Georgian period, James Wyatt (1748–1813). The Mall, with its lime trees lining both sides of the **Carrowbeg River**, is one of the country's most charming thoroughfares. From the harbour in the town a 100-seater ferry plies to **Clare Island** – well worth visiting to learn the seafaring expoilts of Grace O'Malley, a 16th-century pirate queen who preyed on cargo vessels. Her massive fort can be seen on the island. In spite of her exploits Grace O'Malley, also known as Granuaile, ended her days peacefully, having obtained protection from Queen Elizabeth I. Her grave is in the Abbey on the island. Clare Island has a population of about 350 and holds much interest for the botanist. It measures 3½ by 1½ miles (5.5km by 2.5km) and has a small hotel and B&Bs. The ferry journey takes 1½ hours from Westport, sailing through the islands of Clew Bay. There is a shorter ferry service of 15 minutes from Roonagh Harbour, Louisburgh.

On the way from Westport to Achill Island the huge disused, arched railway bridge that dominates the little town of **Newport** ㉔ is a sad comment on the social life of this area, and particularly Achill Island. It is all that remains of the railway that once linked the island and Westport but was closed in 1936.

Although Achill has been connected by a bridge to the mainland since 1888, it still retains many of the characteristics of an island. It is dominated by two mountains, skirted by wild moorland. The rest of the land is a dazzling combination of magnificent cliffs, golden strands, purple heather and scattered cottages that look even whiter than they are because of the dark background.

To the north lies one of the most desolate and depopulated areas in Ireland, the boglands of **Erris** that lead to the Erris Peninsula, where **Belmullet** is the principal town. From Belmullet the coast road runs via Belderrig to Ballycastle. Between these two towns it passes the **Ceide Fields**, a Stone-Age excavation

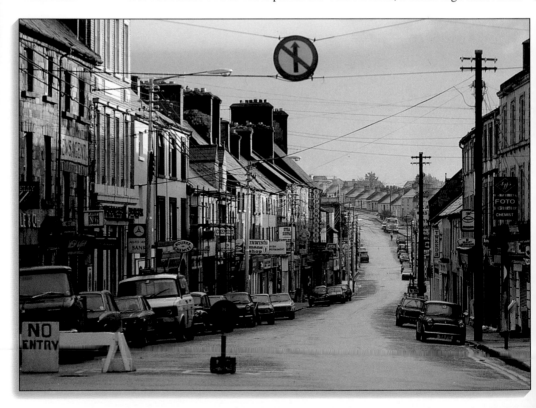

site which can hardly be missed thanks to its giant, pyramid-shaped visitor centre. Opposite the centre, the **Ceide Cliffs** attract geologists and birdwatchers.

The next town is **Killala**, which has a 10th-century round tower. It was here that the French forces landed during the 1798 Rising. Just outside the town is **Moyne Abbey**, founded by the Franciscans in 1460, and a little further to the south, near Ballina, is **Rosserk Friary**, a monastery from the same period. **Ballina ㉕**, Mayo's largest town (pop. 7,000), is good for shopping. Its cathedral is situated beside the ruins of a 15th-century Augustinian Friary. The more pleasant part of the town is along the river on the Sligo road.

Miracle at Knock

The journey coninues through wonderful scenery along the west coast of **Lough Conn** to arrive at **Castlebar**, County Mayo's capital. From here it is worth taking a detour to the village of **Knock ㉖**, where, on a wet evening in 1879, several local people supposedly saw the Blessed Virgin silhouetted on the gable of the local church. Now a 15,000-seat basilica dominates the village and, although no great miracles have been claimed or verified by Catholic authorities, hundreds of thousands of pilgrims, many of them invalids, journey to Knock annually. It was to celebrate the shrine's centenary that the Pope came to Ireland in 1979 at the invitation of the local parish priest, Monsignor James Horan.

Mgr Horan went on to parley £8 million out of a vote-conscious government to finance a runway 10 miles (16 km) from Knock. The resulting "international airport" progressed from being a "foggy, boggy white elephant" to a reasonable success. Before his sudden death, during a visit to Lourdes, Mgr Horan, the Pope's friend, saw Knock achieve its technological miracle.

Map, page 230

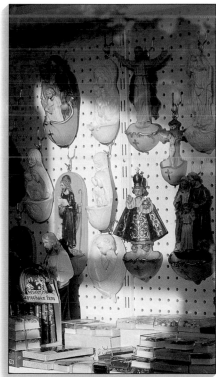

TIP

You can fly directly to Knock from England. Ryanair has daily flights from London Stansted, British Airways Express flies from Manchester, and Aer Lingus flies from Birmingham.

BELOW: a religious procession and selection of sacred souvenirs at Knock.

THE NORTHWEST

*The counties of Sligo, Leitrim and Donegal combine
Stone Age burial sites, a craggy coastline, quiet
fishing villages, and echoes of William Butler Yeats*

Map,
page 260

South-western Sligo, a land of bright lakes and dramatically carved valleys left behind when the last ice age retreated 10,000 years ago, wears its history on its sleeve. Huts from 2,000BC cluster on a plateau high in the **Bricklieve Mountains** west of Lough Arrow. To their west lie the passage tombs of **Carrowkeel Cemetery** where these Stone Age farmers buried their dead. Cairn K catches the rising sun on the year's longest day, yet the main road to Dublin, the N4, is just a mile west. Across it and across **Lough Arrow**, south of Riverstown, beside a modern bungalow, is the 200-ft (70-metre) unexcavated **Heapstown Cairn**. Almost every hilltop has a passage grave, every lake a defensive artificial island, a crannog, every river confluence a castle, a friary, a priory.

North-west, 5 miles (8 km) along the R295, Richard de Burgo, the Red Earl of Ulster, has left us the 10-ft (3-metre) walls and six towers of his castle, built in 1,300, in tiny **Ballymote ❶**. The ruins beside it are of a Franciscan friary where, in 1391, priests wrote the *Book of Ballymote* which enabled scholars to interpret Ireland's ancient Ogham script. At **Collooney**, north again 5 miles (8 km), stands a castle, site of a great battle between the English and the French who had come to support the Irish insurgents in the rebellion of 1798.

Travellers coming from the west, from **Ballina**, can follow the surfers' coast through **Easky** with its 15th-century Rosalee Castle and two Martello towers built to repel Napoleon in the early 19th century. One eclectic diversion is to visit the seaweed baths at **Inishcrone** (Kilcullen's Bath House, tel: 096-36238), another is to take the road south from Easky, past the sparkling waters of Easky Lough deep into the Ox Mountains before joining the N17 at Tobercurry.

PRECEDING PAGES: a deserted beach in Co. Donegal. **LEFT:** Bunglas, Co. Donegal. **BELOW:** sheep shearer at work.

Prehistoric sites

At **Carrowmore ❷**, 5 miles, (8 km) south-west of the eponymous county town, Sligo, the 6,000-year-old Bronze Age graves of Ireland's largest Megalithic cemetery (Visitor Centre, 071 61534, admission fee, closed Oct–Apr, site open all year) are easily approached, scattered across the hussocky fields, whilst up above them, on the horizon, west, on top of 1,078-ft (328-metre) Knocknarea, is the vast cairn, 200ft (70 metres) long by 35ft (11 metres) high, consisting of 40,000 boulders. It is named **Mebh's** (pronounced *Maeve's*) **Cairn**, supposedly for the 1st-century AD Mebh of Connaught whose lust for glitz, baubles and fine clothes would put many a modern royal princess in the shade. Her fall, when, coveting the Brown Bull of Cooley, she sent her army north on a cattle raid "The Taín", is recorded in the Irish equivalent of the *Iliad*, the *Ulster Cycle*. The advised approach is from the south. In the National Museum

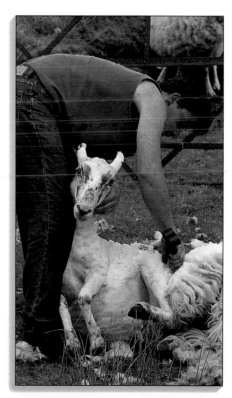

in Dublin is a splendid casket supposed to have held the tooth St Patrick lost the when he tripped over the entrance stone to 10th-century Killaspugabone Church on **Strandhill beach**, 5 miles (8km) west of Sligo by the R282 past Sligo Airport.

But **Sligo** town , with its associations with the poet, playwright and Abbey Theatre co-founder William Butler Yeats, is the county's tourist magnet. It's a fair enough market town, with the river Garavogue cutting though it, with excellent pubs and delicatessens, diverting narrow streets, plus beaches to the west, mountains to the north, and the ruins of a Dominican friary.

But Yeats, who spent most of his childhood here, is the main attraction. In the **Municipal Art Gallery** (County Library, Stephen Street, 071-45847, closed Sat–Tues, Sept–June) hang drawings and painting by that excellent artist, his brother Jack B. Yeats, given to vigorous impressionist watercolours, oils and drawings of country fairs and horse races. There are also fine Paul Henrys and George (A.E.) Russells, the latter one of Yeats's fellow mystics.

"The best lack all conviction, while the worst Are full of passionate intensity."
—W. B. Yeats

Next door you will find the **Sligo County Museum & Yeats Memorial Collection**, (071-42212, closed Sat pm, Sun and Mon). There are many Yeats letters, a complete collection of his poems, photographs and his Nobel Prize citation. The **Yeats Memorial Building** (Yeats Society, Wine Street, Douglas Hyde Bridge, 071-42693) is the venue for the Yeats International Summer School. A bronze statue to the poet, portraying him half swan, half stern cobra, stands nearby.

BELOW: the dolmen at Carrowmore.

Seasoned travellers, after asking in the tourist office for directions to the offices of the local solicitors **Argue and Phibbs**, checking out the Yeats connections, and fingering the finest of woollens and tweeds in Dooney's shop on

O'Connell Street will settle – with a volume of Yeats, or a copy of the local paper, the *Sligo Champion*, to hand – into the dark recesses of a snug in **Hargadon's Pub** almost opposite, for a pint of stout and a sandwich. The bar could be the model for many another spirit-grocers in the west of Ireland. The paper lists local pubs with traditional music and gives the programmes for the adventurous **Hawk's Well Theatre** (Temple Street) and its nearby competitor the **Blue Coat**. You can make your own sandwiches from supplies at Cosgrove's Delicatessen (Market Street) and plan a Yeats picnic.

The elusive Innishfree

To the east, the L16/R288 follows the 24-mile (40-km) circuit of beautiful **Lough Gill** ❹, swinging south, just into county Leitrim, at the elegant restored 17th-century lakeside **Parke's Castle** (Fivemile Bourne, 071-64149, admission fee, closed mid-Sept–mid-June) to Dromahair and the 15th-century **Creevylea** abbey ruins. The final stage of the journey, a visit to Yeats's **Lake Isle of Innishfree** is only for the determined. A small boat is sometimes available in summer from the shore, a 3-mile (5-km) walk from the main road.

The Yeats brothers spent their holidays at often windswept **Rosses Point**, 4 miles (6 km) north-west on the R291. The view across to Knocknarea is inspiring; mid-channel is a seafarer's marker, the **Metal Man**, according to the sour Yeats "the only Rosses Point man who never told a lie."

North of Sligo, 5½ miles (9 km) on the N15 is tiny **Drumcliff** ❺, at the foot of the majestic cliffs of Benbulben. Although he died in France, Yeats by his own request was re-interred here in the dour little Protestant Church of Ireland's graveyard, citing the spot in his poem which begins: *Under Ben*

**Map,
page 260**

ABOVE: Lough Gill.

BELOW: Co. Sligo's
untamed landscape
near Mullaghmore.

ABOVE: Lissadell House, which Yeats immortalised.

Bulben's head" and finishes with the celebrated words inscribed on his tomb: "*Cast a cold eye/ On life, on death, / Horseman, pass by!*"

The adjoining round tower is evidence of St Columba's AD575 monastery, whilst on the 10th-century **high cross** it is *just* possible to make out the bible stories of Cain and Abel, Adam and Eve. **Glencar Lough**, east on the N16 and half in county Leitrim, has a most dramatic setting.

Literary haunts

Branching west, 4 miles (6 km) along the northern shore of Drumcliff Bay, is **Lissadell House ❻** (071-63150, admission fee, closed Sun and mid-Sept–May). It is languid, shabby even, and was built in 1832 for the Gore Booths, whose Arctic explorer son Henry mortgaged the house to help Famine victims in 1845–46. Even if the house were to crumble, Yeats has immortalised it: "*The light of evening, Lissadell, / Great windows open to the south, / Two girls in silk kimonos, both / Beautiful, one a gazelle.*" The girls were poet Eva and her sister Constance, later to become Countess Markievicz, friend of Michael Collins. Constance, although sentenced to death for her heroic part in the 1916 Easter Rising, was the first woman to be elected to the British House of Commons. She never took the seat, preferring Ireland's equivalent, the Daíl.

Earlier literary diversions may be contemplated at **Cooldrumman**, half way between Drumcliff and Lisadell. Here, in the **Battle of the Books**, AD561, 2,000 monks of various factions, and their supporters, died in an argument as to whether St Finian was right in citing Derry's St Columba for breach of copyright.

BELOW: the harbour at Mullaghmore.

Further north off the N15, turn west at Grange for superb **Streedagh Strand** with Carriag na Spáinneach, Spaniard's Rock, where three ships of the Spanish Armada foundered in 1588. Most of the shipwrecked, cold and starving, were put to the sword. Some re-grouped, joined the *Gerona*, only to suffer similar fates at Port na Spániagh, Dunluce, county Antrim. The little road east from Grange leads up Benbulben.

Mullaghmore ❼ is a picture-postcard, holiday harbour village from some perfect childhood. The beach is golden, bright boats rock by the pier, waves splash on Mullaghmore Head. But Lord Mountbatten was assassinated here in his boat, with innocent youngsters, by the IRA in 1979. The fairytale Cassiebawn Castle was his holiday home.

On **Innishmurray**, 4 miles (6 km) offshore, there are the still stunning remains of St Molaise's 6th-century monastery, three churches within a 12-ft (4-metre) high dry-stone wall – just about the only survivors of Viking raids in the 9th century. If the crossing from Mullaghmore, or Rosses Point, was rough enough, travellers might seek out the island's other curiosity, its cursing stones.

Leitrim: Rescued by water

North of Mullaghmore, Leitrim is allowed to just dip its toes into 2½ miles (4 km) of the Atlantic, before the shore line reaches the **Drowes**, one of the best of salmon rivers and the boundary with Donegal. Ten miles (16 km) inland and Leitrim's border is with Fermanagh in Northern Ireland. Another 20 miles (32 km) east and its northern border is with Monaghan. At **Lough Allen**, its biggest lake, there are scarcely 5 miles (8km) of Leitrim soil between Monaghan north, and county Roscommon south.

Thus it has been too easy to dismiss this tiny county of lakes and rushes, meandering rivers, bumpy roads, crumbling farmhouses, low hills, neglected fields, as "Ireland's Cinderella". Sligo even takes credit – via Yeats – for Lough Gill and for **Glencar** ❽ with its waterfall immortalised in Yeats's poem *The Stolen Child*, though the two counties share them. Fermanagh is more associated with salmon-rich **Lough Melvin** than Leitrim on its southern shore, and the same can be said for the magic of **Lough Macnean Upper**, which is similarly divided.

The great famine of 1845–46 hit the county hard, and emigration has continued ever since. The unflinching novels of John McGahern, who lives at Mohill, catch the area's air of rural desperation. But as the attractions of the unspoilt environment begin to mean as much as the pull of the beaches, Leitrim has much going in its favour. A glance at the map shows a necklace of lakes linking the great rivers Shannon and Erne via the Ballinamore-Ballyconnell Canal – now more prosaically marketed as the **Erne Shannon Waterway.**

From spring to winter, the banks of the lakes and rivers – where cows drink hock-high amongst the flag irises – are dotted with the big green umbrellas of visiting fishermen after bream, eel, perch, pike, roach and rudd. Hired cruisers flying Austrian, British, Dutch, French and German ensigns ply the canal, their crews clinking their gin 'n' tonic glasses, their skippers nautical in caps,

Map, page 260

The county takes its name from the village of Leitrim, whose Gaelic name, Liatroim, means Grey Ridge.

BELOW: tranquillity in Leitrim's lanes.

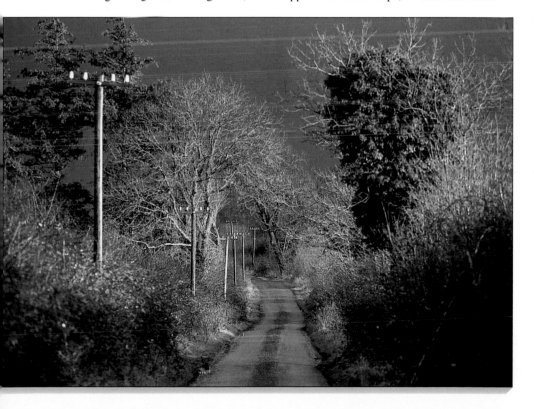

binoculars at the ready. Heron poise in the reed mace, great crested grebe dive before the bow wave. Amid the uncut watermeadows, amateur botanists count sedges, birdwatchers tick off another species of warbler, cup their ear for the cry of corncrake and cuckoo.

Thus small villages such as **Drumshanbo** on the R280 to the south of Lough Allen, **Carrick-on-Shannon** ❾, the county town 8½ miles (13 km) south, **Drumsna**, just south, where Anthony Trollope wrote his first novel, *The McDermotts of Ballycloran*, and **Roosky** 9 miles (14 km) south again, have found prosperity. The new money has brought music back to the pubs, turned old market houses into heritage centres and tourist offices, and refurbished town piers and lake fishing stands.

In the **Leitrim Heritage Centre and Museum** at **Ballinamore** visitors learn that the original canal had been a nonsense, built too late for the Canal Age; only a dozen or so boats ever traversed its original stone-built locks. Near the canal, fragments of the old Sligo Leitrim and Northern Counties Railway, whose initials were interpreted locally as the Slow Late and Never Completely Reliable, can be traced.

Dromahair's **Breffni Castle** ruins are the setting for the complex tale of Dervorgilla, Ireland's Helen of Troy, involving elopements, convent retreats, local chiefs, England's Henry II and Welsh barons. **Manorhamilton** has a ruined mansion and a Wild Rose Colleen beauty contest and **Carrigallen** has a flourishing theatre, the **Corn Mill**. A diversion from fishing could be **Lough Rinn House** (078-31427, admission fee, closed mid-Sept–May), once home to the Earl of Leitrim and now an open demense with visitor centre 10 miles (16 km) east of Carrick-on-Shannon.

Carrick-on-Shannon has developed into one of Ireland's major cruise boat centres.

BELOW: wall mosaic, Carrick-on-Shannon.

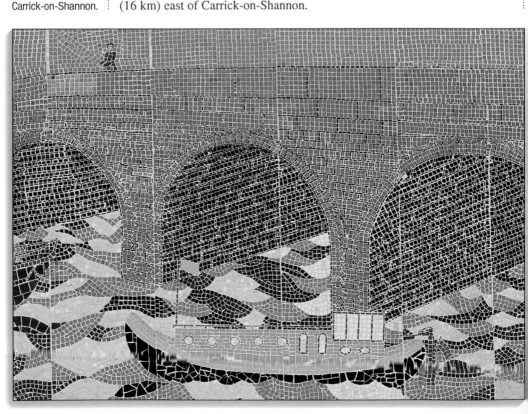

Donegal

The Atlantic storms into Donegal's rocky coves, rumbling round white boulders up in banks beside the sheep cropped grass. Rusty winches, skeletal memories of long-lost fishing enterprises, paint red the stone of crumbling piers. Dreamers and poets, and stressed-out business persons from Continental Europe, put thatch back on the roofs of old stone cottages, whilst locals, seemingly with no planning constraints erect new bungalows higgledy piggeldy, despoiling (for the tourist) the silent landscape of empty valleys, purple mountains, rushing streams, towering sea-cliffs.

Donegal's people, like Leitrim's, will argue that they are hard done by. In Donegal, tenuously linked to the rest of the Republic by a slender isthmus, they say Dublin forgets them, and that only tourism generated by Northern Ireland's middle classes (and a handful of foreigners) keeps them going. Certainly much of the county harks back to another age: tiny fields bound by dry-stone walls, the hay cut by scythe then tossed in cocks; a scattering of sheep, woolly dots on a distant, bare, impossibly steep, mountainside.

Off pot-holed village streets, monosyllabic, big knuckled, red-faced solid farmers – mountainy men – suck on tobacco pipes, read the death notices in the *Donegal Democrat* in sepulchral pubs, their children off in Amerikay, or Glasgow, or the hotel bar across the square, swaying to country and Irish – a more lachrymose version of country and western. And the tourist season, though it packs pubs, hotels and rented cottages, is short enough with a winter such as Donegal's around the corner after harvest.

Bundoran ⑩ is a brash resort, kiss-me-quick and windy. Rossnowlagh, its smaller quieter cousin, is a base for surfers and – in the friary – the Donegal Historical Society Museum (072-51267, free). In the one-time garrison town of **Ballyshannon**, where the waters of the Erne are tamed to produce hydro-electricty, pretty Georgian houses survive and literary folk commemorate the town's most famous son, poet and bank official William Allingham, remembered for his verse *Up the airy mountain,/ Down the rushy glen,/ We daren't go a-hunting / For fear of little men.* During the recent Troubles, northern visitors – mainstay of the county's tourism – shunned the area, tearing that armed IRA terrorists might indeed be hiding out in the lonely glens and off-season chalets.

The county town

Donegal ⑪, the lively county town, has a busy triangular "Diamond" market square, congested with tourist traffic all summer. The town's history has a familiar ring. Its **castle** (073-22405, admission fee, closed Oct–Apr), once an O'Donnell stronghold, was redesigned, as was the town itself, by the Brookes, planters who took over the land after the O'Donnells were deported in the so-called "Flight of the Earls" at the turn of the 17th century. In the now ruined O'Donnell-financed Franciscan abbey, south on the estuary of the Eske, monks compiled, in the 1630s, *The Annals of the Four Masters*, tracing Ireland's history back to the time of Noah's granny.

Complementary to tourism, the weaving and mak-

Map, page 260

ABOVE: a distinctive Donegal pub sign.

BELOW: gossip is the stuff of life in a Donegal village.

ing up of tweeds is the town's main industry, and Magee's, the town's largest shop, is the industry's principal outlet. A mile south, Donegal Craft Village (Ballyshannon Road, 073-22053, closed Sun out of season) demonstrates weaving and other craftworks.

Three miles (5 km) south of Donegal town, at Laghy, the R232 runs southeast for Pettigoe from where the R233 bears north 3 miles (5 km) across desolate bogland to **Lough Derg** , with its tiny **Station Island**, focal point for a major act of pilgrimage, St Patrick's Purgatory. The island, now covered with buildings, looks from a distance like some Canaletto painting and the pilgrims commemorate the 40 days Ireland's saint spent on it, praying, fasting and expelling evil spirits. There can be few Irish Catholics over the age of 40 who have not spent, sometime between June and August, the required three days of ritual there, walking barefoot, repeating prayers, and consuming nothing but black tea and dry toast.

Craggy coastline

The road west from Donegal town runs past **Bruckless,** where there are live oysters and mussels for sale, then through the fishing port of **Killybegs** where hefty trawlermen, drinking amongst the Victorian villas, give the town a raffish, frontier air. **Kilcar** 7 miles (11 km) on along the craggy, beautiful coastline, is another vacation, traditional music and tweed centre somewhat overshadowed by **Ardara** 20 miles (33 km) north. However, it is rewarding to continue further west through quiet **Carrick**, then turning south for the precipitous drive past **Teelin** to Carrigan Head at the eastern end of 2,000-ft (650-metre) **Slieve League** whose sheer cliffs drop a scary 765ft (235 metres) into

TIP

During the pilgrimage season, from 1 June to 15 August, only pilgrims are admitted to visit Station Island.

BELOW:
Donegal Castle.

Map,
page 260

the indigo sea beyond. An alternative is to leave transport at Teelin, walking the signposted One Man's Pass in the same direction. The views from **Amharc Mór** are, when not shrouded in mists, spectacular – and vertiginous.

Glencolumbkille ⓭, further west in the lowlands at the head of Glen Bay, represents a landmark in the development of a particular kind of Irish tourism. The idea was devised here that the draughty, cold traditional thatched white-washed cottage could be up-graded, given central heating, pine furniture, shower, television and fridge and clustered into a marketable group. Purists dismiss it, while its protagonists argue that it sustains life and employment in distressed rural communities. Four cottages in the village's **Folk Village Museum** (073-30017, free, closed Oct–Easter, plus Sat and Sun Easter–May) present traditional life over the centuries; one cottage, the Shebeen, sells sea-weed and fuschia wines – but no poteen.

Tiny **Port**, difficult to reach in the next valley north, demonstrates what happens when a village dies, but most travellers continue north-east the 16 miles (26 km) to **Ardara**, then **Glenties** ⓮, both awash in season with Belfast's holidaymakers buying Guinness, tweeds, Aran sweaters, salmon flies for the Owena and Owentocker rivers, and tapping their toes to fiddlers. Glenties' **St Conall's Heritage Centre** (075-51265, admission fee, closed Sept–May) is in its Georgian courthouse.

North, the N56 continues to Dungloe, capital of the **Rosses**, a raggedly charming peninsula of islands, trout lakes and inlets. From **Burtonport**, 4 miles (6 km) north-west, a 25-minute ferry service (075-21532) runs to **Aranmore** island 3 miles (5 km) offshore, with its 900 souls, dry stone walls and holiday cottages. Ferries for bare and windswept **Tory Island** ⓯, now a

One of the village's buildings, the National School replica, has a display on Rockwell Kent, an American painter who captured many local scenes.

BELOW: the harbour at Burtonport; peat digger, Horn Head.

ABOVE: the gardens
at Glenveagh Castle.

popular tourist destination, run the 15-mile (24-km) sea journey regularly from **Bunbeg** almost 15 miles (24 km) by the coast road north and from **Meenlaragh** round the **Bloody Foreland** near Gortahork. Home once to Balor, the one-eyed God of Darkness, Tory gave its name (meaning outlaw) to Britain's right-wing political party when it opposed James II in 1680.

This area, like Gweedore to the north, is traditionally Irish-speaking. It witnesses a pilgrimage more modern than Lough Derg's, when, on several summer Sundays, up to 8,000 fans – mostly women "of a certain age" – track 10 miles (16 km) north of Burtonport to the Viking Hotel (075-43295) to receive "a wee cup of tea in your hand" from **Kincasslagh**'s most famous son, the sentimental country-and-Irish singer Daniel O'Donnell.

The dramatic mountain north of Dunlewey is **Errigal**, Donegal's highest at 2,466ft (752 metres). The peak south is Slieve Snacht, 200ft (60 metres) less.

Twenty-one miles (37 km) north on the N56, **Dunfanaghy**'s fame rests on its popularity with Northern Ireland's golfers who take time off from the links to drive back south to Falcarragh, then east 8 miles (13 km) along the R255 to walk through the 10,000 acres (400 hectares) of always open **Glenveagh National Park** ⑯ (074-37008, admission fee visitor centre and castle, closed Oct–Easter). The park was given to the nation by Henry McIlhenny, who made his fortune from Tabasco Sauce. With its castle and its formal French and Italian gardens mixing with the wild mountains, the park has a further surprise in the Regency-style **Glebe House Gallery** (074-37071, closed Oct–Easter), housing paintings by Degas, Renoir, Picasso and the primitive painters of Tory Island. **Gartan Lough,** 3 miles (5 km) south via a narrow bog road, is much photographed, but its stunning beauty will elude many a lens.

BELOW: Tory Island.

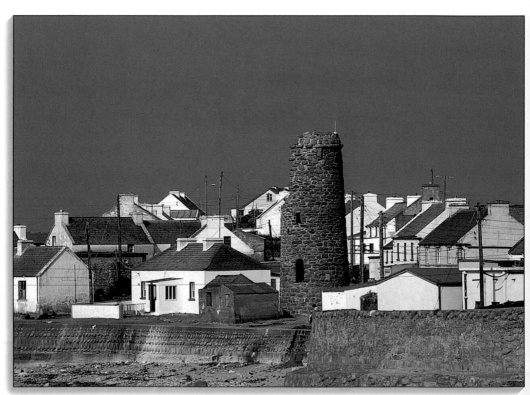

Letterkenny ⑰, the county town, 10 miles (16 km) to the southwest, is useful as a base because it has ATMs, hole-in-the-wall cash machines being pretty scarce in rural Donegal. A little restaurant (ask in the Tourist Office, because its name changes) is on the site of Laird's Hotel where Wolf Tone, patriot of the 1798 rebellion, was arrested over breakfast.

A choice of routes

The traveller could go north from Letterkenny, or follow the N56 south-east from Dunfanaghy, then taking the R245 north chasing the **Atlantic Drive** past the golfer's haven of **Rosapenna** around **Mulroy Bay** with its farmed mussel rafts and salmon cages, around windswept **Fanad Head**, then south again to **Rathmullan** ⑱, from whence, in 1607, the leading clan chiefs took flight by ship for Spain. Their story is recalled in the **Flight of the Earls Heritage Centre** (074-58131, closed Oct–Easter and Sun am).

Beyond, 7 miles (11 km) is charming preserved, conserved, restrained, riverside Ramelton, its past explained in the **Ramelton Heritage Centre** (074-51273): thence to Letterkenny again.

From here it's a tempting run north, for 16 miles (26 km), to the 4,000-year-old **Grianán of Aileach**, a really spectacular circular stone enclosure atop a 800-ft (240-metre) mound. Its name is translated, controversially, as "sun-palace".

Even more tempting now is the drive 40 miles (64 km) north to Ireland's most northerly point, **Malin Head** on the Inishowen Peninsula. The great estuary south is that of the river Foyle, on which sits Northern Ireland's second (and most vibrant) city, Derry.

Map, page 260

The flight of the most powerful Irish clan princes in 1607 was more than just another setback for the Irish cause: it effectively marked the end of Gaelic supremacy.

BELOW: Malin Head; the ancient Grianán of Aileach.

THE NORTHEAST

The evidence of Northern Ireland's civil strife is there to see,
but even more evident are gorgeous lakes and glens,
a stunning coastline and a wealth of golf courses

Map,
page 260

Twenty-five years ago it was hard to tell when you had crossed the border from the Republic into Northern Ireland. Perhaps you noticed that the post boxes and telephone booths were no longer green but red. Or that the road surface had suddenly improved and deduced that British rather than Irish taxes had financed it. But that was about all. No passports were required. A few crossings had Customs posts, but most people were casually waved through.

In the 1970s the differences became marked. Passports were still not required, but many lanes which used to weave across the border and back again, as unpredictably as a St Patrick's Day drunk, were blocked by wedges of reinforced concrete a metre thick. On authorised roads, the visitor's first glimpse of Northern Ireland was of a British Army checkpoint, a concrete bunker with bullet-proof glass and silver anti-sniper screens, manned by a soldier wearing a flak jacket and carrying an automatic rifle. It was an unsettling sight. At some crossings, as one soldier asked you for some means of identification, an unseen colleague inside the bunker tapped your car registration number into a terminal linked to a computer at police headquarters. This was programmed with details of all suspect vehicles and within seconds you were cleared – or arrested.

After the IRA ceasefires in 1994 and 1997, the security became much less obtrusive. Although many could not believe that peace was permanent, most barriers were removed from towns throughout Northern Ireland and efforts were made to make everything look as normal as possible. If things *looked* peaceful, it was reasoned, peace would be encouraged.

Where's the border?

One reason it is so difficult to be sure of the border's exact location is that it snakes its way along 18th-century county boundaries through farming land that is sometimes bleak, more often breathtakingly beautiful. It takes little account of natural boundaries, such as rivers, or of the cultural differences that separate Republican-minded Roman Catholics and British-oriented Protestants. A priest may find part of his parish on one side of the border, the rest on the other. Houses straddle it so that, as the joke has it, a man may sleep with his head in the United Kingdom and his heart in the Republic of Ireland.

Political expediency accounts for the absurdities. It had been intended to redraw the border rationally after partition in 1920, and a Boundary Commission was set up to advise. But in the end the British and Irish governments, both hoping to avoid further trouble, suppressed the commission's report and left things as they were. Had they decided differently, much of the subsequent conflict might have been averted.

Northern Ireland
telephone numbers
dialled from outside
the country must be
prefixed by Britain's
international code, 44.

ABOVE: Derry's walls
were completed in
1618 at a cost of
£8,357.

Many confusions were created. Whereas the ancient Irish province of Ulster consisted of nine counties, the new state of Northern Ireland, popularly known as Ulster, consisted of only six: **Antrim**, **Down**, **Armagh**, **Derry**, **Fermanagh** and **Tyrone**. Yet the three counties which went to the Republic – **Donegal**, **Cavan** and **Monaghan** – are still bound to the other six by firm family and trading ties. To many locals, therefore, the border is an abstraction. And indeed it's hard to take it wholly seriously when the states it divides can't even agree about its length, the Republic claiming it is 280 miles (448 km) long and the Northern Ireland authorities adamant that it is 303 miles (485 km).

Since this book's concern is the convenience of travellers rather than tribal loyalties, we have included Donegal in the previous chapter and will here roam freely within the remaining eight counties of ancient Ulster. And it *is* possible to roam freely without seeing much evidence of sectarian conflict. As the Northern Ireland Tourist Board likes to point out, its bailiwick consists of 1,200 golf holes with a number of towns and villages scattered among them.

Old Derry's walls

Across the border from Donegal, the county of **Londonderry** – the name of whose chief city, in a pointed rejection of the city's imperial links, the local nationalist majority legally shortened to **Derry ⑲** – is famously friendly. Even in its sectarian squabbles, it is far less implacable than Belfast. The 19th-century Scottish historian Thomas Carlyle called it "the prettiest looking town I have seen in Ireland" and, though the Troubles seriously scarred it, recent refurbishment has restored its attractiveness. But the city, finely situated on the **River Foyle**, doesn't set out to be a calendar girl; it prefers to provide exhilarating

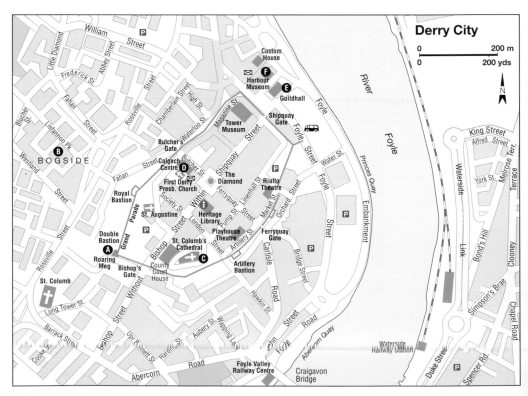

Derry City

0   200 m
0   200 yds

company, and it succeeds. There has been a renaissance in community activity, especially in the arts, and enthusiasts will tell you that Derry is the first city in Western Europe to face up to the realities of the high-unemployment post-industrial age.

The city's growth was financed by London guilds, which in 1614 began creating the last walled city in Europe. Its purpose was mercantile success and you can still see traces of its former economic confidence in the ornamental facades of the old shirtmaking factories, which provided the city with its livelihood for generations. The walls, 20 ft (6 metres) thick and complete with watch-towers and cannon such as the 18-pounder **Roaring Meg ⒶA** (dating from 1642), are marvellously intact. (Tours 01504-267284 with fee, otherwise free access.)

Two 17th-century sieges failed to breach the walls, earning the sobriquet "maiden city". Some say the city still has a siege mentality, a theory reinforced by the IRA's daubed slogan "You are now entering Free Derry." This was the name given to the **Bogside ⒷB**, a densely populated Roman Catholic housing estate, when its inhabitants barricaded it against the police in 1969. Their grievances were old ones. After Ireland's partition in 1920, the city's governing Unionists had fixed constituency boundaries to ensure a "permanent" majority for themselves in what was a mainly nationalist area – an artificial majority that wasn't overturned until the mid-1990s. Feeling isolated from the prosperous eastern counties, Derry's citizens built up both a wonderful community spirit and a resentment that finally boiled over.

The most famous siege – which is still commemorated by Protestant marches today – took place in 1689, when the Catholic forces of James II, the last of England's Stuart kings, blockaded the Protestant supporters of William of Orange for

Map, page 280

The famous "Londonderry Air" was based on an old folk melody. It became "Danny Boy" when an English songwriter, Frederic Edward Weatherly (1848–1929), added lyrics.

BELOW: the view from the walls; the statue to Peace.

15 weeks, almost forcing them into submission. About 7,000 of the 30,000 people packed within the city's walls died of disease or starvation. One member of the besieged garrison chillingly recorded the selling prices of horseflesh, dogs' heads, cats, and rats "fattened by eating the bodies of the slain Irish." The city's eventual relief is depicted on the siege memorial window of **St Columb's Cathedral** 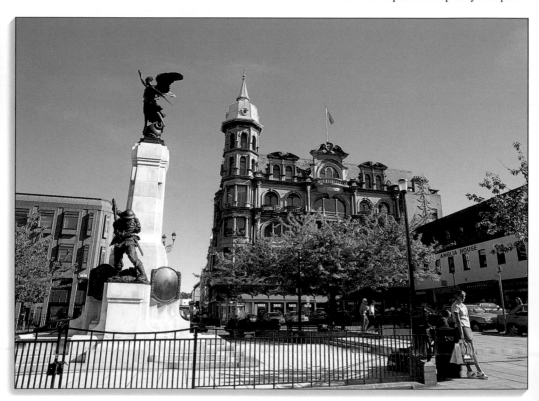 (London Street, 01504-267313, admission fee) a graceful 17th-century Anglican church built in "Planters' Gothic" style. The chapter house contains siege relics. Outside the walls, off Bishop Street Without, **St Columb's** (01504-42303, admission free), built 1784, known as the Long Tower Church, has a lavish interior.

For those interested in the city's turbulent history, the award-winning **Tower Museum** (Union Hall Place, 01504-372411, admission fee, closed Sun and Mon) skilfully uses audio-visuals and photography to tell its story from both sides of the sectarian divide. The **Calgach Centre** 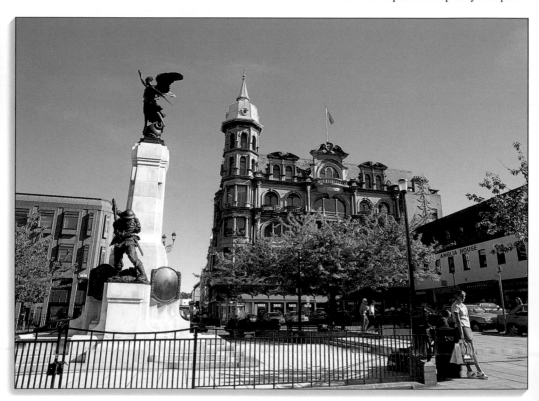 (4–22 Butcher Street, 01504-373177, closed Sun and Mon winter) also presents the span of the city's history whilst the Heritage Library (14 Bishop Street Within, 01504-269792, closed weekends) has genealogical research facilities.

Streets from the city's original four gates (Shipquay, Ferryquay, Bishop's and Butcher's) converge on **The Diamond**, a perversely square-shaped market place at the top of Shipquay Street, the steepest main thoroughfare in Ireland. At the bottom of the street, the **Guildhall** 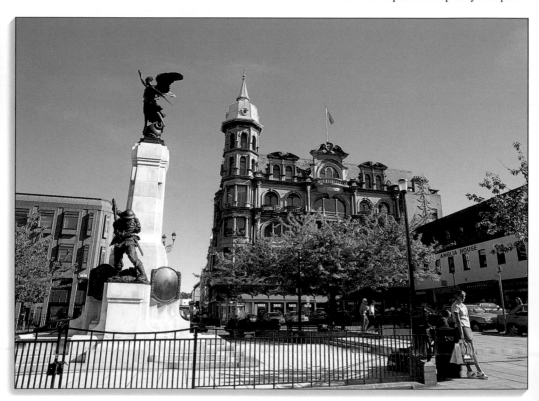 (Guildhall Place, 01504-365151, admission free, closed Sun), one of those Tudor-Gothic structures popular in Northern Ireland, clearly shows the influence of the London merchants. Its grandeur has been stained by the Troubles too. A Republican entering as a newly elected councillor turned out to be the same man who had blown part of it up 13 years pre-

St Columb (c. 521–597), also called Columba and Columcille, founded Derry around 546 and later set up a community on Iona, off Scotland's west coast. His feast day is 9 June.

BELOW:
The Diamond.

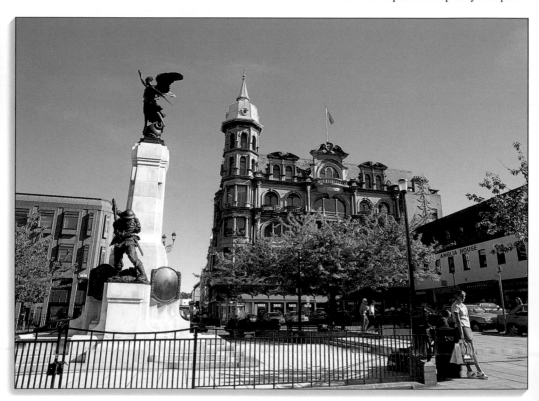

viously. He had made a political statement by carrying in the bomb, he explained, and he was making the same political statement now.

Behind the Guildhall is **Derry Quay**, celebrated in song by hundreds of thousands of emigrants who sailed down the Foyle from here, bound for a new life in America. The city's maritime past is covered in the **Harbour Museum** (Harbour Square, 01504-377331, admission free, Closed Sun); displays include a replica of a 30-ft (9-metre) curragh in which St Columba sailed to Iona in AD563. Its railway past is explored in the **Foyle Valley Railway Centre** (Foyle Rd. 01504-265234, admission fee, closed Monday, plus Sunday in winter). The **Earhart Centre** 1½ miles north-west on B194 (Ballyarnet, 01504-354040, admission free) focuses on one incident in aviation's past – the day Amelia Earhart, the first woman to fly solo across the Atlantic, landed here in 1932.

The Gordon (London Street, 01504-374004), Orchard (Orchard Street, 01504-269675) and Context (Artillery Street, 01504-373538) are fine contemporary art galleries (closed Mondays), whilst touring and homespun ballet, drama and opera play the Foyle Arts Centre (Lawrence Hill, 01504-266657), the Playhouse (Artillery Street, 01504-268027), St Columb's Theatre (Orchard Street, 01504-262880) and the Rialto (5 Market Street, 01504-260516).

Small-town Tyrone

Thirteen miles (21 km) southwest of Derry City, in county Tyrone on the A5 is **Strabane ㉑**, a border town paired with Lifford on the Donegal side. It was here in Gray's Printing Press (49 Main Street, 01504-884094, admission fee, closed Oct–Mar plus Thur, Sun and bank holidays), preserved by the National Trust, that John Dunlap, printer of America's Declaration of Independence, learned

The dramatist George Farquhar (1678–1707) was born in Derry. His best plays are The Recruiting Officer and The Beaux' Stratagem.

BELOW: echoes of the old working-class town.

ABOVE: Andrew Jackson, one of 11 US presidents with roots in Ulster.

his trade. Three miles (5 km) to the southeast, signposted off the B47, is a white-washed cottage, the ancestral home of US president Woodrow Wilson (Dergalt, 01662 243292, admission fee, closed Oct–March).

Sion Mills, 3 miles (5 km) south of Strabane, is a village whose name betrays its origins. The linen-workers' old cottages are charming. The Parish Church of the Good Shepherd is a striking Italian-style edifice, contrasting sharply with the modern architecture of St Teresa's Catholic Church, whose facade displays a large image on slate of the Last Supper.

As you drive into **Omagh** ㉑, the county town of Tyrone, 16 miles (25 km) along the A5, the religious fragmentation of Northern Ireland is immediately apparent. On the right is the Presbyterian Church (Trinity); on the left, the Methodist Church; next, St Columba's Church of Ireland; then the Gothic spires of the Roman Catholic Church of the Sacred Heart, a poor man's Chartres Cathedral. There are many more. The joining of the Rivers Camowen and Drumragh to form the Strule make the location pleasant enough, but Omagh is more a town for living (and praying) in than for visiting. In its shops, alongside the usual linen souvenirs, are plaques and statuettes made of turf (peat). This is cut from the **Black Bog** between Omagh and Cookstown, 27 miles (43 km) to the east.

American connections

During tough times in the 1800s, the area's strong Scots-Presbyterian work ethic spurred many to seek their fortune in America. The results were remarkable and Northern Ireland claims that 11 US presidents have had roots in the province: Andrew Jackson, James Knox Polk, Andrew Johnson, James Buchanan, Ulysses S. Grant, Chester Alan Arthur, Grover Cleveland, Benjamin Harrison, William McKinley, Theodore Roosevelt and Woodrow Wilson. Genealogists pore over old documents, hoping to add more names, and many Americans visit to seek out ancestral homes.

BELOW: the Ulster-American Folk Park.

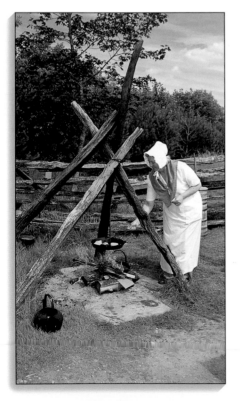

The Mellon banking family of Pittsburgh, having traced their roots to 4 miles (6 km) north of Omagh, off the A5, endowed the **Ulster-American Folk Park** ㉒ on the site at Camphill (01662-243292, admission fee, closed Sat and Sun, Oct–Easter). To illuminate the transition made by the 18th-century emigrants, craftsmen's cottages, a schoolhouse, a blacksmith's forge and a Presbyterian meeting-house from the Old World have been rebuilt on a peat bog alongside log cabins, a Pennsylvania farmstead and a covered wagon from the New World. Peat is kept burning in the cottages, adding to the authenticity, and there are demonstrations of candle-making, fish-salting and horse-shoeing.

An indoor exhibit recreates the main street of an Ulster town at the turn of the century, its hardware shop displaying foot warmers and lamp wicks, its medical hall containing Bishop's Granular Effervescent Citrate of Magnesia and Belladonna breast plasters. A replica of an emigrant ship links the continents. There's not a whiff of Disney, thanks to attention to detail, though the American "half" looks more prosperous than it was in reality for the original settlers.

Also north of Omagh (7 miles/11 km on the B48) the outdoor **Ulster History Park** (016626-48188, admission fee, closed Sat and Sun Oct-Mar), traces back 10.000 years by means of reasonably realistic recreations of the built environment, from Neolithic huts and ring-forts to round towers and planters' houses.

Map, page 260

Relics of old industries

There's nothing Northern Ireland likes better than history, and almost every village in Tyrone – **Castlederg**, **Creggan**, **Donaghmore**, **Fivemiletown**, **Newtownstewart** – has its heritage centre. The most interesting, a little further along the B48, near **Gortin**, is the **Sperrin Heritage Centre** ㉓ (274 Glenelly Rd., Cranagh, 016626-481422, admission fee, closed Nov– Mar), which includes the history of local gold-mining and lets you try your luck panning in an iron pyrite stream.

With the eclipse of Ulster's once-flourishing linen industry, hard times have again come to villages such as **Draperstown** (built in 1618 by the London Company of Drapers) in the archaeologically rich, blue-tinged **Sperrin Mountains**. Near **Maghera**, a working linen mill (Wm. Clark and Sons, Upperlands, 01648-42214) may be visited by arrangement. The fortunes of towns like **Dungannon**, 13 miles (21 km) south of Cookstown and once the seat of the great O'Neill clan, have faltered too.

Signposted from the M1 motorway, exit 13, 7 miles (11 km) east of Dungannon, is the always open **Peatlands Park** (Peatlands Park Centre and Railway, 01762-851102, fee for railway which is closed Oct–Mar), a unique preservation of the flora and fauna of an Irish bog which can be viewed from a miniature railway. Three miles (5 km) to the northeast, **Coalisland's Corn Mill Heritage Centre** (Lineside, 01868-748532, admission fee, closed Sat and Sun

Ireland's linen industry began in 1698 when Louis Crommelin brought over a group of Huguenots from France to escape the wars of religion during Louis XIV's reign.

BELOW: the Mellon Homestead at the Ulster American Folk Park.

ABOVE: The poet
Seamus Heaney
grew up in Bellaghy.

BELOW: Lower
Lough Erne.

Oct–May) commemorates coal-field and canals that never fulfilled their promise. Eleven miles (18 km) south of Dungannon, **Benburb Heritage Centre** (Milltown Rd., 01861-549752, admission fee, closed Oct–Mar and Sundays and Mondays) traces linen's history.

Twenty-five miles (40km) east of Omagh, **Cookstown** ㉔, the exact middle of Northern Ireland, is renowned for its main street, 2 miles (3 km) long and 160 ft (50 metres) wide, and can be located from miles away by the 200-ft (61-metre) spire of the Gothic-style Catholic church. The town (population 6,700) has a strong tradition of nationalism, often refined in its many old-fashioned pubs. Local livestock sales give a good insight into the rough amiability of the rural Ulster character. Four miles (4 km) west, the water-powered **Wellbrook Beetling Mill** (Wellbrook, 016487-51735, admission fee, closed Oct–Mar and Tuesdays) demonstrates arcane processes of linen polishing.

Just east of the town an 18-hole golf course (200 Killymoon Rd., 01648-62254) occupies the grounds of **Killymoon Castle**, designed in 1803 by John Nash, architect of London's Regent Street. Some years ago, a farmer bought the castle, then derelict, for £100.

Many Neolithic graves and stone circles are sprinkled around both towns. The best are at **Beaghmore**, (free access) 10 miles (16 km) west of Cookstown, off the A53. Villages such as **Clogher** and **Coagh**, **Moneymore** and **Pomeroy** are noted for fine traditional musicians and a variety of ecclesiastical architecture. There's a run-down air about some, the result of chronic unemployment. But it's as well to remember writer John Broderick's advice in *The Pilgrimage*: "The city dweller who passes through a country town and imagines it sleepy and apathetic is very far from the truth: it is watchful as the jungle." The poet Seamus

Heaney, now a Nobel Laureate, is celebrated near his native village (**Heaney Library**, Bellaghy Bawn, Bellaghy, 01648-386812, admission fee, closed Sun am). Much of Heaney's poetry derives its imagery and colloquial language from his rural upbringing in this part of Northern Ireland.

Ulster's lakeland

To the southwest, **Fermanagh**, adjacent to Monaghan and Cavan, has many things in common with them, particularly its tempo. Politically it is part of Northern Ireland and is the province's lakeland playground: a third of it is under water. But political divisions are less of a barrier these days: the restoration of the Ballinamore–Ballyconnell cross-border canal means that you can now travel all the way here from Limerick by inland waterway.

The county town, **Enniskillen ㉕**, a Protestant stronghold since Tudor times, is built on an island between two channels of the River Erne as it flows from **Upper** to **Lower Lough Erne**. In summer, pleasure boats ply (MV *Kestrel*, Round O Jetty, 01365-322822, daily May–Sept) the lakes, and western Europeans cruise them in hired craft (Erne Charter Boat Association c/o Fermanagh TIC, Wellington Rd. Enniskillen, 01365-323110). The town's strategic importance is shown by **Enniskillen Castle** (Castle Barracks, 01365-325000, admission fee, closed Sat, Sun and Mon am, plus Sat–Mon Oct–Mar) the earliest parts dating from the 15th century and the imposing water gate from the late 16th century. The castle houses two museums, one specialising in prehistory, the other in military relics.

Enniskillen is rich in small bakeries and butcher's shops, and there's a gossipy atmosphere as farmers mix with townsfolk in Blakes of the Hollow, one of

Map, page 260

One of the worst terrorist outrages in Ulster took place in Enniskillen when a bomb exploded during a Remembrance Day service at the war memorial in 1987, killing 11 people.

the North's finest pubs. A secret is soon shared in such a place. Confusingly, the main street, best viewed from the head of the 108 stairs of Cole's Monument (Forthill Park, 01365-325050, admission fee, closed Oct-Mar and mornings) changes its name six times between the bridges at either end.

A true taste of the region's flavour can be gained by circling Lower Lough Erne by road or by boat. **Devenish Island** ㉖ is reached by ferry (boat fare and admission fee, accessible Apr–Sept, except Mondays) from Trory Point, signposted 3 miles (5 km) north of the town at the A32/B82 junction. It is the best known of the lough's 97 islands because of its elaborate and well-preserved round tower, which you can climb by internal ladders. Close by are the decorative ruins of the 12th-century Augustinian Abbey of St Mary. Three miles (5 km) south of Kesh on the B82, along the lough's north shore, a ferry departs (Castle Archdale Park Marina, 013656-21731, ferry fare, admission free, June–Sept only) for **White Island** with its 12th-century church along one wall of which are lined up eight mysterious pagan statues, discovered only in the 20th century. Their origins fox experts; some speculate that seven may represent the deadly sins.

On the outskirts of Enniskillen, to the northwest, is Portora Royal School, founded in 1608. Its most famous pupils were Oscar Wilde and Samuel Beckett.

Ancient monuments

A few miles further, past the village of **Kesh**, with its modern sailing school and fortified police station, is the strangest of all the ancient stone figures: the two-faced Janus statue on **Boa Island** ㉗, which is joined to the mainland by a bridge at each end. In most countries, such a find would have been turned into a major tourist attraction. Here, you have to watch for an easily missable road sign pointing to "Caldragh Cemetery" (free access), then tramp through cowpats down a farm lane until you come across a field full of overgrown, moss-covered gravestones, in the middle of which lurks the inscrutable Celtic figure. The lack of refurbishment makes the place feel splendidly eerie; you notice the figure's sexual arousal and the hollow in its head and wonder whether that hollow once held sacrificial blood.

BELOW: an ancient two-faced Janus figure on Boa Island.

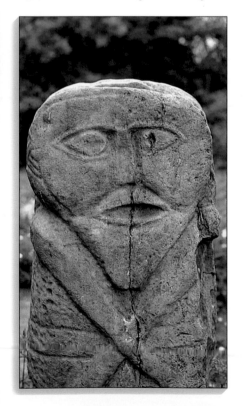

A second Janus figure was discovered on the little island of **Lustybeg**, near Kesh. There are holiday chalets for hire on this island.

Following the lough's shoreline, you reach **Pettigo**, an old plantation town once the railhead for pilgrims visiting the holy sites at **Lough Derg,** across the border in Co. Donegal. The River Termon, running through Pettigo, marks the border and is said to be stuffed full of bilingual trout. It is also said that when a man had his skull fatally cracked during a fist fight in the middle of the bridge a surveyor had to be called to determine whether he had died within the jurisdiction of the Northern police or the Republic's gardai. An oak tree on one side of the bridge was planted in 1853 to mark the British victory at Sebastopol. A statue on the other side commemorates four IRA men who died fighting the British in 1922.

Castle Caldwell, on the A47 4 miles (6km) east of Belleek a ruined 16th-century castle by the loughside nearby, has become the centrepiece of a Forest Park (details 013656-31253, free access, daily dawn to dusk), popular with picnickers and bird watchers. Worth seeing is a "Fermanagh cot", a 30-ft (10-metre) wooden barge used for transporting cattle and sheep to and from the islands of Upper and Lower Lough Erne. A fiddler who, the worse for drink, fell off a barge and drowned is remembered on a fiddle-shaped monument with a cautionary verse that ends: *On firm land only exercise your skill. There you may play and safely drink your fill.*

The border touches the River Erne again at **Belleek** ㉘, where anglers assure you that you can hook a salmon in the Republic and land it in Northern Ireland. You can sense how tightly knit the town is by reading the advertisements on a restaurant's table-mats. On one, a local businessman offers to provide you with souvenirs, confectionery, Sindy dolls, cigarettes, and his personal services, day and night, as a funeral director. The village is famous for its lustrous **Belleek pottery**, manufactured from felspar imported from Norway. Half-hour tours (Belleek Pottery, 013656-58501, admission free, closed weekends) of the working factory are available. The pottery's Visitor Centre opens on summer weekends.

You can take the scenic drive back to Enniskillen along the south side of the lough, stopping 5 miles (8 km) north-west of Derrygonnelly on the A46 at **Lough Navar Forest Park** (details 013656-41256, free access, daily, dawn to dusk), where a lookout point offers a panorama of five counties. At **Tully**, off the A46, 3 miles (5 km) north of the village, is one well-preserved 17th-century castle (admission fee, closed Oct–Mar) whilst at **Monea**, 7 miles (11 km) north-west of Enniskillen on the B81, is another with free access at all times.

"Over 300 million years of history" – impressive even by Irish standards – is the slogan used to promote **Marble Arch Caves** ㉙ (Marlbank Scenic Loop,

Map, page 260

ABOVE: home of Belleek pottery.

BELOW: the ancient Marble Arch Caves.

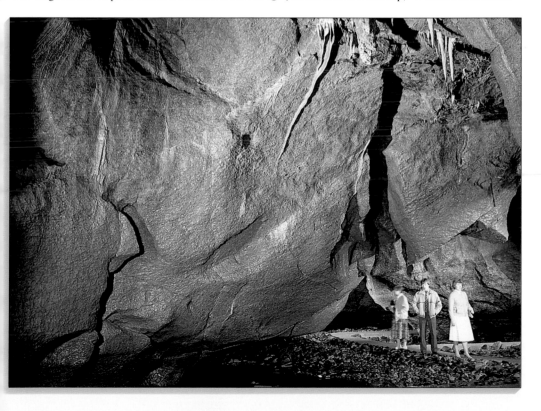

Florencecourt, 01365-348855, admission fee, accessible Mar–Sept, weather permitting), an extensive network of limestone chambers, containing remarkable stalactites. A 75-minute tour includes an underground boat journey. The "Moses Walk" is so called because the dammed walkway has been created through a lake, with more than a metre of water on either side. Twelve miles (20 km) south-west of Enniskillen, the caves are reached by following the A4 south-west for 3 miles (5 km), then following signposts after branching off on the A32 in the direction of Swanlinbar.

Florence Court (National Trust, 01365-348249, admission fee, closed Oct–Mar and Thur all year), is a beautiful 18th-century mansion 4 miles (6 km) back. Contents include fine rococo plasterwork and 18th-century furniture. The grounds include an ice house, a water-powered sawmill and a walled garden.

Two miles (3 km) southeast of Enniskillen on the A4 is Ireland's finest classical mansion, **Castle Coole** (National Trust, 01365-322690, admission fee, closed Oct-Mar and Thur all year). Completed in 1798, it is a perfect example of late 18th-century Hellenism and has furniture dating from before 1830. The park lake's flock of graylag geese was established here 300 years ago.

Cavan's cruising

Across the border to the south of Enniskillen, landlocked County Cavan, emptied by emigration, bridges the two Irelands by providing the source of two great rivers: the **Shannon,** which flows south to the Atlantic, and the **Erne,** which flows north into Fermanagh's magnificent lakes. Both rivers are ideal for cruising. Most of the county's scattered towns and villages have small hotels which cater for visiting fishermen. The grandiose scheme to re-open the Ballinamore-

BELOW: Castle Coole, Co. Fermanagh.

Ballyconnell canal linking the two river systems has been completed. Pleasure trips along the canal are on offer, on demand (Brennan Boats, Ballinamore, 078 44079).

Cavan town ㉚ is the site of a 14th-century Franciscan friary, of which only a belfry tower remains. The Roman Catholic Cathedral, in contrast, dates from 1942. Cavan Crystal (Dublin Road, 049-31800, admission free) offers glass-blowing displays.

A tour going west and north from Cavan would take in **Arvagh**, a peaceful village 14 miles (22 km) south-west on the R198 by Lough Garty; **Cornafean**, north off the R198, 4 miles (6 km) from Cavan where Corr House has a fascinating collection of curios such as three-legged pots and cow bells housed in a converted pighouse; 17th-century **Cloughoughter Castle** on an island in Lough Oughter and nearby **Killeshandra** where the R199 crosses the R201; **Dowra**, on the R200 near the Black Pig's Dyke, thought to be an ancient frontier earthwork; **Swanlinbar**, with its faded, once-a-spa charms, on the Border; **Blacklion**, on Lough Macnean 33 miles (52 km) north-west on the N3/R200, a hamlet surrounded by many prehistoric ringforts and cairns including a beehive-shaped sweat house, a Celtic form of Turkish bath; and **Butlersbridge**, 4 miles (6 km) north on the N3 near which Ballyhaise House, now an agricultural college, has a rare 1733 oval saloon and two storeys vaulted over in brick.

A tour going east and south would cover: **Cootehill**, 16 miles (26 km) east on the R118 which has a splendid Palladian house (Bellamont House, 049-52461, admission free by appointment) built for the Coote family in 1730 in Bellamont Forest; south-east 13 miles (21 km) on the R192 to **Shercock**, where the playwright Richard Brinsley Sheridan once lived; **Kingscourt**, whose Catholic

Map, page 260

Cavan's tourist office is on Farnham Street and is open all year Mon–Sat 9am–5pm. Tel: (049) 31942.

BELOW: Ballyconnell, Co. Cavan.

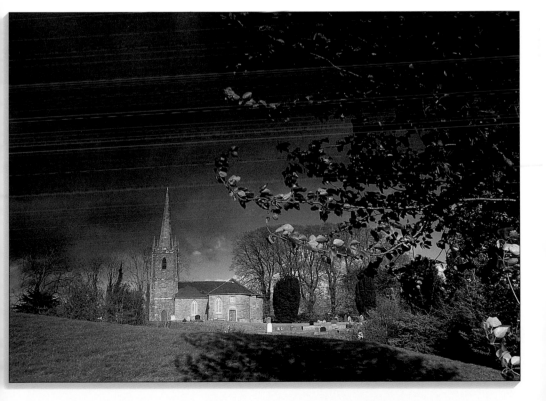

church has some renowned stained glass; **Bailieborough**, on the R165, which has a fine main street; **Virginia**, 19 miles (33 km) south-west on the N3, planned as a garrison town in 1610 and now a handsome, peaceful place with Cuilcagh House, owned by playwright Tom McIntyre (private), where Dean Swift began *Gulliver's Travels* 3 miles (5 km) east; and **Ballyjamesduff**, with a well-designed market house.

The area is rich in folk traditions. In the late 1960s, for example, thousands flocked from all over Ireland to **Lough Gowna**, a remote hamlet where a 17-year-old boy was reputed to have great powers of healing through being "the seventh son of a seventh son" and could supposedly cure even serious ailments by laying his hand on the afflicted.

Monaghan's mix of monotonous low hills and poor small farms was well captured by the novelist and poet Patrick Kavanagh (1905–67), who grew up here on a farm at Inishkeen.

BELOW: making music in a Monaghan pub.

Mild Monaghan

To the northeast, in Monaghan, is the small agricultural town of **Clones** ㉛ (pronounced *Clone-ess*), whose most famous son is Barry McGuigan, the "Clones cyclone" who became world featherweight boxing champion in 1985. The town's commercial centre is Fermanagh Street, signalling the town's former significance for the farmers of south Fermanagh. But, just as partition destroyed its role as an important railway hub, so the Troubles have hit trade as northerners have become more reluctant to cross the border. Also, the two tills on most shop counters hint at the effect of two different currencies. Since the Irish pound (or *punt*) broke its link with the British pound in the 1970s, it has often been the weaker of the two, making prices in the South uncompetitively high compared to those in the North; but at other times the punt has risen, making northern shops attractive to southerners.

Clones has an ancient lineage. The remains of a 12th-century Augustinian abbey (known as "**the Wee Abbey**") can be seen in Abbey Street. An ancient cross in the marketplace shows scenes from the Bible, such as the Fall of Adam and Eve and the Adoration of the Magi. The cemetery has an early **round tower**, 75 ft (23 metres) high and rather dilapidated, and an early Christian carved **sarcophagus**, the key to which can be obtained from nearby Patton's pub. Several Georgian houses are a reminder of the town's greatest period of prosperity, in the 18th century. Another sign of the vanished "Ascendancy" era are the "big houses", once the homes of the well-to-do Anglo-Irish, many of which have fallen into disrepair.

Monaghan is a quiet, trim county of snug farmhouses and tranquil market towns, and lakes and rivers that draw fishermen. Its administrative centre, **Monaghan** ㉜, 12 miles (19 km) northeast of Clones, has a **Market House** dating from 1792, an imposing 19th-century Gothic Revival cathedral (**St Macartan's**) an award-winning **County Museum** (047-82928, closed Tues) highlighting prehistoric relics and local arts and crafts. The **Garage Theatre** (047-81592) mounts excellent touring productions. To the north, 5 miles (8 km) on the R185, by Glaslough is reputedly haunted **Castle Leslie** (047-88100) bed-and breakfast home of the literary Leslie family.

To the south, east of **Newbliss**, 10 miles (16 km) on

the R188, at **Annamakerrig House** is the **Tyrone Guthrie Centre** (047-54003), an international haven for professional writers. Six miles (10 km) east is Rockcorry where John Gregg invented Gregg's Shorthand, America's favourite. The poet and novelist Patrick Kavanagh grew up 10 miles (16 km) east of attractive **Carrickmacross**, at tiny Inishkeen, where a riverside **museum** (042-7810, closed Tues) celebrates his work. Traditional local lace is sold in Carrickmacross. **Ballybay** and **Castleblayney** are unremarkable except for their proximity to **Lough Major** and **Muckno Lake**, both filled with a variety of coarse fish and surrounded by nature trails and picnic sites.

Bandit country

To the northeast and crossing the border again brings you to County Armagh, traditionally known as the Apple Orchard of Ireland, and more recently, its southern acres, thanks to terrorist activity near its border with the Republic, by the less inviting sobriquet of Bandit Country.

Its county town of **Armagh** ㉝ (always called a city despite a population of just 12,000) symbolises many of Northern Ireland's problems. Its two striking cathedrals – one Protestant, one Catholic, both called **St Patrick's** – sit on opposite hills like, someone once said, the horns of a dilemma. The two communities reside in separate parts of the city, behaving for the most part as if they were living on different planets.

Armagh is known for its dignified Georgian architecture. At one end of an oval **Mall** – where cricket is played in summer, rugby football in winter – is a classical courthouse, at the other a jailhouse. The charmingly arcane Ionic-pillared **County Museum** (The Mall, 01861-523070, admission free, closed Sun

Map, page 260

The Book of Armagh, a Latin manuscript of the Old Testament and two lives of St Patrick transcribed in 807, is kept in the library of Trinity College, Dublin.

BELOW: Armagh's two St Patrick's Cathedrals – one Catholic (left), the other Protestant.

ABOVE: the Navan Fort, an ancient site.

and bank holidays) contains many local artifacts, as well as records of Ireland's worst railway disaster, which happened in 1889 just outside Armagh; 80 Sunday School excursionists died when 10 uncoupled carriages ran down a steep incline into the path of a following train. Nearby, the **Royal Irish Fusiliers Museum** (Sovereign's House, The Mall, 01861-522911, admission free, opening times vary), exhibits a variety of regimental uniforms, medals and flags.

Access is free into the ordered gardens of the adjacent **Observatory** which also boast Ireland's only **Planetarium** (College Hill, 01861-523689, admission fee, closed Sun). Its Eartharium allows you to view cities in close-up via spy satellites and forecast the weather and its outdoor Astropark has a scale model of the solar system.

Two miles (3 km) west of the city, off the A28, is the high-tech **Navan Centre** (01861-525550, admission fee, closed Sun am in winter) celebrating Emain Macha, Ulster's Camelot around 600BC. Until recent restorations, it was a neglected hilltop; now it comes complete with hands-on computers and audio-visual interpretation facilities. Access to the hilltop itself is free.

The **Palace Stables Heritage Centre** (Friary Road, admission fee, closed Sunday am in winter), past the ruins of a 13th-century friary, at the former archbishop's palace, recreates the building's daily life in 1776 and offers carriage rides. In the city centre **St Patrick's Trian** (English Street, admission fee, closed Sunday am all year) explains St Patrick's connections with the city and cashes in on Dean Swift's habit of holidaying nearby with a "Land of Lilliput" presentation aimed at children.

BELOW: Saturday afternoon cricket on Armagh's Mall.

The city is surrounded by neat villages, reached through a network of pleasant lanes. Each May, the countryside around **Loughgall** is radiant with apple blos-

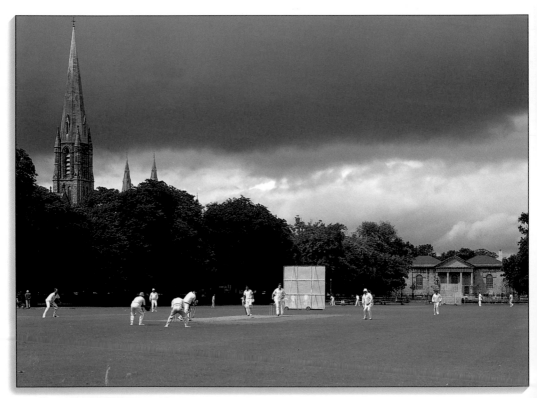

som. In the village the **Dan Winter Ancestral Home** (9 The Diamond, Derry-loughan Road, 01762-851344, admission free, Sunday pm only) displays details of the founding of the Orange Order. Near **Markethill**, in **Gosford Forest Park** (01861-551277, admission fee, closes at dusk), Gosford Castle is a large turreted mock-Norman edifice built of local granite. **Bessbrook** is a model linen-making town, created by a Quaker and therefore lacking a pub.

Crossmaglen has a remarkably large market square, containing a bronze monument to the IRA; this village was in the front line of battles between the IRA and the security forces. Remarkably, after enduring many bloody sectarian murders, Crossmaglen has begun promoting tourism with some success in the 1990s. On the B30, 8 miles (13 km) towards Camlough, the thatched **Mullaghbawn Folk Museum** (01693-888108, admission fee, open only Sun pm in winter) preserves a traditional farmhouse of past centuries. The village of **Tynan** has a 10th-century sculptured stone cross, 13 ft (4 metres) high.

Between Armagh and Belfast is a chain of towns built on commerce. **Portadown** ㉞, 10 miles (16 km) to the northeast, has found its role scaled down from that of a major railway junction to a prosperous market town noted for rose growing and coarse fishing. Linen manufacturing has diminished, as it has in **Lurgan**, 6 miles (10 km) further along the A3. In the 1960s it was decided to link the two towns to form the "lineal city" of **Craigavon**, thereby reducing congestion in Belfast; but the new city's population never arrived and civic pride has kept the separate identities of Portadown and Lurgan very much alive despite the mushrooming between them of housing estates, schools and countless traffic circles. Lough Neagh's wildlife is well explained in the **Lough Neagh Discovery Centre** (Oxford Island, 01762-322205, admission fee, closed Sun am Oct–Mar). Lough trips on the *Master McGra'* (Marina, Oxford Island, 016937-72950, not Oct–Easter) are available.

Seven miles (11 km) west of Portadown, off the B28, two National Trust mansions – 17th-century **Ardress House** (01762-851236) and 19th-century **The Argory** (01868-784753) charge admission fees and keep Trust opening times, closing weekdays in Apr, May and Sept, all Tuesdays and Oct–Mar.

Echoes of the Brontës

Banbridge ㉟, 10 miles (16 km) south of Lurgan, has a peculiar main street, bisected by an underpass taking through traffic, with sections of road on either side serving a varied collection of small shops.

To its south-east, off the B10, is "**Brontë Homeland**", promoted from the Brontë Interpretive Centre (Drumballyroney, Rathfriland, 018206-31152, admission fee, closed Nov–Feb and Mon all year), a confusingly signposted trail invented by the tourist authorities to capitalise on the fact that Patrick Brontë (or Brunty or Prunty), father of the novelists Charlotte, Emily and Ann, was born in a cottage at Emdale, 3 miles (5 km) southeast of Loughbrickland. The family's fame was cemented in Yorkshire, not in Emdale, and there's nothing here to conjure up the claustrophobia of *Wuthering Heights* or *Jane Eyre*. But the drive through country lanes so narrow that the hedges almost meet is worth

Map, page 260

Bullet, a variant of Cork's road bowling, is played in summer and autumn in the winding lanes around Armagh. The idea is to propel an iron ball over a 4km distance in the least number of throws. Motorists should be vigilant.

BELOW:
Kinnego Marina, Lough Neagh.

taking and, if you lose track of Patrick Brontë's trail on Ballynaskeagh Road, or Ballynafern or Lisnacroppin, it doesn't much matter.

The river valleys are peppered with the tall chimneys of disused linen mills so for access to the history and impact of what was the province's major industry go north-west along the Lagan valley to the impressive **Irish Linen Centre and Lisburn Museum** (Market Square, **Lisburn**, 01846-663377, admission fee, closed Sun am) with its hand-loom weaving workshop. Fascinating day and half-day summer tours, passing blue-flowered flax meadows and visiting linen processors modern and arcane, are available.

Newry ㊱, 19 miles (10 km) to the south-west of Banbridge, is a bustling border town, disfigured by the Troubles but, thanks to the resilience of the Northern Irish, a cheery enough place. Its mercantile history is recalled by a canal, one of Britain's oldest, detailed in **Newry Museum** (Arts Centre, Bank Parade, 01693-66232, admission free, closed Sun–Tues) and 12 miles (19 km) north on the A27 in **Scarva Visitor Centre** (Main Street, 01762-832163, admission free, closed Nov–Feb and all Mondays).

Four miles (6 km) west of Newry, on the A25, the thatched 18th-century **Derrymore House** (National Trust, 01238-510721, phone for details) recalls a more sheltered world.

ABOVE:
Derrymore House.

Seaside relaxations

The atmosphere lightens as you travel either 5 miles (8 km) southwest to **Slieve Gullion Forest Park** (016937-38248, admission fee, summer dawn to dusk, closed winter), where a forest drive winds up to two mountain-top Stone Age cairns, or southeast to the respectable little resorts of Warrenpoint and Rostrevor,

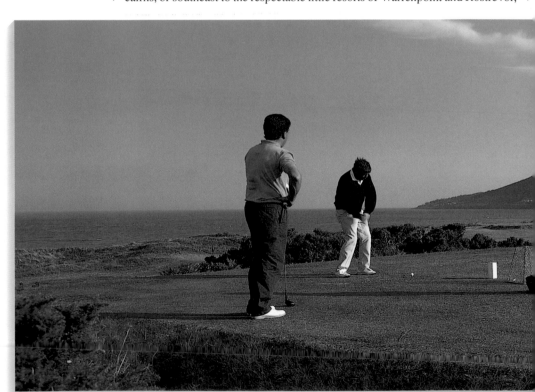

overlooking Carlingford Lough. **Warrenpoint** ③ has two piers (good for fishing), a spacious square and a half-mile promenade lined with trees. **Rostrevor**, a favoured retirement spot sheltered by high hills, has more of a Victorian atmosphere. A summertime ferry plies the lough (*Maiden of Mourne*, Carlingford Lough Cruises, 016937-72950) crossing to Omeath in the Republic. A steep half-mile walk up the slopes of **Slievemartin** brings you to **Cloghmore**, a "Big Stone" supposedly hurled by the Irish giant Fionn MacCool at a rival Scot. The geological explanation for this misplaced piece of granite is more mundane, having to do with glacial drift.

Skirting round the **Mourne Mountains**, past 14th-century **Greencastle** takes you to the active fishing village of **Kilkeel**, capital of the so-called "Kingdom of Mourne." Its winding streets, stepped footpaths and old houses are alluring. There's a choice here: you can proceed along the coast via **Annalong**, a smaller fishing village with old cottages and a **cornmill** (Marine Park, 013967-68736, admission fee, closed weekdays Easter–May and Sept–Oct and all winter) with waterwheel, or you can turn inland into the Mournes.

Meandering in the Mournes

The Mournes are "young" mountains (like the Alps) and their chameleon qualities attract walkers. At one moment the granite is grey, then it changes to pink. You walk by an isolated farmhouse, and within moments you find yourself in the middle of a wilderness. One minute, the Mournes justify all the songs written about them; the next, they become plain scrubland and unexceptional hills. The weather has a lot to do with it. Off the B27 the remote **Silent Valley** (Head Road, 01232-746581, admission fee) cradles a large dam which supplies Belfast

Map, page 260

Welcome to **MOURNE** Area Of Outstanding Natural Beauty

BELOW: Royal County Down Golf Club.

and Co. Down with water. **Slieve Donard**, the highest peak at 2,796 ft (850 metres), has exhilarating views.

As you reach the foothills of the Mournes, turn right just before Hilltown towards **Newcastle ❸**. This is east Down's main resort, with a fine, sandy beach, an inordinate number of cake shops, and the celebrated Royal County Down Golf Club. It tries for amusement arcade jollity, but is too small and picturesque to be truly vulgar. Several forest parks – **Donard**, **Tollymore**, **Castlewellan** (admission fees) – are good for riding (by pony or bicycle) or walking. This is an area that invites you to unwind, that doesn't understand people who are in a hurry.

Five miles (8 km) inland from Newcastle, **Castlewellan** is a picturesque village with a wide main street. Nine miles (14 km) to the west, **Rathfriland** is a steep-streeted plantation town with lively livestock sales and, as elsewhere in Ulster, kerbstones painted red, white and blue to show political allegiance.

As an alternative to heading into the Mournes from Newcastle, one can continue round the coast, via, at **Dundrum,** Ireland's finest Anglo-Norman castle to **Ardglass**, where several smaller, ruined castles hint at its strategic importance in the Middle Ages to unwelcome kings visiting from Britain. It is an important herring fishing centre.

Seven miles (11 km) inland to the northwest is **Downpatrick ❹**, which has a Georgian air and a cathedral supposedly built on the site of St Patrick's first stone church. The saint himself is said by some to be buried here; **Down County Museum** (The Mall, 01396-615281, free, closed Sun–Mon Oct–May) explains the proposition. The Christian theme continues, off the A7 a mile north-west at placid riverside Cistercian **Inch Abbey** (admission fee). The **Struell Wells** (free access always), off the B1, 1½ miles (3 km) east of the town, are evidence of pagan worshippers long before Christianity.

North of the town there begins a prosperous commuter belt, populated by well-spoken professional people who put their money into making their homes ever more comfortable. The source of their prosperity and the commercial magnet to which they are drawn each working day lies to the north: Belfast.

The Ards Peninsula

Comber ❹, 17 miles (27 km) to the north at the head of Strangford Lough, was a linen town and still has a working mill. The town centre retains its old character, despite the developers, with single-storey cottage shops and a square. **Castle Espie** (Wildfowl and Wetlands Trust, 78 Ballydrain Road, 01247-874146, admission fee) is base for Ireland's largest collection of ducks.

Strangford Lough, an environmental conservation area, is noted for its myriad islands, most of which are sunken drumlins, the smooth glacial hillocks which characterise the Co. Down rolling landscape. There are rocky shores on this side of the lough at places like **Whiterock Bay**. **Mahee Island**, accessible by a bridge, has a golf course and the remains of **Nendrum Abbey** (free access to site always, museum fee, closed Monday), an early monastery.

You can reach the **Ards Peninsula**, a 23-mile (37-

BELOW:
Strangford Lough.

km) long finger dotted with villages and beaches, by means of a regular car ferry which chugs a slanted course from **Strangford** ❹, 8 miles (13 km) from Down-patrick, across to Portaferry. The Vikings are said to have had a trading post at Strangford in the 9th century. Nearby is **Castle Ward House** (01396-881204, admission fee, closed Thursdays and Oct–March and weekdays Apr–June and Sept), an 18th-century Georgian mansion, once the home of the Lord of Ban-gor. Overlooking the lough, the house has two "fronts" in differing styles (clas-sical and gothic) because the Lord and his Lady had diverging tastes. There are wildfowl in the 700-acre (280-hectare) grounds and the **Strangford Lough Wildlife Centre** is located at the water's edge. There's also a Victorian laun-dry, two small 15th-century castles and an adventure playground for children.

The ferry across the mouth of the lough deposits you where the sunsets are as fine a sight as anywhere in the world and where the local lobster and the **Exploris** (Castle Street, 012477-28062, admission fee, closed Sun am), North-ern Ireland's only sea aquarium, are not to be missed.

Nine miles (14 km) north of Portaferry along the A20 is the one-street town of **Kircubbin**, a boating centre with a small pier jutting into Strangford Lough. Two miles (3 km) inland takes you to the **Kirkistown Circuit**, a wartime air-port and the home of car racing in Northern Ireland. Motor sport has a keen fol-lowing in Northern Ireland; motorcycle racing and rallying can take place on public roads closed by Act of Parliament for the events.

Four miles (6 km) further north on the A20 is the pretty village of **Greyabbey** is the site, with "physick garden", of a Cistercian abbey dated 1193, and one of the most complete of its type in Ireland (Grey Abbey, admission fee, closed Oct–Mar). Two miles north of the village is **Mount Stewart** (012477-881204,

Map, page 260

Emulating England's Glyndebourne, Castle Ward mounts three weeks of opera each June. Picnic hampers welcome.

BELOW: a windy day near the Irish Sea.

admission fee, closed Nov–Mar, weekdays Apr, June and Sept, and all Tues) another National Trust treasure, an 18th-century house which has several fine gardens and a mild microclimate which fosters delicate plants untypical of the area. The rhododendrons are particularly fine, and the gardens contain a variety of statues of griffins, satyrs, heraldic lions and the like. Mountstewart House was the birthplace of Lord Castlereagh, England's foreign secretary during the Napoleonic Wars. The **Temple of the Winds**, an 18th-century folly in the grounds, was built by James Stewart, a rival of Robert Adam, and is modelled on another in Athens. It offers a splendid view of the lough.

Newtownards ㊷, a sprawling commuter town at the head of Strangford Lough, belies its name; it's an old town, dating back to the 17th century. It was an old market town and still is a bustling shopping centre with a blend of traditional shops and a covered shopping centre. There is a fine sandstone town hall and other buildings of historical interest include **Movilla Abbey** on the site of a 6th-century monastery about 1 mile to the east of the town. The airfield, a centre for amateur fliers (Ulster Flying Club, 01247-813327), stages a spectacular annual display of aerobatics. The **Somme Heritage Centre** (233 Bangor Road, 01247-823202, admission fee, closed Mon Sept–June and Sunday am always), on Bangor Road, reconstructs elements of the 1916 battle in which many Ulstermen died.

Overlooking the town is **Scrabo Tower** (Scrabo Country Park, 01247-811491, closed Fri Oct–May and 28 Jan–11 Feb), a 19th-century memorial to the third Marquess of Londonderry, offering splendid vistas of the lough and the soft-hilled countryside and good walks in the nearby **Killynether Wood**.

Donaghadee ㊸, 8 miles (13 km) to the east, is notable for its much-painted

The First Battle of the Somme, in 1916, cost more than 1 million lives. Ulster regiments were heavily involved and their sacrifice is still cited by Unionist politicians wishing to demonstrate Northern Ireland's loyalty to Great Britain.

BELOW: Donaghadee.

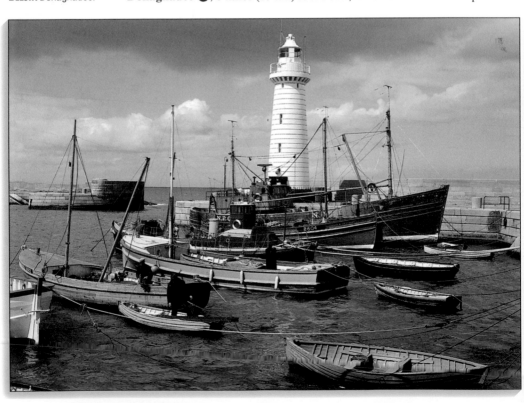

harbour and lighthouse, and summer boat trips (Nelson's Boats, 01247-883403) up Belfast Lough and to **Copeland Island** (a bird sanctuary), just offshore. The twisting road passes 18th century **Ballycopeland Windmill** (Millisle, 01247-861413, closed Sunday am and Mon and Oct–March) and quieter beaches at **Ballywalter** and **Ballyhalbert**, and the fishing port of **Portavogie**, which has occasional evening quayside fish auctions.

Popular resort

Bangor ㊹ was orginally a small seaside resort, noted for its abbey. The expensively rejuvenated seafront still has to gentrify some of its collection of fast-food bars and souvenir shops to do justice to the spanking new marina packed with yachts and cruisers. Rowing around the bay in hired punts and fishing trips from the pier are evergreen attractions. The town has a leisure centre with heated swimming and diving pools. For some reason, perhaps the bracing sea air, Bangor is favoured by evangelists who trawl for souls along the sea wall by the little harbour. The **North Down Heritage Centre** (Castle Park Avenue, 01247-271200, closed Sunday am always, and Monday Sept–June) could provide a refuge.

The old Bangor has been overgrown by acres of new housing developments and shopping centres, many of them inhabited by people who work in Belfast. It is a busy shopping town with a weekly open-air market, plenty of pubs and eating places, and parkland. The best beach is nearby **Ballyholme Bay**, a sandy arc which becomes very crowded when the sun shines.

If you leave Bangor by the A2, a signposted detour to the right will take in the beaches of **Helen's Bay**, the nearby wooded **Crawfordsburn Country Park**

Map, page 260

One of Bangor's first mentions in history is linked to a Viking raid in AD 839.

BELOW: all the fun of the fair at Bangor.

(01247-853621, free), and the picturesque village of **Crawfordsburn** with its charming **Old Inn**. Such havens are unusual so close to a city the size of Belfast.

The "Gold Coast"

The A2 from Bangor to Belfast runs through what locals enviously describe as the **"Gold Coast"**. This is stockbroker country, where lush lawns meet mature woodland. Hillside sites, overlooking the shipping lanes, have traditionally lured the well-heeled. **Cultra**, 6 miles (10 km) from Bangor, has leafy lanes, splendid houses, and the resplendent **Culloden Hotel**. They go in for yachting, golf and horse riding around here. Nowhere is more removed from the TV image of Northern Ireland. **Holywood**, an ancient religious settlement a mile further on, enjoys a quiet prosperity since it was bypassed. Nothing much happens here, apart from summer jazz and rumours of the odd dance around the Maypole, but it has pleasant shops, and good pubs and restaurants.

Nearby, at Cultra Manor is the award-winning **Ulster Folk and Transport Museum** ❹❺ (01232-428428, admission fee, closed Sunday am all year, plus Sat am Oct–March), which brings social history to life. Farm-houses, cottages, churches and mills have been painstakingly reconstructed – often brick by brick from their original locations. Freshly made soda bread, a local speciality, is sometimes baked over a traditional peat fire. On another part of the site the Transport Museum has its own fascination; exhibits range from horse-drawn chariots right up to a prototype of the ill-fated Belfast-built De Lorean sports car (the company crashed but the car lived on in the *Back to the Future* movies). The brilliant Ulster engineer Harry Ferguson, a pioneer of flying, tractors and four-wheel-drive cars, is the prize example of the remarkable local contribution to air, sea and land transport.

From here it's straight into Belfast (*see next chapter*).

North of Belfast

If you aren't in the mood for city life, however, a good ring-road system will take you through the city to the north shore of Belfast Lough and the suburbs of **White-abbey** and **Greenisland**, with some opulent housing.

Carrickfergus ❹❻, 12 miles (19 km) north from Belfast along the A2, is yet another market and dormitory town. Its big synthetic-fibre plants are empty now – a contemporary monument to its industrial past. The imposing 12th-century Norman **Castle** (The Harbour, 01960-351273, admission fee, closed Sunday am) beside the harbour, scene of gun-running exploits early in the 20th century, still attracts attention for its authenticity. It is a real castle in every sense, with a portcullis, ramparts looking out over the sea, chilling dungeons, cannons and a regimental museum in the keep. Looking to the new age of leisure, the town's **marina** has 300 berths. The parish church of St Nicholas (with stained-glass windows to Santa Claus) is 12th-century. The **Knight Ride and Heritage Plaza** (Antrim Street, 01960-366455, admission fee, closed Sunday am) provides the kind of monorail ride through history which can give interpretive centres a bad name. The preserved Carrickfergus Gasworks (Irish Quarter West, 01960-351438, admission fee, open Sunday pm only, June

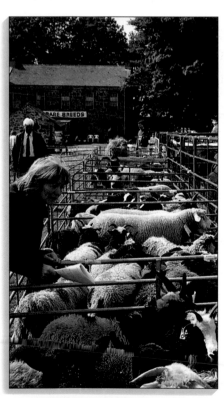

ABOVE: a plaque at Carrickfergus.
BELOW: rare breeds on show at the Ulster Folk and Transport Museum.

Aug) will fascinate the mechanically minded. A mile to the east, the **Andrew Jackson Centre** (Boneybefore, 01960-366455, admission fee, closed Sat and Sun pm) is a reconstruction of the thatched cottage home of Andrew Jackson, the seventh President of the United States.

The countryside north of Carrickfergus becomes rich meadow land, with the sleepy seaside town of **Whitehead,** base for the Railway Preservation Society of Ireland (22 Town Lane, Islandmagee, 01960-353567, occasional steam excursions). The town nestles at the mouth of the lough, with a seashore walk to the Black Head lighthouse. Beyond this begins the peninsula of **Island Magee**, with unspoilt beaches and caves, which wraps around Larne Lough. From here, the road runs into unlovely **Larne ⓐ**, a port with frequent ferries to and from Stranraer in Scotland (70 minutes away). The Larne and District Historical Centre (2 Victoria Lane, 01574-279482, free, closed Sun and Mon) has a historical centre featuring photographs from 100 years ago.

The Antrim Coast Road

The rewards of continuing along the coast are spectacular views of brown moorlands, white limestone, black basalt, red sandstone and blue sea along the **Antrim Coast Road**. A notable engineering achievement, it is explained in the Larne Interpretive Centre (Narrow Gauge Road, 01547-260088, free, closed Sun). The road, designed in 1834 by Sir Charles Lanyon as a work of famine relief, opened up an area whose inhabitants had previously found it easier to travel by sea to Scotland than overland to the rest of Ireland.

At various points, you can turn into one or other of Antrim's celebrated nine glens – **Glenarm, Glencloy, Glenariff, Glenballyeamon, Glenaan, Glencorp,**

Map, page 260

Ulster Unionists opposed to a Roman Catholic-dominated united Ireland unloaded a large consignment of German-made rifles in Larne harbour in 1914. World War I shelved the problem for a few years.

BELOW:
Carrickfergus Castle, recalling the Norman Conquest; a round tower overlooking Larne Lough.

Glendun, **Glenshesk** and **Glentaisie** – and into another world. It's a world of weather-beaten farmers in tweeds and baggy trousers; a world of sheep sales conducted by auctioneers who talk like machine guns; a world with a baffling dialect that turns an ewe into a *yow* and "six" into *sex*; a world where poteen, the "mountain dew", is distilled in lonely places. It's not hard to track down this illicit (and potentially lethal) alcohol. "It's floating about," they'll tell you. "In fact it's practically running down the streets."

Ballygalley ④⑧, at the start of the famous scenic drive, has a 1625 fortified manor house (now a hotel) and, inland from the coast road, a well-preserved old mill and pottery. **White Bay** is a picnic area around which small fossils can be found. **Glenarm** has a beautiful park adjoining a fussy castle, home of the Earls of Antrim. **Carnlough** has a fine harbour and, running over its main street, a white bridge built in 1854 to carry limestone from the quarries to waiting boats. The Londonderry Arms hotel (also 1854) retains the charms of an old coaching inn. An eponymous literary summer school at Garron Tower 5 miles (8 km) north celebrates John Hewitt, an acerbic dissenter poet.

An Irish song-and-dance festival is held each July in the village of **Waterfoot**. This is also the entrance to **Glenariff Glen**, a deep wooded gorge dubbed by Thackeray "Switzerland in miniature". Wild flowers carpet the upper glen in spring and early summer, and slippery rustic footbridges carry walkers over the Glenariff River, past postcard-pretty waterfalls.

About 1½ miles (2 km) to the north, **Cushendall**, "capital of the glens", was created largely by a wealthy 19th-century landowner, Francis Turnly. His most striking structure was the four-storey red sandstone **Curfew Tower**, built as "a place of confinement for idlers and rioters". The village has a good beach and is

ABOVE: roaming the Glens of Antrim.

BELOW: Cushendun.

a popular sailing centre. Just to the north is **Layde Old Church**, dating back to the 13th century and containing some ancient vaults. Six miles (10 km) further on, **Cushendun** ㊾ is a village of charming Cornish-style white cottages, graceful old houses and friendly pubs, has been captured on countless canvases and the entire place is protected by the National Trust.

The northern coast

Crossing the towering **Glendun Viaduct** (1839), one passes the ruins of **Bonamargy Friary**, founded around 1500. A vault contains the massive coffins of several MacDonnell chieftains who stood out successfully against the forces of England's Queen Elizabeth I. Nearby, **Corrymeela Community House** is an inter-denominational conference and holiday centre, whose idealism shines out amid Northern Ireland's prevailing political cynicism.

The best time to visit **Ballycastle** ㊿ is during the **Auld Lammas Fair**, held on the last Monday and Tuesday of August. Then this unspoiled town turns into one throbbing market place as farmers with impenetrable accents bring their livestock in from the glens and hundreds of stalls sell souvenirs, bric-a-brac, dulse (dried, edible seaweed) and yellowman (a sweet confectionery). The big attraction is the *craic* – pronounced "crack" (a Scots-Irish word for talk, enlivened by a glass or two of Bushmills). It's great fun – an authentic folk event that owes nothing to the manipulations of tourist boards. The **Ballycastle Museum** (59 Castle Streeet, 012657-62024, free, closed Oct– June) concentrates on the folk social history of the Glens.

A sea-front memorial marks the spot where, in 1898, Guglielmo Marconi first seriously tested wireless telegraphy. He made his historic transmission between here and **Rathlin Island** ㊿, 8 miles (13 km) off the coast towards Scotland's Mull of Kintyre. The boomerang shaped island, whose population has slumped from 2,000 to 100 since 1850, makes its living from farming and fishing and attracts geologists, botanists and birdwatchers; there is a reserve (012657-63935) managed by the Royal Society for the Protection of Birds, an estimated 10,000 birds of 175 species, 79 of them breeding. With the new ferry (012657 620242) installed, uncertainties about the 50-minute sailings being affected by weather and high seas are hopefully over. But whether the decrease in isolation will benefit the island's environment is another matter. There is one pub and one hotel – but no policeman, and no need for one.

Five miles (8 km) west, off the A2, is the **Carrick-a-rede Rope Bridge** (May-September, 012657 31159), 65 ft (20 metres) wide swinging over a 80-ft (24-metre) chasm to an island salmon fishery. Past Whitepark Bay is **Dunseverick Castle,** the slight remains of a 6th-century fortress perched on a high crag overlooking a fishing harbour.

The Giant's Causeway

The castle is at the eastern end of the **Giant's Causeway** 52, an astonishing assembly of 37,000 basalt columns, mostly perfect hexagonals formed by the cooling of molten lava. Dr Samuel Johnson, when asked by

The Auld Lammas Fair is Ireland's oldest, dating back to 1606, when a charter was first granted.

BELOW: eating seaweed, a delicacy at Ballycastle's Auld Lammas Fair.

Map, page 260

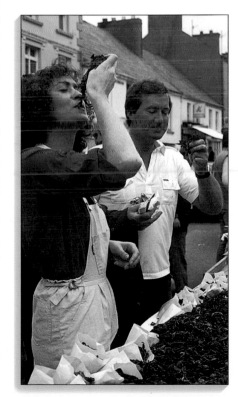

his biographer James Boswell whether this wonder of the world was worth seeing, gave the immortal reply: "Worth seeing? yes; but not worth going to see." It was a shrewd judgment in the 1770s when roads in the region were primitive enough to turn a journey into an expedition; indeed, the existence of the Causeway hadn't been known at all to the outside world until a gadabout Bishop of Derry stumbled upon them in 1692. Today this geological curiosity is accessible to the most monstrous tourist coaches, but it can still disappoint some visitors, who expect the columns to be bigger (the tallest, in the **Giant's Organ**, are about 12 metres) or who find that their regularity only diminishes their magnificence. It remains worth seeing, though. The formal approach is via the Causeway Centre (Causeway Head, 012657-31855, car park fee) 2 miles (3 km) north of Bushmills on the B146.

The world's oldest distillery

The distillery at **Bushmills** ⑤ (Distillery Road, 012657-31521) a couple of miles away, boasts the world's oldest whiskey-making licence (1609). Old Bushmills, Black Bush and Bushmills Malt, made from local barley and the water that flows by in St Columb's Rill, can be tasted after a tour. Connoisseurs tend to prefer the classic Black Bush to the more touted (and expensive) malt. The main difference between Scotch whisky and Irish whiskey, apart from the spelling, is that Scotch is distilled twice and Irish three times.

About 2 miles (3 km) along the coast road are the romantic remains of **Dunluce Castle** (closed Mon and Sun am, Oct–Mar). Poised on a rocky headland besides sheer cliffs, the 14th-century stronghold is immense and dramatic. The novelist William Makepeace Thackeray wrote of "those grey towers of Dun-

BELOW: Dunluce Castle; the Giant's Causeway.

Map, page 260

luce standing upon a leaden rock and looking as if some old old princess of old old fairy times were dragon guarded within." It was abandoned in 1641, two years after part of the kitchen collapsed into the sea during a storm, carrying many of the servants to their death. In the graveyard of the adjacent ruined church are buried sailors from the Spanish Armada galleass *Girona*, which was wrecked on nearby rocks in 1588 with 1,300 men on board and was located on the seabed in 1967. Many of the *Girona*'s treasures are in the Ulster Museum, Belfast.

Next along the coast are two seaside resorts. **Portrush ㊹** is the brasher, tackier, offering amusement arcades, burger bars, karaoke pubs, souvenir shops, guest-houses, a children's adventure play park, boats trips for sea fishing and viewing the Causeway and two championship golf courses. The **Dunluce Centre** (01256-824444, admission fee, closed Sat and Sun am, mid-Sept– Mar) offers virtual-reality "myths and legends"). **Portrush Countryside Centre** (Landsdowne Crescent, 01256-823600, free, closed Oct–Mar) has rock pool animals in a touch tank. **Portstewart** is the quieter, a tidy Victorian town with a huge strand, excellent for beach casting but plagued by speeding cars which, unaccountably, are allowed free access. Long-distance walkers can pick up the **North Antrim Coast Path** at Portstewart Strand; it forms part of the Ulster Way and extends eastwards for 40 miles (64 km) to **Murlough Bay**. Nearby **Coleraine** is an unimaginative market town whose traffic schemes make little of its setting on the wide River Bann or of the fact that man's earliest settlement in Ireland was found at the 200-ft (60-metre) **Mount Sandel** in its southern suburbs. However, its university's **Riverside Theatre** (Colmore Road, 01265-51388) imports interesting productions during term.

The Royal Portrush Golf Club is Northern Ireland's finest; it has one 9-hole and two 18-hole courses. Tel: (01265) 822311.

BELOW: Portstewart.

A choice of routes

Here, you can either continue westwards towards Derry City or proceed south towards Aldergrove Airport and Belfast.

Along the first choice, the A2 towards Derry City, on a windswept headland at **Downhill** ⑤, the massive roofless ruin of **Downhill Castle** (1780) dominates the skyline. Its **Mussenden Temple** (Mussenden Road, Castlerock, 01256-848728, free, closed Oct–Mar and weekdays Apr–June and Sept), is perched precariously near a 200-ft (60-metre) cliff and housed an eccentric bishop's library and possibly his mistress; it was inspired by the temples of Vesta at Tivoli and Rome. **Downhill Forest** has lovely walks, a fish pond and waterfalls.

An inscription on Mussenden Temple reads: "It is agreeable to watch, from land, someone else involved in a great struggle while winds whip up the waves out at sea."

Beyond is **Magilligan Strand**, Ireland's longest beach. Along its magnificent 7 miles (11 km) of sand dunes can be found teal, tern, mallard, snipe, wild geese, and 120 different kinds of seashells. At the beginning of the strand is a **Martello Tower** with walls 10 ft (3 metres) thick, built during the Napoleonic wars. A ferry is proposed to Greencastle in Donegal.

The alternative route is southwards through the relatively prosperous farming country "east of the **Bann**". This long, under-used river, which flows from the southeast of the province through Lough Neagh and into the Atlantic near Portstewart, is a rough and ready political dividing line between the western counties of Londonderry and Tyrone, with their preponderance of nationalists and Roman Catholics, and the eastern counties of Antrim and Down, with their Unionist/Protestant majority. In a thriving market town like **Ballymoney** ⑤, 17 miles (27 km) southwest of Ballycastle, archaic words that would have been familiar to Shakespeare crop up in everyday conversation – a legacy of the Scots Presbyterians planted as settlers in the 1800s.

BELOW: the Mussenden Temple.

As elsewhere in Ulster, churches loom large. There's one on each of the four roads leading into a small village like **Dervock**, for instance, 4 miles (6 km) north of Ballymoney and ancestral home of America's President William McKinley (assassinated in 1901). Legend says that this strategic siting of churches keeps the Devil out. Locals suggest it probably keeps him in. Off the B96, 20 miles (33 km) south, the restored **Arthur Ancestral Home** (Dreen, Cullybackey, 01266-44111, admission fee, closed Sun and Sept–Apr) commemorates Chester Alan Arthur, US president from 1881 to 1885, whose father emigrated from it in 1815.

Ballymena ⑤, 19 miles (30 km) southeast of Ballymoney, is the staunchly Protestant business centre of Antrim and, as a result perhaps of the strong Scottish influence, has been unkindly called the meanest town in Ireland.

Water sports on Lough Neagh

Antrim ⑤, the county town, 11 miles (18 km) to the southeast, has more to see. There's an almost perfectly preserved round tower, more than 1,000 years old, in Steeple Park, and the **Antrim Castle Gardens,** (Masserene Demense, 01849-428000) are laid out like a mini-Versailles. They run down to the shore of **Lough Neagh, whose** 17-mile length and 11-mile breadth (27 by 18 km) make it the largest inland sheet of water in the British Isles. **Pogue's Entry** (Church Street, 01849-

Map, page 260

428331) recalls the life of Alexander Irvine who became a missionary on New York's Bowery.

Because of the lough's marshy edges, it has surprisingly few access points. But recreational facilities for sailing and water-skiing are at last being developed, with marinas at **Oxford Island** (south shore) and **Ballyronan** (west shore). The *Maid of Antrim* (Sixmilewater Marina, 01849-463133, June–Sept) offers one-hour cruises. A large eel fishing industry is based at **Toome**. Until it became a fishermen's cooperative, gun battles used to take place on Lough Neagh between the police's patrol boats and the vessels of organised poachers.

A less fraught view of the lough can be had, in summer, from the steam locomotives on **Shane's Castle Railway** (01849-428216), a narrow-gauge track on a private estate on the north shore near **Randalstown**. There's a deer park and nature reserve here too.

Near **Crumlin** ⏱, to the south of Antrim, is **Station 597** (Langford Lodge, Gortnagallon Road, 01849 423896, admission fee, closed Dec–Easter, plus Sat and Sun am) designed to appeal to veterans of the US 8th Army Air Force based here in World War II. There are medals, maps and audio-visuals.

Wonderfully atmospheric, **Patterson's Spade Mill** (751 Antrim Road, Templepatrick, 01849 433619, admission fee, closed Oct–Mar and weekdays Apr, June and Sept) is the last working water-powered spade mill in Ireland. And you can buy a spade, always remembering the Ulster saying about people who "dig with the other foot" – a reference from the days when the shapes of spades were very localised and a stranger's home and therefore, by inference, his religion could be told from the cut of his spade. Some obsessions in Ulster don't change much over the centuries.

TIP

To fish in Lough Neagh, you first need a rod licence from the Foyle Fisheries Commission (Tel: 01504 42100). You may then need a further permit from an angling club.

BELOW: Shane's Castle narrow-gauge railway.

MEN WHO MARCH

Parades and bunting, bands and bibles... it's hard to escape these provocative rituals during July and August. Just what is the marching season all about?

Northern Ireland is unique in its flourishing popular culture: there are bands in every village and every housing estate, and nowhere else in the UK do normally discreet citizens sing and dance in the streets. There are many processions throughout the year, and some quiet church parades, but the prolonged marching season in July and August can heighten sectarian tensions.

The main Orange procession, which celebrates the 1690 Battle of the Boyne in which William III (William of Orange) cemented the Protestant heritage, takes place on 12 July. On 13 July, the Black Men (the Orange Order's elite) dress up in period costume to re-enact King Billy's routing of the Catholic King James II in the "Sham Fight" at Scarva, County Down. On 12 August the Apprentice Boys march through Derry City in memory of 13 apprentices who closed the city's gates against the forces of James II.

THE GREEN ORANGEMEN

Lady's Day, in honour of the Madonna, Mary Mother of God, is held on 15 August by the Ancient Order of Hibernians, who are sometimes known as the Green Orangemen. (Green symbolises Catholic Ireland, orange Protestant Ulster.) Like their Orange counterparts, the Hibernians mix prayer with pageantry.

Before the current Troubles began in 1969, many hoped that such pageantry would become less political and more of a tourist attraction. Instead, it appears to Catholics a sign of "triumphalism" and to Protestants as another nationalist provocation.

◁ **THE BIG PARADE**
In Belfast, the main 12 July Orange parade is a massive affair that can take up to four hours to pass any given point. It attracts followers from all over the world, including Glasgow, Liverpool, Canada, Australia and New Zealand.

△ **WEARING THE GREEN...**
The Ancient Order of Hibernians dates its origins to 1565 when persecuted Irish Catholics formed armed bands to protect their priest. The order united in its present form in 1838. Its main march takes place on 15 August.

◁ DRUMMING IT IN

The booming Lambeg drum, named after a village near Belfast, is often cited by nationalists as an obvious example of the Orangemen's triumphalist attitude towards Catholics. The "loyalists" say they march – or "walk" – simply to demonstrate their loyalty to the Protestant faith and to the British monarch.

▽ THE GREEN MACHINE

By rejecting the use of force to gain a united Ireland after World War I, the Hibernians lost ground to extremists, and today they number only about 20,000. There are probably five times as many Orangemen. Both Orders enjoy hymns and "blood and thunder" party tunes.

▽ CATCHING THEM WHEN THEY'RE YOUNG

Many Northern Irish children, who learn sectarian songs along with nursery rhymes, start marching at an early age. But fewer than 10 percent of Ulster schoolboys are lodge members today, compared with more than one-third 30 years ago.

△ ...AND THE ORANGE

The Orange Order dates back to the late 18th century when Protestant formed groups to defend their land from raids by its former Catholic owners. They celebrate the victory of William of Orange over the Catholic James II in 1690.

WHY THE BANDS ARE BIG BUSINESS

The world-famous flautist James Galway started his career in a Belfast band, and there can be few other parts of Europe where such a high percentage of the population plays a musical instrument.

Despite the years of conflict, enthusiasm for bands and music remains as jubilant now as it ever was. In late spring and early summer, motorists driving through the leafy lanes of the Ulster countryside must be prepared to round a corner and confront columns of men in bowler hats solemnly drumming and tootling their way to a local contest.

Scottish and Gaelic pipers compete with ecumenical harmony, at their own expense and "for the glory of it", in villages and small towns throughout summer. With a set of pipes costing around £1,500, that means there may be £2.5 million worth of pipes keening at a typical contest.

There are celebrated brass bands, like the Templemore and Britannia. Fife and drum, flute and even the tin whistle are favoured by the young, with accordians for girls. The musical range is colourful and varied: Irish or Scottish folk songs, "blood and thunder" party tunes (Orange or Green), military marches and hymns.

There are few places in the West where folk traditions remain so central to everyday life as in Ulster.

BELFAST

Forget the television coverage. This is a city of unexpected charms, mixing splendid Victorian architecture with a genuine hospitality

Map, page 316

A part from one unique feature, Belfast is an unremarkable, medium-sized, post-industrial city on the western fringes of Europe. Its unique feature is that, as the capital of Northern Ireland, it has made world headlines for 30 years. Its setting, in a saucer of green hills and spanning the mouth of the **River Lagan** as it flows east into the Irish Sea, is charming. There are serried rows of red-brick terraces, a worthy, white stone and marble City Hall. The Linen Conservation Area attests to the source of its founding wealth and man-made fibre factories in surrounding towns continue textile's traditions. Massive cranes dominate the skyline where the Harland and Wolff shipyards produced the doomed *Titanic* and now, much reduced, maintain other traditional engineering skills. Short Brothers aerospace company remains a contender in the weapons race.

Belfast (pop. 400,000) looks little different from a provincial English city. Donegall Place, its "main street", is lined with UK multiple stores such as Marks & Spencer and Boots. And Britain's monarchy is well represented on the map. The first major bridge to link the city east and west was named Queen's for England's Victoria. The university is named Queen's for her too. Albert, her consort, gave his name to a monolithic, now leaning, clocktower. The Royal Botanic Gardens provide an island of calm. Windsor Park stages soccer internationals.

But 30 years of the "troubles" and 800 years of English colonial rule have set the city apart. In the blue-collar enclaves, the gable ends of red-brick houses are bright with murals. In one area, this "folk art" portrays hooded figures brandishing Kalashnikov rifles and the green, white and orange of the Irish Republic's tricolour flag; in another area, it features King Billy (England's William III) crossing the Boyne on his white horse.

A brief history of Belfast time

The city's history is brief, by European standards. When John de Courcy, an Anglo-Norman freebooter, marched north to take Ulster from Gaelic hands in 1177, the place was known for little more than its approach to the crossing point (*béal feirsde* in Gaelic) at the mouth of the Lagan. The 12th-century Irish horsemen, bareback, stirrup-less, were no match for de Courcy's mail-armoured lancers. De Courcy's aides built a strategic castle, fought over for centuries and remembered now only in a city crossroads, Castle Junction. In Elizabeth I's reign, Protestant Tudor England, at war with Spain, fought Catholic Ireland. The Virgin Queen's favourite, Lord Essex, built a fort at Fortwilliam and, in the fashion of the times, put to the sword the Irish he invited to dinner. Although he planned a corporate town here, Essex failed in this

PRECEDING PAGES: Belfast City Hall. **LEFT:** the City Hall's ornate dome. **BELOW:** the new Waterfront Hall.

Belfast

0   300 m
0   300 yds

Cave Hill Country Park & Zoological Gardens

Gaol & Courthouse

Clifton Street
Westlink
Clifton House
Great George's Street
St. Patrick Street
Little Patrick Street
Sinclair Seamen's Presb. Church
Clarendon Dock
Donegall Quay
Queen's Quay
Abercorn Basin
Queen's Road
Harbour Office
Isle of Man Ferry Terminal
Sea Cat Terminal
Lagan Bridge
Sydenham Road

Peter's Hill
Carrick Hill
Donegall Street
York Street
Academy Street
Talbot St.
Dunbar Link
Corporation Street
Albert Sq.
General Post Office
Custom House
Lagan Lookout Centre
Queen Elizabeth II Bridge
Middlepath St.
End
Mountpottinger Rd.

Gardiner St.
North Street
Royal Av.
North Street
Belfast Central Library
St. Anne's Cathedral
Waring St.
Hill St.
Donegall Quay
Queen's Quay
Albert Memorial Clock
Queen's Bridge
Queen's Bridge
Bridge End
Strand
Parliament Buildings; Stormont

Westlink
Durham Street
Smithfield Market
Northern Bank
Rosemary St.
Bridge St.
High Street
Ulster Bank
St. George
Victoria Street
Albert Sq.
Q
Short Strand

Castle Court Shopping Centre
P
Bank St.
Castle Street
O Kelly's Cellars
Corn-market
Ann Street
Arthur Sq.
Oxford Street

Old Museum Arts Centre
College Sq. North
Linen Hall Library
N
Donegall Pl.
Donegall Sq. N.
Chichester Street
Waterfront Concert Hall
Q
Lagan Bank Road

M Royal Belfast Academical Institution
Wellington Pl.
A City Hall
East Street
May Street
Royal Courts of Justice
Lanyon Pl.
Central Station
Bridge End
Street

Howard St.
Donegall Sq. S.
West
St. George's Market
East Bridge Street

Grosvenor Road
K Grand Opera House & Cirque
Crown Liquor Saloon
L
Franklin St.
Alfred Street
St. Malachy
C
Friendly St.
River Lagan

J Europa Hotel
Gt. Victoria St. Station
Bedford St.
B Ulster Hall
Linen Hall St.
Eliza St.
Welsh St.
Steward Street

Hope St.
Ormeau Avenue
Cromac Street
McAuley St.
Embankment

Sandy Row
D Ormeau Baths Gallery
Dublin Road
P
Wellwood St.
Lindsay Street
Ormeau
Ormeau Park

Blythe Street
Donegall Pass
Golf Course
Ravenhill Road

Shaftesbury Sq.
Botanic Station
Vernon Street
Ardenlee Av.

Donegall Road
City Hospital Station
Arts Theatre
Bradbury Pl.
Botanic Avenue
I Empire Music Hall
McClure Street
Balfour Avenue

Belfast City Hospital
Lisburn Road
Lr. Crescent
Cromwell Road
Mt. Charles St.
University Street
Fitzroy Avenue
Farnham St.
Ormeau Road

Queen's Film Theatre
H Union Presbyterian Theological College
Rugby Rd.
University Street
Jerusalem Street
Agincourt Street

E Queen's University
Ulster Museum G
Rugby Rd.
Rugby Avenue
Golf Course

Elmwood Avenue
College Gardens
Wellesley Avenue
Stranmillis Road
Royal
F Botanic
Gardens
Eglantine Avenue
Malone Road
Queen's University Sports Complex
Annadale Embankment
Stranmillis Embankment
Elgin Street
Delhi Street
Ava Street
Park Road
Ravenhill Road

venture and the task was left to Arthur Chichester, a robber of tax collectors, who was rewarded for deploying a scorched-earth policy against Irish resistance. He built a "towne of good forme" and it was all his, by its charter of incorporation, by 1613.

It was another Chichester of flawed character who made possible the modern city. For such were the extravagances of George Augustus Chichester, Lord Belfast – otherwise known as Gambling George – that he was in a debtors' prison before he succeeded to the title of 2nd Marquis of Donegall, and possession of the city, in 1799. Twenty years later much of his lands were leased in perpetuity, the rest sold on his death to meet massive debts.

Donegall Place, which was still shopless, a mix of mansions, orchards and falconries, was thus opened up to speculators who found their champion in architect Sir Charles Lanyon. A flamboyant ruthless and corrupt speculator, philanderer and Conservative MP, Lanyon made his first fortune marrying the boss's daughter and later became Mayor of Belfast.

At a time when financial services were less than regulated, banks which Lanyon designed had the solidity of an Italian merchant prince's palace. His County Gaol, County Courthouse and Custom House dignified authority. His Deaf and Dumb Institution glorified its benefactor, his Queen's College echoed Oxford's dreaming spires, and his Presbyterian College offered diligence and obedience. His Queen's Bridge underlined the monarch's majesty, his viaducts made permanent the railways of commerce, and his 14 churches beckoned God's blessing down upon the worthy. To understand what made Belfast what it is, a tour of his buildings is more than a useful aid, and it is possible to build a walking tour loosely around the Lanyon Trail.

The city centre

Belfast's imposing **City Hall** (Donegall Square, tel. 320202, admission free, tours Wednesday am), with its imported marbled interior, isn't Lanyon's. It was designed by Brumwell Thomas, a Londoner, who had to sue the Corporation for his fees, and was built in the early years of the 20th century. The domes of its exterior and of its Council Chamber – laid out as to the manner of Westminster's House of Commons – pay tribute to the great English architect, Sir Christopher Wren. Northern Ireland's first House of Commons sat there in 1921–22, its Whispering Gallery has heard many a whisper, many a roar, and the assorted statuary speaks of a time when Britain's Empire ruled far and wide.

The best view of Thomas's work is not of the front with its dumpy statue of Queen Victoria, but rather of its rear, from down **Linen Hall Street** running parallel to **Bedford Street** in the **Linen Conservation Area,** still resonant with linen warehouses whose style is typified by Lanyon's work at number **35–37**. The nearby **Ulster Hall** (30 Bedford Street, tel: 323 900), once a music hall, hosts weekly Ulster Orchestra concerts, boxing matches, rock gigs and beerfests. Its annex, the **Group Theatre**, is the base for the province's amateur drama movement, but alternates their plays with avant garde professional

Map, page 316

TIP

If telephoning from outside Belfast, prefix all numbers in this chapter with the code 01232 (outside the country: 44-1232).

BELOW: Belfast's high street fashion.

productions, bewildering senior citizen season ticket holders. East of Linen Hall Street runs **Alfred Street** with its wonderfully castellated red-brick Catholic **St Malachy's Church** . The creamy fan-vaulted ceiling, a wedding cake upturned, would have served well the cathedral it was intended to be. In 1886 the tolling of its bell was deemed to interfere with the maturing of whiskey in Dunville's then adjacent distillery. The bell was removed.

Where Linen Hall Street meets **Ormeau Avenue**, by the BBC building, Belfast's tiny red-light district operates at night on street corners by the city's newest modernist art space, the **Ormeau Baths Gallery** (18 Ormeau Avenue, tel: 321402, admission free, closed Sun and Mon), which makes good use of an imaginative conversion of an 1887 public bath house.

The Golden Mile

No one knows where the city's much vaunted **"Golden Mile"** begins – or ends. Christened thus by a Tourist Board flaneur in the troubled tourist-free 1970s, it is an ever-changing 20-hour-a-day banlieu of bistros, restaurants, theme bars, ethnic eateries, pizza parlours, burger bars and design houses. It encompasses, roughly, a triangle whose base runs from Donegall Place's Linen Hall Library to College Square North's avant-garde, community-based **Old Museum Arts Centre** (7 College Square North, tel: 235053, closed Sun). Its east side is the Bedford Street–Dublin Road–Bradbury Place axis. Its apex is Queen's University. Its west side is definitely Great Victoria Street. By 3am the thoroughfare is impassable as disco clubs disgorge.

Although the Golden Mile may not rival London's Covent Garden, it does

offer variety. **Morrison's**, on Bedford Street, was the first bar to market itself as a recreation of the Edwardian rural spirit grocery store. **Dempsey's** opts for glitz and **Lavery's Gin Palace** in **Bradbury Place** melds 1960s drop-outs with '90s clubbers. Amongst the ethnics, crepuscular **Archana** does a firey balti and of the bistros, **La Belle Epoque** is a quiet haven of French provincial food. Its partner, **Frogities** in **Bradbury Place** dispenses with bookings, seeking younger customers. **Bishop's** dispenses fine fish and chips, mushy peas, pots of tea, slices of white bread, unselfconscious in its post-modernism.

Tom Caldwell's Gallery (40 Bradbury Place, tel: 232226, admission free, closed Sun) markets Irish landscapes and still-lifes to the well-to-do, whilst the **Fenderesky** (2 University Road, tel: 325245, admission free, closed Sat–Mon), in the enterprising Scots baronial-style granite **Crescent Arts Centre** (tel: 242338), offers the best of contemporary Irish painting. The Centre itself, though obsessed with New Age-ery, runs a discerning line up of jazz, Latin American music, dance, cabaret and experimental theatre.

The university area

Queen's University **E**, its blue-tinged red brick at its best near dusk, is one of Lanyon's delights, a pinnacle of Early Victorian, appropriating the Tudor of Oxford's Magdalen College. Its quad, open all hours, is rich in cherry trees and looks superb in May's blossom-time. The Visitor Centre (tel: 245133) keeps office hours. Across University Road, a gilded cockerel tops the spire of Italiante **Elmwood Hall**, a deconsecrated church, home to the Ulster Orchestra and a core venue for the University's adventurous autumnal Belfast Festival at Queen's (25 College Gardens, tel: 665577), which had become formulaic and middle-brow for years until it was re-born in 1997 under direc-

Map, page 316

Queen's College, named in honour of Queen Victoria, was established in 1849 and incorporated as a separate university in 1908. Pressed for space, it has taken over most of the houses in the vicinity.

BELOW: graduation, Queen's University.

tor Sean Doran. Work by Robert Wilson, John Cage, Silviu Pucarete, Bill Viola and Hans Peter Kuhn has become standard fare. The **Queen's Film Theatre** (7 University Square Mews, tel: 244857) is an art-house cinema and the **Bell Gallery** (13 Adelaide Park, 662998, phone first) deals in Irish landscapes.

South of the University, the **Royal Botanic Gardens ⑤** (tel: 324902, admission free, closes at dusk) contain another Lanyon gem, his curvilinear **Palm House** (tel: 324902, admission free, closed Sat and Sun mornings). It dates from an era when the city's botanist clergymen preached to the far-flung Empire's corners, returning home with exotic plants sealed safe in micro-climate jars devised by a local inventor. Balloons once ascended here, edifying the tradesmen classes. Now Belfast-born Van Morrison rocks its Midsummernight's dream concerts.

On the park's Stranmillis Road boundary, north of the area's bistros, the excellent **Ulster Museum ⑥** (Botanic Gardens, tel: 381251, admission free, closed Sat and Sun morning) houses well-presented displays of Irish art from the Bronze Age to today's, and explains the island's geological, biological, sociological and industrial histories. The natural science areas, plus the treasures rescued from the north coast wreck of the Spanish Armada galleas *Gerona*, are splendid. The museum shop sells replicas of these treasures, most poignant of which is a fine gold ring bearing the inscription *No tengo mas que dar te* – "I have nothing more to give you". Past the museum there are impressive views across the city of the white Portland stone of the former Parliament Buildings at Stormont.

East, past the Palm House, in College Park, is another Lanyon creation, **Union Presbyterian Theological College ⑪** (108 Botanic Avenue, tel: 325374, admission by arrangement), fronted by Doric columns and built of beautiful, now neglected, Scrabo stone from County Down. The Corinthian-columned library and chapel housed Northern Ireland's first Parliament in the 1920s while the grandiloquent permanent buildings at Stormont were being completed.

Evening entertainment

North again is raffish tree-lined **Botanic Avenue**, its café-bars, Eastern restaurants, bookshops, book makers, world trade bric-a-brac emporiums, charity shops, delicatessens and launderettes providing necessities of life for the chattering and student classes. Its **Empire Music Hall ⑪** (42 Botanic Avenue, tel: 328110), another deconsecrated church, features Thursday night stand-up comedy and from the participants' ironic patter visitors learn much about local politics. Opposite, the **Belfast Civic Arts Theatre** (25–41 Botanic Avenue, tel: 324936) leavens homespun indigenous plays with excellent touring drama. **Vincent's** is fine for espressos, **Madison's** has live music and an up-front decor worthy of Barcelona.

At the Avenue's northern extremity, those with a predilection for antique warehouses or biker shops can turn east down **Donegall Pass** which also boasts two of the city's most authentic Chinese restaurants,

ABOVE:
the Ulster Museum.

BELOW:
Botanic Gardens.

the up-market Cantonese **Manor House** and budget **Sun Kee.**

As one crosses bleak, detritus-ridden **Shaftesbury Square**, it's worth glancing up at the **Elizabeth Frink sculpture**, the city's finest alfresco artwork, on the south wall of the Ulster Bank. The well-heeled will stop off at Paul and Jeannie Rankin's award-winning **Roscoff**, its minimalist decor, exhilarating food, a contrast to its low-income surroundings. **Deane's** in **Brunswick Street** is its only comparable rival.

Architectural gems

Great Victoria Street, which runs north off Shaftesbury Square, offers more eateries and also, near its northern end, several of Belfast's best-known tourist honey-pots. The first, the **Europa ❿**, a 179-room hotel of accepted international standards, is proud of its self-imposed sobriquet of "Europe's most bombed". As well as 24-hour room service, there's 24-hour security.

The **Grand Opera House & Cirque ⓚ** (tel: 241919), with its plush brass and velvet, its gilded elephant heads and its excellent acoustics, was designed by theatre architect Frank Matcham and opened in 1895 with a pantomime, *Bluebeard*. Pavlova, Beerbohm Tree, Orson Welles, Sarah Bernhardt, Donald Wolfit – and Laurel and Hardy – trod the boards until it fell into disuse, victim to changing tastes. Rescued by conservationists in the 1970s and rendered sumptuous once more, it re-opened with a pantomime, *Cinderella.*

It has occasionally been damaged by IRA bombs, as has the **Crown Liquor Saloon ⓛ**, across the road (46 Great Victoria Street, tel: 249476, admission free, pub hours) with its magnificent tiled interior. Both delights are now fully restored. No visit to the city is complete without a pint (or pot of coffee), a

Map, page 316

The Crown Liquor Saloon, described by the poet John Betjeman as a "many-coloured cavern", was built in 1885 by Banbridge-born Patrick Flanagan

BELOW: the Grand Opera House.

plate of local oysters and a dish of champ (mashed potatoes) taken in one of the Crown's beautifully carved private snugs (where stage door Johnnies once propositioned chorus girls) before an evening of grand opera, rock, Shakespeare or contemporary drama at the Opera House. The Crown is classic enough to have been taken under the wing of the National Trust. **Robinson's**, **Flannagan's**, **Spinners'** and **Beaten Docket** are other local bars offering ersatz versions of this Victorian experience.

Another attraction, in Great Victoria Street's continuation, **College Square East**, is incomprehensibly ignored by most tourist literature. This is the view, across its cricket square lawns, of the city's finest building, Sir John Soane's dignified dark red brick **Royal Belfast Academical Institution** Ⓜ. The best view of this best view is from north-facing bedrooms in Jury's Inn hotel. The green statue facing the green sward, known locally as the "Black Man" since that was the colour of its predecessor, is of Henry Cooke, a rabble-raising 19th-century Presbyterian prebend. The baroque Portland stone building north, is, in local argot, the College of Knowledge – more correctly, the **College of Technology**.

A celebrated library

East along **Wellington Place**, the **Linen Hall Library** Ⓝ (17 Donegall Square North, tel: 321707, closed Sun) is all brass and mahogany, with its unique collection of printed "troubles" ephemera, is a must for visiting researchers. Its first librarian, Thomas Russell, was hanged for his part in the United Irishmen's revolution of 1798. Both Linen Hall Library and Marks & Spencer's frontage three blocks east were designed by Lanyon's firm.

Thomas Russell, the Linen Hall Library's first librarian and a prominent member of the United Irishmen, was hanged in 1803 for participating in an attempted uprising.

BELOW: the Crown Bar, preserved by the National Trust.

To the north is **Donegall Place** with its street-scape of British chain stores. Off it, past **Castle Junction**, west down **Bank Street**, are **Kelly's Cellars ⊙**, dating from 1780. Though considerably refurbished, the bars retain much of the charm which appealed to Henry Joy McCracken and other Protestant leaders of the United Irishmen as they caroused and plotted here in 1798.

East along Castle Lane towards Cornmarket is another essential of Ulster life, its street evangelists preaching round the bandstand in polygonal **Arthur Square** where the designs for the **Masonic Buildings, Nos 13-21**, came from Lanyon's office. And so east, along tacky **Ann Street**, dodging left into one of the entries which once made a warren of the area leading into **High Street**, where merchant ships tied up until the late 18th century. In **Pottinger's Entry,** at no 17, is the excellent **Morning Star** bar, the last of the many oyster houses which once thronged these narrow lanes, catering for sailors and thespians, for this was the city's theatrical district in times past.

Across **High Street**, north, is **Rosemary Street** where, at **No. 33, William Drennan**, founder of the United Irishmen was born and where, at No. 41, in the 1783 elliptical box-pewed interior of the **First Presbyterian (Non-Subscribing) Church**, the oldest place of worship within the city, lunchtime recitals provide lacunas of calm.

Lanyon's handsome 1845 makeover of what was the city's first public building, the 1769 **Exchange and Assembly Rooms**, now the **Northern Bank**, decorates the corner of **Bridge** and **Waring** Streets. The **Northern Ireland Tourist Board's** welcoming **Information Centre** is further up scruffy **North Street,** at no 59. Behind it, the landscaped **St Anne's Square** with sculpture by John Kindness, faces 1898 **St Anne's Church of Ireland**

Map, page 316

BELOW: Castlecourt Shopping Centre.

One consequence of years of anti-terrorist planning is that many Belfast streets have become traffic-free.

BELOW: the leaning Albert Clock.

(Protestant) Cathedral in **Lower Donegall Street**, designated an urban conservation area for the detail on its houses and warehouses.

Catalyst Arts (5 Exchange Place, tel: 312737), the most adventurous of the city's visual arts spaces, is housed in a converted shirt factory and empty shops in the surrounding area, particularly **North Street Arcade**, are frequently taken over by experimental visual artists. The **Duke of York**, in **Commercial Court**, is amongst the last of the journalists' pubs in the city's Fleet Street. The others are the **Front Page** opposite the Irish News building and the **A1** in Waring Street. The presses of the Catholic Nationalist *Irish News* (113-117 Upper Donegall Street) and the city's evening paper, the *Belfast Telegraph* (124 Royal Avenue, tel: 264000), still unionist with a small 'u' but carrying news of both communities, operates on a corner near **Belfast Central Library** (tel: 243233, closed Sat pm and all Sun).

Lanyon enthusiasts will walk north-west up Clifton Street past spare elegant **Clifton House**, the Charitable Society's Poor House of 1771, to his **Gaol** and **Court House** ⓟ, facing each other across Crumlin Road.

Echoes of maritime history

Returning east from Donegall Street, cobbled **Hill Street** with its fashionable **Nick's Warehouse Wine Bar** points towards **Waring Street's** ornate **Ulster Bank,** rich in the extravagant carvings of Thomas Fitzpatrick whose stone work figures decorate so many of the city's buildings. **Skipper Street**, with the **Crow's Nest**, one of the city's two gay bars (the other, **The Parliament** is on nearby **Dunbar Link**) leads back to **High Street** with the **Albert Memorial Clock** ⓠ, a leaning tower that is Belfast's answer to London's Big Ben, and elegant Georgian **St George's Church** on the left, and Lanyon's Northern Bank (now **First Trust**) just beyond on **Victoria Street.** Lanyon's **Custom House**, is in **Custom House Square**, on the river bank, behind. His **Sinclair Seamen's Presbyterian Church, Corporation Square,** with its astonishing interior of ship's prow pulpit, binnacle font and lifeboat shape collection boxes, is worth the short stroll north through forbidding Tomb Street, Steam Mill Lane. A wee dram in Pilot Street's **Rotterdam Bar**, a prime music venue brushing shoulders with Lagan's re-gentrification, may also revive the soul. The ornate **Harbour Office** (Corporation Square, tel: 234422, admission by arrangement) has unique reords of the city's maritime history.

From here, upstream, the Lagan's banks are witness to a declaration of confidence in the future, millions having been spent, via the state-sponsored Laganside Corporation, on gentrifying quays from **Clarendon Dock** southwards. A derelict docklands is becoming an area of stylish offices and designer street furniture. The **Lagan Lookout Centre** (Donegall Quay, tel: 315444, admission fee, closed Sat and Sun mornings) relates the harbour's history. It bridges the river at **Queen's Square** where **McHugh's Bars**, once in the centre of the city's red-light district where painter Stanley Spencer's brother played piano, claim to be the city's oldest extant building. South is Victor

Robinson's new, circular **Waterfront Hall** (Lanyon Place, Oxford Street, tel: 334400), now the city's premier concert and conference space, provides an astonishing vista from Chichester Street, past the **Royal Courts of Justice.**

One **Oxford Street Gallery** (tel: 310400, closed Mon and Sat), hothouse of contemporary figurative and landscape painting, almost faces the Hall as does **Magennis's Whiskey Café** in May Street. Belfast's Hilton and British Telecom's headquarters rise beside it, whilst **St George's Market** at the corner of Oxford Street and Cromac Square, is next on the ambitious regeneration schedule. Up river, on **Ormeau Road**, opposite **Ulster Television**, the huge **Gasworks** is also included in the plan.

However, walkers following the Lanyon Trail may return east to base via **Victoria Square**, for its two excellent old-fashioned pubs, **Bittle's** and the **Kitchen Bar**, or by **Chichester Street** with its occasional fine Georgian house and the **Garrick Bar**, favoured by barristers and such. Around the city the carved heads above the ground-floor windows of one-time warehouses speak of its Victorian citizens' aspirations, no more so than in **Donegall Square South**, where the figures represent Columbus, Homer, Humboldt, Jacquard, Michelangelo, Newton, Shakespeare and Peace.

On the outskirts of the city

A taxi (or bus) will be necessary to reach two areas of interest on the edge of the city. The first, **Cave Hill Country Park** , is where, by McArt's Fort United Irishmen planned the 1798 rebellion. In the park, there's a **Heritage Centre** inside the Scots Baronial-style **Belfast Castle** (Antrim Road, tel: 776925, free access) designed by Lanyon's son John (it's now a restaurant

The Royal Courts of Justice were built in 1933 as a gift to the city by the British government, which had grudgingly accepted that the partition of Ireland wasn't going to be a short-lived affair.

BELOW:
Belfast Castle.

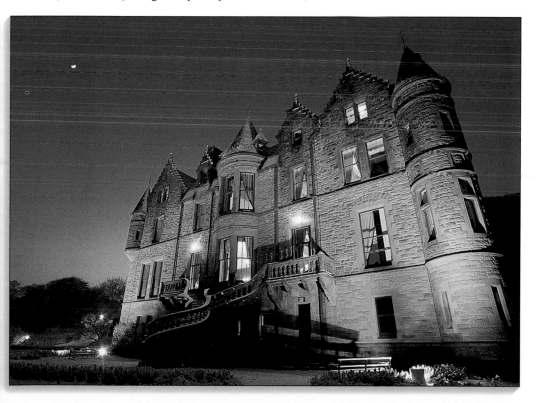

complex) plus the **Zoological Gardens** (Antrim Road, tel: 776277, admission fee) beyond. Set in a picturesque landscape, the zoo is praised for its breeding programmes and underwater sea lion viewing, but not everyone believes that caged tropical animals are entirely happy in Ireland's temperate climate. The **Cavehill Gallery** (18 Old Cavehill Road, tel: 776784, phone first) concentrates on living Irish painters.

The second area of interest is the much-televised **Parliament Buildings** at Stormont, 6 miles (10 km) to the east along the Newtownards Road. Echoing the pomp of Buckingham Palace, the seat of the disbanded Northern Ireland government is set in 300 acres (120 hectares) of lawns and trees and has a front drive a mile long. In the grounds is the smaller, baronial **Stormont Castle**, where the Ulster prime minister lived before Britain assumed direct control in 1972. For security reasons, it is not possible to visit either building.

Package up your Troubles

Accepted wisdom insists that a visitor will never come to harm on the city's streets. Despite tribal animosities, the people have a natural warmth, a welcoming abrasive wit. In truth, Belfast is amongst Europe's safest cities, offences by what its long-suffering police force terms ODCs – ordinary decent criminals – being far below that for most English or American cities. This is partly because the terrorist organisations assumed responsibility for dispensing swift and vicious justice (such as knee-capping) to persistent offenders in the areas they controlled, and the visitor should tread tactfully in such working-class, headline-grabbing enclaves of the Catholic Falls Road and the Protestant Shankill Road. For those keen on viewing the areas of

ABOVE: army patrol.
BELOW: Lord Carson guards the approach to Stormont; children in front of the "Peace Line" barricade.

greatest conflict, **Translink**, the State transport company has a series of afternoon **CityBus** tours which broaden the Belfast experience.

Belfast: A Living History takes in *all* the city's troubles, from the Viking long boats to the terrors of the past 30 years. This tour includes "Green" Falls and "Orange" Shankill plus the "Peace Line" in between. The commentary is admirably impartial. For the less adventurous, the **Belfast City Tour** traces the history and development, with stops at Parliament Buildings and the Zoo. The **Look At Linen** tour focuses on Belfast's staple industry.

Instructive, too, are the city's taxi-cabbies. Yellow Pages provide telephone numbers and there is hardly a driver who won't, for a negotiated price, lay on a tour of his favourite horrors, complete with a colourful commentary.

The curious system of the city's "**black taxis**" can also operate to the visitor's advantage. Whilst a small number of London-style cabs operate normally from ranks at City Hall, another system persists, a hangover from the 1970s when buses were terrorist targets. Fleets of second-hand London taxis were imported to serve, under paramilitary control, districts which had become no-go areas for buses. Now made legal, they run regular routes into the ghettos, each cab departing only when jam-packed full.

Cabbies meeting the trains at the city's less than central **Central Station** on East Bridge Street try to pack 'em in too, and it takes a determined passenger to insist on solitude. Non-confrontational alternatives are: to telephone for a radio-controlled taxi which will look like an ordinary saloon car bearing the taxi firm's logo; to change trains and continue to the really central Great Victoria Street Station; or to take the York Street Station courtesy bus, but drop off in the city centre. And, yes, it is safe for a stranger to walk the streets.

Map,
page 316

TIP

If you're tempted to air your views on Ulster's future, don't. Debates become heated and an unbiased opinion is deemed not to exist.

BELOW: Republican mural hails Irish revolutionary leader James Connolly. **OVERPAGE:** the sun sets at Ferrycarrig, Co. Wexford.

INSIGHT GUIDES
Travel Tips

Insight Guides portray destinations in depth, providing the complete picture and the top photography

Insight Pocket Guides focus on the best choices for places to see and things to do and include large fold-out maps

Insight Compact Guides' portability makes them the perfect books to carry with you for on-the-spot reference

Three types of guide for all types of travel

INSIGHT GUIDES Different people need different kinds of information. Some want *background information* to help them prepare for the trip. Others seek *personal recommendations* from someone who knows the destination well. And others look for *compactly presented data* for on-the-spot reference. With three carefully designed series, Insight Guides offer readers the perfect choice. Insight Guides will turn your visit into an experience.

The world's largest collection of visual travel guides

CONTENTS

Getting Acquainted

The Place 330
Time Zones 330
Climate 330
The Economy 331
Language.............................331
Government 331

Planning the Trip

Visas and Passports.............331
What to Bring.......................331
Money Matters.....................331
Getting There 332
Public Holidays 332

Practical Tips

Emergencies........................333
Media and Communications..334
Postal Services 334
Telephoning Abroad 334
Tourist Offices......................335
Tracing Your Roots 335
Embassies 336

Getting Around

Public Transport 336
DART & suburban rail map....337
Driving & Car Rental 337
Horse-drawn Caravans ... 338
Dublin Literary Tours............339

Where to Stay

Dublin..................................340
Southeast Region.................342
Southwest Region................343
Midwest Region 344
Midlands Region 345
Far West Region...................346
Northwest Region 347
Northeast Region 348
Belfast 350

Eating Out

Dublin..................................351
Southeast Region.................353
Southwest Region................354
Midwest................................356
Midlands & Far West............357
Northwest Region 358
Northeast Region 358
Belfast 360

Nightlife

Late Spots, Dublin................361
Late Spots, Belfast...............362

Culture

Theatre 362
Music...................................363
Art Galleries 363

Festivals

Calendar of Events...............365

Outdoor Attractions

Relics...................................367
Beauty Spots 367

Shopping

What to Buy..........................368
Shopping Hours 369

Sports

Spectator Sports 369
Golf......................................369
Angling 370
Adventure Sports 371
Birdwatching........................371
Hill walking, climbing............371

Further Reading

General 372
Other Insight Guides.............372

Getting Acquainted

Note: The international dialling code for the Republic of Ireland is **353**. For Northern Ireland, it is **44**.

The Place

Ireland is a small country, just 170 miles (275 km) across at its widest point and 301 miles long (486 km). If you happen to be sailing single-handed across the Atlantic, look for it between 51½° and 55½° north latitude and 5½° and 10½° west longitude.

The warm drifting waters from the Gulf Stream ensure an equable climate and the winds from the Atlantic bring enough rain to guarantee that the proverbial 40 shades of green remain bright.

Six counties in the north-eastern sector, part of the ancient province of Ulster, are now Northern Ireland and come under the United Kingdom's jurisdiction; they occupy 17 percent of the island's landmass.

The island consists of a central plateau surrounded by isolated hills and mountains. The highest peak is Carrantuohill in Co. Kerry, at 3,412 ft (1,040 metres). The longest river is the Shannon, at 159 miles (256 km). The biggest lake is Lough Neagh in Northern Ireland, at 153 sq. miles (396 sq. km).

Although Ireland has a network of 57,000 miles (92,000 km) of roads, it has one of Europe's lowest traffic densities. Its population density is low, too, with just over 3.6 million people in the Republic (44 percent of them under 25) and 1½ million in Northern Ireland.

The People

The Irish are a mixed race. Originally waves of settlers arrived over a period of 5,000 years from Britain and Europe. The predominant element consisted of Celts, tribes who came from central Europe by way of France, arriving in Ireland in the 7th or 8th centuries BC.

They are known to have been a combative people, their warriors high-spirited and boastful, and their strong story-telling abilities relied heavily on elements of the supernatural. These characteristics are still evident in Ireland, where Celtic culture survived after it was driven out of most of Europe by the Romans.

Another strong influence, especially in the east, was that of the Anglo-Normans. They first invaded in 1170, and were followed by settlers from England, Wales, and Scotland.

The population, which expanded rapidly during the 18th and early 19th centuries, reached 8.1 million in 1841. The great potato famine, which began in 1845, led to mass starvation and emigration, particularly to North America. Ireland's population density is the fifth-lowest in Europe.

The Republic still has a distinctly rural orientation. Less than 59 percent of the population lives in towns of 1,000 inhabitants or more. More than one in five people live in the capital, Dublin, together with its seaport of Dun Laoghaire. The next biggest cities are all ports: Cork, Limerick, Waterford and Galway.

More than 90 percent of the Republic's citizens profess to Roman Catholicism. In Northern Ireland, two-thirds are Protestant, one-third Roman Catholic.

Time Zones

Ireland follows Greenwich Mean Time. In spring, the clock is moved one hour ahead for Summer Time to give extra daylight in the evening; in autumn it is moved back again to GMT.

At noon according to GMT, it is: **4am** in Los Angeles; **7am** in New York; **1pm** in western Europe; **8pm** in Singapore; **l0pm** in Sydney; **midnight** in New Zealand.

Many visitors find that time passes more slowly in Ireland. A visitor once asked if the Irish attitude to time could be expressed by the word *mañana*. He was told: "Oh, we've nothing as urgent as that here."

The 4 Provinces

Ireland consists of four ancient provinces – Ulster, Munster, Leinster and Connacht – but these are purely historical and have no administrative significance today. Since they're often referred to, though, it's useful to know which of the 32 administrative counties technically belong in which province:

Ulster: Cavan, Donegal, Monaghan (all in the Republic); Antrim, Armagh, Derry, Down, Fermanagh, Tyrone (all in Northern Ireland).
Munster: Clare, Cork, Kerry, Limerick, Tipperary, Waterford.
Leinster: Carlow, Dublin, Kildare, Kilkenny, Laois, Longford, Louth, Meath, Offaly, Westmeath, Wexford, Wicklow.
Connacht: Sligo, Mayo, Galway, Roscommon, Leitrim.

Climate

Although Ireland lies at roughly the same northerly latitude as Newfoundland, it has a mild, moist climate, because of the prevailing south-westerly winds and the influence of the warm Gulf Stream along its western coast. As no part of the island is more than 70 miles (110 km) from the sea, temperatures are fairly uniform over the whole country.

Average air temperatures in the coldest months, January and February, are mainly between 4°C and 7°C (39°F–45°F). The warmest months, July and August, have average temperatures between I4°C and I6°C (57°F–6I°F), but occasionally reaching as high as 25°C (77°F). The sunniest months are May and June, with an average of between 5½ and 6½ hours a day over most of the country. The sunniest region is the extreme southeast.

Parts of the west of the country, with annual rainfall averaging 59 inches (1,500mm), are twice as wet as the east because of the prevailing Atlantic winds.

The Economy

The Republic's gross national product is around IR£28 billion and its principal trading partner is Britain, followed by Germany, France and the United States. Racehorses, whiskey, handwoven tweed, handcut crystal glass, and agricultural products are among the best-known exports.

The country imports more goods than it sells, but the gap in the balance of trade is closed by its substantial earnings from tourism and foreign investments. Tourism in particular continues to grow: the Republic's 3.6 million people welcome 4.7 million visitors a year.

Government

The Republic is a parliamentary democracy, with two Houses of Parliament, an elected president who is head of state and a prime minister (*Taoiscach*, literally "leader") who is head of government. In 1998 the Republic abandoned its constitutional claim to the six counties of Northern Ireland, which is part of the United Kingdom and is directly ruled from London pending the transfer of limited power to an elected assembly.

The national symbol is the shamrock, a three-leafed plant which is worn on the national holiday, 17 March, to honour Ireland's patron saint, St Patrick. This "wearing of the green" tradition has been successfully exported as thousands of sprigs of shamrock are despatched by Irish families each March to relatives all over the world.

The Language

The Republic of Ireland has two official languages, English and Irish (Gaelic). English is spoken everywhere, but while many people throughout the country know Irish, it is the everyday language of fewer than 100,000 people in remote areas known as Gaeltachts, mainly in the far west.

Intrepid linguists may wish to wrap their tongues round the following Gaelic phrases:

Dia dhuit/God be with you.
To which the reply is:
Muire dhuit/God and Mary be with you.
Conas tá tú/How are you?
To which the hoped-for reply is:
Tá mé go maith, go raibh maith agat/I am well, thank you.
Slán agat/Goodbye.
To which the desirable reply is:
Slán leat agus go n-éirí bóthar leat./Goodbye and may the road rise to meet you.

Planning the Trip

Visas and Passports

Passports are required by everyone visiting the Republic except British citizens. Visas are not required by citizens of European Union countries, Australia, Canada or the United States.

What To Wear

Casual clothing is acceptable almost everywhere in Ireland, including smart hotels and restaurants. Because of the unpredictability of the weather, pack an umbrella, some rainproof clothing and a warm sweater, even in summer.

But bring the suntan cream as well: when the summer sun shines, the ozone-laden winds from the Atlantic can intensify the burning effect of its rays.

Electricity

220 volts AC (50 cycles) is standard. Hotels usually have dual 220/110 voltage sockets for electric razors only. To use their own small appliances, visitors may need a plug adaptor (best purchased in their home country) to fit Ireland's 3-pin flat or 2-pin round wall sockets.

Currency

The Irish pound (or punt), usually written IR£ to distinguish it from the pound sterling, is divided into 100 pence. The coins used are Ip, 2p, 5p, 10p, 20p, 50p and £1. The notes are

IR£5, IR£l0, IR£20, IR£50, and IR£l00. The Republic joined the European Single Currency system in 1999 and the euro will replace the pound.

In Northern Ireland, British currency is used. Exchange rates vary but many shops in Border areas will accept either currency.

In the Irish Republic, banks are open 10am–4pm, Monday–Friday. Branches in small towns may close from 12.30pm to 1.30pm. Most Dublin banks are open until 5pm on Thursday. In Northern Ireland, bank opening hours are l0am–3.30pm, Monday–Friday.

British visitors to Northern Ireland can cash personal cheques with a bank card. But British visitors to the Republic and European visitors to both parts of Ireland need Eurocheques and Eurocards. Travellers cheques are accepted at all banks, money-change kiosks and many hotels.

Access (alias MasterCard) and Visa are the most commonly acceptable credit cards, followed by American Express and Diners Club. But many small guesthouses and bed-and-breakfast places will expect payment in cash.

Getting There

By Air
There are three major international airports in the Republic of Ireland, at Dublin, Cork and Shannon. The busiest by far is Dublin, with annual traffic of about 5 million passengers.

There is a regular bus service from Dublin Airport (Tel: 01-705 2222) to the main bus station in the city centre, taking about 30 minutes. The bus from Cork Airport (tel. 021-313131) to the city takes about 10 minutes. From Shannon Airport (Tel: 061-171444) there is a regular bus service to LImerick city operating between 8am and midnight. It takes about 40 minutes.

Frequent flights from UK airports also arrive at regional airports such as Kerry, Waterford and Knock. There are connections from Dublin and/or Shannon to many destinations in Britain and Europe, including London, Glasgow, Manchester, Liverpool, Amsterdam, Brussels, Copenhagen, Dusseldorf, Frankurt, Las Palmas, Madrid, Malaga, Milan, Moscow, Paris, Rome and Zurich, as well as to transatlantic destinations such as New York, Boston, Atlanta, Chicago and Havana.

Carriers serving Ireland from the US are Aer Lingus, Aeroflot and Delta Airlines. Aer Lingus flies direct from Boston, Chicago, Newark and New York to Dublin and Shannon. Flying time from New York to Dublin is six hours; from Chicago 7 hours. Delta flies from Atlanta to Dublin and Shannon, and Aeroflot flies direct from Miami, Chicago and Washington D.C. to Shannon. To contact **Aer Lingus** in the United States tel. 800 223 6537; to contact **Delta Airlines** tel. 800 241 4141; to contact **Aeroflot** tel. 800 867 8874.

Public Holidays

- **January** New Year's Day (1)
- **March** St Patrick's Day (17)
- **March/April** Good Friday, Easter Monday
- **May** May Day (first Monday), Spring Bank Holiday (last Monday, *N. Ireland only*)
- **June** First Monday (*Republic of Ireland only*)
- **July** Orangeman's Day (12) *Northern Ireland only*
- **August** Summer Bank Holiday (First Monday in the Republic, last Monday in Northern Ireland)
- **October** Last Monday (*Republic of Ireland only*)
- **December** Christmas Day (25), St Stephen's Day (26)

The main airlines connecting Ireland to the UK and the European mainland are Aer Lingus, Ryanair and British Airways. To contact **Aer Lingus**: tel: 844 4777 in Dublin, 327155 in Cork, 245151 in Belfast, 181-899 4747 in London, 69 69073264 in Frankfurt, 1-4862 1212 in Paris, 6 481 8518 in Rome. **Ryanair** can be contacted on 677 4422 in Dublin and 0171-435 7101 in London. **British Airways** and **British Airways Express** fly from Heathrow, Gatwick and various provincial airports in England and Scotland to Dublin, Cork, Waterford, Shannon, Knock, Carrickfinn (Donegal) and Kerry County Airports; to contact BA Express in Ireland tel. 1800 62 67 47; in the UK tel. 0345 222111. **Air France** has direct flights from Paris to Dublin and Cork; in Ireland tel. 01-677 8899.

Amongst the other airlines operating from the UK, **Virgin** (tel: 01293 747146) offers a smooth daily flight from London City Airport to Dublin, matched by **British Midland**'s (tel: 0345 554554) daily flights from London Heathrow and East Midlands

Belfast International Airport (at Aldergrove) in Northern Ireland (tel: 01232-245151) has flights to most main British destinations and to Paris and Amsterdam; there's a frequent British Airways shuttle service between Aldergrove and London's Heathrow. Belfast Harbour Airport (tel: 01232-457745), close to the city centre, has domestic flights to Scotland and England. **Student/youth fares** operate all year round between Britain and Ireland. Contacts: Campus Travel, London (Tel: 0171-730 3402) and STA Travel, London (Tel: 0171-361-6161).

By Sea
Many ferry services connect

Ireland to Britain and to France. These include: Larne to Stranraer and Belfast to Cairnryan (both in Scotland); Belfast to Liverpool (England) and Douglas (Isle of Man); a faster Seacat service from Belfast to Stranraer; Dublin to Holyhead (Wales); Rosslare to Fishguard and Pembroke (Wales); Cork to Swansea (Wales); Rosslare to Cherbourg and Le Havre (France); Cork to Le Havre and Roscoff (France). The fastest crossing from Holyhead to Dun Laoghaire is by Stena Sealink Line's catamaran service, which takes 99 minutes, as does to Stena Line Lnyx crossing from Rosslare to Fishguard.

Details of services and operators are liable to change, so check with the following operators in the UK:

Irish Ferries, Reliance House, Water Street, Liverpool L2 8TP. Tel: 0151-227 3131. *Also at*: 150 New Bond Street, London W1Y 0AQ. Tel: 0171-491 8682. Also 0990-171717. *Services*: Holyhead–Dublin North Wall (3 hours 15 minutes); Pembroke–Rosslare (4 hours). Also offers three sailings a week between Rosslare and the French ports of Le Havre and Cherbourg (Tel: Rosslare 053-33158 or Dublin 01-661 0511).

Stena Line, Charter House, Park Street, Ashford, Kent TN24 8EX. Tel: 01233-647047. Also 0990-707070. *Services*: Holyhead– Dun Laoghaire (1 hour 39 minutes) ;

Fishguard–Rosslare 3 hours 30 minutes or 1 hour 30 minutes); Stranraer–Belfast (3 hours 15 minutes or 1 hour 45 minutes by HSS).

Swansea Cork Ferries, Ferryport, Kings Dock, Swansea SA1 8RU. Tel: 01792-456116. *Services*: Swansea–Cork (10 hours).

P & O European Ferries, Cairnryan, Stranraer, Wigtownshire DG9 8RF. Tel: 01581-200276. *Also at*: Channel House, Channel View Road, Dover, Kent CT17 9TJ. Tel: 01304-203388. *Services*: Cairnryan–Larne (2 hours 15 minutes or 1 hour by Jetliner).

SeaCat Scotland, SeaCat Terminal, West Pier, Stranraer, Wigtownshire DG9 7RE. Tel: 0345-523523. *Services*: Stranraer–Belfast (1 hour 30 minutes).

Isle of Man Steam Packet Company, P.O. Box 5, Imperial Buildings, Douglas, Isle of Man IM99 1AF. Tel: 01624-661661. *Services*: Isle of Man–Dublin (2 hours 45 minutes).

By Bus

Bus companies run through services from various points in England and Wales via the ferries. The ride to Galway from London, for example, takes around 17 hours by **National Express/Irish Bus** (Tel: 01-836 6111 in Dublin or 0171-730 8235 in London) or **Slattery's Coach Service** (Tel: 066-21611 in Tralee or 0171-482 1604 in London).

Practical Tips

Emergencies

Medical Services

Medical insurance is highly advisable for all visitors. However, visitors from EC countries are entitled to medical treatment in Ireland, North and South, under a reciprocal arrangement.

With the exception of UK citizens, visitors for EC states should obtain form E111 from their own national social security office. These forms entitle the holders to free treatment by a doctor and free medicines on prescription. If hospital treatment is necessary, this will be given free in a public ward. UK visitors need only go to a doctor (or, in an emergency, a hospital), present some proof of identity (e.g. driving licence) and request treatment under EC health agreement.

For **emergency services**, such as police, ambulance, fire service, lifeboat and coastal rescue, tel: 999 (in either part of Ireland) and ask for the service you need.

The **Samaritans**, who help lonely, depressed and suicidal people, can be contacted on 1850 609090 and in Northern Ireland on 0345 909090.

Other Useful Numbers

Poisons Information Service, Dublin. Tel: 837 9964/837 9966.
Alcoholics Anonymous, Dublin. Tel: 453 8998/679 5967; Belfast 681064.
Rape Crisis Centre, Dublin. Tel:

Factfile on the Irish Sea

The Irish Sea (*Muir Éireann* in Irish) is 130 miles (210 km) long and 150 miles (240 km) wide. Its total area is roughly 40,000 sq. miles (100,000 sq. km) and its deepest point is 576 ft (175 metres). It connects with Atlantic waters through St George's Channel in the south (between Ireland and Wales), where tidal currents reach up to 4 knots, and the North Channel in the north (between Northern Ireland and Scotland). Geologists believe it was created by rifts at least 70 million years ago and could be as old as 1.6 million years.

The principal fish caught are herring in summer and whiting in winter, and there is some trawling for cod.

661 3923 or 1800 778888 and Belfast 249696.

Aids Helpline Dublin. Tel: 872 4277, Mon–Fri 7–9pm, Sat 3–5pm.

Gay Switchboard Dublin. Tel: 8721055, Sun–Fri 8–10pm, Sat 3.30–6pm.

Lesbian Line Dublin. Tel: 872 9911, Thur 7–9pm.

Media

Newspapers

The Irish devour newspapers, and have no fewer than five morning newspapers to serve the island's population of 5 million. The *Irish Times* and the *Irish Independent* are published in Dublin. The *Examiner* is published in Cork.

The *Times*, the most serious and comprehensive, is best for foreign news, arts and business. It has a great letters page. It avoids political affiliations, but has a broadly liberal bias, and is part of a syndicating group that includes the *Guardian* in the UK, *Le Monde* in France and *El País* in Spain. The *Independent* broadly supports the Fine Gael party and aims for a hard-hitting style. The *Examiner* is the staple diet of business and farming people in the southwest. Two morning papers are published in Belfast: the Unionist/Protestant *Newsletter* and the nationalist/Catholic *Irish News*; it can be fascinating and instructive to compare their treatments of a controversial story.

There are three evening papers: the *Evening Herald* (from the Independent stable in Dublin), the *Echo* (Cork) and the *Belfast Telegraph*. All contain lots of sport, gossip and showbiz.

The *Independent* has a Sunday version; also published from Dublin are the *Sunday Tribune* which aims to be a serious paper of political analysis, arts review, etc., the *Sunday World*, a lurid tabloid

(pin-ups, shocks, scares, scandals, etc) and the *Sunday Business Post*, which concentrates on business and politics. The London *Sunday Times* Irish edition is published in Cork and distributed nationally. From Belfast, there is *Sunday Life* from the Telegraph stable.

Since all the British dailies and Sundays are readily obtainable on both sides of the border, even the most news-hungry visitor should be satisfied in this newsprint-mad country. However, UK readers can expect an "Irish edition" of their favourite paper, with a focus on Irish topics.

There are nearly l00 local papers, which may be entertaining and informative if you are interested in a particular region, or interested in newspapers.

Magazines

Hot Press is a lively local pop culture paper. *In Dublin* is useful for telling you what's on at the theatre, cinema, etc.

Radio and television

The national broadcasting service, Radio Telefis Eireann (RTE) has three TV channels (one of them, T na G, broadcasting exclusively In the Irish language) and two radio stations. Ireland's first independent television network, was launched in 1998 to provide an alternative to RTE – "a middle-of-the-road service aimed at Middle Ireland".

In addition, the British TV channels (both BBC and commercial channels) can be received over much of the country – which accounts for the unsightly height of television aerials. Several satellite channels, including Sky and Screensport, are widely available via cable.

On Radio, RTE1 is the main station for news, current affairs and drama; RTE2 has a staple output of pop music. There are also a number of independent

local radio stations.

Northern Ireland has full BBC radio and TV coverage with many local programmes. Ulster Television provides a commercial service, as does Downtown Radio (MW) and Cool FM.

Postal Services

At the time of writing, letters weighing less than 20 grammes (approximately the weight of an envelope containing up to three regular A4 sheets of paper) cost 32p within Ireland and to all European Union countries. Postcards cost 28p. To all other destinations, surface mail letters cost 44p, postcards 37p. The basic air letter rate is 52p, but pre-stamped air letters are sold at post offices for 45p.

Philatelists may obtain information on Irish stamps from the Controller, Philatelic Section, GPO, Dublin 1.

In Northern Ireland, British postal rates apply: 26p for a letter sent first-class to anywhere in the British Isles (or less than 20 grammes within the EC), and 20p for letters sent second-class. Air-mail letters to destinations outside Europe cost 43p or 60p, depending on weight.

Telecoms

The international dialling code for the Republic of Ireland is **353**. Northern Ireland's is **44**.

The Republic's phoneservices are operated by a state-owned company, Telecom Eireann. A local call from a public telephone costs 20p. Longer-distance calls to most places within Ireland can be dialled direct; area codes are listed in the front of the telephone directories. Have plenty of coins ready. About 50 percent of public phones are card phones.

Phone Cards are widely available from post offices, news-agents and supermarkets and are sold in denominations of

10, 20 and 50 units.

International calls can be dialled direct from private phones, or dial 114 for the international operator. To contact the local operator, dial 10.

The long-distance services of AT&T, Sprint and MCI are also available.

Telephone services in Northern Ireland are operated by British Telecom; dial 100 for the operator. Local calls from public booths cost 10p. For the weather forecast, tel: Belfast 8091. Mercury has been setting up a rival network, as in Britain.

Tourist Offices

Irish Tourist Board Offices
General postal enquiries: Irish Tourist Board, PO Box 273, Dublin 8, Ireland. Fax enquiries: 01-475 8046.

The following are the principal offices for the various regions and are open throughout the year. Many other local offices are open only in the summer months. A full list is available from any tourist information office.

Internet Site:
http://www/Ireland.travel.ie

DUBLIN & ENVIRONS
Dublin City: Dublin Tourism, Suffolk Street, Dublin 2. Tel: 605-7700; fax 605-7757
Dublin Airport: Tel: 844 5387.
Dun Laoghaire: St Michael's Wharf. Tel: 280 6984.

SOUTHEAST REGION
Rosslare Harbour: Tel: 053-33622; fax: 053-33421.
Wexford: Crescent Quay. Tel: 053-23111; fax: 053-41743.
Cashel: Town Hall. Tel: 062-

Tracing your Roots

The number of visitors to Ireland who want to uncover half-forgotten roots in the "ould sod" has mushroomed. The Hibernian Research Company, Ireland's largest genealogical agency, says it receives 150–200 enquiries a week.

It gives free advice on how to go about tracing your own ancestry, but most people prefer to hire one of its panel of trained genealogists to do the time-consuming research. There is no fixed charge – clients pay for time, not results – but expect to pay IR£150 and upwards. Tel: Dublin 4966522; Fax: 4973011.

Whether you intend to do your own research or hire a professional, it is important to gather as much information as possible in your home country. Try to find out the name of your emigrant ancestor; his or her place of origin in Ireland, as precisely as possible; approximate dates of birth, marriage and death; religion; occupation and social background; names of children. Look for old diaries, letters or family bibles.

In the US National Archives, Irish-Americans can often find their ancestor date and port of arrival in the New World. Immigrant records and shipping lists show the country, age and trade of the immigrant and the port of departure. Australian records are helpful because many immigrants arrived on state "assisted passage" schemes.

In Ireland, all centralised records for the 26 counties of the Republic are stored in Dublin. The main sources are as follows:
The National Library, Kildare Street, has an extensive collection of journals of local historical societies, trade directories, old newspapers, private papers and letters. Patient, helpful staff.
The National Archives (formerly the Public Record Office), in the Four Courts, was damaged

badly in a fire in 1922 at the outbreak of the Civil War and many invaluable documents were lost (but, contrary to rumour, not all).
The General Register Office, Joyce House, Lombard Street, has the civil registrations of all births, marriages and deaths since 1864.
The Register of Deeds, Henrietta Street, has deeds relating to property and marriage settlements dating from 1708. Most of these concern the gentry of the time.
The Genealogical Office, in Kildare Street, includes the State Heraldic Museum. The office records and designs coats of arms and will carry out research for a fee.
The State Paper Office, Dublin Castle, is of special interest to Australians because it houses records of people sentenced to be transported there. There is no stigma attached to this, since the crime concerned was often petty or notional, or simply that of supporting the rebel cause.

Many individual counties have now set up local genealogy companies. Initial assessments tend to cost around £15 and you can track them down through local libraries.

In **Northern Ireland**, records are held at the Public Record Office, 66 Balmoral Avenue, Belfast 9. Derry has opened a genealogy centre in Butcher Street called The Fifth Province, with records from 1642 to 1922. The Ulster American Folk Park in Omagh holds thousands of documents in its Centre for Emigration Studies (Tel: 01662 256301; Fax: 01662 242241).

In both North and South, records are often kept at parish level, some going back over 200 years. For a list of approved research agencies, contact the Genealogical Office, 2 Kildare Street, Dublin 2 (Tel: 6618811).

61333; fax: 062-61789.
Kilkenny: Rose Inn Street. Tel:
056-21755; fax: 056-63955.
Waterford: 41 The Quay. Tel:
051-75788; fax: 051-77388.

SOUTHWEST REGION
Cork City: Tourist House, Grand
Parade. Tel: 021-27325; fax:
021-273504.
Skibbereen: The Square. Tel:
028-21766; fax :028-21353.
Killarney: Town Hall. Tel: 064-
31633; fax: 064-34506
Tralee: Ashe Memorial Hall,
Denny Street. Tel: 066-21288.
(no fax)

MID WEST REGION
Limerick City: Arthur's Quay.
Tel: 061-317522; fax: 061-
317939. **Ennis:** Clare Road. Tel:
065-28366; fax: 065-28366
Shannon Airport: Tel: 061-
61664; fax: 061-471664.
Midlands Region
Mullingar: Dublin Road. Tel:
044-48650; fax 044-40413.
Birr: Emmet Square. Tel: 509-
20110. (no fax)
Athlone: 17 Church Street. Tel:
0902-94630. (no fax)
Far West Region
Galway City: 1 Victoria Place,
Eyre Sq. Tel: 091-563081; fax:
091-565201.
Westport: The Mall. Tel: 098-
25711; fax: 098-27609.
Northwest Region
Sligo: Áras Reddan, Temple
Street. Tel: 071-61201; fax:
071-60360.
Letterkenny: Derry Road. Tel:
074-21160.; fax: 074-25180.

NORTHERN IRELAND & ABROAD
Northern Ireland: 53 Castle
Street, Belfast, BT1 1GH. Tel:
01232-327888. Fax: 240201.
Foyle Street, Londonderry. Tel.
& Fax 01504-369501.
Britain: 150 New Bond Street,
London W1Y OAQ. Tel: 171-493
3201. Fax: 493 9065.
US & Canada: New York: 757
Third Avenue, New York, NY
10017. Tel: 212-418-0880. Fax:
371 9052.

Australia & New Zealand:
Sydney: 5th level, 36 Carrington
Street, Sydney, NSW 2000. Tel:
02-9299 6177. Fax: 9299
6323. Auckland: c/o Walsh's
World Ld., Dingwall Building,
Auckland 1. Tel: 9-379 3708.
Fax: 9-309 0735.

NORTHERN IRELAND TOURIST
BOARD OFFICES
Belfast: 59 North Street,
Belfast BT1 1NB. Tel: 246609.
Fax: 312424.
Dublin: 16 Nassau Street,
Dublin 2. Tel: 679 1977. Fax:
679 1863.
Britain: 11 Berkeley Street,
London W1X 5AD. Tel: 0171-
355 5040. Fax: 0171-409
0487. 135 Buchanan St.,
Glasgow G1 2JA. Tel: 204
4454. Fax: 204 4033.
United States: 551 5th Avenue,
New York, NY 10176. Tel: 212-
922 0101. Fax: 922 0099.
Canada: 111 Avenue Road,
Suite 450, Toronto M5R 3J8.
Tel: 416-925 6368. Fax: 925
6033.

Embassies

DUBLIN
Australia: Fitzwilton House,
Wilton Terrace, Dublin 2. Tel
676 1517.
Britain: 31 Merrion Rd, Dublin
4. Tel 205 3700.
Canada: 65 St Stephen's
Green, Dublin 2. Tel 478 1988.
Israel: 122 Pembroke Road,
Dublin 2. Tel 668 0303.
United States: 42 Elgin Rd,
Dublin 4. Tel 668 8777.

BELFAST
American Consulate General,
Queen's Street, Belfast. Tel
01232-328239.

Getting Around

Public Transport

In the Republic, the State transport authority, CIE, is the
umbrella body for three companies: Dublin Bus (serving the
city), Bus Eireann (serving
provincial areas from Dublin)
and Irish Rail (operating inter-
city trains as well as the DART,
the Dublin Area Rapid Transit
system).

Timetables for bus and train
services, including details of
various money-saving commuter
and tourist tickets, are sold in
newsagents. The public transport network caters adequately
for travel between major centres, but plan ahead with care if
your itinerary takes you to
smaller towns. Once off the
main routes, small towns and
villages may only be served by
a couple of buses a week. For
information, tel: 873 4222
(Dublin Bus); 836 6111 (Bus
Eireann); or 836 6222 (Irish
Rail). You can dial a recorded
timetable for most mainline rail
destinations (look in the telephone directory under Coras
Iompair Eireann).

In Dublin city, the DART rail
service is the most efficient
way to travel, but it runs, alas,
only along the coastal strip from
Howth to Bray. The city's bus
service can be maddeningly
unpredictable, so try to be
philosophical.

CIE city buses also serve
Cork, Galway, Limerick and
Waterford

Eurailpasses are valid for bus
and train travel in the Republic,

excluding city services. A free ferrylink is provided by Irish Continental Line from Le Havre and Cherbourg in France to Rosslare. These tickets must be bought in advance from offices of the participating railways. CIE offers reduced-rate

Rambler passes providing unlimited travel on buses and/or trains, excluding city services, for either 8 or 15 days. Tickets can be bought from any bus or train station in the Republic, or through a travel agent abroad.

In Northern Ireland, trains run from Belfast northwest to Derry via Ballymena and Coleraine; east to Bangor; and south to Dublin via Newry. Information from Northern Ireland Railways, Belfast Central Station. Tel: 899411. Bus services in Belfast and throughout Northern Ireland are operated by Ulsterbus. Tel: Belfast 333000/320011.

Private Transport

Driving

This can still be a real pleasure in Ireland, as the roads are the least congested in Europe. Drive on the left is the rule on both sides of the border, although there is a predilection in some rural areas for the middle of the road. Drivers and front seat passengers must wear seat belts.

In the Republic, the speed limit is either 30 miles per hour

or 40 mph or 50 mph in urban areas, and 60 mph on country roads, with 70 mph permitted on motorways. On-the-spot fines of £50 can be issued for speeding offences. Drink driving laws are strict. It is an offence to drive with a concentration of alcohol exceeding 80mg per 100ml of blood. In Northern Ireland, the limit for country roads is 60 mph, and 70 mph is allowed on motorways and dual-carriageway trunk roads.

CAR RENTALS
Irish Republic

At the height of summer, hire cars can be harder to find than gold at the end of the rainbow, so book in advance. If you're heading west, the smaller the car, the better – the most alluring lanes are the narrowest. It pays to shop around – a recent survey revealed that rental prices were significantly lower outside the Dublin area. You must be over 23 with two years' full licence and under 76 to hire a car in the Irish Republic.

All the companies listed here are members of the Car Rental Council and operate a code of practice drawn up by the council and the Irish Tourist Board.

DART and Suburban Rail Network

Dundalk
Drogheda
Laytown
Mosney
Gormanston
Balbriggan
Skerries
Rush-Lusk
Donabate
Malahide
Portmarnock
Bayside
Sutton
Howth Junction
Howth
Kilbarrack
Raheny
Harmonstown
Connolly Station
Killester
Tara St
Pearse Station
Lansdowne Road
Sandymount
Sydney Parade
Booterstown
Blackrock
Seapoint
Salthill & Monkstown
Dun Laoghaire
Sandycove & Glasthule
Glenageary
Dalkey
Killiney
Shankhill
Bray
Greystones
Kilcoole
Wicklow
Rathdrum
Arklow

— DART
— SE Suburban
— N Suburban
○ interchange station

Taxis

There are metered taxis at railway stations, ports and airports in Dublin, Belfast, Cork, Limerick and Galway. Elsewhere, fares are by arrangement with the driver in advance. In cities and towns you can book a taxi by telephone. Look in the *Golden Pages* classified telephone directory under "Taxis".

In Dublin, taxis are not hailed in the street. You must go to a taxi rank, phone a taxi rank, or phone one of the many radio-linked taxi companies. There are taxi ranks at St Stephen's Green, College Green, O'Connell Street, and Westland Row, among other places.

Radio cab firms include **Airport Express**, Santry, Dublin 9, Tel: 8361111; **Blue Cabs**, 41 Westland Row, Dublin 2. Tel: 6761111; **City Group**, North Frederick Lane, Dublin 1. Tel: 8727272; **National Radio Cabs**, Citywide. Tel: 8365555 (Northside) and 4544070 (Southside); **Pony Cabs**, Tel: 8360144 North City, 4966777 Ranelagh, 2691000 Donnybrook; **Southside Cabs**, Stillorgan. Tel: 2836622/2805545; **Swords Cabs**, 2 North Street, Swords. Tel: 8406600; and **Taxi Radio Link**, 24 Aungier Street, Dublin 2. Tel: 4781111.

Note that all Dublin area telephone numbers need an 01-prefix if dialled from outside the area.

Argus Rent A Car, Terenure, Dublin 6. Tel: 490 4444. Deliveries to Dublin airport, ferry ports and hotels.

Atlas Car Rentals, arrivals hall, Dublin Airport. Tel: 844 4859.

Avis, Dublin Airport. Tel: 605 7555; Shannon Airport. Tel: 061-471094; Cork Airport. Tel: 021-281111; Killarney. Tel: 064-36655; Galway. Tel: 091-568886.

Budget Rent-a-Car, Dublin City. Tel: 837 9802; Dublin Airport. Tel: 844 5919; Shannon Airport. Tel: 061-471688; Killarney. Tel: 064-34341. Galway. Tel: 091-566376.

Cahills Motors, Howth Road, Raheny, Dublin. Tel: 831 1944.

Dan Dooley Rent-a-Car, Knocklong Co. Tipperary. Tel: 062-53103; Shannon Airport. Tel: 061-471098; Dublin Airport. Tel: 844 5156; Dublin city. Tel: 677 2723.

Diplomat Cars, Knock Airport. Tel: 094-67252. (International franchise: Budget Rent-a-Car.)

Eurodollar, arrivals hall, Dublin Airport. Tel: 260 3371; Shannon Airport. Tel: 061-472633; Cork Airport. Tel: 021-344884.

Hamill's Rent-a-Car, Mullingar. Tel: 044-48682/44500. Delivery to Dublin, Shannon and Knock airports and Dublin ferry terminals.

Hertz Rent-a-Car, Leeson Street Bridge, Dublin. Tel: 660 2255; Dublin Airport. Tel: 844 5488; Shannon Airport. Tel: 061-471369; Cork Airport. Tel: 021-310111.

Murrays Europcar Rent-a-Car, Baggot Street Bridge, Dublin. Tel: 668 1777; Dublin Airport. Tel: 844 4179; Shannon Airport. Tel: 061-471618; Cork Airport. Tel: 021-966736; Kerry Airport. Tel: 066-64666. Killarney. Tel: 064-31237. Galway. Tel: 091-562222;

Knock Airport. Tel: 0778-33029. Rosslare Harbour. Tel: 053-33634; Waterford. Tel: 051-77314.

O'Mara's Rent-a-Car, Athlone, Co. Westmeath. Tel: 0902-92325; Shannon. Tel: 061-92325; Dublin. Tel: 429313; Galway. Tel: 091-564663.

Windsor Rent-a-Car, South Circular Road, Rialto, Dublin. Tel: 454 0800; Monkstown, Co. Dublin. Tel: 284 2688; Dublin Road, Bray. Tel: 284 2688. Delivery to Dublin Airport and to Dublin and Dun Laoghaire ferry terminals.

Northern Ireland

Avis Rent-a-Car Great Victoria Street, Belfast. Tel: 01232-240404; Belfast International Airport. Tel: 018494-422333; Belfast City Airport. Tel: 01232-452017; Coleraine/City of Derry Airport. Tel: 01265-43654; Larne. Tel: 01574-260799.

Budget Rentacar, Belfast. Tel: 01232-230700; Belfast City Airport. Tel: 01232-451111.

Europcar, Belfast City Airport. Tel: 01232-450904; Belfast International Airport. Tel: 018494-423444.

Hertz Rent-a-Car, Belfast International Airport. Tel:

018494-422533; Belfast City Airport. Tel: 01232-732451; Larne Harbour. Tel: 01574-278111.

Lochside Garages, Tempo Road, Enniskillen. Tel: 01365-324366.

McCausland Car Hire, Grosvenor Road, Belfast. Tel: 01232-333777; Belfast International Airport 01849-422022; Belfast City Airport. Tel: 01232-454141.

Cycling
This is an excellent way to see the countryside at a leisurely pace, provided you aren't anxious to cover too much ground (the modern disease). Throughout the Republic, specially appointed Rent-a-Bike dealers hire out sturdy Raleigh Tourer bicycles: a list of them is available from the Irish Tourist Board and the bikes can sometimes be delivered to airports. Expect to pay upwards of £30 a week for rental.

For details of organised biking holidays with bike hire, route maps and pre-booked accommodation contact:
Rent A Bike Holidays, 58 Lower Gardiner Street, Dublin 1. Tel: 01-872 5399, fax 836 4763.

In Dublin, you can also hire a

Hiring a Horse-drawn Caravan

Horses and caravans are available for hire in Counties Cork, Kerry and Wicklow. You can expect to cover only about 10 miles (16 km) a day – but going slowly is just the point, of course, giving you plenty of time to appreciate the countryside, meet and talk to passers-by and let your inner rhythms settle down to a more sensible pace. Feeding, grooming and harnessing the horse is time-consuming too, and quite hard work.

The caravans, which have gas cookers, are mostly for four people, with berths that convert into seating for daytime. Utensils, crockery, etc are provided. Fastidious people should note that caravans do not have toilets (well, didn't you want the real thing?). In high season, expect to pay from £400 to £500 a week; allow about £7 a night for overnight parking.

Operators include **Clissman's Horse-Drawn Caravans** in Co. Wicklow (tel: 0404-48188; fax: 48288) and **Slattery's Horse-Drawn Caravans** in Co. Kerry (tel: 066-21722, fax: 26001). Further details from the Irish Tourist Board.

bicycle from **C. Harding**, 30 Bachelors Walk (on the north quays west of O'Connell Bridge), tel: 873 2455; **Dublin Bike Hire**, 27 North Great George's Street, tel: 878 84/3; and **Mike's Bikes**, Dun Laoghaire Shopping Centre, tel: 280 0417.

Horse Riding
Equestrian Holidays Ireland
have details of residential and non-residential riding holidays around the country. Choose between post to post trail riding staying in a different guest house every evening, or equestrian centres with on-site accommodation and indoor and outdoor riding facilities.

For a detailed brochure, contact Bord Fáilte or Equestrian Holidays Ireland, Whispering Pines, Crosshaven. Co. Cork. Tel: 021-831950, fax 831679.

Inland Waterways
The three main waterways for cruising are the River Shannon, navigable for 150 miles (240 km) downstream from Lough Key, Co Roscommon; the Grand Canal, which runs westward from Dublin across the central plain to the Shannon, and is joined in Co Kildare by a branch line running south to the River Barrow; and the River Erne, navigable for 50 miles (80 km) from Belturbet, Co Cavan through Upper and Lower Lough Erne to Belleek, near Enniskillen, Co Fermanagh. All three waterways are marvellous for fishing, birdwatching, rowing, photography, or just pottering peacefully along.

In the Republic, six approved companies offer cabin cruisers for hire on the River Shannon, and two on the Grand Canal. All are affiliated to the Irish Boat Rental Association, and full details are included in Bord Fáilte's *Cruising Ireland* brochure. In Northern Ireland,

six companies approved by the Erne Charter Boat Association operate on Lough Erne; ask for the *Holidays Afloat* brochure from the Northern Ireland Tourist Board.

Cruisers range in size from two berths to eight; all have refrigerators and gas cookers; most have heating, hot water and showers; dinghies, charts and safety equipment are included. Experience in handling a boat is an advantage, but instruction is provided for novices.

Disabled Travellers
For people with mobility problems, the National Rehabilitation Board publishes a booklet, *Dublin: A Guide for Disabled Travellers*. It is full of practical information and available from the NRB, 25 Clyde Road, Dublin 4, tel: 01-874 7503, fax 874 7490. or the tourist board.

Dublin Literary Tours
A **Bloomsday Walking Tour** based on James Joyce's *Ulysses* starts from the Post Office. Contact Beatrice Healy on 01 4545943. A **Bloomstime Ulysses Bus Tour** is led by experts and staff of the James Joyce Centre (Tel: 01-8788547). A general two-hour **Georgian/Literary Walking Tour** of Dublin starts at Bewley's Museum in Grafton Street, and is run by Dublin Footsteps (Tel: 01-4960641).

Where to Stay

The Choice

It is possible to pay as much as IR£200 or more for a room in a top-rated hotel, or as little as IR£12 for "bed and breakfast" in a family home which takes visitors. Dearer is not necessarily better, of course, but generally speaking the more you pay, the more facilities are on offer.

Apart from what you can afford to pay, you may decide that you don't need a hotel with suites available, night service, two restaurants, a health complex and uniformed attendants at every turn. Or you may simply dislike large, grand hotels and prefer small, family-run places with a bit more character, even if the bathroom is down the hall and the menu is pot luck. And a remarkable number of B & Bs now have rooms with "en-suite" shower or bath and some – especially farmhouses – offer first-class food. B & Bs are not necessarily budget options: large rooms decorated with antiques in stately homes like

When to plan ahead

Accommodation is seasonal in the more remote areas. Many places close from October or November to mid-March or Easter in the smaller villages of the southwest, far west and northwest areas. It is advisable to book ahead in July and August, especially in scenic and coastal areas.

Bantry House may cost the same as a good hotel, but the experience will be much more memorable.

Both the Irish Republic and Northern Ireland classify hotels on broadly the same grading system, as follows:

AP: Top-grade hotels, some in former castles; all rooms have private bathrooms and suites are available. High-quality restaurant.

A: Hotels, ranging from modern, purpose-built premises to converted period houses, offering a high standard of comfort and service. With few exceptions all rooms have private bathrooms.

BP: Medium-priced hotels, ranging from small, family-run places to larger, more commercial operations. Most rooms have private bathrooms.

B: Mostly family-run hotels, with limited but satisfactory range of food and comfort. Some rooms have private bathrooms.

C: Simple but acceptable accommodation and services.

Guesthouses: This is a category for B & Bs with over five rooms. Some but not all guesthouses have restaurant facilities, and those public facilities that you would expect in a hotel, such as residents' lounge, may be limited or non existent. Guesthouses are not licensed to sell beer and spirits (unless the guesthouse is also a pub), but some have wine licences.

Bed & Breakfast: B & B accommodation is offered in many private family houses, both in towns and in the countryside. Evening meals are normally provided if notice is given before noon. The newer B & Bs have often been designed for that purpose, and will have bathrooms en suite, and, in major towns, direct dial phones and TV.

Hostels: The Irish Youth Hostel Association (An Oige) has 37 hostels in the Republic, with fees varying from £IR5.50 to

What prices include

Prices indicated are based on the rate per person sharing a double room. Single rooms can be hard to find, and usually carry a premium. Guesthouses and B & Bs are both listed under the B & B category.

£IR9.50. Hostels in Northern Ireland are run by the Youth Hostel Association of Northern Ireland. Members of the International Youth Hostel Federation can use any of these. Independent Holiday Hostels is an umbrella organisation for about 150 privately owned hostels. These are relaxed places, with none of the rules and curfews imposed by An Oige. As well as traditional dormitory accommodation, many also have private double and family rooms, and offer cooked breakfast as an optional extra, as well as kitchen facilities. For a brochure contact the IHH Office, 57 Lower Gardiner Street, Dublin 1. Tel: 01—836 4700; fax: 836 4710. Some hostels prefer not to belong to any organisation. All independent hostels are privately owned, and can vary from scenic organic farms to a tiny town house stacked with bunk beds. The atmosphere is generally friendly, and you will soon learn about the best places by talking to fellow travellers. The one drawback is a tendency to overcrowding in July and August and at festival times.

Budget accommodation: The Irish student and youth travel company USIT runs Kinlay House year-round centres in Dublin (tel: 01-679 6644), Galway (091-65245) and Cork (021-508966). Prices start at below £IR10. During the long vacation from mid-June to mid-September, they also offer self-catering apartments in UCD Village, Belfield Campus, Dublin

4 (01-269 7111) and at Brookfield Holiday Village, College Road, Cork (021-344032) with prices starting at under £IR20.

Self-catering accommodation: This is available throughout Ireland in houses, cottages (some thatched), apartments, caravans and even a few castles (suitable for groups). If you are looking for a "traditional Irish cottage" be warned that many on offer are newly built in artificial "clusters", and used solely for holiday rentals. Be sure you are getting what you want when you book. There are also many caravan and camping parks for those who like to take their accommodation with them.

If touring the Republic, you can ask one of the local tourist information offices to book ahead for you. A small charge is made for telephone costs.

Dublin

££££ (over £150 a night for a double room).

Berkeley Court Hotel, Lansdowne Road, Dublin 4. Tel: 6601711, fax: 6617238. Ugly, concrete-shoebox exterior, but luxurious inside. Sited in Ballsbridge near the famous Lansdowne Road international rugby ground.

The Burlington, Upper Leeson Street, Dublin 4. Tel: 6605222, fax: 6608496. Ireland's largest hotel and conference centre. Located near "The Strip", although the number of nightclubs on the once legendary Leeson Street is now dwindling. The bar is a popular spot for *après*-rugby match knees-ups.

The Clarence, 6–8 Wellington Quay, Dublin 2. Tel: 6709000, fax: 6707800. City-centre, riverside location, backing onto Temple Bar. Recently refurbished and redesigned with stylish restraint, this place delights the eye as well as the stomach (the restaurant is first-class). Owners include members of the U2 rock group, clientele is self-consciously hip.

Conrad International Hotel, Earlsfort Terrace, Dublin 2. Tel: 6765555, fax: 6765424. Recently-built, American-style, gleaming five-star hotel across the street from the National Concert Hall and just a few metres from St Stephen's Green. Telephones even in the bathrooms.

Gresham Hotel, Upper O'Connell Street, Dublin 1. Tel: 8746881, fax: 8787175. Once rivalled the Shelbourne as Dublin's grandest hotel, but has suffered somewhat from the decline of O'Connell Street. Still characterful and atmospheric.

Shelbourne Hotel, St. Stephen's Green, Dublin 2. Tel: 6766471, fax: 6616006. Long established as Dublin's most prestigious hotel, with plenty of old-world atmosphere. The lounge is a great place for afternoon tea, the Horseshoe Bar is popular with some of the city's "heavy hitters".

Westbury Hotel, Clarendon Street, off Grafton Street, Dublin 2. Tel: 6791122, fax: 6797078. Modern, luxury hotel right in the city centre with a shopping mall next door. First-class food.

£££ (over £90 a night double)

Bewley's Principal Hotel, 19–20 Fleet Street, Temple Bar, Dublin 2. Tel: 6708122, fax: 6708103. The legendary café group has branched into the accommodation market. An old-fashioned intimate hotel with every modern facility. Plus fresh Bewley's coffee.

Buswell's Hotel, Molesworth Street, Dublin 2. Tel: 6764013, fax: 6762090. Former Georgian townhouses used as a hotel since the 1920s. A haunt of politicians because of its proximity to Leinster House. Recently refurbished.

Camden Court Hotel, Camden Street, Dublin 2. Tel: 4759666, fax: 6627244. Large new hotel located 10 minutes' walk from the city centre. Modern interior and planned facilities include a leisure centre.

Central Hotel, Exchequer Street, Dublin 2. Tel: 6797302, fax: 6797303. Arguably more characterful than some of the bigger, pricier places, with interesting paintings on the walls. Close to Grafton Street.

The Davenport Hotel, Merrion Square, Dublin 2. Tel: 6073500, fax: 6615663. Luxurious hotel in the heart of Georgian Dublin. Sited near the National Gallery of Ireland, Trinity College and Grafton Street.

Hibernian Hotel, Eastmoreland Place, Dublin 4. Tel: 6687666, fax: 6602655. Luxurious old house in Ballsbridge offering high level of personal service. First-rate food.

Tip: Book ahead

It can be difficult to find a bed in Dublin at high season, so advance booking is advised. Check prices before booking.

Longfield's Hotel, Lower Fitzwilliam Street, Dublin 2. Tel: 6761367, fax: 6761542. Charming small hotel in heart of southside Georgian Dublin. Good food in basement restaurant.

Mont Clare Hotel, Clare Street, Dublin 2. Tel: 6616799, fax: 6766064. Excellent location on the corner of Merrion Square, close to National Gallery and main southside shopping areas.

The Morgan Hotel, 10 Fleet Street, Temple Bar, Dublin 2. Tel: 6793939, fax: 6793946. New hotel in the heart of Temple Bar. High-tech facilities; all rooms have hi-fi systems and video players, ISDN lines and Internet access.

Temple Bar Hotel, Fleet Street, Dublin 2. Tel: 6773333, fax: 6773088. Sited in trendy Temple Bar area with its bustling night-life. Great location if you're not a light sleeper.

££ (over £60 double)

Aberdeen Lodge, Park Avenue, Dublin 4. Tel: 2838155, fax: 2837877. Well-equipped guesthouse in pair of Edwardian houses on elegant road.

Albany House, Harcourt Street, Dublin 2. Tel: 4751092, fax: 4751093. Elegant house in the heart of Georgian Dublin. Bedrooms are decorated with period prints and antiques.

Anglesea Town House, Anglesea Road, Dublin 4. Tel: 6683877, fax: 6683461. Privately run guesthouse in Edwardian villa in Ballsbridge. Famous for its breakfasts.

Chestnut Lodge, Vesey Place, Dun Laoghaire. Tel: 2807860, fax: 2801466. Fine Regency house in quiet, leafy terrace near Dun Laoghaire. Family-run.

Hotel St. George, 7 Parnell Square, Dublin 1. Tel: 8745611, fax: 8745582. Comfortable hotel in two converted Georgian houses. Close to the Hugh Lane Municipal Art Gallery, Gate Theatre, and O'Connell Street.

Hotel Isaacs, Frenchman's Lane, Dublin 1. Tel: 8550067, fax: 8365390. Small, efficient, friendly place handily situated close to Connolly Station and Busaras (central bus stations).

Jurys Christchurch Inn, Christchurch Place, Dublin 8. Tel: 4540000, fax: 4540012. Newish, less expensive addition to a long-established chain of hotels. Well located for the old city and Temple Bar.

Merrion Hall, Merrion Road, Dublin 4. Tel: 6681426, fax: 6684280. Rambling, cosy Victorian guesthouse near the Royal Dublin Society grounds. Good breakfasts.

Mount Herbert House, Herbert Road, Lansdowne Road, Dublin 4. Tel: 6684321, fax: 6607077. Family-run guesthouse in an extended Victorian house near Lansdowne Road stadium. Children's playground.

Number 31, Leeson Close, Dublin 2. Tel: 6765011, fax: 6762929. Interesting, friendly guesthouse based in two houses, one modern, one Georgian. Just off Leeson Street, known for its basement nightclubs.

River House Hotel, 23–24 Eustace Street, Temple Bar, Dublin 2. Tel: 6707655, fax: 6707650. Few hotels are closer to the action in the hip Temple Bar area. Opposite the Irish Film Centre, and near art and photographic galleries, pubs and restaurants.

£ (under £60 double)

Abraham House, Lower Gardiner Street, Dublin 1. Tel: 8550600, fax: 8550598. Hostel in two large Georgian houses. Double rooms, dormitories, private parking. Cheap.

St. Aiden's Guesthouse, Brighton Road, Dublin 6. Tel: 4902011, fax: 4920234. Good guesthouse in a pleasant south-side suburb of Rathgar.

Avalon House, Aungier Street, Dublin 2. Tel: 4750001, fax: 4750303. Well-located hostel near Grafton Street and Temple Bar. Single rooms, double rooms, family rooms, dorms. Cheap.

Carraige House Guesthouse, Lusk, Co. Dublin. Tel: 8438857, fax: 8438933. Cosy, welcoming guesthouse with extensive award-winning gardens. Leisure centre free to guests.

The Cumberland Lodge Town House, York Road, Dun Laoghaire, Co. Dublin., Tel: 2809665, fax: 2843227. Recently restored Georgian house situated in a scenic suburb south of the city centre. Elegant rooms and extensive car parking.

Dorchester House, North Circular Road, Dublin 1. Tel: 8385204, no fax. Two restored

Georgian houses in central northside location.

Kinlay House, Lower Edward Street, Dublin 2. Tel: 6796644, fax: 6797437. Close to Christ Church Cathedral, backing onto Temple Bar. Singles, doubles, 4–6 bedded rooms, dorms. Cheap.

The Oliver St. John Gogarty, Anglesea Street, Temple Bar, Dublin 2. Tel: 6711822, fax: 6717637. Recent addition to the budget end of the accommodation market, and offering bright and airy rooms in the heart of trendy Temple Bar.

Othello Guesthouse, Lower Gardiner Street, Dublin 1. Tel: 8554271, fax: 8557460. Handy, inner north-city location near the principal rail and bus stations. Well equipped.

Southeast Region

CAHIR, CO. TIPPERARY

Kilcoran Lodge, Cahir. Tel: 052-41288, fax 41994. Former hunting lodge in its own grounds on the main N8 with views over the Knockmealdown Mountains. ££.

CASHEL, CO. TIPPERARY

Cashel Palace Hotel, Main Street, Cashel. Tel: 062-62707, fax 61521. Queen Anne-style Bishop's palace sumptuously converted into fine hotel. View of the Rock from back rooms. ££££.

GLEN OF AHERLOW, CO. TIPPERARY

Aherlow House Hotel. Tel: 062-56153, fax 56212. Hunting lodge surrounded by pine forest

and overlooking the Galty mountains. Good base for walking and climbing. ££.

GOREY, CO. WEXFORD

Courtown Hotel, Courtown Harbour, near Gorey. Tel: 055-25108, fax 055-25304. Small hotel run by owner-manager, with indoor heated pool in family-oriented seaside resort. ££.

Marlfield House, Gorey. Tel: 055-21124, fax 21572. Grand Regency house with first-class restaurant in large conservatory. £££.

KILKENNY, CO. KILKENNY

Hotel Kilkenny, College Road, Kilkenny. Tel: 056-62000. Modern hotel and leisure complex built around old home. Conservatory, indoor pool, jacuzzi. ££.

ROSSLARE, CO. WEXFORD

Hotel Rosslare, Rosslare Harbour. Tel: 053-33110; fax 33386. Modern cliff-top hotel overlooking Rosslare Bay and ferryport. ££.

Kelly's Resort Hotel, Rosslare Village, Co. Wexford. Tel: 053-32144, fax 32222. Beachfront resort hotel established 1895, and run by the Kelly family ever since. Outstanding sports facilities and excellent food. £££.

THOMASTOWN, CO. KILKENNY

Mount Juliet Estate, Thomastown. Tel: 056-24455, fax 24522. Elegant 18th century house on its own sporting estate which includes a Jack Nicklaus golf course, equestrian centre and tennis centre. ££££.

What the tourist boards offer

In most places, prices vary according to season. Full details of current rates are given in Bord Fáilte's accommodation brochure, which can be purchased at any Irish tourist board office. The Northern Ireland Tourist Board publishes *Where to Stay*, also on sale at any of its branches. The *Hidden Ireland* brochure lists large and often grand family homes throughout Ireland which take visitors. In these, you are paying for ambience as well as accommodation. **Contact addresses: page 333.**

WATERFORD, CO. WATERFORD
Dooley's Hotel, Waterford. Tel: 051-873531, fax 870262. Family-run hotel with good food and lively bar in centre of town on the quays of the River Suir. ££.

WEXFORD, CO. WEXFORD
Ferrycarrig Hotel, Ferrycarrig Bridge, near Wexford. Tel: 053-22999, fax 20982.. Stylish modern hotel in attractive setting by Slaney River 5km/3 miles outside town on the Enniscorthy road. £££.

BED AND BREAKFAST
ANNESTOWN, CO. WATERFORD
Annestown House, Annestown. Tel: 051-396160, fax 396474. Cliff top house on coastal road between Tramore and Dungarvan with private paths to the beach. Tennis and billiards. £.

INISTIOGE, CO. KILKENNY
Berryhill, Inistioge. Tel. & fax: 056-58434. Creeper-clad, elegant farmhouse dating from 1780, with views over the River Nore, log fires, and private salmon fishing. Exceptionally comfortable and well-decorated rooms. ££.

KILKENNY TOWN, CO. KILKENNY
Butler House, Patrick Street. Tel: 056-65707, fax 65626. Once the Dower House of Kilkenny Castle, this town-centre Georgian house overlooking extensive gardens combines period elegance with contemporary design. ££.
Lacken House, Dublin/Carlow Road, Kilkenny. Tel: 056-65611, fax 62435. Award-winning restaurant with owner-chef offers comfortable, well-equipped rooms in small Georgian house. £ .

WEXFORD TOWN, CO. WEXFORD
Faythe Guest House, Swan View, Wexford. Tel: 053-22249. No fax.. Simple. town house. Views over Wexford Harbour. £.

Southwest Region

BANTRY, CO. CORK
Seaview House Hotel, Ballylickey, Bantry. Tel: 027-50073, fax 51555. Elegant but relaxed country house hotel set in wooded grounds on the edge of Bantry Bay. ££.

CORK CITY
Arbutus Lodge Hotel, Montenotte. Tel: 021-501237, fax 502893. Small hotel in early 19th-century town house with fine gardens and collection of modern Irish art. Outstanding restaurant and wine list. ££
Hayfield Manor Hotel, Perrott Avenue. Tel: 012-315600, fax 316839. Cork's newest luxury hotel is built in the country house-style on carefully landscaped grounds near University College. A haven of tranquillity five minutes' drive form the centre. ££££.

What the codes mean

- **£** = under £30 per person
- **££** = £30–£60 per person
- **£££** = £60–£90) per person
- **££££** = over £90 per person

Jury's Hotel, Western Rd. Tel: 021-276622, fax 274477, Large, modern low-rise hotel beside the River Lee, 5 minutes' walk from centre. £££.
Rochestown Park, Rochestown Road, Douglas, Co. Cork. Tel: 021-892233, fax 892178. Situated in the south suburbs, convenient for airport and ferry port this is a pleasant modern hotel with indoor pool built around an old manor house in lovely wooded grounds. ££.

DINGLE, CO. KERRY
Dingle Skellig, Co. Kerry. Tel: 066-51144, fax 066-51501. Imaginatively designed modern hotel on the water's edge. Sea view on request. Indoor heated pool. £££.

GOLEEN, CO. CORK
Barley Cove Beach Hotel, Goleen. Tel: 028-35234, fax 35100. Popular family hotel beside sandy beach on Mizen peninsula. ££.

KILLARNEY, CO. KERRY
Cahernane Hotel, Muckross Road. Tel: 064 31895, fax 34340. Once the shooting lodge of the Earl of Pembroke, this characterful old house has a lakeside location 1 kilometre outside town. Most bedrooms are in a modern wing. £££.
Great Southern Hotel, Killarney. Tel: 064-31262, fax 31642. Monumental Victorian railway hotel adjacent to town centre. Swimming, tennis, sauna and Irish entertainment nightly from May to September. £££.

KINSALE, CO. CORK
Blue Haven Hotel, Kinsale. Tel: 021-772209, fax 774268. Small, family-run hotel in town centre noted for its sea food restaurant. £££.

MALLOW, CO. CORK
Longueville House, Co. Cork. Tel: 022-47156, fax 47459. Relaxed family-run country house in a magnificent classical-style 18th-century house overlooking the Blackwater River midway between Cork and Killarney. The restaurant is renowned. £££.

RING OF KERRY, CO. KERRY
Ard-na-Sidhe, Caragh Lake, Killorglin. Tel: 066-69105, fax 69282. Luxurious lakeside Victorian mansion with antiques, open fires and extensive gardens. £££.
Butler Arms Hotel, Waterville. Tel: 066-74144, fax 066-74520. Well-established, informal family-run hotel overlooking the sea. Golf, tennis, fishing, horse riding. ££.
Great Southern Hotel, Parknasilla. Tel: 064-45122, fax 45323. Imposing, 19th-century

mansion with extensive semi-tropical gardens. Private golf-course, swimming, riding, tennis, fishing, water-skiing. £££.
Park Hotel, Kenmare. Tel: 064-41200, fax 41114. Luxurious, impeccably decorated hotel in grand 1897 greystone building with 11 acres of gardens. Excellent food. ££££.
Sheen Falls Lodge, Kenmare.. Tel: 064-41600, fax 41386. Kenmare's newest luxury hotel is in a rambling lodge on a 300-acre waterside estate. Award-winning restaurant. ££££.

BED AND BREAKFAST
CORK CITY
Isaac's, 48 MacCurtan Street. Tel: 021-500011, fax 506355. cheerful budget hotel and hostel in boldly converted warehouse. Handy for both bus and train stations. £.
Victoria Lodge, Victoria Cross. Tel: 021-54223, fax 542572. Imaginatively converted early 20th-century monastery in mature gardens with private car park. Five minutes' drive from city centre on bus route. £.

DINGLE, CO. KERRY
Cleevaun Country House, Lady's Cross, Milltown. Tel & fax: 066-51108. Modern house a mile outside town on Slea Head road with views over Dingle Bay. Extensive breakfast menu. £.

KANTURK, CO. CORK
Assolas Country House, Kanturk. Tel: 029-50015, fax 50795. Romantic 17th-century house with sweeping riverside gardens owned and managed by the Bourke family. Idyllic. Restaurant is renowned for imaginative cuisine. £££.

KILLARNEY, CO. KERRY
Kathleen's Country House, Tralee Road, Killarney. Tel 064-32810, fax 32340. This well-appointed modern guesthouse run by energetic owner-manager

Kathleen O'Regan Sheppard is five minutes drive from town on the Tralee road. Dinner by arrangement. ££.
Victoria House, Muckross Road. Tel: 064-35430, fax 064-35439. Bright, modern guest-house a mile outside town near the gateway to the National Park. £.

KINSALE, CO. CORK
Kilcaw Lodge, Pewter Hole Cross. Tel: 021-774155, fax 774755. Situated just outside town on the main road from Cork Airport this newly built guest house offers private parking, a welcoming open fire and country pine bedrooms. £
Old Bank House, Pearse Street, Co. Cork. Tel. 021-774075, fax 774296. High standard of comfort in boldly converted Georgian town house. ££

MIDLETON, CO. CORK
Ballymaloe House, Shangarry, Midleton. Tel: 021-652531. One of Ireland's leading guest houses, virtually indistinguishable from a luxury hotel, Ballymaloe is a large, impeccably run and stylishly decorated Georgian house, owned by farming family. Renowned for its kitchen which pioneered imaginative use of fresh local produce. £££.

What the codes mean

- **£** = under £30 per person
- **££** = £30–£60 per person
- **£££** = £60–£90) per person
- **££££** = over £90 per person

RING OF KERRY
Caragh Lodge, Caragh Lake, near Glenbeigh. Tel: 066-69115, fax 69316. Secluded fishing lodge in lovely lakeside gardens. Boating, tennis, fishing. Dinner can be pre-booked. ££.
Sallyport House, Glengarriff Road, Kenmare. Tel. 064-42066, fax 42067. Exceptionally comfortable family home on

the edge of town overlooking Kenmare harbour. Interesting antique furniture. ££.
Smuggler's Inn, Cliff Road, Waterville. Tel: 0667-4422. Small, family-run guesthouse. Good food. ££.
Tahilla Cove Country House, near Sneem. Tel: 064-45204, fax 45104. Secluded waterside retreat with a 14 acre estate, run by the friendly Waterhouse family. Fully licensed. Home cooked dinner. ££.

Mid West Region

ADARE, CO. LIMERICK
Dunraven Arms Hotel, Adare. Tel: 061-396209, fax 396541. Historic old inn in beautiful village. Equestrian and golf holidays a speciality. £££.
Woodlands House Hotel, Knockanes, Adare. Tel: 061-396118, fax 396073. Friendly, family-run modern hotel with a lively bar and a busy local trade. Good touring base. ££.

BALLYVAUGHAN, CO. CLARE
Gregan's Castle, Co. Clare. Tel: 065-77005, fax 77111. An elegant country house hotel in extensive gardens at the base of the Burren's famous Corkscrew Hill with breathtaking views over Galway Bay. A little formal for some tastes, for others it is an oasis of sophistication. ££££.
Hyland's, Co. Clare. Tel: 065-77037, fax 77131. Rambling, much extended family-run hotel in village centre with a lively bar and busy restaurant. ££.

ENNIS, CO. CLARE
Old Ground Hotel, Ennis. Tel: 065-28127. Spacious, ivy-clad hotel partly 17th-century, with a quiet but central location 30 minutes from Shannon Airport. Lively local trade and lots of golfers. £££.

ENNISTYMON, CO. CLARE
Falls Hotel, Ennistymon. Tel:

065-71004. Family-owned and managed large spa hotel near waterfalls on River Inagh on the edge of a quietly attractive old world village. Retains charm and atmosphere in spite of its relatively large size (130 rooms). ££

KINVARA, CO. GALWAY
Merriman Inn, Kinvara. Tel; 091-638222, fax 637686. A large thatched building dating from 1997 in the centre of this attractive little fishing village, the Merriman shows modern Irish design at its best. ££

LAHINCH, CO. CLARE
Aberdeen Arms Hotel, Lahinch. Tel: 065-81100, Fax 81228. Attractively modernised Victorian hotel in seaside village with long sandy beach and dunes. Popular with golfers. ££.

LIMERICK CITY
Castletroy Park, Dublin Road. Tel: 061-335566, fax 061-331117. This well-designed modern red brick hotel is on the edge of town near the university campus. While catering admirably for the business traveller, the hotel also has superb leisure facilities and a lively pub-bistro. £££.
Jury's Inn, Lower Mallow Street, Mount Kennett Place. Tel: 061-207000, fax 400966. A large, modern hotel that charges per room, this is part of Jury's budget chain, and is by far the best value in this price range in central Limerick. It overlooks the River Shannon and is part of Limerick's long over-due dockside development. £.

LISDOONVARNA, CO. CLARE
Sheedy's Spa View Hotel, Lisdoonvarna. Tel: 065-74026, fax 74555. Small family-run hotel with turf fires. The main attraction is the exceptional food cooked by the owner's son and served in the Orchid Room Restaurant. ££.

Ballinalacken Castle, Co. Clare. Tel & fax: 065-74025. A converted shooting lodge with a modern bedroom wing, located beside the ruined castle for which it is named, on the coast road outside town. Superb views of the Atlantic and the Aran islands. ££.

QUIN, CO. CLARE
Ballykilty Manor Hotel, Quin. Tel: 065-25627, fax 25654. An appealing first stop for Shannon arrivals. Relaxed, informal Georgian manor in wooded grounds on River Rine (good trout and salmon fishing). ££

NEWMARKET ON FERGUS, CO. CLARE
Dromoland Castle Hotel, Newmarket on Fergus. Tel: 061-368144. Former seat of the O'Briens of Thomond, direct descendants of the High King of Ireland, Brian Boru, Dromoland is now an American-owned luxury hotel. Private golf course and lake, clay shooting, and horse riding on the estate. Interior decor is atmospheric and stylish. ££££.

BED AND BREAKFAST
BALLYVAUGHAN, CO. CLARE
Cappabhaile House. Ballyvaughan. Tel. and fax: 065-77260. Large, unpretentious stone-faced bungalow on the edge of the Burren purpose-built for the B&B business. Family-run restaurant. Walking distance to lively village pubs. £.

BRUREE, CO. LIMERICK
Ballyteigue House, Bruree. Tel. & Fax: 063-90575. Georgian family home in country location just off Cork road about one hour from Shannon. Log fires and a warm welcome. Dinner at 7pm by arrangement – bring your own wine. £.

CLARECASTLE, CO. CLARE
Carnelly House, Clarecastle. Tel: 065-28442, fax 29222. Lovely Queen Anne-style

Georgian house near Dromoland Castle in 100 acres of farm and woodland. A real taste of gracious living at the very top end of the B&B market. Dinner by arrangement. £££.

KILRUSH, CO. CLARE
Old Parochial House, Cooraclare. Tel.: 065-59059, fax 065-77040. Spacious, informal period house on the edge of small seaside village. £.

KINVARA, CO. GALWAY
Burren View Farmhouse, Doorus. Tel: 091-37142, fax 0905-42952. Simple, restful farmhouse accommodation well off the beaten track with peaceful sea and mountain views of the Burren and Galway Bay. Evening meal by arrangement. £.

Midlands Region

ATHLONE, CO. WESTMEATH
Hodson Bay Hotel, Athlone. Tel: 0902-92444, fax 0902-92688. Large, nicely modernised hotel with a superb location on the water's edge at Lough Ree just west of Athlone on the N61 Roscommon road. ££.

BANAGHER, CO. OFFALY
Brosna Lodge Hotel, Banagher. Tel. 0509-51350, fax 0509-51521. Simple hospitality in a lively Shannonside village. £.

BIRR, CO. OFFALY
County Arms Hotel, Birr. Tel: 0509-20791. Small, owner-managed hotel in converted Georgian mansion. ££.
Kinnitty Castle, Kinnitty. Tel: 0509-37318, fax 37284. Exuberant, turreted Gothic castle about 9 miles outside Birr in the foothills of the Slieve Bloom mountains, this is a genuine Irish castle experience with everything on a vast scale. £££.

MULLINGAR, CO. WESTMEATH
Bloomfield House Hotel, Belvedere, Mullingar. Tel: 044-

40894, fax 43767. Friendly hotel in old, castellated house on the shores of Lough Ennell that once served as a convent boarding school. Good value in pleasant, unspoilt countryside. ££.

ROSCOMMON, CO. ROSCOMMON
Abbey Hotel, Abbeytown. Tel: 0903-26240, fax 26021. Modern hotel in venerable castellated shell parts of which date from the 18th century. Peaceful location surrounded by lawns. ££.

BED AND BREAKFAST
BIRR, CO. OFFALY
Spinners Town House, Castle Street, Birr. Tel & fax: 0509-21673. A row of five Georgian town houses near the town centre have been refurbished as a restaurant and guest house. Excellent value. £.

BORRISOKANE, CO. TIPPERARY
Ballycormac House, Aglish. Tel: 067-21129, fax 21200. Pretty country cottage run by American gourmet cooks, Herb and Christine Quigley. Dinner, bookable in advance by residents only, is a highlight here. ££.

MOUNTRATH, CO. LAOIS
Roundwood House, Mountrath. Tel: 0502-32120, fax 32711. Informal hospitality in an 18th-century Palladian villa close to the Slieve Bloom mountains. Popular with walkers. Dinner by arrangement. ££.

NENAGH, CO. TIPPERARY
Saint David's Country House, Puckane. Tel: 067-24145, fax 24388. Picture-book pretty Victorian lakeside lodge refurbished to unusually high standard. Restaurant, bar. Fishing and horse riding in the grounds. £££.

TERRYGLASS, CO. TIPPERARY
Tír na Fiúise (Land of Fuchsia), Borrisokane. Tel. & fax: 067-

22041. Quiet farmhouse well off the beaten track popular with those seeking rural solitude. Interesting breakfast menu. Good walking country near scenic Lough Derg. £.

Far West Region

ACHILL, CO. MAYO
Ostan Gob A'Choire (Achill Sound Hotel), Achill Island. Tel: 098-45245, fax 45621. This splendidly scenic island is connected to mainland Mayo by a causeway. Accommodation is simple, but you can expect some form of traditional entertainment most evenings in July and August. £.

ARAN ISLANDS, CO. GALWAY
Ostan Inis Oirr, Lurgan Village, Inisheer. Tel: 099/75020, Fax: 75099. Whether you fly or take the ferry, this simple modern hotel makes a comfortable base for exploring the smallest of the Aran Islands. Traditional music nightly in the bar. £.
CASHEL BAY, CO. GALWAY

What the codes mean

- **£** = under £30 per person
- **££** = £30–£60 per person
- **£££** = £60–£90 per person
- **££££** = over £90 per person

Cashel House Hotel, Cashel Bay. Tel: 095-31001, fax 31077. Elegant, antique-filled country hideaway in lovely gardens over-looking bay and backed by the hills of Connemara. £££.

CLIFDEN, CO. GALWAY
Ahbeyglen Castle, Clifden. Tel: 095-21201, fax 21797. Turreted mock castle on beautiful site on outskirts of "capital of Connemara." Good sports facilities including an outdoor heated swimming pool. ££
Erriseask House, Ballyconneely. Tel: 095-23553, fax 23639.

This small modern country hotel set amidst some of Connemara's best coastal scenery is impeccably run by Swiss brothers Christian and Stefan Matz. Stefan's cooking has a high reputation. £££.
Rock Glen Manor House, Clifden. Tel: 095-21035, fax 21737. Elegant shooting lodge in quiet location 1.6km outside Clifden on the shores of Ardbear Bay. Cosy. Good food. ££.

CONG, CO. MAYO
Ashford Castle, Cong. Tel: 092-46003, fax 46260. A castellated fairy-tale castle, standing on the isthmus between Lough Corrib and Lough Mask. American-run with high very standards of comfort and decor. Private golf course, tennis, fishing, boating, horse riding and shooting are part of the "total resort" experience. Ronald and Nancy Reagan stayed here on their presidential visit to Ireland in 1984. ££££.

GALWAY CITY
Ardilaun House Hotel, Taylor's Hill. Tel: 091-521433, fax 521546. Charming old world hotel is quiet, leafy location midway between Galway city and Salthill. £££.
Brennan's Yard Hotel, Lower Merchant's Road. Tel: 056-568166, fax 568262. Interesting warehouse conversion in city centre's newly revitalised dock area. ££.
Glenlo Abbey Hotel, Bushy Park. Tel: 091-526666, fax 527800. Luxuriously converted monastery on the banks of Lough Corrib 4km from city centre, surrounded by its own golf course. ££££.
Great Southern Hotel, Eyre Square, Galway. Tel: 091-564041, fax 566704. Grand old railway hotel on city's main square, still a major landmark and social centre. Indoor pool, health complex. £££

Jury's Galway Inn, Quay Street. Tel: 091-566444, fax 568415. Large modern building on edge of the River Corrib in the fashionable heart of the city, Jury's Inn is relatively anonymous but offers excellent value and location. £.

LETTERFRACK, CO. GALWAY
Rosleague Manor Hotel, Letterfrack. Tel: 095-41101, fax 41168. Beautifully situated Georgian house in scenic Connemara with grounds running down to the sea. Relaxed country house hotel atmosphere. £££.

OUGHTERARD, CO. GALWAY
Connemara Gateway Hotel, Oughterard. Tel: 091-82328. Well-run, imaginatively designed modern hotel. Swimming, tennis. £££.
Sweeney's Oughterard House, Oughterard. Tel: 091-552207. In spite of its main road location, this 200-year-old country house hotel retains an attractive, slightly faded, old world charm. Tea can be taken in the pretty gardens while a beautiful stretch of the Owenriff River runs in front of the hotel. ££.

RECESS, CO. GALWAY
Ballynahinch Castle Hotel, Ballinafad. Tel: 095-31006, fax 31085. A historic house full of character, splendidly sited in the wilds of Connemara at the foot of one of the "Twelve Bens", overlooking the Owenmore River. Private salmon fishing. £££.

WESTPORT, CO. MAYO
Hotel Westport, Westport. Tel: 098-25122, fax 26739. Comfortable, modern two-storey hotel with spacious rooms a short walk from town centre. Surrounded by gardens with pleasant rural views. Good sports facilities. ££.
Olde Railway Hotel, The Mall, Westport. Tel: 098-25166, fax

25090. Family-run hotel on a tree-lined riverside mall in town centre, more than 200 years old. Thackeray called it "one of the prettiest and comfortablest inns in Ireland." ££.

BED AND BREAKFAST
ARAN ISLANDS, CO. GALWAY
Mainistir House, Inishmore. Tel: 099-61169, fax 61351. B&Bs abound on all three Aran Islands, and you can book a room when booking your ferry or flight. This one is something different - a hostel with private double or twin rooms where owner Joël d'Anjou has built up a reputation for imaginative cooking both at breakfast and dinner. £.

BALLINA, CO. MAYO
Mount Falcon Castle, Ballina. Tel: 096-21172, fax 71517. Greystone mansion offering legendary hospitality in relaxed surroundings. Produce from own farm served at host's table. Private fishing. ££

CLIFDEN, CO. GALWAY
Maldua Guesthouse, Galway Road. Tel: 095-21171, fax 21739. Modern family-run guest house in peaceful surroundings 1.25 kilometres outside Clifden. £.
The Quay House, Clifden. Tel: 095-21369, fax 21608. Beautifully located on a tranquil quay below the busy town, the large harbourmaster's house dating from 1829 has been converted into a stylish and characterful country house and restaurant. ££.

GALWAY CITY
Adare Guest House, 5 Father Griffin Place. Tel: 091-582638, fax 583963. Well-located, unpretentious accommodation with private parking three minutes' walk from city centre. £.
Norman Villa, 86 Lower Salthill. Tel. & fax: 091-521131. Victorian townhouse with bold decor combining antique furniture and

contemporary art. Brass beds, Irish linen, easy walking distance of town centre. £.

LEENANE, CO. GALWAY
Delphi Lodge, Leenane. Tel: 095-42211, fax 42296. Romantic Georgian country house in remote Connemara valley. Lovely lakeside setting, private fly fishing, elegant but informal atmosphere. Freshly prepared dinner daily at 8pm. ££.

Northwest Region

BRUCKLESS, CO. DONEGAL
Bruckless House, Bruckless. Tel: 073-37071. An 18th-century farmhouse with gardens, woods. Sea views. Home cooking. £

CARRICK-ON-SHANNON, CO. LEITRIM
Bush House, Carrick-on-Shannon. Tel: 078-20014. Fax: 078-21180. One of Ireland's oldest country town hotels. ££

CARRIGART, CO. DONEGAL
Hotel Carrigart, Carrigart. Tel: 074-55114. Fax: 074-55250. Roadside hotel in French Mansard style offering excellent value. Heated pool, squash, sauna, solarium. ££

DUNFANAGHY, CO. DONEGAL
Carrig-Rua Hotel, Dunfanaghy. Tel: 07 36133. Fax: 07-436277. Efficient, family-run hotel. Good value. ££

DUNKINEELY, CO. DONEGAL
Castlemurray House, St John's Point, Dunkineely. Tel: 073-37022. Stylish restaurant with rooms. ££

KILLYBEGS, CO. DONEGAL
Bayview Hotel, Main Street, Killybegs. Tel: 073-31950. Fax: 073-31856. Overlooking busy harbour. Swimming pool. ££

LETTERKENNY, CO. DONEGAL
Mount Errigal Hotel, Letterkenny. Tel: 074-22700. Fax:

074-25085. Modern facilities include sauna, leisure centre. ££

LOUGH ARROW, CO. DONEGAL
Rock View Hotel, Lough Arrow, Castlebaldwin. Tel: 079-66073. Popular with anglers, who get good tips from owners. £.

LOUGH ESKE, CO. DONEGAL
Ardnamona, Lough Eske. Tel: 073-22650. Fax: 073-22819. Famed for its wild rhododendron gardens. An 18th-century house with south-facing bedrooms. ££
Harvey's Point Country Hotel, Lough Eske. Tel: 073-22208. Fax: 073-22295. Modern luxurious lakeside complex. Sports facilities. Recommended restaurant with rooms. ££

MALIN, CO. DONEGAL
Malin Hotel, Malin. Tel: 077-70645. Fax: 077-70770. This is Ireland's most northerly hotel, family owned and run in rural location. £

MOHILL, CO. LEITRIM
Glebe House, Mohill. Tel: 078-31086. Fax: 078-31886. In 40 acres (16 hectares) of farmland, a splendid guest-house. £

PORT-NA-BLAGH, CO. DONEGAL
Port-na-Blagh Hotel, Port-na-Blagh. Tel: 074-36129. Fax: 074-36379. A grand setting overlooking Sheephaven Bay. Good value. £

RATHMULLAN, CO. DONEGAL
Pier Hotel, Rathmullan. Tel: 074-58178. Fax: 074-58115. Family-run, home cooking. £
Rathmullan House, Rathmullan. Tel: 074-58117/58188. Fax:

074-58200. Country house on shores of Lough Swilly. Beautiful gardens. Period-style bedrooms. ££

ROSSNOWLAGH, CO. DONEGAL
Sand House, Rossnowlagh. Tel: 072-52366. Fax: 072-52100. The way seaside hotels used to be. £

ST ERNAN'S ISLAND, CO. DONEGAL
St Ernan's House, St Ernan's Island, near Donegal Town. Tel: 073-21065. Fax: 073-22098. This hotel is beautifully situated on a small, wooded island reached via a causeway. £

SLIGO TOWN, CO. SLIGO
Sligo Park Hotel, Pearse Road, Sligo. Tel: 071-60291. Fax: 071-69556. Modern hotel, formerly part of the Jury's chain. Reasonably priced. £

The Northeast

Because this is a sizeable area, entries are grouped according to county.

COUNTIES CAVAN, SLIGO, MONAGHAN
Coopershill, Riverstown, Co. Sligo. Tel: 071-65108. Handsome Georgian country house. Period fittings. Woodland settings. Family-run. £
Cromleach Lodge Country House Hotel, Castlebaldwin, Co. Sligo. Tel: 071-65155. Fax: 078-65455. Restaurant with spacious airy bedrooms. Purpose-built. £
Hilton Park, Clones, Co. Monaghan. Tel: 047-56000. Fax: 047-56033. In the Madden family since Samuel, a friend of Dr

Samuel Johnson, bought it in 1734, £
Markree Castle, Coolooney, Co. Sligo. Tel: 071-67800. Fax: 071-67840. Eclectically run castellated mansion in gardens and parkland. ££
Slieve Russell Hotel & Country Club, Ballyconnell, Co. Cavan. Tel: 049-26444. Fax: 049-26474. A phenomenon. Luxury interior contrasting with hilltop convent-like exterior. Swimming pool, jacuzzi. Fine food. ££
Temple House, Ballymote, Co. Sligo. Tel: 071-83329. Victorian restyling of lakeside Georgian mansion overlooking 13th-century Templar castle in 1,000-acre (400-hectare) grounds. ££

COUNTY ANTRIM
Adair Arms Hotel, Ballymoney Road, Ballymena. Tel: 01266-653674. Fax: 01266-40436. Traditional town-centre hotel. ££
Antrim Arms Hotel, Castle Street, Ballycastle. Tel: 012657-62284. Fax: 012657-62284. Fairly basic. ££
Bay Hotel, 20 Strand View Park, Cushendun. Tel: 0126 674-267. Magnificent setting on coast. Unclassified. ££
Bushmills Inn, 25 Main Street, Bushmills. Tel: 012657-32339. Fax: 012657-32048. Conveniently near the world's oldest whiskey distillery. ££
Country House Hotel, Kells. Tel: 01266-891663. Fax: 01266-891477. City standards in heart of country. ££
Dunadry Hotel & Country Club, 2 Islandreagh Drive, Templepatrick. Tel: 018494432474. Fax: 01849-433767. Attractive old building. Close to airport. ££££
Fullerton Arms, 22 Main Street, Ballintoy. Tel/fax: 012657-69613. Modernised coaching inn. B&B. £
Galgorm Manor, 136 Fenaghy Road, Ballymena. Tel: 01266-001001. Fax: 01266-880080. Riverside gentleman's residence, converted. ££££

The lowdown on High Tea

This is a concept, common in hotel restaurants, which foxes many visitors. High tea is served between 5pm and 7pm and typically consists of sausages or a lamb cutlet, with a plate of cakes and scones. There's often a choice of freshly baked bread. High tea is different from afternoon tea, which is served between 3pm and 5pm and consists of a pot of tea plus sandwiches or cakes.

Leighinmohr House Hotel, Ballymena. Tel: 01266-652313/ 656669. Suburban hotel specialising in parties and weddings. ££

Londonderry Arms Hotel, Carnlough. Tel: 01574-885255/ 885458. Fax: 01574-885263. Old coaching inn that once belonged to Sir Winston Churchill. The present proprietor was a devotee of the great steeplechaser, Arkle, and set up a miniature museum in his honour. It includes a portrait of the horse by the Glens of Antrim painter, Charles McAuley. ££

Magherabuoy House, 41 Magherabuoy Road, Portrush. Tel: 01265-823507. Fax: 01265-824687. Near resorts with fine beaches. ££

Magheramorne House, 59 Shore Road, Larne. Tel: 01574-279444. Fax: 01574-260138. Close to ferry port. ££

Marine Hotel, 1 North Street, Ballycastle. Tel: 012657-62222. Fax: 012657-69507. Lacking in personality, but excellent views. Popular for weddings. ££

Templeton Hotel, 882 Antrim Road, Templepatrick. Tel: 018494-32984. Fax: 01849-433406. New lodge-style hotel en route to airport. ££££

Rathlin Guest House, Rathlin Island. Tel: 012657-63917. Reached by boat from Ballycastle, weather permitting. £

Thornlea Hotel, 6 Coast Road, Cushendall. Tel: 012667-71223/71403, Fax: 012667-71362. Comfortable hotel in the "capital of the glens". ££

COUNTY ARMAGH

Charlemont Arms, 63 Lower English street, Armagh. Tel: 01861-522028. Fax: 01861-526979. At the centre of this Georgian city. £

Dean's Hill, 34 College Hill, Armagh. Tel: 01861-524923. Guesthouse calm as the deanery it once was. £

Drumsill House, 35 Moy Road, Armagh. Tel: 01861-522009.

Fax: 01861-525624. Woodland setting, good food, a mile north west of city centre. ££

Seagoe Hotel, Upper Church Lane, Portadown. Tel: 01762-333076. Fax: 01762-350210. Good food. ££

What the codes mean

- **£** = under £30 per person
- **££** = £30–£60 per person
- **£££** = £60–£90 per person
- **££££** = over £90 per person

COUNTY DOWN

Brook Cottage Hotel, 58 Bryansford Road, Newcastle. Tel: 013967-22204. Fax: 013967-22193. Good food. ££

Burrendale Hotel & Country Club, 51 Castlewellan Road, Newcastle. Tel: 013967-22599. Fax: 013967-22328. Good food. ££

Dufferin Arms Coaching Inn, 35 Main Street, Killyleagh. Tel: 01396-828229. Fax: 01396-828755. Stout walls, log fires and village gossip. ££

Enniskeen House Hotel, 98 Bryansford Road, Newcastle. Tel: 013967-22392. Fax: 013967-24084. Good food. ££

Glassdrumman Lodge, 85 Mill Road, Annalong. Tel: 013967-68451. Fax: 013967 67041. Exquisite small hotel on edge of Mournes. £££

Killyleagh Castle Towers, Killyleagh Castle, Killyleagh. Tel/fax: 01396-828261. Victorian self-catering apartments in 17th-century turreted castle. Van Morrison gives summer concerts in the poolside gardens. ££

La Mon House, 41 Gransha Road, Castlereagh. Tel: 01232-448631. Fax: 01232-448026. Country hotel with pool quite close to Belfast. £££

Marine Court Hotel, 18 Quay Street, Bangor. Tel: 01247-451100. Fax: 01247-451200. Overlooking new marina. £££

Portaferry Hotel, 10 The Strand. Tel: 012477-28231.

Fax: 012477-28999. Overlooks Strangford narrows. Good seafood. ££

Old Inn, 15 Main Street, Crawfordsburn. Tel: 01247-853255. Fax: 01247-852775. Pleasant hotel, good food. £££

Slieve Donard Hotel, Downs Road, Newcastle. Tel: 013967-23681. Fax: 013 967-24830. Mansion on beach with pool and superb view of Mourne Mountains. £££

Strangford Arms, 92 Church Street, Newtownards. Tel: 012-47 814141. Fax: 01247-814 141. Country town hotel. £££

Sylvan Hill House, 76 Kilntown Road, Dromore. Tel/fax: 01848-692321. Listed Georgian country house B&B, splendid mountain views, home cooking. £

COUNTY FERMANAGH

Colebrook Park, Brookeborough. tel: 01365-531402. Fax: 01365-531686. Titled family's home now open for B&B. ££££

Jamestown House, Magheracross, northeast of Ballinamallard. tel: 01365-388209. Fax: 01365-388322. Gentleman's riverside Georgian residence. Trout fishing at the door, fine food on the table. £

Killyhevlin Hotel, Dublin Road, Enniskillen. Tel: 01365-323481. Fax: 324726. Good food. Lakeland setting. ££

Lough Erne Hotel, Main Street, Kesh. tel: 013656-31275. Fax: 013656-31921. Good food. ££

Mahon's Hotel, Enniskillen Road, Irvinestown. Tel: 013656-21656. Fax: 01656-21656. Good food. ££

Ortine Hotel, Main Street, Lisnaskea. Tel/fax: 013657-21206. B&B in village location. £

Rosskit, Garrison. Tel: 01365-658231. Fax: 01365-658955. Fisherman's waterbank haven. ££

Tempo Manor, Tempo. Tel: 01365-641450. Fax: 01365-541202. Rambling Victorian house in 11-acre (4.5-hectare) garden. ££

COUNTY LONDONDERRY
Ardtara Country House, 8
Gortead Road, Upperlands,
Maghera. Tel: 01648-44490.
Fax: 01648-45080. Deep in
Seamus Heaney country. House
of distinction with distinctive
cuisine. £££
**Beech Hill Country House
Hotel**, 32 Ardmore Street,
Derry. Tel: 01504-49279. Fax:
01504-45366. Four-poster
beds, elegant grounds, excel-
lent kitchen. £££
Camus House, 27 Curragh
Road, Coleraine. Tel: 01265-
42982. A B&B that will appeal
to salmon fishers, £
Edgewater Hotel, 88 Strand
Road, Portstewart. Tel: 0126
583-3314/3688. Fax: 0126
583-832224. Overlooks magnificent sandy beach. Jacuzzi. ££
**Radisson Roe Park Hotel &
Golf Resort**, Roe Park,
Limavady. Tel: 015047-22222.
Fax: 015047-22313. Spacious
conversion of Charles Lanyon
mansion. £££
Trinity Hotel, 22 Strand Road,
Derry. Tel: 01504-271271. Fax:
01504-271227. The city's
newest (and only) city-centre
business-orientated hotel. ££

COUNTY TYRONE
Blessingbourne, Fivemiletown.
Tel: 013655-21221. B&B.
Victorian version of an
Elizabethan lakeside manor,
with mullioned windows and car-
riage museum. £
Grange Lodge, 7 Grange Road,
Dungannon. Tel: 01868-784
212. Fax: 01868-723891. A
charming guesthouse famed for
its good food. ££
Royal Arms Hotel, 51 High St,
Omagh. Tel: 01662-3262.
Convenient for touring. ££
Valley Hotel, 60 Main Street,
Fivemiletown. Tel: 013655-
21505. Good food. ££

Belfast

Ash-Rowan Town House, 12
Windsor Avenue. Tel: 01232-

661758. Fax: 01232-663227.
Guesthouse with Irish linen
sheets. Victorian furniture. Has
character. ££
Culloden Hotel, 142 Bangor
Road, Holywood. Tel: 01232-
5223. Fax: 01232-426777.
Plush hide-away for top people
in baronial-style mansion with
wooded grounds outside the city
on Belfast Lough shore. ££££
Duke's Hotel, 65 University
Street. Tel: 01232-236666.
Fax: 01232-237177. New mid-
market hotel in university area,
10-minute walk to city centre.
£££
Europa Hotel, Great Victoria
Street. Tel: 01232-32700. Fax:
01232-327800. Large hotel
with conference suites in heart
of city. Once a popular target for
bombers, now a watering hole
for expense-account executives
and pressmen. ££££

What the codes mean

● **£** = under £30 per person
● **££** = £30–£60 per person
● **£££** = £60–£90 per person
● **££££** = over £90 per person

Forte Posthouse, 300
Kingsway, Dunmurry. Tel:
01232-301234. Fax: 01232-
626546. Still known locally as
the Conway, a very comfortable
top-class pad in a southern suburb. £££
Holiday Inn Express, 106
University Street. Tel: 01232-
311909. Fax: 01232-311909.
Fax: 01232-815516. At the
lower end of the Holiday Inn
range. Impersonal, but fills a
gap in the university area. ££
Holiday Inn Garden Court, 15
Brunswick Street. Tel: 01232-
333555. Fax: 01232-232999.
Bright renamed hotel (was the
Plaza), aimed at the middle
market, and right in the centre
of it all. £££
Jury's Inn, Fisherwick Place.
Tel: 01232-533500. Fax:
01232-533511. Centrally locat-

ed near the city's tourist honey-
pots, the Grand Opera House
and Crown Liquor Saloon. £££
Madison's, 59 Botanic Avenue.
Tel: 01232-330040. Fax:
01232-328007. A stylish café-
restaurant and bright rooms are
the attractions of this new venture in an off-campus milieu. ££
Old Rectory, 148 Malone Road.
tel: 01232-667882. Former rectory B&B, handy for South
Belfast. Off-street parking. ££
Regency Hotel, 8 Lower
Crescent. Tel: 01232-323349.
Fax: 01232-320646.
Inexpensive busy hotel within
easy walking distance of restau-
rants and nightlife. ££
Renshaws Hotel, 75 University
Street. Tel: 01232-333366.
Fax: 01232-333399. Another
new hotel in studentland, with
bistro bar. Small, but conve-
niently placed. ££
Stormont Hotel, 587 Upper
Newtownards Road. Tel: 01232-
658621. Fax: 01232-480240.
Smart hotel beside former
Parliament buildings and govern-
ment offices. ££££
Wellington Park Hotel, 21
Malone Road. Tel: 01232-
38111. Fax: 01232-665410.
Smart suburban hotel, with
disco, close to university. £££

Guesthouses
Ash-Rowan, 12 Windsor
Avenue. Tel: 01232-661758.
Good-quality accommodation to
south of university. ££
Botanic Lodge, 87 Botanic
Avenue. Tel: 01232-327682.
Handy location in busy area. £
Helga Lodge, 7 Cromwell Road.
Tel: 01232-324820. Terraced
house B&B also close to the
action. £
YMCA, Malone Road. Tel:
01232-668347. Hostel near
university and museums. £
Windermere House, 60
Wellington Park. Tel: 01232-
662693. A short walk from uni-
versity area. £

Where to Eat

The Choice

You will find many superb natural ingredients on offer in Irish restaurants – fresh and smoked salmon, trout, prawns, oysters, succulent beef, pork and lamb – above all, perhaps, delicious and chewy wholemeal and soda bread. But you will find few dishes that are specifically Irish, partly because the country has no tradition of *haute cuisine* and partly because the people tend to associate traditional fare such as Irish stew of boiled bacon and cabbage with the poor old days. These may be humble dishes, but they are also wholesome and delicious. Keep an eye out, too, for the ever-growing range of Irish cheeses, many of which are first-class.

Eating out in Ireland is not cheap, though it is getting cheaper. In the cities and towns there is no shortage of fast-food places offering everything from hamburgers to fish-and-chips or sweet-and-sour chicken. At the other end of the scale there are plush, expen-sive restaurants, often attached to hotels or pubs. A welcome new development is the increasing trend towards bar food at lunch time and in the early evening. The meal will be served at your bar room table featuring a substantial but moderately priced main course (around £5) and a limited choice of starters and desserts.

The restaurant scene has undergone a revolution for the better in the past decade. Many young cooks who have trained in the best kitchens of Europe and America have returned home determined to make the best of Ireland's wonderful raw ingredients. They have opened restaurants – often small, unprepossessing establishments – where you will eat succulent, fresh produce cooked simply and well, and you will find that the fresh Irish air gives you the appetite of a lifetime.

But you can still be unlucky enough to pay inflated prices to eat overcooked and over-dressed food (probably from a menu with misspelt French names) in pretentious surroundings. If this happens, please complain. Many Irish people hate to make a fuss, and bad restaurants survive as a result.

Where To Eat

Irish Republic
The symbols at the end of each entry provide a rough guide to prices, based on the average cost of a three-course evening meal, excluding wine, **£** = less than IR£15 per head; **££** = between IR£15 and IR£20 per head; **£££** = more than IR£20 per head. Lunch is usually cheaper.

Where no area code is given, the telephone number is in the Dublin exchange (01- prefix when dialling from another area). Numbers are given only where booking is possible.

Dublin

EXPENSIVE

Dobbins Wine Bistro, 15 Stephen's Lane, Dublin 2. Tel: 6764675. First choice of movers and shakers for power lunches. Dinner tends to be a boisterous affair; the louder the dinner the more successful the evening is the policy of management. Excellent food. £££
Eden, Meeting House Square, Temple Bar, Dublin 2. Tel: 6705372. Minimalist decor and well-defined flavours combine to make this restaurant a very sophisticated experience. £££
Ernies, Mulberry Gardens, Donnybrook, Dublin 4. Tel: 2693300. A restaurant beloved of socialites and name-droppers. But don't hold that against this dining insitution whose reputation is also built on magnificent food. Intimate atmosphere. £££
King Sitric, Harbour Road, Howth, Co. Dublin. Tel: 8325235. Seafood restaurant with no excuse for not having fresh fish. It's positioned beside one of the most scenic harbours in Dublin, with a view of Ireland's Eye. £££
L'Ecrivain, 190A Lower Baggot Street, Dublin 2. Tel: 6611919. A restaurant worth splashing out on. Delicious French-inspired food and an adventurous menu. It's advisable to book ahead for this hugely popular restaurant. £££
Le Coq Hardi, 35 Pembroke

The Drink of Choice

The most famous Irish drink is Guinness, that dark stout first produced by the 34-year-old Arthur Guinness in 1759. Ask for "a pint" in a Dublin pub and Guinness is what you'll get, black to within an inch and a half of the rim, creamy topped and served with ceremony.

Now owned by the London-based conglomerate Diageo, Guinness is brewed in 50 countries and sold in another 100. But nowhere does it taste better than in Ireland where it is stored in carefully controlled conditions. The slogan "Guinness is good for you" was killed by advertising regulators, but the toast is still "*Slainte!*" ("Health").

Road, Dublin 4. Tel: 6689070. Swish French restaurant with huge snob value. The place to be seen indulging in delicately prepared food complimented by a prestigious wine list. £££

Les Frères Jacques, 74 Dame Street, Dublin 2. Tel: 6794555. Quality French food at affordable prices – provided you don't go mad with the tempting wine list – ensure that this restaurant has an enduring appeal to locals who keep going back.£££

Lobster Pot, 9 Ballsbridge Terrace, Dublin 4. Tel: 6680025. Long-established seafood restaurant near the city centre in which you'll feel immediately at home. Fresh seafood served in mouth-watering sauces. £££

Mermaid Café, 69 Dame Street, Dublin 2. Tel: 6708236. Recent arrival which is fast becoming the hippest place in town. A stylish restaurant with nothing in common with a truckers' stop-over. £££

Old Mill, 14 Temple Bar, Merchant's Arch, Dublin 2. Tel: 6719262. One of the first restaurants to open in the trendy Temple Bar area of Dublin. Has succeeded in fighting off new and stylish rivals Eden and Trastevere. £££

Patrick Guilbaud, Upper Merrion Street, Dublin 2. Tel: 6764192. Dublin's best-known French restaurant, producing classic cuisine with immense attention to detail. The prices are commensurably high. £££

Peacock Alley, Fitzwilliam Hotel, St. Stephen's Green, Dublin 2. Tel: 4787000. Without doubt the "hottest" restaurant in Dublin. Chef Conrad Gallagher is the darling of food critics besotted by his experimental Mediterranean cooking. £££

Siam Thai Restaurant, Gasyard Lane, Malahide, Co. Dublin. Tel: 8454698. Popular restuarant in a pretty seaside village. Excellant Thai food. £££

Tea Rooms, The Clarence Hotel, Wellington Quay, Dublin 2. Tel:

6709000. International celebrities head to this restaurant part-owned by members of the U2 pop group. You can expect a lot of gossip columnists to turn up in tow. More refined than rock 'n' roll, this restaurant was awarded the Beck's Taste of Temple Bar Award. £££

Trocadero, 3 St. Andrew Street, Dublin 2. Tel: 6775545. A Dublin institution with thespians and late-night revellers. A constant buzz and air of excitement sometimes make food irrelevant in this culinary hotspot. £££

Wongs, 436 Clontarf Road, . Dublin 3. Tel: 8334400. Also at 7 Sandford Road, Ranelagh, Dublin 6. Tel: 4967722. Good Chinese food in restaurants with an emphasis on relaxation and good service. £££

What the codes mean

- **£** = less than IR£15 per head
- **££** = between IR£15 and IR£20 per head
- **£££** = more than IR£20 per head

MODERATE

Cafe En Seine, 40 Dawson Street, Dublin 2. Tel: 6774369. Where anyone with any ideas about being someone goes. In other words, a stylish hangout for wannabees. ££

Cedar Tree, 11A St. Andrew Street, Dublin 2. Tel: 6772121. Lebanese restaurant popular with serious foodies and late-night revellers. Ultra-relaxed atmosphere – don't be surprised if the diners start dancing on the tables. ££

Chez Jules, 16 D'Olier Street, Dublin 1. Tel: 6770499. French bistro-style restaurant. Expect to share a table with strangers. ££

Chandni, 174 Pembroke Road, Dublin 4. Tel: 6681458. Cosy Italian restaurant where the

dependably good food is reflected in the dependably good prices. ££

Cooke's Café, 14 South William Street, Dublin 2. Tel: 6790536. Atmospheric restaurant serving Mediterranean/Californian cuisine. Pleasantly close to a range of good pubs around Grafton Street. ££

Da Vincenzo, 133 Upper Leeson Street, Dublin 4. Tel: 6609906. Highly regarded Italian restaurant offering a standard tomato and olive oil-inspired menu. ££

Fitzer's Café, RDS Ballsbridge, Dublin 4. Tel: 6671301. Also at 51 Dawson Street, Dublin 2, Tel: 6771155. Also: 40 Temple Bar, Dublin 2. Tel: 6790440. Also: National Gallery of Ireland, Merrion Square, Dublin 2. Tel: 6614496. This restaurant chain offers a variety of attractive locations, each serving the same cosmopolitan and delicious dishes. ££

101 Talbot, 100–102 Talbot Street, Dublin 1. Tel: 8745011. Italian/Continental fare in a connvivial restaurant. The pre-theatre dinner menu is great value if you are heading to the Abbey Theatre, located around the corner. ££

Mao, 2 Chatham Row, Dublin 2. Tel: 6704899. Favourite among top models who have made something of a second home out of this groovy Indonesian restaurant. Great green curry washed down with an Indonesian beer. ££

Mongolian Barbeque, 7 Anglesea Street, Dublin 2. Tel: 6704154. Groovy American franchise in trendy Temple Bar. Choose your own stirfry ingredients which are cooked on a public hot plate. A boisterous, "cool" restaurant. Not for the self-conscious. ££

Nico's, 53 Dame Street, Dublin 2. Tel: 6773062. Old-fashioned romantic restaurant for when you've proposed marriage on the Ha'penny Bridge. Tasty Italian dishes by candlelight. Plush setting. ££

Pizza Stop, 6 Chatham Lane, Dublin 2. Tel: 6796712. Authentic Italian restaurant located in the heart of the shopping district. Popular any time of the day or night. ££

Rajdoot Tandoori, 26 Clarendon Street, Dublin 2. Tel: 6794274. Excellant Tandoori dishes in the restaurant which set the standard for authentic Indian cooking in Dublin. Good atmosphere. ££

Señor Sassi's, 146 Leeson Street, Dublin 4. Tel: 6684544. Reasonably priced Mediterranean dishes in a brasserie-style restaurant. ££

Shallmar, 17 South Great Georges Street, Dublin 2. Tel: 6710738. Relaxed and inexpensive Balti House downstairs; upstairs offers a more upmarket and extensive Indian menu. Very reliable. ££

Yamamori Noodles, 71 South Great Georges Street, Dublin 2. Tel: 4755001. Japanese restaurant, and probably the best place for noodles in Dublin. Predominantly cool clientele. ££

INEXPENSIVE

Bad Ass Café, 9 Crown Alley, Dublin 2. Tel: 6712596. Sinead O'Connor worked here as a waitress before finding fame. Not as cool as it used to be but still serving good pizzas, pasta, and salads. £

Blazing Salads, 21c Powers-court Townhouse Centre, South William Street, Dublin 2. Tel: 6719552. Popular vegetarian restaurant. Sugar-free, dairy-free, yeast-free foods. £

Cornucopia, 19 Wicklow Street, Dublin 2. Tel: 6777583. Vegetarian restaurant which makes the best use of fresh produce. Arrive early for lunch to guarantee a seat. £

Isaac's Café, 2 Frenchman's Lane, Dublin 1. Tel: 8363877. Cheerful café attached to the hostel of the same name. £

Juice, 9 Castle House, Dublin 2. Tel: 4757856. Tasty vegetarian dishes, organically produced wines, juice bar. £

Kilkenny Design Shop, 6 Nassau Street, Dublin 2. Tel: 6777066. American tourists arrive here by the tour bus load for the Irish-made crafts and clothes as well as the tasty food dishes. Locals favour the freshly prepared stews and cakes. £

La Med, 22 East Essex Street, Dublin 2. Tel: 6707358. Cafe/restaurant serving Mediterranean meals and snacks. £

McDonald's, 9 Grafton Street, Dublin 2. Tel: 6778393. Also at 50 Lower O'Connell Street, Dublin 1. Tel: 8720050. You've seen one, you've seen them all. £

Periwinkle, Powerscourt Townhouse Centre, South William Street, Dublin 2. Tel: 6794203. Interesting seafood dishes and snacks. Bar service. Lunchtime. £

The Well Fed Cafe, 6 Crowe Street, Dublin 2. Tel: 6772234. Vegetarian restaurant offering plain, wholesome, and mainly tasty, dishes. £

The Winding Stair Bookshop and Cafe, 40 Lower Ormond Quay, Dublin 1. Tel: 8733292. Cheap wholesome food, books to browse through, and soothing jazz sounds. Perfect. Lunchtime. £

Delicatessens

The Big Cheese Company, St. Andrews Lane, Dublin 2. Tel: 6711399. Exciting new addition to Dublin delicatessens offering a selection of amazing cheeses complemented by equally enticing wines. The type of delicatessen where you leave with olive oil and chocolate bars.

Magill's, 14 Clarendon Street, Dublin 2. Tel: 6713830. Offering produce from every corner of Ireland including cheese, meats, and freshly prepared salads. Reflects the growing interest in international cuisine among locals in its interesting selection of imported goods.

Caviston's, 59 Glasthule Road, Sandycove, Dublin 4. Tel: 2809120. Visit this seafood deli on an empty stomach and you'll end up in a state of dizzy confusion; the overwhelming temptations include a fresh fish and seafood counter, a cheese display, and any type of cooked meat you'd like to devour.

The Douglas Food Company, 53 Main Street, Donnybrook, Dublin 4. Tel: 2694066. Swanky deli offering freshly prepared meals to fit any occasion.

Pick of the pubs in Dublin

The Brazen Head, 20 Lower Bridge Street, Dublin 8. The city's oldest pub, recently revamped and a popular venue for live music.

Davy Byrne's, 21 Duke Street, Dublin 2. James Joyce immortalised this city-centre pub in *Ulysses*. Good lunches, art deco surroundings.

Doheny & Nesbitt's, 5 Lower Baggot Street, Dublin 2. Atmospheric interior, dark and faded. Popular with politicians and journalists.

McDaid's, 3 Harry Street, Dublin 2. Gothic pub, once a morgue. Small but very lively, favoured by youngish clientele.

Neary's, 1 Chatham Street, Dublin 2. Faded Victorian elegance and genteel ambience. Liked by theatrical and showbiz types.

Southeast Region

BALLYHACK, CO. WEXFORD

Neptune Restaurant, Ballyhack. Tel: 051-389284. Seafood restaurant on the Wexford side of the Passage East Car ferry from Waterford, which combines a lunchtime cookery school with an evening dinner trade. Steak, lamb and vegetarian specials also offered. ££

CASHEL, CO. TIPPERARY
Chez Hans, Rockside, Cashel. Tel: 062-61177. Serious continental cuisine is served by owner-chef Hans-Peter Matthias in a converted Wesleyan chapel right under the famous Rock. £££
The Spearman, 97 Main Street, Cashel. Tel: 062-61143. Once a grocery shop, now a stylishly-designed restaurant, the owner-chef John-David Spearman serves wholesome home-cooked food; excellent soups and pasta, and a very special Irish stew. £
GOREY, CO. WEXFORD
Marlfield House, Gorey. Tel: 055-21124. Regency house in 35 acres of woodland and gardens. Award-winning restaurant in splendid, spacious conservatory. Booking essential. £££

KILKENNY TOWN
Cafe Sol, William Street. Tel: 056-64987. Cheap and cheerful cafe-style restaurant opposite the town hall with plenty of healthy options including home baking, warm salads, fresh pasta and fish of the day. £.
Lacken House, Dublin Road. Tel: 056-61085. Dedicated owner-chef serves freshly prepared food using seasonal local ingredients in elegant Georgian cellar restaurant. ££.
Ristorante Rinuccini, 1 The Parade. Tel 056-61575. The basement of a Georgian townhouse opposite Kilkenny Castle is an Irish-Italian venture, the chef being Italian. Classic veal, seafood and pasta dishes are given an Irish accent. A harpist entertains some evenings. £££.

KILMORE QUAY, CO. WEXFORD
The Silver Fox, Kilmore Quay. Tel: 053-29888. Unpretentious seafood restaurant with a reputation for the freshness of

its locally-landed catch which may include crab, oysters and prawns. Non-fish eaters also catered for. £.

NEW ROSS, CO. WEXFORD
Galley Cruising Restaurant, New Ross. Tel: 051-21723. Dine while cruising on the scenic River Barrow. Emphasis on seafood and fresh local produce. ££.

WATERFORD CITY
Dwyer's, 5 Mary Street. Tel: 051-77478. Talented owner-chef offers imaginative dishes in a cosily converted police barracks in the town centre. ££.
The Wine Vault, High Street. Tel: 051-853444. Informal, bistro-style cooking in old townhouse noted for its interesting wine list. Seafood, steak and chicken, game in season. Basement wine shop. ££.
Waterford Castle, The Island, Ballinakill. Tel: 051-78203. Luxury hotel restaurant in restored Fitzgerald castle, reached by winch ferry across estuary of River Suir. Oak panelled dining room hung with oil paintings and suitably impressive haute cuisine. £££.

WEXFORD TOWN
The Granary, Westgate. Tel: 053-23935. The heavy beams and pillars of this converted granary give a cosy old world atmosphere, while the menu offers a good selection of local seafood and game in season. ££.

Southwest Region

BALLYDEHOB, CO. CORK
Annie's, near Skibbereen, Co. Cork. Tel: 028 37292. Now a West Cork institution, this tiny restaurant in popular mountain village uses the bar across the road as a reception area. Fresh local ingredients simply but tastily prepared, and served with hearty home-made brown

bread and unusually tempting desserts. £££.

CORK CITY
Arbutus Lodge, Montenotte. Tel: 021-501237. Victorian town house with a country house ambience, renowned both for its exquisite food and its extensive wine cellars. The Gallery Bar and patio (lunchtime only), specialising in seafood, is far less expensive than the main restaurant. £££.
Crawford Gallery Café, Emmet Place. Tel: 021 274415. Convivial dining on Ballymaloe-style food (see below) in atmospheric art gallery setting. ££.
Isaac's, 48 MacCurtain Street. Tel: 021-503805. Young owner-chef in partnership with the Arbutus people has created Cork's most buzzing eating place in a high-ceilinged old warehouse. Eclectic menu combining Far Eastern and Mediterranean influences. £.
Lovett's, Churchyard Lane, Well Road, Douglas. Tel: 021-294909. Well established restaurant in inner suburb where you can eat with varying degrees of formality, from the bar food lunch (£) to a la carte or fixed price dinner in the main restaurant (£££), or char-grilled specialities in the Brasserie (££). Interesting wine list, strong on Bordeaux.
The Gingerbread House, Paul Street Piazza. Tel; 021-276411. By day a self-service cafe with excellent coffee, cakes, homemade ice cream and sandwiches, a more substantial bistro-style evening menu is served from 6 to 10.30. £

BANTRY, CO. CORK
Blairs Cove, Durrus. Tel: 027-61127. French-run stone-walled restaurant in stables of Georgian mansion overlooking Dunmanus Bay. Grand piano doubles as sweet trolley. Dining in summer on heated and covered terrace with fountain.

Open-fire rotisserie. £££.
**O'Connor's Seafood Bar and
Restaurant**, Wolfe Tone Square.
Tel: 027-50221. Simple bar
restaurant with fishing nets and
floats hung in the window which
serves the local product, Bantry
Bay mussels, in various guises.
Also does leaping fresh "fish
and chips". £.
Shiro Japanese Dinner House,
Ahakista, Durrus. Tel: 027-
67030. Japanese-German couple Kei and Werner Pilz produce
authentic Japanese food in the
unforgettable surroundings of
their Victorian lodge on the
beautiful Sheep's Head peninsula. Advance booking essential. £££.

DINGLE, CO. KERRY
Beginish Restaurant, Green
Street. Tel: 066-51588. Small,
elegant town house with talented owner-chef in the kitchen.
Outstanding seafood dishes featuring freshly-landed fish and
lobster, lightly sauced, plus a
choice of meat and fowl. £££.
Doyle's Seafood Bar, John
Street. Tel: 066-51174. Bright
red exterior, cosy kitchen restaurant within. Speciality lobster,
chosen live from tank in the bar.
Menu chosen daily from catches
landed by the Dingle fishermen
and simply prepared. £££.

KENMARE, CO. KERRY
An Leath Phingin Restaurant,
35 Main Street. Tel: 064-
41559. Chic, minimalist-
designed modern restaurant
serving North Italian cuisine
including excellent home-made
pasta and crispy pizzas using
unusual combinations of fresh
local produce. £.
Park Hotel, Kenmare. Tel: 064-
41200. First-class modern Irish
cuisine in spacious dining room
overlooking the rolling lawns of
one of Ireland's premier country
house hotels. £££.
La Cascade, Sheen Falls Lodge.
Classic French cuisine in airy
modern restaurant overlooking

natural waterfalls. £££.
Lime Tree, Shelbourne Street.
Tel: 064-41225. An old schoolhouse near the Park Hotel is
now a busy restaurant with an
imaginative, up-to-the-minute
menu. ££.
Packie's, Henry Street. Tel:
064-41508. Ingenious bistro-
style menu based on traditional
Irish cooking combined with
continental influences. Small
town centre venue with open
fire and local artists' work on
display. ££.

What the codes mean

- **£** = less than IR£15 per
  head
- **££** = between IR£15 and
  IR£20 per head
- **£££** = more than IR£20 per
  head

KILLARNEY, CO. KERRY
Gaby's Seafood Restaurant, 27
High Street. Tel: 064-32519.
Gert and Marie Maes run one
of Ireland's oldest seafood
restaurants, a popular landmark
in Killlarney's town centre. The
atmosphere is pleasantly
informal with red checked table
cloths, and the seafood is the
freshest. ££.
Foley's, 23 High Street. Tel:
064-31217. Busy restaurant
behind a quiet bar. Plush art
nouveau-style decor and pleasantly old-fashioned menu
featuring classic French seafood
and local steaks, lamb and
duckling. £££.
The Strawberry Tree, 24
Plunkett Street. Tel: 064-
32688. Tiny first floor restaurant done out in Irish-cottage
style. Owner-chef Evan Doyle
produces memorable up-market
versions of traditional Irish dishes like corned beef and bacon
and cabbage. £££.

KINSALE, CO. CORK
Blue Haven, Pearse Street. Tel:
021-772209. Renowned sea-

food restaurant in quiet, elegant
room overlooking a tiny garden
and fountain. Busy bar food
trade until 9pm . £££.
Casino House, Coolmain Bay,
Kilbrittain. Tel: 023-49944. Not
a casino, but an attractively
converted farmhouse on the
R600 midway between Kinsale
and Timoleague. Light, tasty
menu in relaxing surroundings
freshly prepared by German-
Yugoslav owner-chef Michael
Relja and served by his wife
Kerrin. ££.
Crackpots, 3 Cork Street. Tel:
021-772847. Open fires and a
lively atmosphere are complemented by a pleasantly eclectic
menu. Owner Carol Norman
also makes and sells ceramics,
hence the name. £.
Jim Edwards, Market Quay. Tel:
021-772541. Busy town centre
pub restaurant renowned for
generous portions of steak and
seafood. Bar food (£) also available. £££.
Man Friday, Scilly. Tel: 021-
772260. Popular. Short walk
uphill from town centre serving
popular food – steaks, sole on
the bone, prawn cocktail – well
cooked, generous portions. £££.
The Vintage, Main Street. Tel:
021-772502. One of the original "front parlour restaurants"
now under Swiss management
with a rather hushed ambience
and a seriously luxurious five
course set menu featuring local
seafood and game in season.
£££.

MALLOW, CO. CORK
President's Restaurant,
Longueville House, near Mallow.
Tel: 022-47156. Impressive
1720 Georgian mansion overlooking the Blackwater River
with restaurant in large
Victorian conservatory. Food
mainly from farm, garden and
river. Wine from Ireland's only
vineyard. £££

MIDLETON, CO. CORK
Ballymaloe House, Shanagarry.

Tel: 021-652531. The farming Allen family pioneered the use of fresh local produce including herbs and vegetables from their own garden, local meat, and fish from nearby Ballycotton, and continue to serve delicious, simply prepared food in restful country house surroundings. Trade secrets are passed on at the neighbouring Ballymaloe Cookery School (Kinoith House, Shanagarry, Tel: 021- 646785). £££.

WATERVILLE, CO. KERRY
Smugglers Inn, Cliff Road. Tel: 066 74422. Informal cliff-top restaurant adjoining the bar with excellent sea views. A wide choice of fresh local seafood is on offer, including John Dory, wild salmon, squid and lobster along with Kerry lamb, duckling and steaks.

YOUGHAL, CO. CORK
Aherne's Seafood Bar and Restaurant, 163 North Main Street. Tel: 024 92424. Long-established family-run bar and restaurant serving delicious fish dishes. Use the bar for a quick meal from the all-day menu (£), such as their famous seafood pie, or linger in the more formal restaurant over classically pre-pared seafood. £££

Mid West Region

ADARE, CO LIMERICK
The Wild Geese, Adare. Tel: 061-396451. Quaint thatched cottage in village centre previously known as the Mustard Seed (see Ballingarry) uses fresh local produce in classical French cuisine. £££.

BALLINGARRY, CO LIMERICK
The Mustard Seed at Echo Lodge, Ballingarry. Tel: 069-68508. Two elegant dining rooms in a flamboyantly decorated country house 8 miles west of Adare are presided over by owner Dan Mullane whose attention to detail is legendary. Chef David Norris's elaborate cuisine combines Mediterranean and Oriental influences. £££.

BUNRATTY, CO LIMERICK
MacCloskey's, Bunratty House Mews, Bunratty. Tel: 061-364082. Excellent restaurant in basement of 17th-century house overlooking Bunratty Castle and Folk Park serving a set five course dinner menu. French-Irish cuisine. £££.

DOOLIN, CO. CLARE
Bruach na Haille, Roadford. Tel: 065-74168. Doolin's longest

established restaurant is in a pretty riverside cottage complete with low beams and ornate dressers. Local lobster, simply prepared seafood and Irish specials like Beef in Guinness or steak with Irish whiskey sauce. ££.
O'Connor's Pub. Tel: 065-74168. Famed for traditional music sessions after 9pm, by day O'Connor's serves hearty home-cooked bar food including wild Doolin salmon and a great Irish stew. £.

ENNIS, CO. CLARE
The Cloister, Abbey Street. Tel: 065-29521. Historic pub with low ceilinged rooms and open fires serving bar food midday and evening (£), and a more elaborate dinner menu in the stone-flagged main restaurant which incorporates a 13th-century abbey's kitchen. ££.

KINVARA, CO. GALWAY
Merriman Inn, Kinvara. Tel: 091-638222. Star chef Michael Clifford serves his celebrated and subtle brand of Irish cuisine in this strikingly designed new hotel's spacious and relaxing dining room. ££.
Moran's of the Weir, Kilcolgan, Clarinbridge. Tel: 091-96113. A plate of fresh oysters beside the weir outside this pictur-esque thatched cottage is a quintessential West of Ireland experience. Crab, prawns, smoked salmon and mussels. ££

LIMERICK CITY
Quenelle's Restaurant, Corner of Mallow Street and Henry Street. Tel: 061-411111. Adven-turous cooking in five course dinner menu by owner-chef at charming city centre restaurant overlooking river. £££.

LISDOONVARNA, CO. CLARE
Orchid Room, Sheedy's Spa View. Tel; 065-74026. Chef Frankie Sheedy trained at Dromoland Castle and serves a surprisingly elaborate, robustly

A Who's Who of Irish Whiskies

The comparative affluence and sophisticated tastes of recent years have stimulated the demand for Ireland's more traditional whiskies as well as Scotland's rarer malts. There are 15 or so different whiskies on sale in Ireland. John Power's Gold Label is by far the most popular. Next come Jameson, Bushmills, Coleraine (which sells in Northern Ireland), Paddy, Hewitt's and Dunphy's. Murphy's sells mainly in the United States, and Tullamore Dew, a particularly light brand, does well in Europe.

Two popular premium brands are Black Bush (from Bushmills in County Antrim, the world's oldest distillery) and Crested Ten, matured for 10 years in the Jameson stable. At the top of the range are liqueur whiskies, among the most exceptional drinks on earth. Bushmills Malt is a single 10-year-old; Jameson 1780 is aged for 12 years; and Redbreast, also 12 years old, is matured in wood by the house of Gilbey, renowned for its wines, ports and sherries. To put ice in these last three whiskies is an act of sacrilege to an Irishman.

flavoured menu in the small, modestly decorated dining room of his parents' hotel. Daily specials feature local seafood. ££.

Midlands Region

ABBEYLEIX, CO. LAOIS
Preston House Café, Main Street. Tel: 0502-31432. Attractive creeper-clad Victorian town house on the main Cork-Dublin road, the restaurant has a country-style pine decor. Wholesome and appetising home-cooking including home-baked bread. ££.

ATHLONE, CO. WESTMEATH
Wineport Restaurant, Glasson. Tel; 0902-85466. Informal waterside restaurant in wooden chalet beautifully situated on Lough Ree just outside town. Good choice for vegetarians. Game tasting menu in season. ££
Restaurant Le Chateau, Abbey Lane. Tel: 0902-94517. First floor restaurant run by a young husband-and-wife team in a characterful old house behind the castle, Le Chateau has a good reputation for imaginative cooking of fresh local produce. ££.

BIRR, CO. OFFALY
Emmet Restaurant, Dooly's Hotel, Emmet Square. Tel: 0509-20032. Above-average hotel restaurant in nicely preserved Georgian coaching inn. ££.
The Thatch, Crinkle, Co. Offaly. Tel: 0509-20682. Restaurant in thatched pub just outside Birr, offering five course dinner menu with hearty local produce and lighter a la carte choices. ££.

LONGFORD, CO. LONGFORD
The Vintage, Moydow, near Longford town. Tel: 043-22122. Bar restaurant where owner-chef serves freshly prepared local produce for Sunday lunch and dinner. Interesting use of herbs

and vegetables. ££.
MULLINGAR, CO. WESTMEATH
Crookedwood House, Mullingar. Tel: 044-72165. Large country house well off the beaten track 8 miles (13km) north of Mullingar with outstanding family-run cellar restaurant. Game a specialty in winter. Rooms available. £££.

Far West Region

ACHILL ISLAND, CO. MAYO
The Boley House, Keel, Achill Island. Tel: 098-43147. Stone-walled cottage, turf fire, candle light. Five course set menu or a la carte dinner menu. Strong on seafood. You don't need a boat: Achill is linked by a causeway to mainland Co Mayo. ££.

CLIFDEN, CO. GALWAY
Destry Rides Again, Clifden. Tel: 095-21722. Entertaining town centre venue with wacky decor vaguely related to a Marlene Dietrich film. Eclectic, Mediterranean style menu using fresh herbs, local seafood, or venison, lamb or home-cured ham. ££.
Erriseask House, Ballyconeely. Tel: 095-23553. Swiss-run waterside hotel and restaurant 7 miles south of Clifden where owner-chef has gained a fine reputation for well-judged, imaginative cooking. £££.

What the codes mean

● **£** = up to £12 per head
● **££** = £12–£16 per head
● **£££** = over £16 per head

O'Grady's, Market Street, Co. Galway Tel: 095-21450. Long-established traditional seafood restaurant, also serving meat dishes, in centre of tourist "capital" of Connemara. Ask for a table in the cosy main room, not the annexe. £££.

GALWAY
Kirwan's Lane Creative Cuisine, Kirwan's Lane, off Quay Street. Tel: 091-568266. Trendy bistro cuisine with an Irish accent in a sharply designed modern restaurant that will make urban sophisticates feel at home. ££.
McDonagh's Fish Restaurant. Kirwan's Lane. Tel. 091-565 001. For many years a wet fish shop with a few tables serving cooked seafood, McDonagh's is now a fully-fledged classic seafood restaurant, and the best place to try Galway oysters. Also renowned for their seafood platter of hot lobster, scallops, crab claws and prawns. £££. (Their adjacent fish and chip bar serves a wide choice of battered fish. £.)
Nimmo's, Spanish Arch. Tel: 091-653565. Spacious first floor restaurant in an old stone building beside the River Corrib just beyond the Spanish Arch. Swiss chef Stephan Zeltner serves a robust menu featuring plenty of alcohol and cream in the sauces. £££.
Noctan's, 17 Cross Street. Tel: 091-566172. Popular pub with the thriving Galway arts scene. Excellent bar food at lunchtime, separate seafood bistro and bar upstairs. £.
The Malt House, Olde Malte Arcade, High Street. Tel: 091-563993. Chintzy pub restaurant with white rough cast walls tucked away in an alley in the town centre. A place for old reliables like duckling à l'orange, steak or fresh prawns pan fried in garlic butter. ££.

MOYCULLEN, CO. GALWAY
Drimcong House Restaurant, Moycullen. Tel: 091-555115. Gerry and Marie Galvin's stylish country house restaurant 12 miles (19 km) from town on the N59 will be a high point of any gastronomic tour of Ireland. Gerry is an inventive chef with a light touch and the gift of

making it all look – and taste – incredibly simple. Marie tends front of house and grows the many herbs and fresh vegetables that help to make Drimcong so different. Book well in advance. £££.

White Gables Restaurant, Moycullen. Tel: 091-555744. Cottage restaurant on main road but well insulated from traffic by thick stone walls. Owner-chef Kevin Dunne serves light, tasty menus featuring the best of fresh local produce. Homemade bread and imaginative vegetables. ££.

SPIDDAL, CO. GALWAY
Boluisce Seafood Bar, Spiddal. Tel: 091-553286. Bar food and first floor restaurant in lively pub in the centre of Irish-speaking village in Connemara. Cheerful service and generous portions. Steaks, stir fries and local seafood. £–££.

WESTPORT, CO. MAYO
Asgard Tavern and Restaurant, The Quay. Tel: 098-25319. Quayside bar with nautical decor offering simple bar food downstairs and a more formal and wide-ranging menu upstairs with emphasis on fresh ingredients and good value. £–££.
Quay Cottage, The Harbour. Tel: 098-26412. Small, always busy waterside cottage with scrubbed pine tables and a maritime theme. Lashings of excellent seafood plus vegetarian options and plenty of meat choices. ££.

The Northwest

BALLYBOFEY, CO. DONEGAL
The Looking Glass, Kee's Hotel, Ballybofey. Tel: 074-31018. Seasonal menus have local game and seafood. ££

BRUCKLESS, CO. DONEGAL
Castlemurray House, Dunkineely. Tel: 073-37022. French provincial. Recommended. £££

BUNDORAN, CO. DONEGAL
Le Chateaubrianne, Sligo Road. Tel: 072-42160. Traditional fare, good local produce. ££

GREENCASTLE, CO. DONEGAL
Kealey's Seafood Bar. Tel: 077-81010. Fine seafood. Recommended. £££

LETTERKENNY, CO. DONEGAL
Carolina House, Loughnagin. Tel: 074-22480. High standards using fresh local produce. £££
LOUGH ESKE, CO. DONEGAL
Ardnamona House, Lough Eske. Tel: 073-22650. Reliable general menu. £££

MOVILLE, CO. DONEGAL
McNamaras, Foyle Street. Tel: 077-82010. Old-world style, fresh fish a speciality.

ROSSNOWLAGH, CO. DONEGAL
Smugglers Creek, Rossnowlagh. Tel: 072-52366. In 1845 building overlooking Donegal Bay. Specialises in fresh seafood. ££

The Northeast

Most of these entries are in Northern Ireland, where prices are in sterling. The symbols provide a rough price guide, based on the average cost of a three-course evening meal including a 10 percent service charge and VAT, but not wine.
 £ = under £12 sterling,
 ££ = £12 to £16;
 £££ = over £16.

ANNALONG, CO. DOWN
Fisherman, 43 Kilkeel Road. Tel: 013967-68733. Local seafood. £
Halfway House, 138 Glassdrumman Road. Tel: 013 967-68224. Scampi, plaice. £

ARMAGH CITY, CO. ARMAGH
Charlemont Arms, 63 English Street. Tel: 01861-522028, Country cooking. £
Drumsill House, 35 Moy Road.

Tel: 01861-522009. Adventurous menu for country house. Disco. ££

BALLYCASTLE, CO. ANTRIM
Antrim Arms, Castle Street. Tel: 012657-62284. Country cooking. ££

BALLYGALLEY, CO. ANTRIM
Ballygalley Castle. Tel: 01574-83212. Hotel-style general menu. ££
BALLYMENA, CO. ANTRIM
Galgorm Manor, 136 Fenaghy Road. Tel: 01266-881001. Oysters and halibut. ££
Leighinmohr House, Leighinmohr Avenue. Tel: 01266-652313. Country cooking. ££

BANGOR, CO. DOWN
Back Street Café, 14 Queen's Parade. Tel: 01247-453990. Inspired food. £££
Jenny Watts, 41 High Street. Tel: 01247-270401. Good bistro atmosphere. ££
Shanks, Blackwood Golf Club, Crawfordsburn Road. Tel: 01247-853313. Excellent. Recommended. £££

BELLANALECK, CO. FERMANAGH
The Sheelin. Tel: 0136582-232. Buffet £, gourmet evenings (booking essential). Thatched. £££.

BUSHMILLS, CO. ANTRIM
Bushmills Inn, 25 Main Street. Tel: 012657-32339. Good local flavour.
Wind-Rose, Rodgers Quay. Tel: 01960-364192. Bistro. ££

CARNLOUGH, CO. ANTRIM
Londonderry Arms. Tel: 01574-85255. Charming surroundings on Antrim Coast Road. £

CARRICKFERGUS, CO. ANTRIM
Dobbins Inn, 6 High Street. Tel: 019606-51905. Country cooking. £

CAVAN TOWN, CO. CAVAN
The Olde Priory, Main Street.

Tel: 049-61898. Hearty fare.
£££
COLERAINE, Co. LONDONDERRY
Salmon Leap, 53 Castleroe Rd.
Tel: 01265-52992. Game in
season, smoked fish. ££

COOKSTOWN, Co. TYRONE
Otter Lodge, 26 Dungannon
Road. Tel: 016487-65427.
Carvery, à la carte,
Recommended. ££.

CRAWFORDSBURN, Co. DOWN
Old Inn, 15 Main Street. Tel:
01247-853255. Thatched inn
with 18th-century minstrels'
gallery. ££

CULTRA, Co. DOWN
Culloden Hotel. Tel: 012317-
5223. Reliable cooking, grand
hotel style. £££.
Cultra Inn. Tel: 012317-5840.
Country cooking. £

DERRY CITY, Co. LONDONDERRY
Badger's, 16 Orchard Street.
Tel: 01504-360763. Standard
pub grub. £
Beech Hill House, 32 Ardmore
Road, Ardmore. Tel: 01504-
49297. Chef trained at
Belfast's Michelin-starred
Roscoff. £££
Brown's, 1 Victoria Road. Tel:
01504-45180. Modern
European, Kilkeel fish. £££
Everglades, Prehon Road. Tel:
01504-46722. Set meals, à la
carte. ££
Reggie's Seafood Restaurant,
165 Strand Road. Tel: 01504-
262050. Try the panfried fillets
of John Dory. ££

What "country cooking" means

Traditionally Northern Ireland, even more than the Republic, wielded
the frying pan with vigour. The "Ulster fry" – consisting of beef or
pork, sausages and bacon, often with fried potato cakes thrown in –
was a recipe for an early heart attack. The approach these days is
healthier, but outside Belfast and a number of chef-driven restaurants
around the province, the emphasis is still on plain cooking. The term
"country cooking" in these listings implies that you can expect
standard meat, chicken and fish dishes, reliably cooked.
For a fuller discussion, see "A Fresh Approach to Food", page 125.

White Horse Inn, 68 Clooney
Road. Tel: 01504-860606.
Carvery, salmon, steaks. £££

DONAGHADEE, Co. DOWN
Grace Neill's, 33 High Street.
Tel: 01247-882553. Claims
Daniel Defoe and Franz Liszt as
previous customers. ££

DOWNPATRICK, Co. DOWN
Hunt Club, English Street. Tel:
01396-617886. Chef trained at
Belfast's Michelin-starred
Roscoff. Ireland's oldest hunt
club meets here. £££
Rea's, 78 Market Street. Tel:
01396-612017. Old-fashioned
bar. ££

DROMARA, Co. DOWN
O'Reilly's, 7 Rathfriland Road.
Tel: 01238-532209. Seafood.
££

DUNGANNON, Co. TYRONE
Grange Lodge, 7 Grange Road.
Tel: 01868-784214. Home
cooking in country house. Highly
recommended. £££
Inn on the Park, Moy Road. Tel:
018687-25151. Reliable hotel-
style menu. ££.

ENNISKILLEN, Co. FERMANAGH
Franco's, Queen Elizabeth
Road. Tel: 01365-324424. Fun
place for fish. ££
Hollander, 5 Main Street. Tel:
013656-21231. Steaks. £££
McCartney's Inn, 17 Belmore
Street. Tel: 01365-220122.
Beoth. Irish stew. £.

GIANT'S CAUSEWAY, Co. ANTRIM

Causeway Hotel. Tel: 012657-
31226/31210. Standard hotel
menu. £

HILLSBOROUGH, Co. DOWN
Plough Inn, 3 The Square. Tel:
01846-682985. Fabulous fish.
£££

HOLYWOOD, Co. DOWN
Sullivan's, Sullivan Place. Tel:
01232-421000. Bistro seafood.
££

KILLINCHY, Co. DOWN
Balloo House. Tel: 01238-
541210. Fresh fish and game.
Recommended.
Daft Eddy's, Sketrick Island.
Tel: 01238-541115. Good food
with a view.

KILLYLEAGH, Co. DOWN
Bufferin Arms, 35 High Street.
Tel: 01396-828229. Comfort
food in coaching inn. ££

LARNE, Co. ANTRIM
Magheramorne House, 59
Shore Road. Tel: 01574-79444.
Country cooking. ££

LIMAVADY, Co. LONDONDERRY
Radisson Roe Park Hotel, Roe
Park. Tel: 01504-722212.
Good-quality hotel food. £££
MAGHERA, Co. LONDONDERRY
Ardtara Country House, 8
Gorteade Road, Upperlands.
Tel: 01648-44490. Chef trained
at Belfast's Michelin-starred
Roscoff. Elegant rooms. Recom-
mended. £££

MAGILLIGAN, Co. LONDONDERRY
Ballymaclary House, 573
Seacoast Road. Tel: 015047-
50283. An 18th-century country
house. £

NEWTOWNABBEY, Co. ANTRIM
Ginger Tree, 29 Ballyrobert
Road. Tel: 01232-848176.
Japanese. £££
Sleepy Hollow, 15 Kiln Road.
Tel: 01232-342042. Art gallery,
first-class food. ££

NEWTOWNARDS, CO. DOWN
Ganges, 69 Court Street. Tel: 01247-811246. Indian. ££
Gaslamp, 47 Court Street. Tel: 01247-811225. Superb food. £££

PORTAFERRY, CO. DOWN
Portaferry Hotel, 10 The Strand. Tel: 012477-28231. Recommended. ££

PORTRUSH, CO. ANTRIM
Dionysus, 53 Eglinton Street. Tel: 01265-823855. Greek. ££
Ramore Restaurant & Wine Bar, The Harbour. Tel: 01265-823444. Noted for its excellent seafood. ££

RATHLIN ISLAND, CO. ANTRIM
Rathlin Restaurant, The Harbour. Tel: 012657-63939. Good seafood. ££

SAINTFIELD, CO. DOWN
The Barn, 120 Monlough Road. Tel: 01238-510396. Sample starter – salmon and prawn mousse – conveys the flavour. Recommended, booking essential. £££

STRANGFORD, CO. DOWN
Lobster Pot, 11 The Square. Tel: 0139686-288. Good fish. ££

WARINGSTOWN, CO. DOWN
The Grange, Main Street. Tel: 01762-881989. Baked salmon, whiskey steak. Recommended, booking essential. £££

Belfast

Antica Roma, 67 Botanic Avenue. Tel: 01232-311121. Built in style of old villa with great wall paintings and authentic food. £££
Archana, 53 Dublin Road. Tel: 01232-323713. Belfast's authentic balti house. ££
Bananas, 4 Clarence Street. Tel: 01232-339999. Informal, downtown, seafood and vegetarian. ££
Belfast Castle, Antrim Road. Tel: 01232-776925. In restored hall overlooking lough. Serves reliable food. £££
Bengal Brasserie, 339 Ormeau Road. Tel: 01232-640099. Stylish Bangladeshi. £££
Café Society, 3 Donegall Square East. Tel: 01232-439525. Great views from upstairs. Bistro food. ££
Capers, 63 Great Victoria Street. Tel: 01232-247643. Pizza specialists. £
Crown Liquor Saloon, 46 Great Victoria Street. Tel: 01232-249476. Pub grub in restored Victorian saloon. £
Deanes, 38–40 Howard Street. Tel: 01232-560000. Its chef rated a Michelin star in his previous out-of-town restaurant and the food lives up to these standards. £££
Dempsey's Terrace, 43 Dublin Road. Tel: 01232-326432. Bars, bistros and nightclub. £–££
Frog Follies, 103 Great Victoria Street. Tel: 01232-24066.

French provincial. £££
Jharna Tandoori, 133 Lisburn Road. Tel: 01232-381299. Elaborately Indian. ££
La Belle Epoque, 61 Dublin Road. Tel: 01232-323244. Classic French restaurant. £££
Larry's Piano Bar, 36 Bedford Street. Tel: 01232-325061. Pasta, steaks, fish. Dancing on the tables. ££
Manor House, 47 Donegall Pass. Tel: 01232-238755. Authentic Cantonese. ££
Nick's Warehouse, 35 Hill Street. Tel: 01232-439690. Trendy wine bar and restaurant near city centre. ££
Restaurant 44, 44 Bedford Street. Tel: 01232-244844. Small, high-quality. Casseroles, char-grills. £££
Roscoff, 7 Lesley House, Shaftesbury Square. Tel: 01232-331532. Nouvelle cuisine, Irish-style, and the only Michelin Star in the North. £££
Saints and Scholars, 3 University Street. Tel: 01232-325137. Stir-fries, spicy chicken, deep-fried brie. ££
Speranza, 16 Shaftesbury Square. Tel: 01232-230213. Real Italian pizzeria.
Strand, 12 Stranmillis Road. Tel: 01232-682266. Buzzy atmosphere. ££
Summer Palace, 126 Great Victoria Street. Tel: 01232-235 828. Authentic Chinese. ££
Sun Kee, 38 Donegall Pass. tel: 01232-312016. Good Chinese food. ££
Terrace, 255 Lisburn Road. Tel: 01232-381655. Wine bar with smoked salmon, stuffed duck, and the like, well cooked. £££
Truffles, 3a Donegall Square West. Tel: 01232-247153. Steak, chicken. Good for quick lunch in city centre. £
Villa Italia, 39 University Road. Tel: 01232-328356. Italian family restaurant, no lunches, no bookings, but it's good.
Welcome ?? Stranmillis Road. Tel: 01232-681359. Another good Cantonese place. ££

Pick of the pubs in Belfast

The Crown Liquor Saloon, 44 Great Victoria Street. Stained glass, ornate decor, cosy snugs – all preserved by the National Trust.
Kelly's Cellars, 30 Bank Street. Founded in 1720. There's a stone-floored bar downstairs and a beamed restaurant upstairs.
The Front Page, 108 Donegall Street. The church-like upstairs bar is popular with journalists. Live music at night.
The Garrick, 11 Montgomery Street. Another authentic Victorian-style pub, named after the actor David Garrick.
The Morning Star, 17 Pottinger's Entry. Fine old-fashioned bar with good food. Less crowded in the evenings.

Nightlife

Late spots

The Irish have always had their priorities in the right order when it comes to having a good time and their fun-loving attitude can't help but rub off. The recent changes in the city's nightlife reflect the upbeat mood of a city experiencing an economic boom.

If you're under 30 years old and believe in having a good time, the chances are you've heard of Dublin's club scene. Much has been written internationally about how the city has begun to rival groovy European cities for exciting clubs. The reality behind the hype is improving all the time.

You don't have to dance till dawn. Visitors more sophisticated in years can enjoy late-night bars, cabarets, or smart nightclubs where tables positioned away from the dance floor allow for meaningful conversations.

Nightclubs

Annabel's, Burlington Hotel, Upper Leeson Street, Dublin 4. Tel: 6605222. This Leeson Street club is one of the oldest in town and remains unfailingly popular with the older, sophisticated crowd. Smart dress essential.
Howl At The Moon, O'Dwyer's, Lower Mount Street, Dublin 2. Tel: 6762887. This club is attached to a popular pub and attracts punters who decide to keep the night alive as well as people on a serious night out. Classic sounds. Casual dress.
The George, 89 South Great Georges Street, Dublin 2. Tel: 4782983. Probably the city's most popular gay club. The George pub from which the club gets it name is a favourite meeting place among gay men. Stylish dress.
The Kitchen, East Essex Street, Dublin 2. Tel: 6776635. Attached to the Clarence Hotel in which rock band U2 are major shareholders, this is a cool hangout whose door policy isn't as strict as you might expect. Hip-hop, heavy rock sounds are enjoyed by a mainly young and trendy clientele. Trendy gear a must.
La Cave, 28 South Anne Street, Dublin 2. Tel: 6794409. Cosy and compelling late night venue which falls somewhere between a restaurant, wine bar, and nightclub, although there's no dance floor as such. The soothing Latino sounds and intimate atmosphere mean this is a winner with thirty-somethings wanting to kick back. Smart dress.
Lillies Bordello, Adam Court, Grafton Street, Dublin 2. Tel: 6799204. One of the most exclusive clubs in town, and one which prides itself on its VIP lounge where high-profile party animals rub shoulders with fellow celebrities. Membership is compulsory but looking like a celeb can work wonders on the bouncers. Stylish clothes essential.
Club M, Blooms Hotel, 6 Anglesea Street, Dublin 2. Tel: 6715622. If you don't feel like posing and just want to bop the night away. City centre disco playing classic '70s and '80s sounds. Smart dress recommended.
The POD, Harcourt Street, Dublin 2. Tel: 4780225. Ultra-hip club where everyone who is anyone in rock music, the media, and the world of modelling congregate. The dance floor is home to the young and beautiful. You probably already know to wear hip clothes.
Ri-Ra, Dame Court, Dublin 2. No telephone. Groovy club for babes with attitude and cool dudes. Funk, hip-hop, and audio-visual shows. As for clothes, the hipper the better.
Renards, 33 South Frederick Street, Dublin 2. Tel: 6775876. The trendiest club in town when it was called the Pink Elephant , this new version tries hard to live up to its past reputation with particular doormen and a fashion-conscious clientele. Style is all.

Late Bars

Late-night bars are a new phenomenon in Dublin thanks to revised – though still not exactly liberal – licensing laws. The following pubs are open on various nights, mainly weekends, until the crazy hour of 1.30am.
Bleeding Horse, 24 Upper Camden Street, Dublin 2. Tel: 4752705.
Conways, 70 Parnell Street, Dublin 1. Tel: 8732687.
Foggy Dew, 1 Upper Fowne's Street, Dublin 2. Tel: 6779328.
Hogans, 35 Great South Georges Street, Dublin 2. Tel: 6775904.
Mean Fiddler, 26 Wexford Street, Dublin 2. Tel: 4758555.
Mercantile Bar, Dame Street, Dublin 2. Tel: 6707100.
O'Briens, Dame Street, Dublin 2. Tel: 6778816.
Sinnotts, South King Street, Dublin 2. Tel: 4784698.
Turks Head Chop House, Parliament Street, Temple Bar, Dublin 2. Tel: 6792606.
Whelans, 25 Wexford Street, Dublin 2. Tel: 4780766.

Cabaret

Doyles Cabaret, Burlington Hotel, Upper Leeson Street,

Dublin 4. Tel: 6605222. Cabaret inspired by the postcard image of Ireland; lots of pretty *cailíns* doing Irish jigs and handsome men singing Celtic songs. A show with a certain charm for the mature and sentimental. Dinner can be included if you wish. Summer season, Monday to Saturday.

Dublin Viking Feast, Old Smock Alley Theatre, Essex Street West, Dublin 8. Tel: 6796040. Viking-style feast with traditional contemporary Irish music, song and dance. Running during the summer months, bookings essential on 6796040.

Fonntraí, Culturlann na hEireann, Belgrave Square, Monkstown, Co. Dublin. Tel: 2800295. Show with a strong Irish flavour. Musican, singers, storytellers and dancers entertain in the comfortable folk theatre. Runs during the summer months Monday to Thursday. Also a ceili on Friday nights and a ballad session on Saturdays.

Jurys Cabaret, Jurys Hotel, Ballsbridge, Dublin 4. Tel: 660 5000. This cabaret has a strong accent on traditional Irish culture with dancers, singers and comedians. Likely to offer a good performance of *Danny Boy* before the night is over. Dinner included. Summer season, Tuesday to Sunday.

Comedy

Murphy's Laughter Lounge, Eden Quay, Dublin 2. Tel: 8744611. Dublin's first full-time comedy venue is proving successful since opening in 1998 in a disused cinema along the Liffey's northside quay. Top Irish comedians and international comics compete for the loudest laughs. Performances Thursday to Sunday inclusive.

City Arts Centre, 23 Moss Street, Dublin 2. Tel: 6710043. This multi-purpose arts venue is worth checking out for its

occasional comedy slots which provide an opportunity for emerging comics to cut their teeth while established comedians warm up for the Edinburgh Festival.

Belfast

Clubs

Fashions change, but constants on the club beat include:

Madison's, Botanic Avenue. Tel: 330040. Chart music, no jeans.

M-Club, Bradbury Place. Tel: 233131. Commercial dance, a provincial obsession with B-list celebrities and vertiginous cleavages.

Paradise Lost (Europa Hotel), 25 Glengall Street. Tel: 266060. Easy listening, brassy.

Storm (a.k.a. Bob's), Lisburn Road. Tel: 332526. Chart music, no sports wear.

Thompson's Garage, Patterson's Place, Tel: 323762. House and garage music with a glam or scam dress code.

Parliament, 2 Dunbar Street. Tel: 234520. Gay.

Crow's Nest, Skipper Street. Tel: 279924. Gay.

Duke of York, 11 Commercial Court. Tel: 241062. Lesbian on Thursdays.

Jazz

Belfast Boat Club, Lockview Road. Tel: 665012.

Cutter's Wharf, Lockview Road. Tel: 662501. Sunday jazz brunch.

White's Tavern, 2–12 Winecellar Entry. Tel: 243080. Thursdays.

Katy Daly's, 17 Ormeau Road. Tel: 325942. Home to the city's singer-songwriters.

Traditional music

Madden's, 74 Smithfield. Tel: 244144. The real McCoy.

Kitchen Bar, 16 Victoria Square. Tel: 021001. Also authentic

Kelly's Cellars, 30 Bank Street. Tel: 324835. Mid-week. Less purist.

Culture

Theatres

Dublin

Abbey Theatre, Lower Abbey Street, Dublin. Tel: 878 7222. Ireland's national theatre. Founded in the early years of the century by Yeats, Lady Gregory and their collaborators, it quickly won a world reputation with some outstanding plays and a unique style of acting. Many Irish classics feature in its programme. The Abbey's sister theatre, the **Peacock**, is used to try out new, experimental work.

Andrews Lane Theatre, 9-11 Andrews Lane, Dublin 2. Tel: 679 5720. Opened in September 1989 in a converted warehouse and is a popular smaller venue.

Gaiety Theatre, South King Street. Tel: 677 1717. A fine Victorian building, recently restored. The programme includes opera, ballet, pantomime, variety concerts and serious drama.

Gate Theatre, Cavendish Row, Parnell Square. Tel: 874 4045. Founded by the actor Micheál MacLiammoir. The programme includes opera, ballet, pantomime, variety concerts and serious drama.

Lambert Puppet Theatre, Clifton Lane, Monkstown, Co. Dublin. Tel: 280 0974. Where the country's only permanent professional puppet theatre company performs.

Olympia Theatre, Dame Street. Tel; 677 8962. Similar shows to the Gaiety. Once a Victorian music hall.

Players' Theatre, Front Square, Trinity College Dublin is based in the university that produced such dramatists as Goldsmith, Synge and Beckett. TCD also has the Lombard Street Theatre, associated with the university's Samuel Beckett Centre.

Project Arts Centre, East Essex Street, Dublin 2. Tel: 671 2321. Offers new work, often experimental, and innovative revivals from mainly Dublin-based independent companies.

Other Theatres

Belfast: Grand Opera House, Great Victoria Street. Tel: 241919; Lyric Theatre, Ridgeway Street, tel: 381081; Arts Theatre, Botanic Avenue. Tel: 324936.
Cork: Opera House, Emmet Place. Tel: 270022; Everyman Palace, 15 MacCurtain Street. Tel: 503077. both mix touring productions., popular entertainment and local productions.
Derry: Riverside Theatre, University of Ulster, Coleraine, Co. Derry. Tel: Coleraine 51388. New auditorium.
Fermanagh: Ardhowen Theatre, Dublin Road, Enniskillen, Co. Fermanagh. Tel: Enniskillen 25440.
Galway: Druid Theatre Company, Druid Lane Theatre, Chapel Lane, off Quay Street. Tel: 568617. One of Ireland's most successful repertory theatre companies presenting a mix of new work and revivals; Taibhdhearc na Gaillimhe, Middle Street. Tel: 562024. Irish language theatre. Galway's other professional companies, Punchbag and Macnas, share the new Town Hall Theatre with the Druid.
Limerick: Belltable Arts Centre, 69 O'Connell Street. Tel: 319866. Small auditorium.
Sligo: Hawk's Well Theatre, Temple Street. Tel: 61526 and 61518. Modern theatre hosting touring and local shows.
Tralee: National Folk Theatre of Ireland, Tel: 066-23055. Evokes Irish rural tradition in song, dance and mime.

Music

Ireland has some of the most vital traditional music in the world. You can hear it in pubs almost everywhere in the country, but visitors who want to be sure of hearing some good stuff are best advised to attend an organised session, such as one of those presented in summer on Wednesdays and Thursdays at Culturlann na hEireann, the headquarters of Comhaltas Ceoltoiri Eireann (the traditional music association). The address is Belgrave Square, Monkstown, Co. Dublin. Tel: 280 0295. Buses No. 7 and 8 from Dublin city centre stop nearby and the Monkstown and Seapoint DART station is only a short walk away.

The biggest change in Irish popular music over the past few years, particularly among the younger people, is how "club" music has become the new and dominant means of musical expression. In European terms, Dublin is seen as a "clubbing capital" and venues like POD (Place of Dance) and The Kitchen (the nightclub owned by U2) are two of the best places in the city in which to experience the modern musical sound of youthful Ireland. Local DJs are bringing out their own records on their own labels and dabbling in the contemporary genres of music known as Garage, Drum 'n' Bass and Trance.

Dublin's leading folk music club is at Slattery's of Chapel Street. Details of sessions there and at other venues appear in *In Dublin* magazine.

In Dublin also carries details of jazz, rock and classical music events. The top venue for the latter is the National Concert Hall in Earlsfort Terrace, off St Stephen's Green, Dublin.

Art Galleries

DUBLIN AREA

Anyone interested in the visual arts should visit the **National Gallery**, the **Hugh Lane Municipal Gallery**, the **Irish Museum of Modern Art** and the **Gallery of Oriental Art** (Chester Beatty). There are also many smaller exhibition centres and commercial galleries which often contain interesting work.

Bank of Ireland Exhibition Hall, Lower Baggot Street. Tel: 661 5933. Monday–Friday, 10am–4pm. Puts on both modern Irish and international exhibitions.
Combridge Fine Arts, 24 Suffolk Street. Tel: 677 4652. Monday–Friday 9.30am–5.30pm, Saturday 10am–1pm. Conventional land scapes in oil and watercolour.
Douglas Hyde Gallery, Trinity College. Tel: 677 2941 ext: 1116. Monday–Saturday, 11am– 6pm. Contemporary Irish and International painting, sculpture and photography.
Chester Beatty Library, 20 Shrewsbury Road. Tel: 269 2386. Tuesday–Friday 10am–5pm, Saturday 2–5pm. Superb collection of oriental art and manuscripts. Guided tours Saturday and Wednesday 2.30pm.
Gallery of Photography, 44 Essex Street East, Dublin 2. Tel: 671 4654. Irish and international exhibitions; postcards, prints and posters. **Green on Red Gallery**, 58 Fitzwilliam Square, Dublin 2. Tel: 661-3881. Cutting-edge contemporary art.
Guinness Hop Store, Crane Street. Tel: 453 6700. Paintings and installations.
Hugh Lane Municipal Gallery of Modern Art, Parnell Square. Tel: 874 1903. Tuesday–Saturday 9.30am–6pm, Sunday 11am– 5pm.
Irish Museum of Modern Art, Royal Hospital, Kilmainham. Tel: 671 8666. Irish and international art of the 20th century.

Kerlin Gallery, Ann's Lane, South Ann Street, Dublin 2. Tel: 670 9093. Monday–Friday 10am–6pm, Saturday 11am–4.30pm. Contemporary European, Irish artists.

Malahide Castle, Malahide, Co. Dublin. Tel: 846 2516. Monday–Friday 10am–5pm, Saturday 1–6pm, Sunday and Bank Holidays 2–6pm (Apr–Oct); Weekends 2–5pm (Nov-March). Houses a selection from the National Portrait Gallery.

National Gallery of Ireland, Merrion Square West. Tel: 661 5133. Weekdays 10am–6pm (Thursday 10am–9pm), Sunday 2–5pm. Old masters, Irish and international art from the 16th to the 19th centuries.

Oliver Dowling Gallery, 19 Kildare Street. Tel: 676 6573. Monday–Friday, 10am–5.30pm, Saturday 10am–1pm. Paintings and sculptures by Irish and international artists.

Oriel Gallery, 17 Clare Street. Tel: 676 3410. Monday–Friday, 10am–5.30pm, Saturday, 10am–1pm. Has 19th and 20th-century Irish paintings, mostly landscapes. Established names such as Paul Henry, Jack B. Yeats, "AE".

RHA Gallagher Gallery, 15 Ely Place, Dublin 2. Tel: 661 2558. Exhibitions by Irish and international artists in spacious modern gallery.

Rubicon Gallery, 10 St. Stephen's Green, Dublin 2. Tel: 670 8055. Contemporary Irish and international art.

Solomon Gallery, Powerscourt Townhouse Centre, Dublin 2. Tel: 679 4237. Monday–Saturday 10am–5.30pm. Contemporary Irish and international art.

Taylor Galleries, 6 Dawson Street. Tel: 676 6055. Monday–Friday, 10am–5.30pm, Saturday, 11am–1pm. Contemporary Irish painting and sculpture by leading artists.

Temple Bar Studios, 7 Temple Bar, Dublin 2. Tel: 6710073.

Monday–Friday 11.30am–5.30pm, Saturday noon–4pm. Avant garde contemporary Irish and international art.

Tom Caldwell Gallery, 31 Upper Fitzwilliam Street. Tel: 662 4753. Tuesday–Friday, 11am–5pm, Saturday, 11am–1pm. Contemporary Irish artists, especially Northern.

Kilcock Art Gallery, School Street, Kilcock, Co. Kildare. Tel: 628-7619. Tuesday–Friday 10am– 3pm, Saturday 2–5pm.

SOUTHEAST REGION

Butler Gallery, Kilkenny Castle, Kilkenny. Tel: 056-61106. Late 19th-century and 20th-century Irish art.

Garter Lane Arts Centre, O'Connell Street, Waterford. Tel: 051-77153. Exhibitions by lively young artists.

Wexford Art Centre, Cornmarket, Wexford. Tel: 053-23764. General purpose arts centre in 18th-century market house which hosts touring exhibitions.

SOUTHWEST REGION

Cork Arts Society Gallery, Father Matthew Street, Cork. Tel: 021-277749. Tuesday–Saturday, 10.30am–1pm, 2–6pm. Fortnightly exhibitions by Irish artists.

Crawford Municipal Art Gallery, Emmet Place, Cork. Tel: 021-273377. Monday–Friday, 10am–5pm, Saturday 9am–1pm. Irish and European paintings, sculpture, silver, glass.

Frank Lewis, 6 Bridewell Lane, Killarney. Tel: 064-34843. Commercial gallery hosting regular shows by artists living or temporarily working in Kerry.

Keane on Ceramics, Pier Road, Kinsale. Tel: 021-774553. Represents a number of major Irish ceramic artists.

Kent Gallery, Town Park, Kinsale. Tel: 021-774027. Sells work by up-and-coming local artists.

Sheeog Art Gallery, Langford Street, Killorglin. Tel: 066-61220. April–September, December, Monday–Saturday, 10.30 am–6.30pm.

Triskel Arts Centre, 5 Bridge Street, Cork. Tel: 021-272022. Tuesday–Saturday 10am–5.30pm. Exhibitions, plays, poetry readings and music.

West Cork Arts Centre, Old Bank House, North Street, Skibbereen, Co. Cork. Tel: 028-22090. Community arts centre with exhibitions of contemporary paintings, sculpture, ceramics. Directory of local artist and craft makers on request. Interesting shop.

MID WEST REGION

Belltable Arts Centre, 69 O'Connell Street, Limerick. Tel: 061-319866. Monday–Saturday, 10am–9pm. Community arts centre hosting travelling exhibitions and shows by local artists.

Limerick City Gallery of Art, Pery Square, Limerick. Tel: 061-310633. Monday–Friday, 10am– 1pm, 2.30–8pm, Saturday, 10am–1pm. Collection of 18th, 19th and 20th-century oils and watercolours. Local and touring exhibitions.

Dolmen Gallery, Honan's Quay, Limerick. Tel: 061-417929. Monthly exhibitions of contemporary art.

National Self-Portrait Collection, Kneafsey Gallery, Plassey House, Limerick. Tel: 061-333644. Self-portraits of Ireland's leading artists.

MIDLAND REGION

Carroll Art Gallery, 6 Keons Terrace, Longford. Tel: 043-41148. Paintings by leading Irish artists.

Midland Arts Resource Centre, Austin Friar Street, Mullingar. Tel: 044-43308. Community arts centre with visiting exhibitions and work by local artists.

FAR WEST REGION
Bridge Mills Gallery, O'Brien's Bridge, Galway. Tel: 091-565886. Paintings and photographs.
Clifden Art Gallery, Main Street, Clifden, Connemara. Tel: 095-21788. Landscape and other work by local artists.
Design Concourse Ireland, Kirwan's Lane, off Cross Street, Galway. Tel; 091-566016. Retail outlet that acts as a showcase for portfolios and other work by designers and craft makers from all over Ireland
Education Centre, Castlebar. Tel: 094-21769. Monday–Friday, 10.30am–5pm. Irish art and crafts.
Galway Arts Centre, 47 Dominick Street, Galway. Tel: 091-565886. Regular exhibitions by younger artists. Information centre for the lively Galway arts scene.
Kenny Art Gallery, High Street, Galway. Tel: 091-562739. Monday–Saturday, 9am–6pm. Commercial gallery showing original work chiefly by local artists.
Linenhall Arts Centre, Linenhall Street, Castlebar. Tel: 094-23733. Community centre for all kinds of artistic activity including shows of local work.
Northwest Region
Glebe Gallery, Churchill, Co. Donegal. Tel: 074-37071. Derek Hill collection; English-born artist associated particularly with paintings of Tory Island.
County Sligo Yeats Art Gallery, Stephen Street, Sligo. Tel: 071-42212. Monday–Friday, 10am–2pm, 3–5pm, Saturday 10am–1pm. About 100 paintings, including work by John B. Yeats and Jack B. Yeats.
Model Arts Centre, The Mall, Sligo. Tel: 071-41405. Contemporary exhibitions in community art centre based in old school house.
Taylor's Art Gallery, Castlebaldwin. Co. Sligo. Tel: 071-65138. Original work by local artists.

The Gallery, Dunfanaghy, Co. Donegal. Tel: 074-36224. Contemporary work by local artists and others.

NORTHERN IRELAND
Arts Council of Northern Ireland, Bedford Street, Belfast. Exhibitions, bookshop.
Bell Gallery, 13 Adelaide Park. 19th-century and 20th-century Irish artists, Victorian paintings.
Fenderesky Gallery, 4 Malone Road. Contemporary and avant-garde Irish painting.
Gordon Gallery, 36 Ferryquay Street, Derry.
Kerlin Gallery, 99 Botanic Avenue, Belfast. Contemporary Irish work, with sister gallery in Dublin.
Magee Gallery, 455 Ormeau Road. Mostly conventional work by established painters.
Malone House, Barnett Park, Upper Malone Road. Early 19th-century house with permanent exhibition on Belfast parks and first floor art gallery.
Tom Caldwell Gallery, 40-42 Bradbury Place. Living Irish artists.
Ulster Museum, Botanic Gardens, Belfast. Ulster and Irish artists such as Sir John Lavery, Paul Henry, Jack B. Yeats, Colin Middleton.

Festivals

The number of events and festivals, big and small, seems to increase every year. There are folk festivals, music festivals, oyster festivals, potato festivals, regattas, angling competitions, drama festivals, chess congresses, sporting competitions of all kinds, beauty contests, song contests, parades, car rallies, boat rallies, literary festivals, jazz festivals, exhibitions, agricultural shows, horse shows, dog shows, cat shows, commemorations, celebrations, hunt meetings, marathons, summer schools, community festivals, ceilidhs... the list seems endless.

In many cases, dates and venues are variable and some festivals – particularly the smaller, local ones – may appear and disappear from year to year according to the availability of funds, enthusiasm or organisers.

Here is a small selection, listed in calendar order. Exact dates often vary, and local tourist boards can provide precise dates and details.

Calendar of Events

January Races, Leopardstown, Dublin: top-class National Hunt (jumping) meeting. Opening of Point-to-Point season: races run at different venues every Sunday over unfenced courses.
Aer Lingus Young Scientists Exhibition, RDS, Ballsbridge, Dublin. January.
Holiday and Leisure Fair, RDS,

Ballsbridge, Dublin. January.
International Rugby Champion-ship (Ireland versus England, Wales, Scotland, France). Home matches at Lansdowne Road, Dublin. January/February.
Irish Motor Show, RDS, Ballsbridge, Dublin. February.
Ulster Harp National, Down-patrick: steeplechase. Late February/early March.
Ulster Motor Show, King's Hall, Belfast. February annual.
Limerick Theatre and Music Festivals. Early March.
Irish Dancing Championships. February/March.
Dublin Film Festival. March. Irish premieres of a selection of Irish and international cinema.
St Patrick's Day (17 March): Festival of Ireland's national saint. Celebrated throughout Ireland and much of the world, notably in New York city.
World Irish Dancing Champion-ships: venue variable. March/April.
Pan-Celtic week. Gathering of Celts from Brittany, Cornwall, Wales, Scotland and the home turf. Early April. Venue changes every year.
Irish Grand National (steeple-chase), Fairyhouse. Easter Monday.
Circuit of Ireland Car Rally. Easter weekend.
Dublin Grand Opera Society Spring Season, Gaiety Theatre. Late March/April.
Belfast Civic Festival and Lord Mayor's Show. May.
Belfast City Marathon road race. Mass masochism. May.
Northwest 200: fastest motor-cycle road race in Britain or Ireland. Starts from Portstewart, Co. Derry. May.
Bantry Mussel Fair. Homage is paid to Bantry Bay's most suc-culent product. Early May.
Irish 2,000 Guineas (for 3-year-old colts) and 1,000 Guineas (for fillies), both run over one mile. The first classics of the flat-racing season, staged on consecutive Saturdays at the

Curragh in May.
Ulster Classic Fishing Festival, Fermanagh Lakeland. Anglers' cornucopia. May.
Spring Show, RDS, Ballsbridge, Dublin. Major agricultural exhibi-tion and social occasion, with many sideshows for the city slickers. May.
Royal Ulster Agricultural Show, Belfast. May.
Sligo Arts Festival. Street enter-tainment, fireworks, theatre, readings, comedy and music. Late May.
Writers' Week, Listowel, Co. Clare. Late May/June.
Music in Great Irish Houses Festival: held in various man-sions near Dublin. Early June.
Bloomsday Literary Festival, June 16, Dublin. Held on the date on which Joyce's *Ulysses* takes place. Strictly for Joyce buffs, but there is no shortage of those.
Ballybunion International Bach-elor Festival, Ballybunion, Co. Kerry. Irish manhood's answer to the Miss World contest. Seeing is believing. Late June.
Irish Derby (1œ-mile flat-race for 3-year-old colts). Most glam-orous day in the Irish racing calendar. Held at the Curragh. Late June.
Westport Sea Angling Festival, Westport, Co. Mayo. Late June.
Irish Oaks, the Curragh, Equivalent of the Derby for fillies. Early July.
Willie Clancy Summer School, Miltown Malbay, Co. Clare (uillean piping). July.
Ulster Harp Derby, Downpatrick, Co. Down. July.
Orangeman's Day, all over Northern Ireland. 12 July.
International Rose Trials, Sir Thomas & Lady Dixon Park, Belfast. July–September.
Galway Races – heady, often hilarious, holiday horse-racing. Late July/August.
Galway Arts Festival. Massive celebration of international and Irish theatre, film, art, literature and music overlaps with the

races (see above) to create a mighty buzz. Late July/August.
Ulster Steam Traction Rally, Shane's Castle, Antrim. July, huffing and puffing.
Stradbally Steam Rally, Stradbally, Co. Laois. Early August, more huffing and puffing.
Yeats International Summer School. Sligo. Academics, writers and poetry enthusiasts from all over the world assemble to listen and learn. The biggest and oldest of many summer schools taking place in August.
Dublin Horse Show, RDS, Ballsbridge. Greatest event in the show-jumping calendar. August.
Puck Fair, Killorglin, Co. Kerry. Ancient pagan festival at which a goat is crowned. August.
Ulster Flying Club International Rally, Newtownards, Co. Down. August.
The Ould Lammas Fair, Ballycastle, Co. Antrim. The North of Ireland's most popular old fair, at which you traditional-ly "treat your Mary Ann to some dulse and Yellow Man." For elucidation, go to Ballycastle. Last Monday and Tuesday in August.
All-Ireland Amateur Drama Festival. August.
Ulster Grand Prix (motor-cycling), Dundrod, near Belfast. August.
Merriman Summer School, Lisdoonvarna, Co. Clare. A week in August of intense intellectual debate about the nation's culture, liberally laced with drinking and partying.
Rose of Tralee International Festival, Tralee, Co. Kerry. Late August.
Fleadh Ceoil nah Eireann (All-Ireland festival of Irish music, with competitions therein). Venue variable. August.
Matching Festival of Ireland, Lisdoonvarna, Co. Clare. More fun than computer dating. September.

Hurling and Gaelic Football: All-Ireland finals, Croke Park, Dublin. September.
Galway Oyster Festival, Galway city. Late September.
Irish Hot-Air Balloon Championships, Ballymahon, Co. Longford. Late September.
Dublin Theatre Festival. Late September/October.
Dublin Cat Show, RDS, Ballsbridge. October.
Wexford Opera Festival, Wexford town. October.
Cork Jazz Festival, Cork City. October.
Dublin City Marathon, More self-inflicted punishment. Late October.
Belfast Festival, Queen's University, Belfast. Ambitious, event-packed two weeks of music, drama, folksong, cinema, etc. November.
Dublin Grand Opera Society Winter Season, Gaiety Theatre, Dublin. December.

Outdoor Attractions

Relics

Ireland is rich in relics of its fascinating, troubled past. From prehistoric times, there are monuments such as the extraordinary burial chamber at **Newgrange,** Co. Meath, the stone fort, **Grianán Ailigh** (Sun-palace of Aileach), Co. Donegal; the megalithic tomb of **Creevy-keel Court Cairn,** Co. Sligo; or the strange carved stone figures on **White Island,** Lough Erne, Co. Fermanagh.

From the golden age of Celtic Christianity, there are the ruins of great monastic settlements such as **Glendalough,** Co. Wicklow; **Clonmacnois,** Co. Offaly; **The Rock of Cashel** and **Holycross Abbey,** Co. Tipperary; **Mellifont Abbey** and **Monasterboice,** Co. Louth; and **Boyle Abbey,** Co. Roscommon.

From the times when Gaelic chieftains and Norman barons struggled for supremacy, there are hundreds of castles and fortresses: **Kilkenny Castle, Blarney Castle, Bunratty Castle, Cahir Castle, Knappogue Castle, Dunluce Castle,** to mention only a few.

From the centuries of Anglo-Irish Ascendancy, there are many historic and beautiful houses and gardens, such as **Castletown,** in Co. Kildare; **Strokestown House,** Co. Roscommon; **Carriglas Manor,** Co. Longford; **Damer House,** Co. Tipperary; the **State Apartments of Dublin Castle; Lissadell House,** Co. Sligo, celebrated in a great poem by Yeats; **Russborough,** Co. Wicklow, which houses a splendid art collection; **Birr Castle Demesne,** Co. Offaly, with over 1,000 catalogued species of trees and shrubs; **Howth Castle Gardens,** Co. Dublin; **The Japanese Gardens,** Tully, Co. Kildare; and **Mount Usher** and **Powerscourt** gardens, Co. Wicklow.

Then there are splendid national and civic parks and nature gardens, such as **Phoenix Park** and the **National Botanic Gardens** in Dublin city; **Glenveagh National Park,** Co. Donegal; **Killarney National Park,** Co. Kerry; **Fota Estate,** Co. Cork; **Lough Key Forest Park,** Co. Roscommon; **Tollymore Forest Park** and **Castlewellan Forest Park,** Co. Down; and **Gortin Forest Park,** Co. Tyrone.

Beauty spots

Ireland is renowned above all else for its scenery: often lush, sometimes bleak, always memorable. Here is a handy checklist of places of scenic interest, county by county. (Many have little to offer except beauty or

What the tourist boards offer

Bord Fáilte, the Irish Tourist Board, lists a selection of places to visit in its *Christian Ireland* and *Historic Houses, Castles and Gardens* brochures. The Office of Public Works has produced a lavishly illustrated and highly praised publication, *Heritage – A Visitor's Guide,* edited by Eilís Brennan (£9.95 paperback).

The Northern Ireland Tourist Board will also supply details of visitor attractions in its area. **Contact addresses: page 333.**

tranquillity and may not be mentioned in the main text.)
Antrim: Ballintoy, Ballycastle, Carnlough, Cushendall, Cushendun, Giant's Causeway, Glenariff, Portballintrae, Portrush, Waterfoot, Whitehead.
Armagh: Jonesborough, Newtownhamilton.
Carlow: Bunclody, Hacketstown, St Mullins, Tullow.
Cavan: Cootehill, Glengavlen, Shannon Pot, Swanlinbar, Virginia.
Clare: Aillwee Cave (Ballyvaughan), The Burren, Feakle, Kilkee, Lahinch, Lisdoonvarna, Cliffs of Moher, Mountshannon, Scarriff.
Cork: Adrigole, Allihies, Ballylickey, Ballymacoda, Barley Lake (Glengarriff), Blackwater drive, Castletownshend, Dunworley Strand, Glandore, Hungry Hill (Beara Peninsula), Glanworth, Gougane Barra, Keimaneigh Pass, Lough Ine (Skibbereen).
Derry: Castlerock, Draperstown, Glenshane Pass, Magilligan, Portstewart.
Donegal: Buncrana, Bundoran, Clonmany, Dunfanaghy, Dunlewy, Glen, Glencolumbkille, Glenveagh, Gweedore, Lough Swilly, Malin More, Rosapenna, St Patrick's Purgatory, Slieve League.
Down: Annalong, Bangor, Bryansford, Crawfordsburn, Donaghadee, Hilltown, Kilkeel, Newcastle, Portaferry, Rostrevor, Silent Valley, Warrenpoint.
Dublin: Dalkey, Dun Laoghaire, Howth, Killiney, Kilternan, Phoenix Park.
Fermanagh: Belcoo, Boho, Florencecourt (near Enniskillen), Marble Arch Caves, Tempo, Tully Bay.
Galway: Aran Islands, Ballynahinch Lake, Carna, Cashel Harbour, Clifden, Killary Harbour, Kylemore, Leenane, Lough Corrib, Lough Inagh, Lough Mask, Lough Nafooey, Oughterard, Recess,

Roundstone.
Kerry: Ballydavid, Banna Strand, Caragh Lake, Connor Pass, Dingle, Glenbeigh, Glencar, Healy Pass, Kenmare, Killarney, Parknasilla, Valentia Island, Ventry, Waterville.
Kildare: Celbridge, Leixlip, Robertstown, Monasterevin.
Kilkenny: Graiguenamanagh, Inistioge, Thomastown.
Laois: Abbeyleix, Dunamase, Mountmellick, Rosenallis.
Leitrim: Dromahair, Glenade, Kinlough, Lough Allen, Lough Gill, Lurganboy, Manorhamilton.
Limerick: Ardpatrick, Ballylanders, Kilfinane, Montpelier.
Longford: Ardagh, Drumlish, Granard.
Louth: Carlingford, Omeath, Ravensdale.
Mayo: Achill Island, Ballycastle, Belderg, Clare Island, Croagh Patrick, Delphi, Inishbofin, Killary Harbour, Lough Conn, Lough Corrib, Louisburgh, Mulrany, Moyne Castle, Westport.
Meath: Oldcastle, Slane.
Monaghan: Carrickmacross, Castleblayney, Rockcorry.
Offaly: Clareen, Kinnitty, Slieve Bloom mountains.
Roscommon: Boyle, Lough Key, Strokestown.
Sligo: Benbulben, Cliffony, Drumcliff, Easky, Lough Gill, Rosses Point.
Tipperary: Aherlow, Clogheen, The Gap, Mitchelstown Caves.
Tyrone: Gortin, Newtownstewart, Plumbridge.
Waterfold: Ballymacarbry, Cheekpoint, Kilmacthomas, Lismore, Tramore.
Westmeath: Castlepollard, Fore, Glassan, Mullingar.
Wexford: Ballyahck, Bunclody, Curracloe, Kilmore Quay, Rosslare, Scullogue Gap.
Wicklow: Annamoe, Aughrim, Avoca, Bray, Dunmore East, Enniskerry, Glendalough, Glenmalure, New Ross, Poulaphouca, Rathdrum, Roundwood, Sally Gap, Woodenbridge.

Shopping

What to Buy

Traditional crafts still flourish in Ireland, partly as a source of merchandise but partly out of a very Irish sense that the excellence cultivated by past generations is worth nurturing. Cut crystal, a craft which had just about died out, was resurrected in the 1960s and today flourishes in Waterford and elsewhere.

Ireland's internationally renowned wool textile industry has moved its emphasis from the old homespun, handwoven tweed to very finely-woven scarves, stoles and dress fabrics. Linen and lace remain remarkably delicate.

Pottery has been fast developing as a craft industry, and new studios are opening all the time. Basket-weaving remains widespread and provides such souvenirs as table mats and St Brigid crosses.

While Irish crafts have always been well-made, they have not always been particularly fashionable. This is changing, with design improving by leaps and bounds. Whether buying for the wardrobe or for the home, the fashion-conscious will be pleasantly surprised at the variety of styles available nowadays in Irish tweeds, knitwear and linen.

Dublin: The two main areas for shopping in Dublin are Grafton Street and its tributaries; and – less stylish but often better value – the Henry Street area, off O'Connell Street. Recent years have seen a major invasion of the city by British-based multiples such as Marks and Spencer, Boots, Debenhams and Habitat, and Dublin now retains only three indigenous department stores: Brown Thomas, on Grafton Street; Arnott's, on Henry Street; and Clery's, on O'Connell Street.

Don't miss the Powerscourt Townhouse Centre, just off Grafton Street, an 18th-century mansion and courtyard converted into a stylish shopping complex with many crafts and antiques shops and several restaurants. The Kilkenny Shop on Nassau Street, a showcase for Irish crafts and clothes, is also worth a browse. On the same street, Blarney Woollen Mills and Kevin & Howlin stock classic Irish knitwear and tweeds, and the Celtic Note record shop specialises in Irish music. DESIGNYARD, Temple Bar, sells innovative Irish and international jewellery and artefacts.

If you're looking for food, there's an excellent range of Irish cheeses at The Big Cheese Company in Trinity Street; hard cheeses travel best. The Kilkenny Shop in Nassau Street has a selection of Irish-made jams, chutneys, cakes, biscuits and confectionery. Dewley's cafés sell attractive gift-packs of cakes, brack (a fruity loaf traditionally eaten around Hallowe'en), fudge, tea and coffee. Butler's Irish Chocolates in Grafton Street offers many delights for the sweet-toothed.

If you're interested in taking some Irish food home with you, smoked salmon is a good bet (but be sure it's labelled "smoked Irish salmon" as opposed to "Irish smoked salmon"). Air travellers can buy some at the Wrights of Howth shop in Dublin Airport.
Belfast: The main shopping area stretches from Donegall Place, opposite the City Hall, down the wide Royal Avenue, where you'll find most of the big British chain stores such as Marks & Spencer. There's a concentration of such stores in the vast Castlecourt Shopping Centre, located just off Royal Avenue and with a car park attached.

The distinctive Northern Irish gift is linen, which once accounted for much of the province's prosperity. One city-centre outlet is Smyth's Irish Linen at 65 Royal Avenue. For those wanting to know more, the Irish Linen Centre at Lisburn Museum (01846-663377) has displays and demonstrations. (Lisburn is to the south-west of Belfast, down the M1 motorway.)

Shopping Hours

Most shops are open from 9am to 5.30pm. Shopping centres stay open until 9pm on Thursday and Friday. Many small grocery stores are open until late at night and there are a few 24-hour shops in Dublin.

Outside the large cities, there is often an all-day or early-closing (1pm) day once a week. This is usually on Wednesday or Thursday.

Sport

Spectator

Gaelic Football: Cumann Luthchleas Gael, Croke Park, Dublin 3. Tel: 8363222.
Rugby: Irish Rugby Football Union, 62 Landsdowne Road, Ballsbridge, Dublin 4. Tel: 6684601.
Soccer: Soccer Football Assocation of Ireland, 80 Merrion Square, Dublin 2. Tel: 6766864.

Participant

GOLF
Visitors are welcome to play at about 180 golf courses in the Irish Republic. Green fees range from about IR£12 to IR£50 a day (the charge is usually per day, not per round as in many countries). Reductions are available for weekly and monthly rates. Most clubs offer discounts to groups and societies. Some courses have sets of clubs for hire. Caddies are not usually available, except by prior booking. Most clubs hire out pullcarts, but not electric or petrol-driven carts. Visitors are advised to bring only light golf-bags, as they may have to carry their own.

For full details of golf courses, holiday offers, or individual golf itineraries, contact the Golf Promotion Executive, Irish Tourist Board, Dublin 2. *Golfing*, is a new publication available from Irish Tourist Board offices in Ireland and overseas. It includes details of golf accommodation offers, tour operators, golf clubs, access travel and golfing fixtures. the Northern Ireland Tourist Board publishes a leaflet listing the 80 golf courses in Northern Ireland.

SEA ANGLING

Shore fishing (from rocks, piers, beaches and promontories), inshore fishing (in bays and inlets) and deep sea fishing are popular in Ireland all the year round. No permits are required. There are over 250 competitions organised throughout the country from February to November.

Boats can be hired from more than 700 operators around the country. Expect to pay between £15 and £25 per angler per day, or between £150 and £250 for a daily charter. Full details of events and of boats for hire are contained in the Irish Tourist Board publication, *Sea Angling in Ireland,* available for IR£1.50, including postage, from Irish Tourist Board Literature Dept, PO Box 1083, Dublin 8.

COARSE ANGLING

The species of freshwater fish in this category are pike, arch, bream, rudd, tench, dace and various hybrids. The main area for coarse fishing is the Midlands, stretching from the River Erne system in the North southwards through the Shannon basin, the Monaghan and Westmeath lakes, the Grand and Royal Canals, to the Barrow River and Canal and the Munster Blackwater. There is no legal closed season, but a conservation order on pike was introduced in 1990. No licence is required in the Irish Republic.

In Northern Ireland, anglers require an annual general coarse fishing permit and a coarse fishing rod licence (for 15 days or a season) – available from local tackle shops, local hotels, handling agents or the tourist board.

Tackle can be bought but seldom hired in Ireland. Boat hire works out at around £18 per head per day based on six sharing. Pre-packed bait, such as pure breadcrumbs, white maggots and worms can be bought from a number of stocklists, but it is best to pre-order from Irish Angling Services, Ardlougher, Co. Cavan. Tel: 049-26258. If you are bringing your own bait into Ireland, do not pack it in soil or vegetable material, the importation of which is illegal.

GAME ANGLING

The species are salmon, sea trout and brown trout. The season for salmon fishing is from 1 January to 30 September, depending on district. A licence is essential, and usually a fishery permit also – though some loughs, for example Corrib and Conn, are free of permit charge. (Permits are not the same as licences and are paid to individual fishery owners.)

An annual licence costs £25, a 21-day licence £10, a district licence £12 and juvenile and one-day licences £8 and £3 respectively.

A salmon licence and permit also covers fishing for sea trout, which is in season from June to 30 September (12 October in some areas). For brown trout, a licence is required in Northern Ireland only and much of the fishing is free.

Full details are in Bord Fáilte's brochure *Game Angling.*

Under new laws governing brown trout and coarse fishing, a system of co-operatives administers and funds the development of these fisheries through share certificates. The matter is complex and visiting anglers should seek clarification from local tourist offices and angling clubs.

Books & Guides on Angling
The Angler in Ireland: Game, Coarse and Sea, by Ken Whelan. Country House.
Trout and Salmon Loughs of Ireland, by Peter O'Reilly. Unwin Hyman.
Trout and Salmon Rivers of Ireland, by Peter O'Reilly. Unwin Hyman.
Coarse Fishing in Ireland, by Hugh Gough. Unwin Hyman.

Useful Contacts for Anglers

Bord Fáilte (Irish Tourist Board), Baggot Street Bridge, Dublin 2 (tel: 01-6765871, fax: 01-676 4764), and tourist offices in main cities and towns throughout country will provide up-to-date information on every aspect of angling.
Department of Marine and Fisheries Board, Fisheries Administration, Leeson Lane, Dublin 2. Tel: 01-678 5444.
Central Fisheries Board, Balnagowan House, Glasnevin, Dublin 9. Tel: 01-837 9206.
Eastern Regional Fisheries Board (*same as above*).
Southern Regional Fisheries Board, Anglesea Street, Clonmel, Co. Tipperary. Tel: 052-23971.
Southwestern Regional Fisheries Board, Neville Terrace, Massey Town, Macroom, Co. Cork. Tel: 026-41221.
Shannon Regional Fisheries Board, Thomond Weir, Limerick, Co. Limerick. Tel: 061-455171.
Western Regional Fisheries Board, Weir Lodge, Galway. Tel: 091-63118.
Northwestern Regional Fisheries Board, Abbey Street, Ballina, Co. Mayo. Tel: 096-22623.
Northern Regional Fisheries Board, Station Road, Ballyshannon, Co. Donegal. Tel: 072-51435.

Fly-fishing for Irish Trout, by Niall Fallon. Poolbeg.
Guides on game, coarse and sea angling are published annually by the Irish Tourist Board.

ADVENTURE SPORTS

Canoeing, boardsailing, caving, hang-gliding, mountaineering, orienteering, parachuting, scuba diving, sailing, and water-skiing are among the main activities provided for in a growing number of adventure centres located in suitably stunning locations from Cork to Galway to Donegal to Wicklow and beyond.
The reputable centres are affiliated to the Association for Adventure Sports (AFAS); contact: Administrator, AFAS, House of Sport, Long Mile Road, Dublin 12. Tel: 01-509845. Full details are also listed in Bord Fáilte and - Northern Ireland Tourist Board brochures.

Surfing

Notable venues with Atlantic swells, stimulating breezes and foaming surf are at Strandhill and Easkey, Co. Sligo, Lahinch, Kilkee, Doolin Point, along the coast of Co. Clare. Coaching, including surf-board and wet-suit, costs about IR£10 per hour. These specialists operate all year round: Co. Sligo Surf Club, Strandhill, Castle Warriors Surf Club, Easkey, Co. Sligo; Lahinch Surf Club, Lahinch, Co. Clare. The Irish Surfing Association is at Easkey House, Easkey, Co. Sligo. Tel: (096) 49020.

Climbing contacts

For further information and advice on mountaineering, rock-climbing and hill walking, contact the Association for Adventure Sports (AFAS), House of Sport, Long Mile Road, Dublin 12. Tel: 450 1633.

Bird-Watching

There are more than 55 recognised birdwatching sites in Ireland. For details of these, and of the various species to be seen at different times of year, contact the Irish Wildbird Conservancy, 8 Longford Place, Monkstown, Co. Dublin. Tel: 01-280 4322. There are two bird observatories at which visitors can stay. These are Cape Clear Bird Observatory (Bookings Secretary is Mr K. Grace, 34 Dorney Court, Shankill, Co. Dublin); and Copeland Bird Observatory, Co. Down (Bookings Secretary is Mr N. McKee, 67 Temple Rise, Templepatrick, Co. Antrim).

Hill-Walking, Rambling, Climbing

There is surely no need for further propaganda about the unspoilt beauty of Ireland's hills and mountains. Few of them rise above 3,000 ft (1,000 metres), but they have great character and variety, from the soft, bogcovered domes of Wicklow to the jagged peaks of Connemara, the ridges of Cork and Kerry, the strange, basalt outcrops of the Antrim plateau or the sweeping Mountains of Mourne. Most of Ireland's mountains command marvellous views of the sea.
  The best-known long-distance walking path in the Republic is the "Wicklow Way," which extends for about 79 miles (126 km) southwards from Marlay Park, Co. Dublin to Clonegal, Co. Carlow. The route switchbacks along the eastern flanks of the Dublin and Wicklow mountains, the largest unbroken area of high ground in Ireland, very sparsely inhabited. For information on the route and accommodation, and on hillwalking in other mountain regions of the Republic, contact Cospoir (The Irish Sports Council), Hawkins House, Dublin 2. Tel: 873 4700.

The *Walking Ireland* brochure produced by Cospoir and Bord Fáilte, which is available from both organisations, gives full details of the marked long distance walking routes such as the Cavan Way, the Tain Trail around the Cooley mountains and Carlingford in the northeast, the Ulster Way, the Slieve Bloom Way, the Aran Island ways, the Kerry Way, Munster Way, Dingle Way and many more. It also lists Irish walking holiday specialists.
  One of Europe's great long-distance paths, the "Ulster Way", virtually encircles Northern Ireland, stretching for 500 miles (800 km). For information, contact the Sports Council for Northern Ireland, House of Sport, Malone Road, Belfast 9. Tel: 0232-381222.

Further Reading

General

Aalen, F.H.A., Whelan, Kevin, Stout, Matthew (eds.) *Atlas of the Rural Irish Landscape* Cork University Press

Ardagh, John. *Ireland and the Irish*. Hamish Hamilton/Penguin.

Arnold, Bruce. *A Concise History of Irish Art*. Thames & Hudson.

Bardon, Jonathan. *Belfast*. Blackstaff Press.

Beckett, J.C. *The Making of Modern Ireland*. Faber.

Bell, Brian and McAuley, Liam (ed.) *Insight Guide: Dublin*. APA Publications.

Boylan, Henry. *A Dictionary of Irish Biography*. Gill & Macmillan.

Brennan, Eílis (ed.) *Heritage – a visitor's guide*. Office of Public Works.

Brown, Terence. *Ireland: A Social and Cultural History 1922–1985*. Fontana Press/Cornell University.

Cahill, Thomas. *How the Irish Saved Civilization*. Doubleday.

Catto, Mike. *Art in Ulster*, vol 2. Blackstaff Press.

Craig, Maurice. *The Architecture of Ireland*. Batsford.

Danaher, Kevin. *In Ireland Long Ago*. Mercier Press.

Seamus Deane. *Short History of Irish Literature* Hutchinson

Deane, Seamus (ed.) *Field Day Anthology of Irish Writing* Field Day publications, Derry.

Delaney, Frank. *James Joyce's Odyssey – A Guide to the Dublin of Ulysses*. Hodder & Stoughton.

Evans, Estyn. *Irish Folk Ways*. Routledge and Kegan Paul.

Fitzgibbon, Theodora. *A Taste of Ireland*. Pan.

FitzSimon, Christopher. *The Arts in Ireland*. Gill & Macmillan.

FitzSimon, Christopher. *The Irish Theatre*. Thames & Hudson.

Gogarty, Oliver St John. *As I Was Going Down Sackville Street*. Sphere.

Guinness, Desmond. *Georgian Dublin*, Batsford.

Healy, Elizabeth (ed.) *The Book of the Liffey from source to the sea*. Wolfhound Press.

Kearney, Richard (ed.) *The Irish Mind*. Wolfhound.

Kee, Robert. *Ireland – A History*. Weidenfeld.

Lydon, James and MacCurtain, Margaret (eds.). *The Gill History of Ireland* (12 vols.). Gill & Macmillan.

Lyons, F.S.L. *Ireland Since the Famine*. Collins.

MacLysaght, Edward. *Irish Families and their Names and Origins*. Figgis.

MacLysaght, Edward. *Surnames of Ireland*. Irish Academic Press.

McDonald, Frank. *The Destruction of Dublin*. Gill & Macmillan.

Mahon, Derek and Fallon, Peter (eds.). *Penguin Book of Contemporary Irish Poetry* Penguin

Mitchell, Frank. *The Shell Guide to Reading the Irish Landscape* Town House & Country House.

Murphy, Dervla. *A Place Apart*. Murray.

Murphy, Matt & Susan (ed). *Ireland's Bird Life* Sherkin Island Marine Staton publications

Murphy, John. *Irish Shopfronts*. Appletree Press, Belfast.

O'Brien, Maire and Conor Cruise. *Concise History of Ireland*. Thames & Hudson.

O'Canainn, Tomas. *Traditional Music in Ireland*. Routledge & Kegan Paul.

O'Connor, Frank. *A Book of Ireland*. Collins.

O'Connor, Nuala. *Bringing it all Back Home – the Influence of Irish Music* BBC Books.

O'Connor, Ulick, illus. Bewick,

Pauline. *Irish Tales and Sagas*. Granada.

O'Faolain, Sean. *The Irish*. Penguin.

O'Riada, Sean. *Our Musical Heritage*. Dolmen.

Potterton, Homan. *The National Gallery of Ireland*.

Prendergast, Mark. J. *Irish Rock: History, Roots and Perspectives* O'Brien Press

Robinson, Tim *The Stones of Aran: Pilgrimage* Penguin/Viking.

Share, Bernard and Tucker, Alan (ed.) Somerville-Large, Peter. *Dublin*. Hamish Hamilton.

Somerville-Large, Peter. *The Grand Irish Tour*. Penguin.

Stephens, James, illus. Rackham, *Arthur. Irish Fairy Tales*. Gill & Macmillan.

Woodham-Smith, Cecil. *The Great Hunger*. Hamish Hamilton.

Other Insight Guides

Nearly 200 Insight Guides cover the world, complemented by more than 100 Insight Pocket Guides and almost 100 Insight Compact Guides.

Insight Guide: Dublin covers in comprehensive detail the city's history, culture, people, places and attractions.

For those on a tight schedule, *Insight Pocket Guide: Ireland* sets out 17 timed itineraries designed to make the most of your visit. It contains recommendations from a local expert and has a full-size fold-out map showing the itineraries. *Insight Pocket Guide: Ireland's Southwest* takes the same approach to the top tourist region of Cork, Killarney and Kerry.

Insight Compact Guide: Ireland, *Insight Compact Guide: Dublin* and *Insight Compact Guide: The West of Ireland* are the ideal pocket reference works to carry with you as you explore. Text, pictures and maps are all carefully cross-referenced for ease of use. Great value.

ART & PHOTO CREDITS

Picture Spreads

INSIGHT GUIDE IRELAND

Editorial Director **Brian Bell**
Cartographic Editor **Zoë Goodwin**
Production **Mohammed Dar**
Design Consultants **Klaus Geisler, Graham Mitchener**
Picture Research **Hilary Genin**

Index

a

abortion 57
Achill Island 257-258
Act of Union 22
Adare 222
agricultural subsidies 60
Ahern, Bertie 61
Ailwee Cave 226
All-Ireland Fleadh Ceoil 88
Allihies 207
Allingham, William 271
Altar 206
Amharc Mm, 273
Ancient Order of
  Hibernians 310
Andrew Jackson Centre 303
Angel 97
Anglo-Irish Agreement 57
Anglo-Irish rule 142
Anglo-Irish treaty 23, 46
Anglo-Irish War 23
Annalong 297
Annals of Innisfallen 210
Antrim 308
Antrim Coast Road 303-304
Aran Islands 226, 253
architecture 62
Ardara 272
Ardee 168
Ardglass 298
Ardmore 180
Ardmore Studios 96
Ards Peninsula 299
Arklow 175
Armagh city 293–294
art galleries 360
Arvagh 291
"Ascendancy" 47
Ashford 165
Athlone 244
  Castle 244
Athy 169, 182
Atlantic Drive 275
Aughnanure Castle 256
Auld Lammas Fair 305
Avondale 165
Avondale House, Co.
  Wicklow 63

b

"B" Specials 48
bagpipes 87

Bailieborough 292
Ballaghbeama Gap 214
Ballina 259, 265
Ballinamore 270
Ballinasloe 235
Ballinskelligs 212
Ballinspittle, Co. Cork 73
Ballybeg 186
Ballybrit 251
Ballycastle 305
Ballycotton 180
Ballydehob 205
Ballydonegan 207
Ballygalley 304
Ballyhack 177
Ballyholme Bay 301
Ballyhoura Way 187
Ballyjamesduff 292
Ballymacarbery 186
Ballymaloe Country House and
  Restaurant 126, 180
Ballymena 308
Ballymoney 308
Ballymote 265
Ballynahow 212
Ballyronan 309
Ballyshannon 271
Ballyvaughan 226, 228
Baltimore 204
Banagher 237
Banbridge 295
Bangor 301
Bantry 206
Bantry Bay 30
barm brack 127
Barrow, River 169, 184-185
battles
  Clontarf 27, 142
  Kinsale 27
  Boyne, the 22, 28, 167, 219,
    310
  Diamond, the 30
  Somme, the 40
  Vinegar Hill 175
Beara Peninsula 207
Beara Way 208
Beckett, Samuel 95
Belfast 315–327
  Albert Memorial Clock 324
  Belfast Castle 325
  Belfast Central Library 324
  Belfast Civic Arts
    Theatre 320
  Botanic Avenue 320
  Bradbury Place 319
  British troops arrive 50
  buildings 62
  Cave Hill Country Park 325

Central Station 327
City Hall 317
Crown Liquor Saloon 126, 321
Donegall Pass 320
Donegall Place 317
Golden Mile 318
Grand Opera House &
  Cirque 321
Great Victoria Street 321
Group Theatre 317
growth of 38
history of 315
hotels 349
Lagan Lookout Centre 324
Lagan, River 315
Lanyon 317
Linen Conservation Area 317
Linen Hall Library 322
Old Museum Arts Centre 318
Ormeau Avenue 318
Ormeau Road 325
Parliament Buildings 326
Peace Line 53, 327
Pottinger's Entry 323
Queen's University 319
restaurants 127, 357
Royal Belfast Academical
  Institution 322
Royal Botanic Gardens 320
Shaftesbury Square 321
Sinclair Seamen's
  Presbyterian Church 324
St Malachy's Church 318
Stormont Castle 326
Ulster Hall 317
Ulster Museum 320
Union Presbyterian
  Theological College 320
Waterfront Hall 325
World War II raids 49
Zoological Gardens 326
Belleek 289
Belmullet 258
Belvedere House and
  Gardens 241
Benburb Heritage Centre 286
Bennettsbridge 184
Bessbrook 295
birdwatching 205, 270, 301,
  305
Birr 237
  Castle and Demesne 237
Black Head 226
Blacklion 291
Blackrock 161
Blackwater Bog 200
Blackwater Valley 179
Blarney Castle 27, 196

Blarney Stone 15
Blasket Islands 214
Blennerville 215
Blessington 164
Bloody Sunday, Derry 23, 54
Boa Island 288
bodhran 87, 256
Bonamargy Friary 305
Bonaparte, Napoleon 31
Book of Armagh 94, 144
Book of Ballymote 265
Book of Dimma 144
Book of Durrow 144
Book of Kells 26, 94, 144
Book of the Dun Cow 94
Borrisokane 238
Ború, Brian 22, 27
Boundary Commission 45–46,
  279
Boycott, Captain 37
Boyne, Battle of the 22, 28,
  167, 219, 310
Boyne, River 166
Bray 162
Breffni Castle 270
Bricklieve Mountains 265
Brontë Interpretive Centre 295
Bronze Age 26
Bruckless 272
Bruton, John 59
Bundoran 271
Bunratty Castle and Folk
  Park 88, 221
Burren, The 62, 226, 228–229
  Burren Centre 225
Burtonport 273
Bushmills 306
  Bushmills whiskey 121

C

Caher 187
  Caher Castle 187
Cahercommaun 229
Caherdaniel 213
Cahersiveen 211
Caldragh Cemetery 288
Caledon 50
Cape Clear 205
Cappoquin 179
Caragh Lake 211
Carlingford 168
Carnlough 304
Carrick-a-rede Rope Bridge 305
Carrick-on-Shannon 270
Carrickfergus 302
Carrickmacross 293
Carrigaholt 225

Carriglas Manor 243
Carrowbeg River 258
Carrowmore 265
Carson, Sir Edward 39, 169
Casey, Bishop Eamonn 74
Cashel 186
Castle Caldwell 288
Castle Coole 290
Castle Matrix 223
Castle Ward House 299
Castlebar 259
Castlecove 213
Castlepollard 242
Castletown House 169
Castletownbere 207
Castletownshend 204
Castlewellan 298
Catholic Church *see Roman
  Catholic Church*
Catholic Emancipation Bill 33
Catholic Relief Acts 29
Cavan 291
Cavendish, Lord Frederick 38
Cead Mile Fáilte 15
Ceide Fields 258
Celbridge 169
Celtic beliefs 71
Ceoltoírí Chualann 88
Charles Fort, Kinsale 201
Charles I 27
Charles II 28
Charleville Forest Castle 240
Chieftains, The 85
Children of Lir 242
Christian Brothers 74
Churchill, Lord Randolph 39
Churchill, Sir Winston 40, 45,
  48
cinema, influence of 96
Clancy Brothers 88
Clare Island 258
Clarinbridge festival,
  Galway 126
Clear Island 205
Clew Bay 257
Clifden 256
Cliffs of Moher 218, 219, 225
climate 330
clocháns 214
Cloghmore 297
Clonakilty 202
Clones 292
Clonmacnois 236
Clonmacnois and West Offaly
  Railway 235
Clonmel 186
Clontarf 162
Cloughoughter Castle 291

Coalisland's Corn Mill Heritage
  Centre 285
Cobh 197
Coffey, Aeneas 119
Coleman, Michael 100
Coleraine 307
Coliemore Harbour 161
Collins, Michael 42, 43, 45,
  203
Collooney 265
Comber 298
Comhaltas Ceoltoírí Eireann 88
Commakesta Pass 213
Commitments, The 80, 97
Connemara 254
Connery, Sean 96
Connolly, James 23, 40-41
Connor Pass 215
contraceptives, laws on 55
cooking 126-127
Cookstown 286
Cooldrumman 268
Coole Park 227
Cooley Peninsula 168
Coomanaspig Pass 212
Cootehill 291
Copeland Island 301
Cork
  Crawford Municipal
    Gallery 195
  Firkin Crane Centre 195
  Lee, River 193
  Opera House 195
  population 193
  Princes Street Market 194
  St Anne's Church 195
  St Finn Barre's
    Cathedral 193
  Tourist Information
    Office 193
  University College,
    Cork 193
Cork Dry Gin 121
Corkscrew Hill 226, 228
Cornafean 291
Corrymeela Community
  House 305
Craggaunowen Project 221
Craigavon 295
Crawfordsburn 302
Creevylea abbey 267
Croagh Patrick 71, 100, 257
Cromwell 22, 28, 162, 167,
  183, 228, 244
Crossmaglen 295
Crumlin 309
Crying Game, The 96–97
Cultra 302

Curracloe Strand 175
Curragh 169, 181
Cusack, Michael 110
Cushendall 304
Cushendun 305
Cyril Fry Model Railway
  Museum 163

d

Dáil Eireann 46, 146
Dalkey 161
Damer House 239
dance 87
Danny Boy 85
Darby O'Gill and the Little
  People 96
Dargan, William 147
Davitt, Michael 37
de Lorean, John 57
de Valera, Eamon 23, 41, 42,
  45, 70
  vision for Ireland 46, 50
Defenders, the 29, 30
Derreen Gardens 208
Derry city 280–283
  1968 civil rights march 50
  Bogside 281
  Foyle Valley Railway Centre
    283
  growth of 281
  Guildhall 282
  Harbour Museum 283
  Roaring Meg 281
  siege of 281
  St Columb's Cathedral 282
  The Diamond 282
  Tower Museum 282
Derrynane House 213
Dervock 308
Devenish Island 288
Devil's Glen 165
Devlin, Bernadette 50
Dingle 214
Dingle Peninsula 214
Disraeli, Benjamin 55
divorce 58
dolphins 225
Donaghadee 301
Donleavy, J. P. 20
Donnelly's Hollow 169
Doolin 226
Downhill 308
Downpatrick 298
Dowra 301
Dowth 166
Doyle, Roddy 97
Draperstown 285

Drimcong House
  Restaurant 127
Drogheda 167
Drombeg Stone Circle 203
Dromineer 238
Drowes, River 269
drug trade 61
Druid Theatre 251
Drumcliff 267
Drumshanbo 270
Drumsna 270
Dublin
  Abbey Theatre 95, 154
  American Embassy 160
  Anna Livia sculpture 155
  Ballsbridge 160
  Bank of Ireland 143
  Belvedere House 158
  Bewley's Oriental Café 144
  Brazen Head 88, 153
  Busaras 154
  Buswell's Hotel 146
  Chester Beatty Library 161
  Christ Church
    Cathedral 151
  Church of the Carmelite
    Fathers 151
  Church of the Most Holy
    Trinity 151
  City Hall 150
  criminal racketeering 61
  Custom House 153
  Dame Street 147
  Dublin Castle 150-151
  Dublin Civic Museum 144
  Dublin Experience 144
  Dublin's Viking
    Adventure 149
  Dublinia 152
  Earlsfort Terrace 146
  Early history 142
  Eden Quay 160
  Fishamble Street 149
  Fitzwilliam Square 62, 147
  Four Courts 159
  Gaelic name 141
  Gallagher's Boxty
    House 126
  Garden of
    Remembrance 157
  Gate Theatre 157
  General Post Office 155
  Georgian buildings 63
  Grafton Street 144
  Guinness's Brewery 152
  Ha'penny Bridge 148
  Half-penny Bridge 153
  Henrietta Street 158

Henry Street 156
High Street 152
hotels 340–341
Irish Museum of Modern
  Art 160
Iveagh House 145
James Joyce Centre 158
Johnston's Court 144
Kildare Street 146
Kilmainham Jail 159
Kilmainham Royal
  Hospital 160
King's Inns 158
Leinster House 146
Liberties 151
Liberty Hall 153
Liffey, River 141
Mansion House 146
Marsh's Library 151
Merrion Square 146
Moore Street 156
Municipal Gallery of
  Modern Art 157
National Concert Hall 146
National Gallery of
  Ireland 146
National Library 146
National Museum 146
National Wax Museum 157
Newman House 145
O'Connell Bridge 143, 153
O'Connell Street 143, 154
O'Donoghue's pub 88
Olympia Theatre 150
Peacock Theatre 154
Phoenix Park 160
Powerscourt Centre 144
restaurants 127, 350–351
Rotunda Hospital 157
Royal College of
  Surgeons 145
Royal Dublin Society 161
Royal Irish Academy 146
Shaw Birthplace 146
Shelbourne Hotel 146
St Anne's Church 146
St Audoen's Church 152
St Mary's Church 159
St Mary's Pro-
  Cathedral 156
St Michan's Church 159
St Patrick's Cathedral 151
St Stephen's Green 145
St Werburgh's Church 69
Tailors' Hall 152
Temple Bar 62, 127,
  148–149
Trinity College 143

University Church 145
Wide Streets
   Commission 63
World of Guinness
   Exhibition 153
Writers Museum 157
Zoological Gardens 160
Duiske Abbey 185
Dún Aengus 254
Dun Laoghaire 161
Dundalk 168
Dundrum 298
Dunfanaghy 274
Dungannon 285
Dungarvan 179
Dunguaire Castle 88, 227
Dunlap, John 283
Dunluce Castle 306
Dunmore East 178
Dunquin 215
Dunseverick Castle 305

e

Earhart, Amelia 283
Easky 265
Easter Rising 23, 40-41, 155,
   160
Eat the Peach 97
Elizabeth I 27
emigration 18, 34, 60, 78, 197
Emmet, Robert 33
Emo Court 239
English, attitude towards 25
Ennis 222
Enniskillen 287
Ennistymon 225
Erlugena, John Scotus 71
Erne Shannon Waterway 269
Errigal 274
expatriates 17
Eyeries 208

f

fairy rings 101
Fanad Head 275
Fastnet Rock Lighthouse 204
feminism 55
Fenians 36
Fianna Fáil 40, 47
   meaning of 46
fiddle players 87
Field, John 151
Field, The 97
Fine Gael 46
Finney, Albert 97
Firbolg, the 25

fishing 241, 269, 366
Flight of the Earls 22
Flight of the Earls Heritage
   Centre 275
Florence Court 290
flying boats 224
folk cures 101
folk music 88
folklore 98
food 125–127
Fota Arboretum 197
Fota Wildlife Park 197
Foyle, River 280
Foynes 223
France, alliance with 30
Fraser, Lady Antonia 242
French Revolution, influence
   of 33
Friel, Brian 95
fuchsia magellanica 203

g

Gaelic Athletic
   Association 110, 112
Gaelic football 110, 112, 115
Gaelic language 60, 93–94,
   254
Gaelic League 22, 39
Gaels 26
Gaeltacht 93, 254
Gallarus Oratory 215
Galway Bay 226, 249, 251
Galway city 249 251
   Druid Theatre 251
   Lynch's Window 249
   population 250
   Race Week 251
   Spanish Arch 250
Galway hookers 227, 253
Galway International Oyster
   Festival 126
Galway, James 311
Gandon, James 143, 153
Gap of Dunloe 210
Gartan Lough 275
Giant's Causeway 305
Gladstone, William Ewart 25,
   36, 39
Glandore 203
Glasnevin 162
Glassan 244
Glebe House Gallery 274
Glen of Aherlow 181, 187
Glenariff Glen 304
Glenarm 304
Glenbeigh 211
Glencar 214, 269

Glencar Lough 268
Glencolumbkille 273
Glencree 165
Glendalough 165
Glengarriff 206
Glenties 273
Glenveagh National Park 274
Glin Castle 224
Golden Age 26
golf 115
Gorey 175
Gosford Forest Park 295
Gougane Barra 206
Graiguenamanagh 185
Grange Stone Circle 222
Grattan, Henry 29, 143
Great Blasket 214
Great Famine 34
Great Rebellion, the 27, 30
Gregory, Lady 95, 154, 227
Greyabbey 299
greyhound racing 113
Grianán of Aileach 275
Griffith, Arthur 39–40, 42, 43,
   45, 46
Guerin, Veronica 61
Guinness 119, 152-153
Guinness, Arthur 28, 152
Guinness Hop Store 119

h

Hallowe'en 100, 127
Handel, George Frederick 149,
   159
hare coursing 113
harp 85
Harris, Richard 97
Haughey, Charles 56–57
Hawk's Well Theatre,
   Sligo 267
Heaney, Seamus 95, 286, 287
Hear My Song 97
Helen's Bay 302
Henry II 27
Henry VI 27
Henry VIII 27
Hidden Ireland 127
Hill of Slane 166
Hill of Tara 168
Holy Island 222
holy wells 71, 101
Holywood 302
Home Rule 36, 38-40, 42
Hook Head Peninsula 177
Horan, Monsignor James 259
horses 105–109
   Galway races 251

Howth 162
    Abbey Tavern 88
    Howth Head 162
humour 15
hunger strikes 42, 55
Hunt Museum, Limerick 220
hurling 110, 112

I

Ilnacullin 207
Inch 214
industry 60
Inishcrone 265
Inisheer 226, 254
Inishmaan 254
Inishmore 254
Inistioge 184
Innisfallen Island 210
Innishmurray 268
IRA, the see Irish Republican
    Army
Ireland's Eye 162
Ireland's Historic Science
    Centre 237
Irish Citizens' Army 40
Irish Coffee 224
Irish Country House
    Association 127
Irish Film Board 97
Irish Free State 45
    creation of 43
Irish Home Rule Party 23
Irish Horse Museum 182
Irish Linen Centre 296
Irish National Heritage
    Park 176
Irish National Land League 22
Irish National League 38
Irish pubs 120
Irish Republic, beneifts of
    European Union 60
Irish Republican Army (IRA) 23,
    42, 48, 50, 53, 54, 279
    ceasefires 59, 61
    in movies 97
    origins of 36
    split in 53
    1956–62 campaign 50
Irish Republican
    Brotherhood 22, 35
Irish Volunteers 29
Iron Age 22
Island Magee 300
Iveragh Peninsula 208

j

Jackson, President
    Andrew 303
James I 27
James II 28, 281, 310
Jameson Heritage Centre 181
Janus figures 288
Japanese Gardens, Kildare 182
jaunting cars 209
Jerpoint Abbey 184
Jerpoint Glass 184
Johnstown Castle Gardens 176
Jordan, Neil 95–97
Joyce, James 93, *95*, 96, 155,
    158, 161

k

Kavanagh, Patrick 95
Kealkil 206
Kells 168
Kenmare 208
Kennedy, John F. 252
Kennelly, Brendan 95
Kerry County Museum 216
Kesh 288
Kierkegaard, Søren 17
Kilbeggan 240
Kilcar 272
Kildare 169, 181–182
Kilfenora 225
Kilfinane 187
Kilkee 224
Kilkeel 297
Kilkenny 181, 183
Kilkenny Rising 35
Killala 31, 259
Killarney 208
    National Park 209
Killary Harbour 257
Killeshandra 291
Killiney 161
Killorglin 211
Killybegs 272
Killymoon Castle 286
Killynether Wood 301
Kilmainham Jail 160
Kilmakilloge Harbour 208
Kilmore Quay 177
Kilnaboy 229
Kilruddery House, Co.
    Wicklow 63
Kilrush 224
King James II 310
King Sitric 151
Kinsale 201
Kinsale Gourmet Festival 127

Kinvara 226
Kircubbin 299
Kirkistown Circuit 299
Knappogue Castle 88, 221
Knock, Co Mayo 71, *75*, 259
Knockmealdown
    Mountains 179
Knowth 166
Kylemore Abbey 257

I

Labour Party 47
Lahinch 225
Lake Isle of Innishfree 267
Lamb's Head 213
Lambeg drums 311
Land League 23, 37
Land reform 36-37
land, ownership of 28
Lane, Sir Hugh 157
Lanyon, Sir Charles 143, 303,
    317, 320, 324
Larkin, James 155
Larne 303
Le Fanu, Sheridan 146
Lecky, William 33
Leenane 257
Lemaneagh Castle 62, 229
Lemass, Sean 49
Letterkenny 275
Liffey, River 141
Limerick 219
    Hunt Museum 220
    King John's Castle 220
    People's Park 220
Lisburn 296
Lisdoonvarna 226
Lismore 179
Lissadell House 268
literature 93
Lloyd George, David 42, 45
Locke's Distillery 240
Longford, Earls of 242
Loop Head 225
Lough Allen 269
Lough Arrow 265
Lough Derg 222, 238, 272,
    288
Lough Derravaragh 242
Lough Ennel 240–241
Lough Gill 267
Lough Gowna 292
Lough Gur 222
Lough Ine 204
Lough Navar Forest Park 289
Lough Neagh 295, 308
Lough Ree 244

Loughgall 295
Louisburg 257
Lower Lough Erne 287
Lusitania 197, 201
Lustybeg 288

m

Macaulay, Thomas
    Babington 25
MacCool, Fionn 98, 100, 297
Macgillicuddy's Reeks 210
MacMurrough, Dermot 22, 27
MacNeice, Louis 17
McAleese, Mary 23, 61
McBride, John 39
McCormack, John 156, 244
McGahern, John 269
McKinley, President
    William 308
McMurrough, Dermot 178
McQuaid, Bishop John 75
Maghera 285
Magilligan Strand 308
Mahaffy, Sir John 93
Malahide 162
Malin Head 276
Malone, Molly 144
Man of Aran 254
Man of No Importance, A 97
Manorhamilton 270
Marble Arch Caves 290
Marian shrines 98
Markievicz, Countess
    Constance 268
Marsh, Archbishop
    Narcissus 151
Martin, Violet 204
Marx, Karl 35
Maynooth 169
Mayo 257
megalithic tombs 206, 229
Mellifont Abbey 167
Michael Collins (film) 96
Midleton 180
Millmount 167
Milltown Malbay, Co. Clare 88
Mitchelstown 187
Mizen Peninsula 206
Monaghan 292
Monasterboice 167
Monasterevin 182
Moore, Thomas 151, 165, 169
Mount Eagle 215
Mount Gabriel 205
Mount Melleray 179
Mount Stewart 300
Mount Usher Gardens 165

Mountjoy, Viscount 154
Mountshannon 222
Mourne Mountains 297
Movilla Abbey 300
moving statues 98
Moyne Abbey 259
Muckno Lake 293
Muckross House 210
Muckross Park 209
Mullaghbawn Folk
    Museum 295
Mullaghmore 268
Mullingar 241
Multyfarnham 242
Murlough Bay 307
Murphy, Dervla 59
Murphy's whiskey 121
music, traditional 85, 226
Mussenden Temple 308

n

Naas 169
National Land League of
    Ireland 37
National Stud 169, 182
nationalism 70
Navan 168
Neeson, Liam 96
Nelson, Lord Horatio 155
Nenagh 238
    Heritage Centre 239
Nendrum Abbey 298
Neolithic period 22
Newcastle 298
Newgrange 26, 166, 229
Newman, John Henry 145, 156
Newport 258
Newry 296
Newtownards 300
Nire Valley Drive 186
Nore, River 184
Normans 27
North Antrim Coast Path 307
North Down Heritage
    Centre 301
Northern Ireland
    abolition of Stormont 55
    Anglo-Irish agreement 57
    community divisions 53
    counties of 280
    growth of economy 50
    housing discrimination 50
    influence of Catholic
        church 53
    joins EEC 55
    roots of US presidents 284
    terrorist death toll 55

Northern Irish Civil Rights
    Movement 23

o

O'Brien, Edna 20, 222
O'Casey, Sean 95, 154, 227
O'Conaire, Pádraic 252
O'Connell, Daniel 22, 33, 35,
    94, 146, 155, 169, 213
O'Connor, Frank 95
O'Flaherty, Liam 254
O'Neill, Captain Terence 50
O'Neill, Hugh 27
O'Riada, Sean 88
O'Shea, Kitty 155
Ogham alphabet 22
Old Head of Kinsale 202
Omagh 284
Orange Order 38, 310–311
    origin of 30
Oxford Island 309

p

Paisley, Rev, Ian 50
Pale, the 142
Parke's Castle 267
Parnell, Charles Stewart 23,
    36, 37–39, 63, 155
partition 43, 45
passage graves 229, 265
passport requirements 331
Patterson's Spade Mill 309
Pearse, Pádraic 23, 40, 69, 252
Peatlands Park 285
Peel, Sir Robert 33
Peep o' Day Boys, the 29, 30
Penal Laws 22
Pettigo 288
Pitt, William 30
Plantation of Ulster 22
*Playboy of the Western
    World* 95, 154, 254
Playboys, The 97
Plunkett, Oliver 167
Pope John Paul II 71
population 78
Port 273
Portadown 27, 295
Portavogie 301
Portmagee 212
Portmarnock 162
*Portrait of the Artist as a Young
    Man* 93, 158
Portrush 307
Portstewart 307
potato cakes 127

potato famine 23
poteen 121, 255, 304
Poulaphouca, Lake 164
Poulnabrone Dolmen 228-229
Powerscourt 165
Progressive Democrats 61
Protestant church, disestab-
  lishment of 36
Provisional IRA 53
Puck Fair 211
pubs 119–122
  Crown Liquor Saloon
    (Belfast) 126, 321
  Doheny and Nesbitt's
    (Dublin) 122
  Durty Nelly's (Limerick) 221
  food 128
  Mulligan's (Dublin) 122
  Neary's (Dublin) 122
  number of 122
Puck Fair 211
public holidays 332
Purple Mountain 210

q

Queen Victoria 39
  plot to kidnap 35
Queenstown Story 197
Quiet Man, The 96
Quin 221

r

Radio Eireann 88
Raleigh, Sir Walter 180, 223
Randalstown 309
Rankin, Jeannie 127
Rathfriland 298
Rathkeale 223
Rathlin Island 305
Rathmullan 275
Rea, Stephen 97
Redmond, John 39, 41, 42
refugee problems 60
religion 69–75
  pagan Catholicism 71
  religious conflict 18
Republic of Ireland
  emigration 60
  founding of 23
  joins EEC 55
  withdrawal from British
    Commonwealth 49
Reynolds, Albert 57, 59
Ribbonmen, the 29
ring forts 229
Ring of Beara 207-208

Ring of Kerry 208-210
Riverdance 61, 80
road bowling 113
Roaringwater Bay 204
Robinson, Mary 23, 57, 60
Rock of Cashel 179, 181, 186
Roman Catholic Church
  abortion 73
  censorship 97
  congregation size 69, 72
  discrimination against 28
  divorce 73
  feminism 74
  influence of 47, 69
  loss of authority 75
  moving statues 98
  schools 70
Roosky 270
Rosaveel 254
Roscoff (Belfast restau-
  rant) 127
Roscommon 244
Roscrea 239
Rose of Tralee Festival 215
Ross Castle 210
Rossbeigh Woods 211
Rosscarbery 203
Rosserk Friary 259
Rosses Point 267
Rostrevor 297
Roundstone 256
round towers 26, 165, 184,
  222, 308
Royal Irish Academy 94
Royal Ulster Constabulary 50
Russborough 164
Ryan's Daughter 214

s

St Finbar's Oratory 206
St Macdara's Island 256
St Patrick 22, 26, 100, 266,
  298
Saltee Islands 177
Salthill 251
Sarsfield, Patrick 219
Scarriff 222
Scarva 310
Scattery Island 224
Schull 206
Scott, Sir Walter 34
Scrabo Tower 300
seafood 125
Shanagarry 180
Shane's Castle Railway 309
Shannon Airport 219
Shannon Harbour 237

Shannonbridge 235
Shaw, George Bernard 17, 93,
  95, 146-147, 157, 227
Shercock 291
Sheridan, Richard Brinsley 94,
  292
Sherkin Island 205
shopping 209, 364
  in Dublin 144, 148
Silent Valley 298
Sinn Féin 23, 40, 42–43, 61,
  153
Sion Mills 284
Skellig Michael 212
Skellig Rocks 208
Skibbereen 204
Slane 166
Slea Head *201*, 214
Slieve Bloom Mountains 238
Slieve Donard 298
Slieve Gullion Forest Park 296
Slieve League 273
Slieve Miskish mountains 207
Sligo 265-266
Sneem 213
Society of United Irishmen 29
soda bread 127
*Some Experiences of an Irish
  RM* 204
Somerville and Ross 95, 204
Somerville, Edith 95, 204
Somme Heritage Centre 300
Spenser, Edmund 223
Sperrin Heritage Centre 285
Sperrin Mountains 285
Spiddal 254
sports 110, 365
Staigue Fort 213
statues, moving 71
Statutes of Kilkenny 22, 93
Stephens, James 35–36
Stormont Castle 48, 326
Stormont parliament, abolition
  of 55
storytellers 100
Strabane 283
Strangford 299
Strangford Lough 298
Strangford Lough Wildlife
  Centre 299
Streedagh Strand 268
Strokestown Park House and
  Famine Museum 243
Strongbow 27, 178
Struell Wells 298
Suck, River 206
Sugar Loaf Mountains 162
Swanlinbar 291

County Mayo region — close up of County Mayo = ↑ ↑

Midlands and Far West Region

Swift, Dean Jonathan 29, 93, 151, 169, 292
Synge, John Millington 95, 154, 227, 254
use of folklore 98

t

Tarbert 224
Temple of the Winds 300
terrorism 36
Terryglass 238
Thackeray, William Makepeace 126, 307
thatched cottages 62
Thatcher, Margaret 55
Thomastown 184
Thoor Ballylee 227
Timoleague 202
tin whistles 87
Tone, Wolfe 22, 29, 159, 206, 275
Torc Waterfall 209
Tory Island 101, 274
tower houses 62, 221, 223, 227
tourism 60
Tralee 215
Tralee and Dingle Light Railway 215
Tramore 178
Travellers 188-189
trawling industry 207
Treaty of Limerick 219
Trevor, William 95, 235
Trim 168
Trollope, Anthony 270
Tuam 33
Tuamgraney 222

Tullamore 240
Tullynally Castle 242
Twelve Pins 256
Tyrone Guthrie Centre 293
Tyrone villages 286

u

U2 (pop group) 60
Uillean pipes 87
Ulster Defence Association 54
Ulster Folk and Transport Museum 302
Ulster History Park 285
Ulster Volunteer Force 23, 39, 54
Ulster, province of 40
Ulster-American Folk Park 284
Ulysses 158, 161
union with Britain (1801) 31
United Irishmen 22, 30, 142, 153
Upper Lough Erne 287

v

Vale of Avoca 165
Valentia 212
Ventry 214
Vikings 22, 26, 142, 149, 178, 236, 268
Vinegar Hill, Battle of 175
Virginia 292

w

Warrenpoint 207
Waterfoot 304
Waterford 177–178

Waterford Crystal Factory 178
Waterville 213
Welles, Orson 157
Wellington, Duke of 146
Westport 257
Wexford 176
Wexford Opera Festival 176
Wexford Wildfowl Reserve 175
whiskey 119–121
brands of 121
White Bay 304
White Island 288
Whiteboys, the 29
Whitehead 303
Wicklow Mountains 164
Wilde, Oscar 39, 93, 146
William of Orange 28, 30, 281, 310
Wilson, President Woodrow 284
World War I 40
World War II 48

y

Yeats, Jack B. 147
Yeats, William Butler 39, 47, 78, 146, 154, 156, *157*, 227, 266
Abbey Theatre 95
use of folklore 98
Yeats Memorial Building, Sligo 266
Youghal 180

The World of Insight Guides

400 books in three complementary series cover every major destination in every continent.

Insight Guides

Alaska
Alsace
Amazon Wildlife
American Southwest
Amsterdam
Argentina
Atlanta
Athens
Australia
Austria
Bahamas
Bali
Baltic States
Bangkok
Barbados
Barcelona
Bay of Naples
Beijing
Belgium
Belize
Berlin
Bermuda
Boston
Brazil
Brittany
Brussels
Budapest
Buenos Aires
Burgundy
Burma (Myanmar)
Cairo
Calcutta
California
Canada
Caribbean
Catalonia
Channel Islands
Chicago
Chile
China
Cologne
Continental Europe
Corsica
Costa Rica
Crete
Crossing America
Cuba
Cyprus
Czech & Slovak Republics
Delhi, Jaipur, Agra
Denmark
Dresden
Dublin
Düsseldorf
East African Wildlife
East Asia
Eastern Europe
Ecuador
Edinburgh
Egypt
Finland
Florence
Florida
France
Frankfurt
French Riviera
Gambia & Senegal
Germany
Glasgow

Gran Canaria
Great Barrier Reef
Great Britain
Greece
Greek Islands
Hamburg
Hawaii
Hong Kong
Hungary
Iceland
India
India's Western Himalaya
Indian Wildlife
Indonesia
Ireland
Israel
Istanbul
Italy
Jamaica
Japan
Java
Jerusalem
Jordan
Kathmandu
Kenya
Korea
Lisbon
Loire Valley
London
Los Angeles
Madeira
Madrid
Malaysia
Mallorca & Ibiza
Malta
Marine Life in the South China Sea
Melbourne
Mexico
Mexico City
Miami
Montreal
Morocco
Moscow
Munich
Namibia
Native America
Nepal
Netherlands
New England
Northern California
Northern Spain
Norway
Oman & the UAE
Oxford
Old South
Pacific Northwest
Pakistan
Paris
Peru
Philadelphia
Philippines
Poland
Portugal
Prague

Provence
Puerto Rico
Rajasthan
Rhine
Rio de Janeiro
Rockies
Rome
Russia
St Petersburg
San Francisco
Sardinia
Scotland
Seattle
Sicily
Singapore
South Africa
South America
South Asia
South India
South Tyrol
Southeast Asia
Southeast Asia Wildlife
Southern California
Southern Spain
Spain
Sri Lanka
Sweden
Switzerland
Sydney
Taiwan
Tenerife
Texas
Thailand
Tokyo
Trinidad & Tobago
Tunisia
Turkey
Turkish Coast
Tuscany
Umbria
US National Parks East
US National Parks West
Vancouver
Venezuela
Venice
Vienna
Vietnam
Wales
Washington DC
Waterways of Europe
Wild West
Yemen

Insight Pocket Guides

Aegean Islands★
Algarve★
Alsace
Amsterdam★
Athens★
Atlanta★
Bahamas★
Baja Peninsula★
Bali★
Bali Bird Walks
Bangkok★
Barbados★
Barcelona★
Bavaria★
Beijing★
Berlin★

Bermuda★
Bhutan★
Boston★
British Columbia★
Brittany★
Brussels★
Budapest & Surroundings★
Canton★
Chiang Mai★
Chicago★
Corsica★
Costa Blanca★
Costa Brava★
Costa del Sol/Marbella★
Costa Rica★
Crete★
Denmark★
Fiji★
Florence★
Florida★
Florida Keys★
French Riviera★
Gran Canaria★
Hawaii★
Hong Kong★
Hungary
Ibiza★
Ireland★
Ireland's Southwest★
Israel★
Istanbul★
Jakarta★
Jamaica★
Kathmandu Bikes & Hikes★
Kenya★
Kuala Lumpur★
Lisbon★
Loire Valley★
London★
Macau
Madrid★
Malacca
Maldives
Mallorca★
Malta★
Mexico City★
Miami★
Milan★
Montreal★
Morocco★
Moscow
Munich★
Nepal★
New Delhi
New Orleans★
New York City★
New Zealand★
Northern California★
Oslo/Bergen★
Paris★
Penang★
Phuket★
Prague★
Provence★
Puerto Rico★
Quebec★
Rhodes★
Rome★
Sabah★

St Petersburg★
San Francisco★
Sardinia
Scotland★
Seville★
Seychelles★
Sicily★
Sikkim
Singapore★
Southeast England
Southern California★
Southern Spain★
Sri Lanka★
Sydney★
Tenerife★
Thailand★
Tibet★
Toronto★
Tunisia★
Turkish Coast★
Tuscany★
Venice★
Vienna★
Vietnam★
Yogyakarta
Yucatan Peninsula★

★ = Insight Pocket Guides
with Pull out Maps

Insight Compact Guides

Algarve
Amsterdam
Bahamas
Bali
Bangkok
Barbados
Barcelona
Beijing
Belgium
Berlin
Brittany
Brussels
Budapest
Burgundy
Copenhagen
Costa Brava
Costa Rica
Crete
Cyprus
Czech Republic
Denmark
Dominican Republic
Dublin
Egypt
Finland
Florence
Gran Canaria
Greece
Holland
Hong Kong
Ireland
Israel
Italian Lakes
Italian Riviera
Jamaica
Jerusalem
Lisbon
Madeira
Mallorca
Malta

Milan
Moscow
Munich
Normandy
Norway
Paris
Poland
Portugal
Prague
Provence
Rhodes
Rome
St Petersburg
Salzburg
Singapore
Switzerland
Sydney
Tenerife
Thailand
Turkey
Turkish Coast
Tuscany

UK regional titles:
Bath & Surroundings
Cambridge & East Anglia
Cornwall
Cotswolds
Devon & Exmoor
Edinburgh
Lake District
London
New Forest
North York Moors
Northumbria
Oxford
Peak District
Scotland
Scottish Highlands
Shakespeare Country
Snowdonia
South Downs
York
Yorkshire Dales
USA regional titles:
Boston
Cape Cod
Chicago
Florida
Florida Keys
Hawaii: Maui
Hawaii: Oahu
Las Vegas
Los Angeles
Martha's Vineyard & Nantucket
New York
San Francisco
Washington D.C.
Venice
Vienna
West of Ireland